MOTHER TROUBLES

MOTHER TROUBLES

Rethinking Contemporary Maternal Dilemmas

Edited by Julia E. Hanigsberg and Sara Ruddick

Beacon Press
Boston

Beacon Press
25 Beacon Street
Boston, Massachusetts 02108-2892
www.beacon.org

Beacon Press books
are published under the auspices of
the Unitarian Universalist Association of Congregations.

Text design by Sara Eisenman and Preston Thomas
Composition by Wilsted & Taylor Publishing Services

Library of Congress Cataloging-in-Publication Data

Mother Troubles : rethinking contemporary maternal dilemmas / edited
    by Julia E. Hanigsberg and Sara Ruddick.
        p.   cm.
    Includes bibliographical references.
    ISBN 0-8070-6787-3
    1. Motherhood.   2. Mothers—Psychology.   I. Hanigsberg, Julia E.
II. Ruddick, Sara, 1935–   .
HQ759.M8732   1999
306.874'3—dc21   99-12363

We dedicate this book
to our daughter and granddaughters
Rachel
and
Lydia and Julia
Who were born while we were making this book

Contents

Introduction

We met in the spring of 1995. Sara was writing about women who use drugs while pregnant and was looking for help. Julia was recommended as a legal theorist who had written about motherhood, including about drug-using pregnant women.[1] A woman who uses drugs when she is pregnant is an archetypal "bad mother," someone who assaults her child in the process of giving birth to her. We quickly discovered that we shared a more general interest in "bad" mothers. Sara had written on teenage mothers who were blamed for having children too young.[2] Both of us had studied mothers who assault their children.[3]

In our early conversations we also recognized each other as mothers' defenders, feminists who wrote on behalf of mothers. We shared our indignation at the injustices to which pregnant women, especially African American women, were subject when suspected of using drugs and at the painful and demeaning policies that discouraged them from seeking the help they could use, not to mention basic prenatal care. We moved on to speak of the ways teenage mothers and unmarried mothers of all ages were held responsible not only for their children's failures but for society's as well. We noted the disproportionate responsibility assigned to mothers when parents harm children, and rued the guilt that mothers bear and that serves them and their children badly.

Defending mothers does not mean taking a mother's part against children, nor does it mean failing to protect children from maternal harm. It does mean listening to a mother as closely as to her children or to anyone's "inner child." Defending mothers does not mean writing against, or in indifference to fathers. We are married to men who are the fathers of our children. We have seen in our own lives what many have written: Men are capable of sharing fully, with love and responsibility, a nurturant parent's work. Our own utopian moments include visions of gender-inclusive, gender-indifferent parenting. But we do not assume that fathers or other males must be present for children to be reared successfully. Moreover, we are aware of the social weight of deeply gendered lives, and of the ways in which too-easy assumptions of genderless equal parenting can harm women.[4]

Most of the mother troubles that have caught our attention, and now appear in this book, are not directly our own. Indeed Julia was not a mother when we met. To be sure, when, during the three years we worked together, one of us became a mother, the other a grandmother, we became used to hearing heavy, head-shaking sighs about our daughter's and granddaughter's "long hours in day care" where we believe the little girls we love are flourishing. Sara remembers living through the story Carol Sanger tells of mothers blamed for work, and even more for ambition unjustified by children's need. But our identification with "bad" mothers runs deeper than these or other particular troubles. As mothers we both know that mother blaming affects all mothers, even those whose children seem blessed with good fortune. Most parents—not just "bad" parents—sometimes willingly, impulsively, or inadvertently harm their children, ignore their needs and pleas, hurt and humiliate them. Any mother who challenges her culture's pervasive mother blaming is also defending herself against blame and self-blame.

"Bad" mothers are scapegoats. By turning from them in horror, by devising laws to control and punish them, we can quarantine our own hurtful, neglectful impulses and acts. Scapegoated "bad mothers" are also often poor, unmarried, and targets of racism, burdens that typically make ordinary mothering extraordinarily difficult. But mothers in every class and social group harm their children. The location of "badness" in particular races, classes, or family arrangements—or in female more than male parents—allows the rest of "us" to deny the harms we have perpetrated as well as those we have suffered.

During the years we have been working together, the government of the United States, already known among technologically advanced capitalist states for its meager support of parents, was ending welfare as "we"—especially poor "single" mothers—have known it. Provincial governments in Canada, while generally more mother-friendly than their American counterparts, were also beginning to curtail important programs on which parents and children depend. As a result, while women of our social class were still not so subtly chastised for leaving children in day care in order to work, other mothers were being forced to work even in the absence of good day care on pain of losing state assistance on which they and their children depend. In ending welfare as we barely got to know it, governments were also undermining an admittedly fragile assumption that parents are meant to take a measure of responsibility for each other's children, that citizens are meant to help any parents and children living among them. To our relief and pleasure, many people, many parents, resist the meanness of their government once they see and understand it. One purpose of this book is to contribute to their resistance.

While we are set to defend mothers against mother blamers, and often enough against the laws and policies of our respective governments, we are also aware that mothers—all mothers maybe, but some mothers especially—harm children. Though the danger of drug use is sometimes systematically exaggerated, a woman using drugs may damage an infant she is carrying to term. Well-intended disciplinarians, enraged parents out of control, or seriously neglectful parents inflict real psychological and physical injury on children. Mothers who harm their children are often filled with bitter regret; but sometimes some mothers, of every class and every social group, seem almost indifferent to the harm they cause. Mothers who harm, however powerless they may be in their lives, are powerful in respect to their young children who are often utterly dependent upon their effective goodwill. Deliberately, helplessly, or inadvertently mothers may use their powers in ways that hurt.

In societies pervaded by mother blame, where many mothers are under siege, there is no easy way to deal with the harm mothers do. We urge— following Dorothy Roberts—that anyone addressing maternal harm *begin* by attending precisely to the circumstances in which mothers fail. Harmful mothers are also often harmed by poverty, racism, violence, sexism, or homophobia. They, as well as more socially fortunate mothers, are often sorely tried by the demands of provocative, mysteriously willful children. Or they may be exhausted simply from trying to make a coherent and safe enough child-world out of the particulars of domestic responsibilities, material demands, work schedules, and personal desires and ambitions.

Attending precisely to circumstances does not mean accepting them. Many of our contributors are determined to change the legal, economic, and political structures that shape mothers' lives, reforming family law, social policies, and cultural institutions so that they serve rather than hinder mothers' work. Although their project is very much ongoing, it is already beginning to undermine any normative models of "mothering" or "fathering" or "families" that exclude some mothers, set others against each other, or mystify or devalue the caregiving that mothers actually provide. Such changes benefit all mothers, including those whose aggression or neglect is largely an expression of circumstances of deprivation and humiliation.

No degree of reform will prevent all maternal harm; as we know, mothers sometimes neglect or assault their children in circumstances that seem distinctly fortunate. We, the editors, do not want to deny the harm mothers do. But, faced with maternal harm, we want to change the questions we ask. This includes changing the questions mothers ask themselves, shifting from the defensive or guilt-ridden cry, "What have I done?" to more open ended and genuinely empirical questions such as "What can I do now? Where can I get help?" We want also to change the questions we ask of other mothers. Many of us deliberately or unwittingly intervene in mothers' lives, acting or refusing to act as lawyers, social workers, policymakers, psychological counsellors, teachers, religious guides, neighbors, family members—as voters, writers, and fellow citizens. As we act—or decide not to act—to prevent harm, we would like to hear angry, punitive questions replaced by more useful ones. Instead of "How could *you* do *that*?" we would like to hear "What is it like for you?" Instead of "How can we punish?" or even "How can we control?" we would rather hear "How can we help?"

In changing the questions we also would like to change the kinds of discussion these questions prompt. In particular we hope for less censorship and self-censorship. Both the desire to censor and the need to resist censorship were brought home to us in an incident that occurred early in our conversations about the issues that later became the focus of this book. Julia brought the draft of a paper she was writing. While unequivocally supporting a woman's right to choose whether to continue her pregnancy, in her paper Julia asked feminists to reflect on the meaning of that choice. Particularly she asked what value, if any, we should place on intrauterine life.[5] Sara's response to the paper was immediately fearful: "You can't talk about that!" In a time when women's reproductive choices were under assault, it seemed dangerous and disloyal even to raise a question about their meaning. Drawing back from our heated exchange, we were surprised by the silences that at least one of us was willing to accept, and to impose. We found ourselves wondering whether a self-censored defense was really stronger than an honestly reflective one. We began to want deliberations among and about mothers less marked by silence and evasion even as we continued to feel the force of the antifeminist and racist culture that silenced us.

Ultimately a feminist politics of motherhood might defend mothers against extraordinary expectations and mean-spirited blame, while at the same time providing a moral framework for recognizing maternal responsibility and articulating standards of maternal judgment. But however honest, compassionate, and informed such a politics might be, it would not yield easy answers. As we worked together, and now continue thinking together, we remind ourselves that many maternal dilemmas cannot be resolved without "moral remainder"—a phrase Hilde Nelson borrows from

Christopher Gowans. Often there are no resolutions that do not leave some wrong outside the circle of rightness we are trying to draw. As Martha Minow recognizes, citing Rabbi Moshe Leib, "The way in this world is like the edge of a blade."

When we first began talking of putting together a book, we intended that most of its contributors would be legal theorists. Julia was herself a legal theorist; Sara had developed an amateur appreciative interest in feminist legal theory. We admired the capacity of legal theorists to focus both on specific cases and on abstract principles, to move easily between particular and general. We thought of legal theorists as "in the world" and yet able to take a reflective distance from it. Moreover, we believe, as Peggy Cooper Davis puts it, that law is a sign of the culture. It therefore offers cultural understanding and provides one purchase for cultural intervention.

Much as we appreciated legal thinking, we also wanted to avoid the defensive simplicity that the adversarial character of the legal system encourages. And we fervently wished, so far as possible, to dissociate our reflections from the drive to punish which the law both expresses and constrains. In dealing with mothers and harm, the recourse to punitive legislation and legal liability should be at best a last resort. Not only the possibility of a guilty verdict, but the ongoing *threat* of social condemnation, public exposure, trial and jail seems more apt to frighten and disable mothers than to help them and to protect their children.

While this collection is grounded by its focus on legal theory, we did not define our project in disciplinary terms. We enlisted thinkers who are trained in philosophy and political theory; in the book as it has emerged a former family court judge may sound like a psychoanalyst, a legal theorist like a philosopher. However, in deciding to ask scholars of religious studies to participate in our project, we did move deliberately outside our own intellectual training and interests to a discipline of which we were largely ignorant.

One of our motives for seeking papers from theorists of religion was to challenge the identification of religion with the Christian—or other fundamentalist—political right. We also recognized, as Bonnie Miller-McLemore and Paula Cooey forcefully remind us in this book, that religious practices are central in the lives of many women and shape many mothers' sense of the meaning of their work. Moreover Sara had maintained an emotional connection to the Christian religion in which she was raised and wanted to include explicitly feminist religious insight in an admittedly secular book.

Most important, for Julia Jewish culture and traditions provide a moral compass, a framework of compassion and justice, and a sense of historical continuity through which to view the world. Both of us felt the need of just such general frameworks, when trying to reckon, compassionately and justly, the needs of mothers and children.

Our efforts to draw theorists of religion into our discussion led to fascinating conversations, conferences, and readings. In the end we came to realize, more than when we began, that it is no easy task simply to "include" a religious perspective within a predominantly secular book. We leave our readers, especially but not only those who are secular, with the question of how to integrate and learn from religious insights within a discussion that does not presume, though it respects, religious heritage or belief.

We now offer a brief guide to the book we have put together, drawn from our particular reading of the essays. We begin with an essay by Eva Kittay that offers a reflective personal account of mothering a profoundly disabled and mentally handicapped daughter. We begin with her essay because we want from the outset to call into question any preconceived ideas about "normal" mothering or about "normal" children. By focusing on what seems a quite "special" child, Kittay illuminates many issues about the practice and meaning of mothering allegedly "normal" children. She speaks, for example, of the need to distribute mothering among many people, about complex relationships with paid caregivers who care for one's children, and of the relationship between parents and doctors or other experts. These issues, problematic for many mothers, acquire a distinctive, often troubled, urgency in the lives of parents of a disabled child.

In her essay, Eva Kittay also casts light on two general philosophical issues. In examining the daily work of caring for her disabled child, she illuminates the pervasiveness and meaning of dependencies and the value of the "dependency work" on which all children rely. In the conclusion of her essay she reflects on the ways that the experience of mothering a seriously disabled child might change and enrich ideas of maternal work and maternal thinking. In particular she questions ideals of mothering which have been couched primarily in terms of fostering the independence of a child. Instead, she suggests, and we endorse, the ideal of developing a child's capacity for love and joy.

In Part 2—"Mothers and Harm: No Easy Answers"—essayists focus on maternal (or parental) actions that allegedly harm children. They consider cases ranging from the failure to protect children from abuse to "abusing children" by using drugs while pregnant, from refusing medical treatment to dying children to leaving children for work or because of divorce, to having children when too young to care for them. The authors articulate the social context in which harm is done, particularly the assumptions about race and class that affect mothers' work and the religious beliefs to which they are subjected or which they hold. Even as they refuse to demonize mothers, each of the essays takes seriously potential harm to children and maternal responsibility for protective care.

The first chapter, by Dorothy E. Roberts, raises the question of how a passionate advocate for mothers thinks about maternal neglect. Her particular focus here is on mothers who fail to protect their children from male violence in the home. Roberts begins by looking at how criminal law imposes affirmative duties on mothers more than on other classes of people. She pays serious attention to public responsibility and to the political circumstances of mothers' lives, including racism, male violence, and poverty. At the same time she does not lose sight of the personal responsibility of mothers whose children (in many cases terrorized and wounded) depend on them. She concludes with what she calls "a political stand on behalf of mothers" which "listens to the child's voice."

Martha Minow offers a reading of the story of the Binding of Isaac, an example of the feminist project of recasting religious texts.[6] She reads as a woman, mother, and child, as a lawyer and teacher of law. And, like Dorothy Roberts, she also finds no easy answers. Taking up the general question of defending other people's children from parental abuse, Minow attends especially to parents who refuse medical treatment for their children out of religious belief. She is troubled both by legal intervention and by failure to rescue children. Her conclusions are ultimately questions, particularly questions about the meaning and dangers of parental sacrifice.

Lynn Paltrow writes from her perspective as a lawyer who defends women prosecuted for "abusing" their "children" by using drugs while pregnant. Paltrow shows how the media uncritically accepts stories of the harm of drug use during pregnancy, particularly how they, as well as prosecutors, some judges, and many politicians, fail to see the racist and class-based underpinnings of the "crack baby" phenomenon. While neither she nor anyone else advocates or even excuses using drugs while pregnant, she insists that our rage to prosecute and punish sets mother against fetus, to the detriment of both. She advocates instead social policies that originate in compassion and a respect for the complexity of women's lives.

Nina Perales discusses one particular instance of "teenage" pregnancy and mothering. While skeptical of legal interventions to punish teenage pregnancy, she is also suspicious of the "cultural defense" that justifies a very young woman's relation to an older man and subsequent pregnancy by appealing to her culture's mores. The case she considers of a young Mexican American, Adela Quintana, reveals the danger of using cultural stereotypes about family, sexuality, and "the foreign" undocumented immigrant to create distinct exculpatory legal categories, in this case for Latina teens made pregnant by adult men. As Perales shows, such a "defense" can effectively deprive a woman of the support she needs. Perales looks to a nuanced analysis that responds to the complexity of the lives of teenage mothers without resorting to cultural essentialism.

Carol Sanger discusses the dilemma of leaving children to work. She places the phenomenon of separating from children in order to work in both historical and class contexts, reminding us of separations that last seasons (for example, migrant workers) or years and may even have endangered children's lives. Her primary concern is with present-day mothers in capitalist societies who leave their children temporarily for work. She notes that some mothers are vilified for working, especially if they don't "need" to, while others (so-called welfare mothers) are castigated for not working. She then argues against accepting the stark class differentials in the way we treat children. Instead she wants to create a social consensus that separating from children in order to work is a respectable and responsible choice for mothers to make and that any mother should be supported in her choice.

In "Always Connect" Hilde Lindemann Nelson assumes that some divorces are desirable or inevitable, and then reflects on the responsibilities divorcing parents have to their children. She recognizes that there may be no way of shaping life after divorce that fails to do harm: There are "no easy answers"—no solution without "moral remainder." But she urges nonetheless that parents attempt to preserve the relationships on which their children depend while also remaining entitled to establish new relationships of their own, including sexual ones. In support of her recommendations she offers a general philosophical account of persons, relationships, and responsibilities that can illuminate many maternal dilemmas.

In Part 3, "Mothers, Families, and the State: Reexamining the Old, Reinventing the New," essayists examine the ways that "mothers," "fathers," and "families" are imagined and thus created by family law, state policy, and religious practice and doctrine, sometimes in conjunction with psychological theories about children's needs. In their essays, the authors examine patriarchal, heterosexist, nativist, and racist conceptions embedded in the defense of various conventional family forms. As they explore deeply embedded gendered norms of mothering (and fathering) along with mechanisms and metaphors for family formation, this group of essays reminds us that mothering and fathering, while intensely personal relationships, are also constructed as well as interpreted within a particular society's legal, cultural, and political frameworks.

Martha Fineman examines the trend in family law toward formal gender neutrality and equality. She establishes the dissonance between legal rhetoric and the social practices of mothering and fathering which remain deeply embedded gendered concepts. Focusing on custody decisions after divorce and welfare law, Fineman exposes an ideology that proclaims fathers' rights, assumes male economic responsibility for families, and idealizes visions of the conventional two-parent, heterosexual nuclear family. She reveals the ways in which this ideology continues to shape law even though women are now expected to be independent economic actors while also remaining the primary caretakers of the vulnerable and dependent. She calls for fundamental social reordering that will acknowledge multiple expectations of women in the home and the workforce, reshape social expectations of men, and demand greater support for caretakers from public institutions.

Lisa Ikemoto's chapter discusses a particular link between welfare "reform" and anti-immigration policies forged, in part, through images of the immigrant mother. She traces a shift in emphasis in social contract from a state's commitment to the liberty and equality of citizens to a citizen's obligations to the state, measured largely in terms of a work ethic. She also explores the changing gendered figurations of immigrant men and mothers in the "living room politics" that helps to create the link between welfare "reform" and immigration policy. As she outlines the nativist, racist assumptions of welfare and immigration policies, she makes clear the material costs that immigrant mothers—especially Asian and Latina mothers—pay for the effects of our dominant "American" discourse.

The next two pieces attend to several issues in the creation and maintenance of families. Mary Lyndon Shanley reflects upon the philosophical bases for determining who has the right and duty to care for children. Her particular focus is the difficulties lesbian co-mothers face in trying to obtain legal recognition of their parental status, and the corresponding complexity of determining the nature (if any) of the rights of sperm donors. In examining court cases about lesbian families Shanley raises fundamental questions about the grounds for establishing parental rights and responsibilities in a world of changing social practices regarding family formation and various new reproductive technologies.

Drucilla Cornell's critique of conventional family structures focuses on the politics of adoption and the lack of feminist engagement with the notion of multiple mothers. She draws particular attention to the imperialist race and class dimensions that exist in the context of international adoptions and to the need for a critical perspective on the patriarchal and heterosexist underpinnings of the typical closed adoption where neither birth mother nor child is provided information about the other. Turning to reform of family law, Cornell calls for a focus on custodial responsibility for children without underpinning such responsibility in heterosexual union or unitary notions of motherhood.

In her chapter Paula Cooey introduces another institution, the conservative Christian church, which in its practice and theology attempts to impose a particular patriarchal, heterosexual family arrangement as both divine and natural. This church ideology, Cooey claims, does not serve even the mothers understandably attracted to its doctrine, let alone the mothers it excludes. Cooey also introduces another cultural force, psychological theory, which, she claims, offers class-based, unrealistic accounts of mothering that undermine maternal self-esteem and may actually contribute to maternal violence. Cooey's general claim is that American society expects the extraordinary of mothers and that the corollary of such extraordinary expectations is the demonization of mothers who fail to meet them. She calls for "social theoreticians and theologians of the left" to provide constructive symbolic interpretations of motherhood that include a focus on the meaning of work inside and outside the home and its relation to spirituality.

Peggy Cooper Davis, a former family court judge, begins by synthesizing case law in the Supreme Court of the United States on the constitutional rights of parents, especially biological, unwed fathers, attending to the ways in which requirements of parenting are gendered. She then turns to mothers suspected of neglecting or abusing their children, focusing on psychological theories that have influenced cultural understandings of children's needs as well as public policy concerning children in public care. Davis argues that cultural conceptions of "The Good Mother" cause social welfare agencies to cut children off from families that fail to meet an impossible standard, leaving them inadequately nurtured by anyone. Drawing upon a variety of theorists, and especially the work of psychoanalyst Jessica Benjamin, she formulates an alternative standard for caretaking adults of the obligation to meet children's needs for love.

In our final section, "Beginning Again: Conversations of Mothers," we turn to two of the original aims of our project. We wanted to encourage honest and realistic discussions of mothering. We also wanted to include a religious perspective in our thinking about mothering.

Bonnie Miller-McLemore deplores the lies about mothering which mothers accept and feminists sometimes tell. But her primary intent is to challenge readers who are grappling with contemporary dilemmas of motherhood to take seriously religious practices, scriptures, and beliefs. She reminds us of the importance of religious practices in many mothers' lives and the persistence of religious ideas even in the thinking of those who count themselves secular. She then draws upon the psychoanalytic self-psychologist Heinz Kohut to argue that some ideals are necessary for mothers, as for people generally. While she endorses "postmodern" suspicions of univocal truth or standards of "goodness," she argues that religious thinking can contribute to the articulation of ideals that mothering requires.

Jennifer Nedelsky's memoir serves as an example of the kind of reflective discussion we had originally envisioned. Speaking in a passionate personal voice, Nedelsky recalls the dilemmas she has encountered as a tenured academic who has come to embrace her own nuclear family, a family form that is also responsible for many of the dilemmas she faces. Her discussion ranges over many subjects: genetic testing, the love affair of mothers and infants, relations with paid "Nannys," the ongoing effort to balance work and family, the political sympathies provoked by mothering which are joined with a kind of practical and emotional withdrawal also provoked by mothering. Uniting these disparate topics is Nedelsky's resolute attempt to document and understand many kinds of silences, including her own, that keep mothers from understanding their own maternal experience.

From the beginning we hoped this book would counter silences about and among mothers. We imagined discussions among people with different "opinions" who listened to each other with care, sought out complexity, and avoided easy answers to stubborn dilemmas. We wanted to replace evasions and pronouncements with real, if halting, talk. Borrowing from Hannah Arendt, Nedelsky stresses the need for mothers to develop a "community of judgment" in which they can express and test their maternal thinking. We hope that this book contributes to creating such communities for mothers and also for their advocates.

1. Sara Ruddick, "Procreative Ethics," prepared for a seminar in feminism and philosophy, Beijing, China, June 1995, published in Chinese in *Chinese Women and Feminist Thought* (Beijing: Chinese Social Sciences Press, 1998); Julia E. Hanigsberg, "Power and Procreation: State Interference in Pregnancy," *Ottawa Law Review* 23 (1991): 35.

2. Sara Ruddick, "Procreative Choice for Adolescent Women," in *The Politics of Pregnancy,* ed. Annette Lawson and Deborah Rhode (New Haven, Conn.: Yale University Press, 1993).

3. Sara Ruddick, "Injustice in Families: Assault and Domination," in *Justice and Care: The Essential Readings*, edited by Virginia Held (Boulder, Colo.: Westview Press, 1995); Julia E. Hanigsberg, "An Essay on *The Piano* and the Search for Women's Desire," *Michigan Journal of Gender and the Law* 3 (1996): 41.

4. The phrase "gendered lives" comes from Martha A. Fineman, *The Neutered Mother, The Sexual Family and Other Twentieth Century Tragedies* (New York: Routledge, 1995); see also Sara Ruddick, "Ideals of Fatherhood," in *Feminism and Families*, ed. Hilde Lindemann Nelson (New York: Routledge, 1997).

5. Julia E. Hanigsberg, "Homologizing Motherhood and Pregnancy: A Consideration of Abortion," *Michigan Law Review* 94 (1995): 371. Now that Julia's article has been published, vitriolic responses from people on both sides of the abortion debate confirm Sara's fears.

6. Minow's article first appeared in a collection of Jewish feminist writing, *Beginning Anew: A Woman's Companion to the High Holy Days* (New York: Touchstone, 1997), an anthology of women's interpretation of Jewish spiritual writing.

PART 1

Prologue

Eva Feder Kittay

''Not *My* Way, Sesha, *Your* Way, Slowly'':
"Maternal Thinking" in the Raising of a Child with Profound Intellectual Disabilities

I — A Personal Narrative

A Child Is Born, Becoming a Mother

The most important thing that happens when a child with disabilities is born is that a child is born.[1]

When Sesha was born, I, along with Jeffrey, her father and my life-partner, fell madly in love with our baby. It was 1969. I was twenty-three, my husband twenty-five, and we were pioneers in the natural childbirth movement. I was reaping the benefits of being "awake and aware."[2] Exhilarated by the vigorous labor of propelling my baby into the world, and amazed by the success of my own body's heaving, I gazed into the little face emerging from me, a face wearing a pout that slowly became the heralding cry of the newborn infant. The nurses cleaned her off, handed her to me and my Sesha melted into my arms. With her full head of black hair, her sweet funny infant's face, and her delicious temperament, this baby was the fulfillment of our dreams. We saw in her the perennial "perfect baby": the exquisite miracle of a birth. It was December 23rd, and all the world was poised for Christmas. But we had our own christmas, our own celebration of birth and the beauty, freshness, and promise of infancy. This birth, and each birth, unique and universal—common, even ordinary, and yet each time miraculous.

Such were my reflections as I lay in my New York City hospital room watching the snow falling, bathing in the glory of a wanted, welcomed baby. Only the hospital wasn't conforming to my mood or my expectations. The staff was being either bureaucratic or inept. I had anticipated seeing my baby shortly after she had been wheeled out of the delivery room, and thought she would soon thereafter join me in my room. "Rooming-in" was an innovation, a concession to new women's voices, to women who wanted to breastfeed and to have their infants by their side, not in a nursery down the hall to be fed on a rigid four-hour schedule. I was to have my baby in my room after a twenty-four-hour observation period. But more than twenty-four hours had passed and no one had brought her in. Why? Could something be wrong? The nurses evaded my questions, and the doctors were nowhere to be found. Finally, I ventured down the hall to the nursery and after encountering still more evasions, eventually found someone with an answer. Sesha had some jaundice ("common, nothing to worry about") and a cyanotic episode of no known origin (that is, she had briefly stopped breathing). She had been examined by a pediatrician, and she seemed fine. I could start nursing her and we could leave the hospital according to schedule. It was four months before anyone thought again about that episode.

As the months wore on, I slowly adjusted to motherhood, and Sesha helped make the adjustment easy. Jeffrey and I shared all aspects of parenting, except the nursing, which I did. One wise nursing book—I no longer recall who wrote it—advised against a baby nurse for the nursing mother. Instead it urged that the father (grandmothers, friends, and paid help, if affordable) should help care for the mother and take over all tasks except the care and feeding of the nursing baby. This would allow her to regain her strength, and to nurse the baby in a rested condition and peaceful frame of mind. I was fortunate enough to be able to follow that advice. In fact, I recognized then and have come to believe still more deeply that this advice contained a profound principle: that to nurture a dependent being well, and without damaging the nurturer, requires that the nurturer herself be nurtured.[3] This advice embodied the egalitarian ideals of marriage and parenthood that I shared with my spouse.

So the two of us embraced our parenthood and were blissful with our new baby. Sesha didn't cry much, fell asleep at my breast at night, and by day slept and munched (though with less vigor than I had expected). While she slept a great deal, when awake she had a wonderful wide-eyed questioning look that made us feel that she was very alert and taking in everything around her. At four months she was developing into a beautiful little baby, very cooperative and oh so sweet. Only she wasn't doing new "tricks." When friends and relatives would ask us what the little prodigy was up to, we'd have curiously little to report. But then, I wasn't interested in how early my child did such and such. All potential sources of anxiety were water on a duck's back: I was the happy mama, content to be gliding through this new period of my life with duckling and mate in tow. Yet it was precisely at this fourth month that a swell of extraordinary proportions engulfed us and interrupted my blissful journey into motherhood.

At this time, friends with a baby approximately Sesha's age visited us, and we were disturbed by the significant difference in the development of the two infants. A physician friend indicated that I ought to visit a pediatric neurologist. (Our own pediatrician responded to my query of why Sesha, at four months, was still not picking up her head, by saying that she must have a heavier head than the average baby and that such a trait is generally inherited from one of the parents. He advised me to go home and measure my husband's head to see if he too had a large head. Like fools, my husband and I pulled out the tape measure and determined that yes, my husband's head was somewhat large. What cowardice propelled this pediatrician to evade his responsibility to be forthright and refer us to a specialist?!) The neurologist we visited must have known right away that Sesha was severely impaired, but he broke the news to us gradually, over a period that lasted nearly two years. In contrast to my pediatrician, this physician was being kind, not evasive. He did not try to falsely reassure us. His efforts to gently ease us into the realization of the extensive damage Sesha had sustained were nonetheless thwarted when, on his recommendation, we visited the star pediatric neurologist on the West Coast while on holiday.

Sesha was six months old, still as lovely and sweet and pliant as one might wish any baby to be. The handsome, well-tanned doctor examined our daughter briefly, and told us without any hesitation that she was and would always be profoundly retarded—at best severely and not profoundly retarded. His credentials as a physician who can correctly predict an outcome remain secure—but his understanding of how to approach parents with such harsh news, surely also an important skill for a physician, is quite another matter. The swell that had been threatening to engulf us for two months now crested, and we were smashed onto a rocky shore with all the force that nature could muster against us. Never will I forget how ill I was in that San Francisco hotel room—how my body convulsed against this indigestible information. My husband had to care for Sesha and me, even as he ached. This doctor's brutal, insensitive way of breaking devastating news to parents is a story I have heard recounted again and again. The pain of the prognosis is matched only by the anger at obtuse and insensitive doctors. In our own case, we had a near repeat performance when, just to be certain of his suspicions, our first and humane physician wanted still one more consultation. We thought that we had now visited the Inferno, and we were prepared to begin the arduous climb back up—to find some equilibrium, some way to live with this verdict. But on our encounter with the third pediatric neurologist we were again told outright—after a five-minute exam—that our daughter was severely to profoundly retarded and that we should consider having other children because "one rotten apple doesn't spoil the barrel." As I type these words nearly twenty-seven years later, I still wonder at the utter failure of human empathy in this physician—one whose specialty, no less, was neurological impairment.

Sesha was never to live a normal life. It would be another year before we completed the tests, the evaluations, the questionings that confirmed those first predictions. We couldn't know or fully accept the extent of her impairment, but some things were clear. We knew it wasn't a degenerative disability and for that, we were grateful. But our worst fear was that her handicap involved her intellectual faculties. We, her parents, were intellectuals. I was committed to a life of the mind. Nothing mattered to me as much as to be able to reason, to reflect, to understand. This was the air I breathed. How was I to raise a daughter who would have no part of this? If my life took its meaning from thought, what kind of meaning would her life have? Yet throughout this time, it never even occurred to me to give Sesha up, to institutionalize her, to think of her in any other terms than my own beloved child. She was my daughter. I was her mother. That was fundamental. Her impairment in no way mitigated my love for her. If it had any impact on that love it was only to intensify it. She was so vulnerable, she would need so much of our love and protection to shelter her from the scorn of the world, from its dangers, from its indifference, from its failure to understand her and her humanity. We didn't yet realize how much she would teach us, but we already knew that we had learned something. That which we believed we valued, what we—I—thought was at the center of humanity—the capacity for thought, for reason, was not it, not it at all.

Portrait of Sesha at Twenty-Seven

Ian's sense of humor is part of what makes him Ian not part of what makes him retarded, even though his cognitive limitations have helped to shape that humor. [This] goes beyond a tolerance of difference . . . to an appreciation of a child's individuality.[4]

I am awakening and her babbling-brook giggles penetrate my semiconscious state. Hands clapping. Sesha is listening to "The Sound of Music." Peggy, her caregiver of twenty-three years, has just walked in and Sesha can hardly contain her desire to throw her arms around Peggy and give Peggy her distinctive kiss—mouth open, top teeth lightly (and sometimes not so lightly) pressing on your cheek, her breath full of excitement and happiness, her arms around your neck (if you're lucky; if not, arms up, hands on hair, which cavemanlike, she uses to pull your face to her mouth). Sesha's kisses are legendary (and if you're not on your toes, somewhat painful).

Sesha was almost twelve before she learned to kiss, learned to hug. These were major achievements. Sesha's chronological age is now that of a young woman. She has the physical characteristics of a teen. She's tall, slender, long-legged, with dark beautiful brown eyes, brown short wavy luxuriant hair, a shy smile that she delivers with a lowered head, and a radiant laugh that will make her throw her head back in delight. Sesha has been beautiful from the day of her birth, through all her girlhood and now into her young adulthood. Her loveliness shines through her somewhat twisted body, the bridge that substitutes for her natural front teeth (lost in a fall at school), her profound cognitive deficits. The first thing people remark when they meet Sesha, or see her photo, is how beautiful she is. I've always admired (without worshiping) physical beauty and so I delight in Sesha's loveliness. The smoothness of her skin, the brilliant light in her eyes, the softness of her breath, the tenderness of her spirit. Her spirit.

No, Sesha's loveliness is not skin deep. How to speak of it? How to describe it? Joy. The capacity for joy. The babbling-brook laughter at a musical joke. The starry-eyed far-away look as she listens to Elvis crooning "Love me tender," the excitement of her entire soul as the voices blare out "Alle

Menschen werden Brüder" in the choral ode of Beethoven's Ninth Symphony, and the pleasure of bestowing her kisses and receiving the caresses in turn. All variations and gradations of joy. Spinoza characterized joy as the increase in our power of self-preservation and by that standard, Sesha's is a very well preserved self. Yet she is so limited. She cannot speak. She cannot even say "Mama"—though sometimes we think she says "Aylu" (our translation, "I love you"). She can only finger-feed herself, despite the many efforts at teaching her to use utensils. She'll sometimes drink from a cup (and sometimes spill it all). She is "time trained" at toileting, which means that she is still in diapers. Although she began to walk at five, she no longer can walk independently—her scoliosis and seizures and we do not know what else have robbed her of this capacity. So she is in a wheelchair. Her cerebral palsy is not severe, but it is there.

She has no measurable I.Q. As she was growing up she was called "developmentally delayed." But delay implies that she will one day develop the capacities that are slow in developing. The jury is no longer out. Most capacities she will not develop at all. Is she then a "vegetable"? The term is ludicrous when applied to her. There is nothing vegetative about her. She is fully a human, not a vegetable. Given the scope and breadth of human possibilities and capacities, she occupies a limited spectrum, but she inhabits it fully because she has the most important faculties of all. The capacities for love and for happiness. These allow those of us who care for her, who love her, who have been entrusted with her well-being to form deep and abiding attachments to her. Sesha's coin and currency is love. That is what she wishes to receive and that is what she reciprocates—in spades.

On the Very Possibility of Mothering and the Challenge of the Severely Disabled Child

My mother would help in the early days and months of Sesha's life. My mother, a warm affectionate woman who miraculously not only survived the Holocaust, but survived it emotionally intact, loves children and especially loves babies. As an only child, I alone could provide her with grandchildren, and Sesha was the first and only grandchild on both sides of the family. All the grandparents were thrilled with Sesha's birth, and deeply saddened at the news that there were suspicions of retardation. We thought that we would slowly introduce them to the idea that the prognosis was as dire as we knew it to be. In the meanwhile, my mother would baby-sit Sesha when both Jeffrey and I were busy and would take her for the night when I had a paper to write for graduate school. We had never brought the grandparents to the doctor's visits, hoping to spare them some of the pain we experienced at each visit, but once it could not be helped. It was on that fateful visit that my mother grasped the full extent of the trauma to Sesha's brain. Upon our return, my mother, in her inimitable and insistent fashion, urged me to place Sesha in an institution.

Of all the traumatic encounters in that first year and a half of Sesha's life, none, perhaps not even the realization that Sesha was retarded, was as painful as these words from the woman I loved most in my life: the woman who had taught me what it was to be a mother, to love a child, to anticipate the joys of nursing, of holding and caring for another, of sacrificing for a child. My model of maternal love asking me to discard my child? Would she have banished me to an institution had I been "damaged"? Surely, she couldn't mean this. But, no, she *insisted*, with conviction, with surefooted rightness that I *had to* put this child out of my life. It made me crazy. I couldn't comprehend it. Only the images and stories of the Holocaust could reclaim for me my mother and her love. Only the knowledge that in those bitter times, a limp was a death warrant. To merely be associated with disability was a death warrant. Of course she was acting like a mother, as someone whose interest was my well-being. I see now that she thought this child would ruin my life, but she was unable to transcend her own maternity and project that quality onto me: to realize that the maternal love and concern she had for me, I had for Sesha. I remained in her eyes a child, a daughter and not a mother with her own daughter. Now I think back and wonder how much of my mother's response was attributable to fear of the unknown (and what was known but in different circumstances), how much was the result of the stigma attached to disability, and how much was resistance to the reality of my maternity? In time, my mother came to understand that we could build a good life with Sesha. She allowed herself to love Sesha with the fullness of a grandmother's love. And in time, I forgave my mother and came to appreciate how her intense, if misdirected, love for me fueled her stubborn insistence that we "put Sesha away."

Of course, parents at that time (1970) did institutionalize retarded children. And this all happened before the horrors of Willowbrook were exposed, although there had been exposés, if not as sensational and gripping as Willowbrook, still chilling enough to give anyone pause before committing their child to an institution. I cannot say what I might have thought if we did not have, as we did (through the good fortunes of family), ample resources to care for Sesha. The image I had of public institutions was that they were merely a dumping ground. No one whose material resources gave them a choice would opt for such putative "care." Private institutions were perhaps less dismal, but nonetheless sad affairs for families who for a variety of reasons, some financial, some psychological and emotional, could not see themselves facing the challenge of raising a mentally retarded child at home. But nowhere in my heart and mind did I find room for that alternative, and in this my husband and I were in complete accord.

It was simply impossible for me to part with my child. This is what I knew of mothering, mothering, at least, that is chosen. A child is born to you. This child is your charge—it is your sacred responsibility to love, nurture, and care for this child throughout your life. Is this "maternal instinct"? I don't know what those words mean. Do all women who become mothers believe thus? Clearly not. Is it then a cultural construct? If so, it is a belief constructed in many cultures, in many historical periods. Perhaps this commitment is rather the condition for the possibility of motherhood—realized differently in different cultures, under different conditions, and differently realized even by women within a single culture, or a single historical period. It may not be inspired by birth, but by adoption, but once a child is "your" child, at that moment you become that child's mother and the duty emerging from that bond is one of the most compelling of all duties. At that point you commit yourself to the well-being of one who is dependent upon you, whose survival, growth, and development as a social being is principally (if never solely) your responsibility. The birth of a child with very significant impairments may test the limit of the commitment that I take to be the very condition for the possibility of mothering. It may do so for some women, under some—adverse—circumstances. In my own understanding this felt conviction is so fundamental that it serves as a benchmark. The extent to which a woman cannot realize it (in the idiom appropriate to her own culture) because of adverse social, political, or economic conditions, to that extent she faces an injustice.[5] I take it, then, that the requirement to be able to mother, that is, to realize the condition for the possibility to mother, constitutes one of the "circumstances of justice."[6]

Mothering Distributed: The Work of Dependency Care

Mothers perceive the mentally retarded child as more of a hardship in direct proportion to the child's incapacitation and helplessness.[7]

Sesha's expansive, affectionate nature is a gift. In comparison studies with autistic children, researchers have found that "the mother's ability and enthusiasm for functioning in the maternal caretaker role are adversely affected by the developmentally disabled child who is *not* affectionate and *not* demonstrative."[8] But researchers have also found (to no one's surprise I hope) that the greater the degree of "incapacitation and helplessness," the greater the burden the child poses. Taking care of Sesha, meeting her daily needs, her medical needs, interpreting her needs and desires, not over the span of twenty-seven months, but twenty-seven years, has posed a substantial challenge.

I never wanted to hire help to care for my child. I believed that with shared parenting it should be possible to care for a child and still pursue an additional life's work. I soon found that I was wrong. All families where each parent takes on work additional to child care and domestic duties require help with child care. Had Sesha been a normal toddler, I would have tried to hunt out the few day care programs that were being established in the 1970s for women like myself who, while not driven by economic necessity, were nonetheless committed to *both* motherhood and some other life's work. But Sesha could not play in the easy way other young children could play. She needed intense stimulation. Her attention faded quickly; if left to her own devices, she'd simply stare off into space. Keeping Sesha stimulated was, and remains, hard work.

For a while Sesha was enrolled in one of the pilot projects in early intervention for the developmentally delayed. She made wonderful progress in the first five months of the program. But Sesha's story, unlike so many I have read about, was not one of continuing development.[9] After several years in that same program the improvements became more and more minimal. While needing child care was something I shared with other mothers, because of my daughter's profound disability I was dependent on housebound help.

Certainly someone could give Sesha perfunctory custodial "care," that is, attend to her bodily needs but without ever seeing the person whose body it is, without tapping into her desires, without engaging her potential, without responding to and returning her affection—her affection which is her most effective means of connecting with others, in the absence of speech and most other capacities required for interpersonal activities. To commit to care for Sesha required an ability to give your heart to a child, who because she would never outgrow the need for your continual care, would not release you from an abiding bond and obligation. While we found a number of talented caretakers, few were willing to yield to the demands of caring for Sesha for an extended time. Caring for Sesha, when done well, is intensive labor and the relationship enabling such care must also already be intensive.

Sesha was four when a woman walked into our lives who came and stayed. How and where we acquired the instincts I don't know, but we knew immediately that Peggy was right. She was scarcely interested in us. Her interview was with Sesha. But she wouldn't take the job. Peggy feared the intensity of the involvement she knew was inevitable. We pleaded and increased the salary. She told me later she would never have taken the job if her agency hadn't urged her to do a trial week. At the end of the week, it was already nearly too late to quit. Sesha had worked her way into Peggy's heart. Twenty-three years later, Peggy told me the following story:

> I had been with Sesha in Central Park and I was working on some walking exercises that the folks at Rusk [Sesha's early intervention program] had assigned. I was working terribly hard trying to get Sesha to cooperate and do what I was supposed to get her to do. I sat her down in her stroller and sat down on a park bench. I realized that I was simply exhausted from the effort. I thought, How am I going to do this? How can I possibly do this job? when I looked down at Sesha and saw her little head pushed back against her stroller moving first to one side and then to another. I couldn't figure out what she was doing. Until I traced what her eyes were fixed on. She had spotted a leaf falling, and she was following its descent. I said "Thank you for being my teacher, Sesha. I see now. Not *my* way, *your* way, slowly." After that, I fully gave myself over to Sesha. That forged the bond.

Sara Ruddick, writing about the relationship between care as labor and care as relationship, remarks: "The work [of caring] is constituted in and through the relation of those who give and receive care." Nowhere is this better illustrated than in this story. And nowhere is the notion that the work of mothering and caring requires thought, understanding—again in Ruddick's words, "maternal thinking"—better illustrated than in this story. Forging the relationship, through this insight into who Sesha is, how she sees the world, made possible the caring labor itself. And a caring labor so infused with the relationship has enhanced the relationship, made it as solid as the bonds of motherhood.

As I write this essay a much older Peggy still cares for a much older Sesha in many of the same ways. But as she ages and Sesha ages we reach the limits of the laboring aspect of caring. The relationship has come to be "in 'excess' of the labor [it] enable[s]."[10] This is a difficult and troubling state of affairs—for us as parents, for Peggy, and if Sesha understands it, for her. Sesha's possible future without Peggy troubles me profoundly—not simply because we have so come to rely on her, but because I cannot bear the thought that such a central relationship in Sesha's life could be sundered.

What is this relationship? "A relationship with no name," as my son so aptly said once. Why has no one spoken of such a relationship? Could our family be so privileged as to be unique? Privileged first in having the resources? Privileged above all in having found such a steadfast companion and caretaker for our daughter? What has this daughter and this relationship taught me about mothering? Can anything be generalized and learned from such a perspective of privilege, on the one hand, and anomaly, on the other?

But neither Peggy nor father nor mother has completely sufficed for the care Sesha requires and we have had to call in others—part-time, usually weekend help—most of whom have stayed with Sesha for years, until their lives called them to move on. With Sesha it takes more than a village. As Sesha has grown older, we have felt the need for more and more help so that we could pursue our roles as professionals, as parents of our son, whose needs and demands were so different, as folks entitled to some leisure, some gratification of aesthetic desires and other accoutrements of the good life, gratification and fulfillment we need not only for their own sake but also so that we can love Sesha without resentment that her overwhelming needs rob us of the satisfactions we might otherwise enjoy. We have moved to a model, which for want of any other adequate term I'll call "distributed mothering." I am Sesha's one mother; but in truth her mothering has been distributed across a number of individuals: father, various caretakers, and Peggy.

In the literature on the care of the disabled child, little attention is given to the team of persons doing the hands-on care of the disabled, whom I have called "dependency workers": those who attend to the very basic needs of a dependent, needs the dependent is incapable of fulfilling on her own behalf. Like the stagehands who serve as Marilyn Frye's (1983) metaphor for the role of women on the stage of world history and culture, the dependency worker is the invisible stagehand in the saga of disability. I hope that the discussion in this set of reflections will open the way to investigating the relationship between dependency work and mothering a disabled child; between dependency work and disability; between the dependency worker and the disabled person.

Peggy and I

Peggy and I are like two metals, of not very dissimilar composition, but tempered under very different circumstances. Ten years and one month my senior, Peggy was born before the war and lived her youth in war-torn Ireland and Britain. I was born after the war, and grew to maturity in the booming economies of Sweden and the United States. We are both immigrants—though she traveled here, willingly, as a young woman, accompanied only by her sister; I came as a young girl, reluctantly, brought by my parents. She was one of thirteen children raised lovingly but in poverty and wartime, with a father off to fight. I was an only child, the precious projection of hope by two survivors of Hitler's murderous rage against the Jews. She was raised to be fiercely independent; I was overprotected. She was raised to be self-reliant and hardy; I was looked over as a fragile flower. She had to make her own way early. I never *had* to make my own way at all. She is always punctual; I am always late. She is a doer; I am a thinker. She insists on routine; I'm incapable of following routine. We are not easily compatible, Peggy and I, but we come together on politics, on compassion, on a love of books, and most important of all on our passion for Sesha.

Peggy and I respect each other. There may even be love there, but we never speak of it. The worst times are when Sesha gets ill. Sesha's disabilities are multiple, which means her illnesses easily compound. An elevated temperature, a small infection, a bit of nausea will lower her threshold for seizures. When the seizures start up, she becomes sleep deprived and that aggravates her condition. Things can snowball quickly. When Sesha is ill, we don't know what bothers her, what hurts her, what the pain feels like. We are deprived of a vital avenue for diagnosis. This makes her terribly vulnerable, and makes us crazy. Peggy in her frustration vents her fear and anger on me. I feel guilty. I am not doing enough; why do I not care for her myself? But I also question why I have to cope with Peggy's anger. How long can I continue to live with this tension? This anger? This pain? Can we continue to care for Sesha in our home? What happens when Peggy leaves? Is Sesha's illness life threatening? What happens when we die?

The threat that Sesha might die, the expectation that we will die—these are always the terminal points for all our questionings concerning Sesha. What is Peggy's terminus? The questions for her are "What happens when I am not here? Why do I stay? Sesha is not my daughter, I am not her mother. What if I don't care for Sesha? Will she die?" Peggy has often said to me, "You can get away from concerns about Sesha with your work. But Sesha *is* my work." Peggy can think of leaving, of quitting. I cannot. But really, can Peggy?

Sometimes I feel that my relationship to Peggy vis-à-vis Sesha is like the patriarchal relation of husband to wife vis-à-vis their children. Peggy accompanies me to doctor's visits with Sesha. Actually, it is more as if I accompany her and Sesha. I deal with the authorities (much as the father does), she undresses Sesha (much as the mother does), although since it is distasteful to me to stand idly by, I "help" (much as an involved father might). I pay the bills, she wheels Sesha out. Some roles we can reverse, others we can't— they are set in the larger practices in which we participate. Whenever and each time I see the analogies, it makes my feminist and egalitarian flesh creep. And yet, I can't see my way out of this. I cannot function without this privilege, and yet I despise it. I cannot see how to live my convictions. Of course, even this dilemma is a great luxury. So many other mothers with children like Sesha have to make much more difficult choices.

II — Maternal Thinking with a Difference

> *Repeatedly, but usually with patience and tact, my father pointed out that sitting with my head down and putting my finger in my eyes jarred people and interfered with their getting to know me. Generally he managed to explain without my feeling ashamed or humiliated. . . . Eating skills were different. Something about teaching me to . . . keep my fingers from touching my food frustrated my parents and made them impatient. They gave in, . . . they were wise to let it go. I did things differently, . . . but . . . there was no point in trying to get me to do everything in life as a person with sight would do it.*[11]

In the literature by and about parents of disabled children, the theme of difference and sameness is persistent. In this essay, *sameness* resonates in the quotation that introduces the personal narrative; *difference* occupies the title. The tension emerges in opposing claims: Parents of disabled children cope as well as parents of normal children; parents of disabled children experience more stress than parents of normal children. There is a sense in which both statements are true. Most mothers and many fathers find the strength to cope with the special burdens of a disabled child—and doubtless more would do so and many would do so better if better resources were available. But read even the cheeriest account, and you will find the enormous cost and pain involved in coming to the point of coping. Nonetheless, every day with even a profoundly disabled child is not a test and it does not require virtual sainthood to be a more than adequate parent to such a child.

What I have learned from the experience of mothering Sesha, and what the many accounts of parenting such a child reveal, is that the differences we encounter redefine sameness. Raising a child with a severe disability is not just like parenting a normal child—but more so. It is often very different. Yet in that difference, we come to see features of raising any child that otherwise escape attention or that assume a new valence. One notices aspects of maternal practice that are not highlighted when we begin our theorizing from the perspective of the mother of the normal child.

Ruddick, considering maternal practice as exercised when children are intact,[12] has identified as the three requirements of maternal work preserving the life of a child, socializing her for acceptance, and fostering her development. And in many important regards these requirements hold for the task of mothering the child with a disability. Nevertheless, the scope and meaning of these practices are altered. In the remainder of this essay, I want to discuss how thinking about caring for dependent persons by thinking of mothering the child with severe disabilities reorients our thinking about the meaning of maternal practices in our social life.

Preservative Love

Preservative love seems to be the most fundamental of all maternal requirements. Disability, however, especially if it is severe and manifests itself early, is too often the occasion for *denying* a child preservative love. This is especially so where resources are too meager to keep even a well child functioning.[13] However, even when material conditions are adequate, the stigma of disability can be sufficient to allow parents of such a child to let the child languish.[14]

Where the commitment to the child has been made, preservative love comes to occupy an often overridingly central place in one's maternal practice. In the case of Sesha, safety and attention to medical needs are the first commandments of her care. Attention to them by her caregivers is paramount. Her fragility elevates this feature of maternal practice and sometimes threatens to overshadow all other aspects of maternal thinking with respect to her.

Preservative love propels parent and child into a medicalized world: corrective procedures for the disability will often involve surgical fixes and even routine illness can go wrong all too easily. Dealings with medical authorities are among the most frequent complaints one hears when listening to mothers of disabled children. One researcher cites one pediatrician as saying, " 'I don't enjoy it . . . I don't really enjoy a really handicapped child who comes in drooling, can't walk and so forth. . . . Medicine is geared to the perfect human body. Something you can't do anything about challenges the doctor and reminds him of his own inabilities.' "[15] In the same study, Rosalyn Darling speaks of the mother of a child with cerebral palsy who says, "[Our pediatrician] didn't take my complaints seriously. . . . I feel that Brian's sore throat is just as important as [my normal daughter's] sore throat."[16]

In my own dealings with physicians, it never occurred to me that any physician wouldn't take my daughter's ailments as seriously as those of a normal child. On the contrary, I have always assumed that a disability gives her a priority because of her fragility and vulnerability. It has never occurred to me that a physician might value her life and well-being less, even though I have had enough negative experiences with the medical profession to make me think otherwise. Perhaps I have needed to refuse to acknowledge such devaluation in sustaining my own preservative love.

The physician who remarked that he didn't "really enjoy a really handicapped child who comes in drooling" still has to understand that regardless of the level of impairment, this child, as every other child, is "some mother's child." It is by virtue of some or several mothering persons' toil and love that this child stands before him. If the physician or other professional is so limited that he cannot see beyond the disabling trait, might he be open to the child's humanity and need through the loving care lavished on this child?

In the struggle to watch over Sesha, to preserve her, to avoid the catastrophe of her death, it is not just the hard wall of medicine I encounter, but her protracted dependency. Preservative love, when directed at the "normally" functioning child, has its most intense period in the early years of the child's life. The individual with severe disabilities does not outgrow her profound vulnerability, nor can she assume the task of her own self-preservation. The effort of preserving a severely disabled child's life is often accompanied by a *lifelong* commitment to *day-to-day physical care* for the child. Dependence is often socially constructed—*all* dependence is not. If you have a fever of 105, the dependence you have is not socially constructed. Sesha's dependence is not socially constructed. Neither "labeling" nor environmental impediments create her dependence—although environment modifications are *crucial* for her to have a decent life.

In responding to this extended dependency, I have had an especially long time to consider what an important feature of human life has been ignored, even expunged from considerations of the exigencies of human life and a social organization that responds to them. Because our own child-hood, and even the childhood of our children, is so fleeting—flying by even as it absorbs us—an amnesia sets in. Consequently, in writing of social orga-nizations, and matters of justice and equality, we too easily think of the child as the future independent being. Because care for Sesha means confronting her irrefutable, inescapable, daily and sustained dependency, my own un-derstanding of what social organization entails, and the place of maternal practice in that social organization, is otherwise oriented. It has made me see that we cannot understand the demands of social organization if we can-not take the fact of dependency as one of the circumstances of justice.

Socialization for Acceptance

Raising children includes more than caring for and protecting them.[17] It means preparing them for a world larger than the family. Mothers who are wary of the social institutions and practices of the society in which they live, and who understand the oppressive nature of these institutions, are reluc-tant to socialize their children to be acceptable in situations that they them-selves view as unacceptable. Yet the most rebellious mother understands that each human is a social being and that some degree of social acceptance is crucial to their own child's well-being.

The task of socializing the child with disabilities also calls upon a notion of "acceptance." But acceptance is now understood against the background of "normalization." Those who are "different" or those who have, to use Helen Featherstone's (1980) term, a "difference in the family" very much want acceptance: acceptance of who they are, if they are disabled; acceptance of the child they love and the family they have created, if they are parents. *Normalization* is often an avenue to acceptance, but by virtue of the disabil-ity, it cannot be the exclusive avenue.

Socializing a disabled child for acceptance may, for instance, encourage a mother to have the child present herself in such a way that the disability is less noticeable—or that the "normal" characteristics of the child are un-derscored. I often find myself far more concerned with the clothes Sesha wears than I would be with my able child, with making sure her clothes or wheelchair are not in any way soiled, with being certain, that is, that Sesha presents a face to the world that is as attractive as possible so that the first response to her is as positive as I can make it be.

There is something very sad about this need—but I believe it is a realistic response to the repugnance (as harsh as that word is) of so many people toward disability. The sadness comes from the recognition of that repulsion, the need to do what I can to counteract it, and the knowledge that a pretty dress is such a superficial way to address the fear and ignorance that the response bespeaks. And yet I do it and feel I must do it, for Sesha, for myself, for our whole family. For Sesha, because I know that she understands when she is approached with a smile, with delight; that she is tickled when people make a fuss over how pretty she looks; that she feels pain at people's indifference to her. For myself, because it is one thing I can do to integrate Sesha into the community of which she is a part, even if her interactions with it are minimal. For my family, because we all feel the pain of the stigma attached to disability. Dressing Sesha nicely, making sure that she goes into the world looking clean and fresh and well cared for, is my way and our family's way of telling the world that this person is loved and cared for, and hoping that the message that she is worth being cared for will be absorbed by others.[18]

Maybe there is a fundamental sense in which a mother cannot fully accept the disability of her child, even as she accepts the child. Conflating these two acceptances is all too easy. One woman recalls how she refused her mother's efforts to get her to "practice walking more 'normally' at home" and to go for physical therapy. In her adulthood, she understood the source of the resistance:

> My disability, with my different walk and talk and my involuntary movements, have been with me all of my life, was part of me, part of my identity. With these disability features, I felt complete and whole. My mother's attempt to change my walk, strange as it may seem, felt like an assault on myself, an incomplete acceptance of all of me, an attempt to make me over.[19]

In the effort to socialize for acceptance, the messages sent to the disabled child, to oneself, and to siblings are hard to decode. Asch asks, "At what point is it all right, even essential to cease working on eliminating those differences disability can cause in appearance and behavior?"[20]

Helen Featherstone cites an instance that brings to the fore the way in which the family normalizes the disabled child, and the outer edge of consciousness that is always alert to the stigma and the non-normality of the situation. She writes of her response to the experience of starting her son Jody, a profoundly retarded boy with cerebral palsy and partial blindness, in a new school:

> On the first day I took him myself, intending to spend the morning.
> As soon as he was comfortably settled in the classroom I withdrew to the
> observation booth. The program pleased me, but after a few moments
> I realized that I felt depressed. . . . I looked at my son as a new teacher
> might. I saw a little boy with severe cerebral palsy and no useful vision.
>   Familiarity and routine blunt our awareness of disability after
> a while. Without meaning to, a stranger can upset this internal bal-
> ance.[21]

I realized as I read that passage that this is why it is so difficult to take Sesha
out in public. I don't want to upset that balance. I don't want to see Sesha as
others see her. I want them to see her as I see her. The blunting of awareness
of disability is part and parcel of a socialization that I, as a mother, have had
to undergo—one that is a prerequisite to my socializing my child.

   This socialization has two parts. First I refuse to see my child as not
"normal"—for what she does is *normal for Sesha*. This is a redefining of normalcy that accepts Sesha in her individuality. Without such acceptance, I
would not be able to present to the world a child *I* find acceptable. At the
same time, I have to see the child as others see her so that I mediate between her and the others—to negotiate acceptability. Where we cannot
mold the child, we may work to shape attitudes and the environment in
which she moves. Socializing for acceptance can mean altering what the
child gets socialized into, and what will count as, or form the grounds of,
acceptance.

   The parental task involves, then, both socializing the child for the acceptance, such as it might be, of the world, and socializing the world, as best
one can, so that it can accept your child. Yet a precondition for both requires
a socializing oneself for the acceptance of the child with her disability and
establishing a sense of normalcy, for oneself and for the face you present to
the world.

Fostering Development

> *I vividly recall a meeting to discuss my son's annual IEP[22] . . . for the com-*
> *ing school year. . . . [W]e found ten professionals of various species arrayed*
> *around the table, each convinced that his or her information was the most*
> *essential to Ian's progress and his parent's edification.*[23]

Most "normal" children are remarkably adaptable and their development
will take place in many different circumstances. The aim of maternal prac-

tice will be to provide, wherever possible, those conditions that are best suited to foster that development. For a child with disabilities, by contrast, development is never a given. It is not only fostering development but *enabling development* that a mother of a disabled child puts her heart and mind to. Enabling the development of a disabled child involves navigating complex straits.

First, finding appropriate facilities and teachers is integral to the task. This is at once an individual and a collective effort. If it were not for the activism of other parents, Sesha's schooling would not have been funded. Although Sesha was never a candidate for mainstreaming, the mainstreaming of less involved children means that Sesha receives a better reception in public. As other disabled children and adults move into their communities, they open vistas for all disabled persons, and facilitate enabling development for even the most profoundly impaired individual.

Second, parents of children with disabilities are dependent upon professional help available for their children—help that was hardly imaginable as little as twenty-five years ago. There are, on the one hand, the imposing (often impressive and sometimes worthless) professional knowledges that are being applied to your child. On the other hand, there is one's deep and intimate knowledge of *this* child, a knowledge that is, however, curtailed by one's limitations in training and expertise. Philip Ferguson[24] fantasizes coming to the next school meeting where a team of professionals sit prepared to discuss his severely retarded son's "individualized educational program" (IEP) with the young man in tow, along with his own numerous friends, his son's friends, and so forth, all with prepared statements they then shower on the assembled experts.

The difficulty of negotiating professional and personal knowledges is compounded by the different virtues that guide professional care and maternal care. As Darling remarks, "While professional responses to disabled children are generally characterized by affective neutrality, universalism, and functional specificity, parental responses are affective, particularistic, and functionally diffuse."[25] No doubt parents generally worry that a professional's "affective neutrality" too often translates as indifference to the particular needs of their particular child. But such "neutrality" can be especially difficult to tolerate when the needs are urgent and when social stigma continues to attach itself to disability, perhaps most of all to cognitive deficits. Affective involvement may be too much to demand of professionals, and without a doubt, an involvement as intense as that of mothering persons should not be expected. Yet parents and professionals need a mutual respect and partnership in order to enable the disabled child to grow and flourish to whatever extent the physical impairment permits. And there is no question in the minds of the many mothers and fathers of disabled children that professionals of all sorts are inadequately trained in the affective requirements of meeting needs of those who are ill or disabled.

The rift between professionals and mothering persons is further aggravated by that aspect of professionalism that assigns the professional a task that is "functionally specific." This means that the professional "focuses exclusively on a part [of the child], indeed a disabled part."[26] To the parent, however, the child's roles as son or daughter, sibling, grandchild, student, playmate, or church member usually supersede his or her disability. This difference is perhaps the source of the greatest dissonance between the mothering person and the professional as they each attempt to ensure a child's thriving.

Professionals also sometimes expect parents to carry out often complex and time-consuming instructions that are unrealistic.[27] Featherstone quotes a professional who became a parent: "Before I had Peter I gave out programs that would have taken all day. I don't know when I expected mothers to change diapers, sort laundry, or buy groceries."[28] "Parents may come to resent professionals who do not take all of these rules or those of their children into account," notes Darling.[29] What she fails to mention is the guilt that their failure to consider this generates in parents. It reinforces (especially within mothers) the sense that their role cuts them out for failure.

A failure in preservative love can result in death or injury. A failure in enabling and fostering development is less visible—but its threat is persistent. It is the continual concern: Am I doing the right thing? Am I pushing too hard? Not hard enough? Are there better, more appropriate programs? How do I balance her needs and those of my other child(ren)? How do I balance the demands of caring for this child and all the other aspects of my life, my life with my partner, my obligations to others? Some of these concerns are common to raising any child. But many of these concerns take on special poignancy when the very possibility of your child developing some fundamental skills to stay alive depends on your making the right decisions. The guilt that you may not be doing enough fuels resentment at those who should understand but never seem to understand well enough.

At the same time that the self-questioning surrounding issues of fostering development can evoke a sense of maternal incompetence, the knowledge that you are providing for an especially vulnerable child, that you are providing as best as you can, becomes a source of pride and accomplishment. But for that pride and sense of accomplishment to be realized, so many conditions need to be fulfilled—you need to know that what you are doing is in fact the best that can be done. This means you need access to knowledge, to financial, medical, and educational resources, to making needed physical modifications in the environment, to technology when appropriate, and to financial security. All these are far from realizable under the conditions in which most mothers of disabled children in the United States and in most of the world find themselves. But in those moments, when I have been fortunate enough to have the best possible situation, I can glean that profound satisfaction. It can vanish in an instant. It can vanish at the next IEP meeting with Sesha's "professional team."

As the disability community is anxious to remind us, handicapping conditions are not simply given by the impairment itself but by socially constructed environments and notions of ability. In reflecting on this point I note an irony: it is a source of great inspiration and insight in the disability community that independent living, as well as inclusion within one's community, should be the goals of education and habilitation of the disabled. But this ideal can also disempower and be a source of great distress if applied with too broad a brush. Even as the disability community, including parent advocates, works toward inclusion and the maximum attainable independence, some of its efforts get congealed in concepts and behaviors that have less desirable consequences. Chief among these are the notions that with concentrated parental effort the child will improve, that providing teams of professionals will "fix" things, and that an appreciable degree of independence is the end result of all the appropriate efforts.

Independence, acceptance, and normalcy are generally the goals of parents of disabled children—not very different from the goals of most parents raising most children. But for parents with a severely or profoundly retarded child, development may no longer have as a goal independent living: lifelong dependence may be clearly an inevitability. So it is in Sesha's case. As we try to feed her soul as well as her body, we look for activities that give her joy, that tap into the diverse pleasures she can enjoy and that will make her function as well as possible. She loves the water, and so we arrange for her to "go swimming." "Swimming" in Sesha's case means walking in lap lanes—the only time she can walk independently without support. Back and forth, giving her pleasure and exercise simultaneously. Music is a perpetual treat, so she has headphones and a walkman that, incidentally, connect her to her teen contemporaries. When we can find the appropriate persons, we supply her with music therapy. We have fought on many occasions for funding for her swim therapy and music therapy. But unlike physical therapy and speech therapy, neither of which are especially applicable to her needs, swim and music therapies are considered luxuries, and not offered to her. They are not seen as necessities because, in part at least, they do not appear to be geared to "independent living."

What does "development" mean for someone like Sesha? Sesha never focused on images. We slowly interested her in images through her love of music. We supplied her with videos of musicals whose music she knew so well. She began to get interested in the screen. She now enjoys ballets and movies such as *Mary Poppins*, *The Sound of Music*, and *Beauty and the Beast*, delighting in the children singing and the cartoon characters dancing. For Sesha, learning to fix her gaze on the video screen—something I seriously discouraged in my able child—was development. No, I don't take independent living as Sesha's goal, as much as I admire it as an aim for so many other disabled individuals. Independent living is a subsidiary goal to living as full and rich a life as one's capacities permit.

I believe that a focus on independence, and perhaps even the goal of inclusion, when inclusion is understood as the incorporation of the disabled into the "normal" life of the community, yields too much to a conception of the citizen as "independent and fully functioning." The disability community has achieved enviable recognition of the needs of the disabled by stressing that it is the combination of inherent traits and environmental enablings that results in capabilities, not inherent traits alone. Without sufficient light, the sighted would all be as incapable of seeing as are the blind—and the sighted would be handicapped because those who have lived a life without sight have developed other capacities by which to maneuver around in their environment. The stress on environmental modification to enhance capabilities is crucial in Sesha's life. Without a wheelchair, she would have only a bed from which to view the world. But no modifications of the environment will be sufficient to make Sesha independent.

I fear that the stress on independence reinstates Sesha as less than fully human. With every embrace, I know her humanity. And it has no more to do with independence than it has to do with being able to read Spinoza. So when we think of mothering a disabled child as enabling and fostering development, we must also reconceive development, not only toward independence, but development in whatever capacities are there to be developed. Development for Sesha means the enhancement of her capacities to experience joy.

A Summation

To conclude, I can only say that, in truth, this essay has no conclusion. The process of mothering will not end, just as marriages are not supposed to end: "till death do us part." Until then I will continue to learn from my daughter, from those who share her mothering with me, and from the unique, but perhaps at times, also generalizable, aspects of this remarkable relationship with an exquisite person we call Sesha.

There are many people to thank—first of all Sesha and Peggy and Jeffrey and Leo—for, well, everything. Next, the many individuals who have helped in fashioning this maternal thinking in the care they have provided Sesha. I want to thank my own mother for the model of maternal thinking she provided and my in-laws for their unwavering support in helping us meet Sesha's needs. I want to thank Sara Ruddick and Julia Hanigsberg for providing me with the inspiration and opportunity to write about my experiences, and Sara Ruddick for her extraordinary editing job. A longer version of this essay appears as chapters 6 and 7 of my book *Love's Labor: Essays on Women, Equality and Dependency* (New York: Routledge, 1999).

1. Philip M. Ferguson and Adrienne Asch, "Lessons from Life: Personal and Parental Perspectives on School, Childhood, and Disability," in *Schooling and Disability—Eighty-Eighth Yearbook of the National Society for the Study of Education, Part II*, ed. Kenneth J. Behage (Chicago: University of Chicago Press, 1989), 108.

2. This phrase comes from Ferdinand Lamaze, *Painless Childbirth: Psychoprophylactic Method* (Chicago: H. Regnery, 1956).

3. This notion is one I have elaborated elsewhere as "the principle of doulia": "Just as we have required care to survive and thrive, so we need to provide conditions that allow others—including those who do the work of caring—to receive the care they need to survive and thrive." Eva Kittay, "Human Dependency and Rawlsian Equality," in *Feminists Rethink the Self*, ed. D. T. Meyers (Boulder, Colo.: Westview Press, 1996); "Dependency Work, Political Discourse and a New Basis for a Coalition Amongst Women," lecture, *Women, Children and Poverty: Feminism and Legal Theory Workshop* (Columbia Law School and Barnard College Institute for Research on Women, 6 June 1995); *Love's Labor: Essays on Women, Equality and Dependency* (New York: Routledge, 1999).

4. Ferguson and Asch, "Lessons from Life," 112.

5. An example of such circumstance is vividly portrayed in Nancy Scheper-Hughes, *Death Without Weeping: The Violence of Everyday Life in Brazil* (Berkeley and Los Angeles: University of California Press, 1992). A gripping study, of the shantytown dwelling of the sugarcane workers of northeastern Brazil. Their situation of abject poverty, of harsh physical conditions, made a hardiness tested in the first months of life a requirement. These mothers allowed their impaired or weakest offspring to die and buried them "without weeping." These women did not see themselves as abandoning the children in a denial of love—the loving gesture was to allow these unfortunate babes to return to Jesus—so these women believed, or so they rationalized. The conviction which I call the condition for the possibility of mothering, and which is embodied in the notion of *preservative* love, reaches a limiting case with these infants who, because they do not thrive, are "allowed to return to the angels."

6. I have in mind Rawls's use of Hume. See John Rawls, *A Theory of Justice* (Cambridge, Mass.: Harvard University Press, 1971), 126; see also Kittay, "Human Dependency and Rawlsian Equality."

7. L. Wikler, "Family Stress Theory and Research on Families of Children with Mental Retardation," in *Families of Handicapped Persons: Research, Programs, and Policy Issues* (Baltimore, Md.: Paul H. Brookes, 1986), 184.

8. Wikler, "Family Stress Theory," 184 (author's emphasis).

9. See, for example, Martha Moraghan Jablow, *Cara: Growing with a Mentally Retarded Child* (Philadelphia: Temple University Press, 1982); Michael Bérubé, *Life as We Know It: A Father, a Family, and an Exceptional Child* (New York: Random House, 1996).

10. Sara Ruddick, " 'Care' as Labor and Relationship," in *Norms and Values: Essays in Honor of Virginia Held*, ed. Joram Haber and Mark Halfon (Totowa, N.J.: Rowman and Littlefield, 1998).

11. Ferguson and Asch, "Lessons from Life," 117–118.

12. Some readers will note that I am using the categories of Sara Ruddick, *Maternal Thinking: Toward a Politics of Peace* (Boston: Beacon Press, 1989). I am also challenging them since, as Jane McDonnell ("Mothering an Autistic Child: Reclaiming the Voice of the Mother," in *Narrating Mothers: Theorizing Maternal Subjectivities*, ed. B. O. Daly and M. T. Reddy, Knoxville: University of Tennessee Press, 1991) has noted, in formulating these categories Ruddick seemed to assume that all children are "intact."

13. Scheper-Hughes, *Death Without Weeping*.

14. For instance, a U.S. physician participating in the Hastings Center Prenatal Testing Project recently reported a case of an infant in his Neonatal Intensive Care Unit with Down's syndrome and an imperforate anus who had a colostomy created which he will need for a year, if not a lifetime. According to this physician, the social worker—who relates that the parents no longer visit the child and have placed him for adoption —believes that the Down's syndrome and associated medical problems are entirely "unacceptable" for the parents because "of a strong cultural bias." Apparently the parents plan to tell family and friends that the child died.

15. Rosalyn Benjamin Darling, "Parental Entrepreneurship: A Consumerist Response to Professional Dominance," *Journal of Social Issues* 44, no. 1 (1988): 149), cites Darling, 1979, 152.

16. Parents of the disabled have decried the excessive medicalization of disability and the pathologizing of parental responses. See, for example, Ferguson and Asch, "Lessons from Life," and Dorothy Kerner Lipsky, "A Parental Perspective on Stress and Coping," *American Journal of Orthopsychiatry* 55 (October 1985): 614–617. Yet parents are also grateful for medical procedures that are now available. For an eloquent statement of the improvements in medical care and habilitation for Down's syndrome children, see Bérubé, "Life as We Know It," especially chapter 2.

17. See William Ruddick, "Parenthood: Three Concepts and a Principle," in *Family Values: Issues in Ethics, Society and the Family*, ed. Laurence D. Houlgate (Belmont, Calif.: Wadsworth, 1998) for a discussion of this distinction.

18. To be sure, dressing her nicely and keeping her in unsoiled clothes is not *the same as* loving and caring for her—but it is sending a message loudly and clearly.

19. Harilyn Rousso, "Fostering Healthy Self-Esteem," *Exceptional Parent* 14 (December 1984): 9, cited in Ferguson and Asch, "Lessons from Life," 117.

20. Ferguson and Asch, "Lessons from Life," 117.

21. Helen Featherstone, *A Difference in the Family* (New York: Basic Books, 1980), 41.

22. "IEP" refers to the "Individualized Educational Program."

23. Ferguson and Asch, "Lessons from Life," 123.

24. Ibid.

25. Rosalyn Benjamin Darling, "Parent-Professional Interaction: The Roots of Misunderstanding," in *The Family with a Handicapped Child: Understanding and Treatment*, ed. M. Seligman (New York: Grune and Stratton, 1983), 148.

26. Ibid.

27. Featherstone, *A Difference in the Family*, 57.

28. Cited in Darling, "Parental Entrepreneurship," 149.

29. Ibid.

PART 2

Mothers and Harm:
No Easy Answers

Dorothy E. Roberts

Mothers Who Fail to Protect Their Children:
Accounting for Private and Public Responsibility

Mothers are held responsible for the harm that befalls their children even when they do not inflict it. The duty imposed on mothers to protect their children is unique and enormous. Mothers have an immediate and unavoidable duty to care for their children from the moment of birth, if not from the moment of conception. When a mother leaves her child locked in the house, playing in a park, or sitting in a car while she goes to work, she alone is arrested for neglect and vilified by the media. Fathers who abandon their children, on the other hand, can escape liability simply by leaving them with the mother. As long as he is not living with the mother, the father is not condemned when his failure to provide or protect harms the child. A father, moreover, is rarely blamed for leaving his child in the care of the mother, even if she is abusive. The investigation of what happened to the child seldom proceeds beyond targeting the mother at fault.

I first grasped the extraordinary scope of maternal responsibility when I began teaching criminal law. To find evidence of this duty, one need only open first-year criminal law casebooks to the omission liability section. The doctrine of omission liability bases criminal culpability on a person's failure to perform a legal duty rather than the usual requirement that she perform an affirmative act. Most of the cases on omission liability, if not all, concern mothers (or women in mothering roles) who failed to care properly for their children. These cases demonstrate that criminal law is more likely to impose an affirmative duty on mothers than on other classes of people. Mothers are far more likely to be punished for *failing to act* than anyone else in our society.

I usually push my criminal law students to determine the extent of the obligation mothers owe their children when we discuss *Commonwealth* v. *Howard*.[1] In *Howard*, a mother was convicted of manslaughter for failing to protect her five-year-old daughter from her boyfriend's deadly abuse. The story is fairly typical for the violent death of a child. Howard's boyfriend had beaten the little girl for a period of several weeks before he killed her. The child died when, during the course of one of these beatings, she fell and hit her head on a piece of furniture. Howard challenged her manslaughter conviction on grounds that the evidence was insufficient to prove that her actions caused her daughter's death. The appellate court upheld her conviction, reasoning that Howard failed to perform her legal duty to protect her child and "knowingly consented" to her boyfriend's abuse.

In class, I raise the possibility that Howard was herself a victim of her boyfriend's violence and that she was afraid that intervening would aggravate his abuse of both her and the child. "Must a mother forgo all self-interest, take on any risk, in order to avoid criminal liability?" I ask my students. "Must she even risk injury to herself in order to ensure her children's safety?" At least one student will invariably respond: "A mother must be willing to give up her own life in order to protect her children from harm."

For a long time, I was sure that some of my students were holding mothers to an unfair standard of care. They made mothers entirely responsible for protecting their children without taking into account the social context in which these women had to mother. Nor did they challenge the assumption that a mother must be the exclusive caretaker of her child. A feminist understanding of these crimes, I tried to teach them, questions the maternal role enforced by these cases and centers on the political circumstances of mothers' lives, including male violence, racism, and poverty. But a feminist symposium at a prominent law school led me to reassess my position. When I presented my paper on "Motherhood and Crime," I was surprised to notice the troubled look on another panelist's face. I expected flabbergasted expressions from audience members who believed that only mothers were responsible for children's welfare, but not from a feminist scholar whose work I admired. I mentioned this reaction to a colleague, who explained, "She has never forgiven her mother for failing to protect her from her father's abuse."

At that moment I pictured a little girl terrorized not only by her father's violations of her fragile body, but also by the horror that her mother—the person who was supposed to cherish, nurture, and defend her—was doing nothing to stop it. I wondered whether my focus on the public responsibility for children's welfare failed to consider seriously enough the personal responsibility of mothers whose children depend on them. Some of these mothers stand by for negligent, unprogressive, and immoral reasons as their children are battered and bruised. Although it is critical to resist the prevailing tendency to privatize children's problems by laying all of the blame on mothers, I did not want to neglect mothers' moral responsibility for their children's welfare.[2]

This essay addresses the duty that mothers owe their children to protect them from harm and the liability of mothers who fail to fulfill that duty. Mothers have been charged with many types of neglect, including giving birth without proper medical assistance and raising their children with inadequate food and shelter. Some mothers are considered neglectful for giving their children too little attention by going to work; others for teaching their children a lifestyle of dependency by not going to work. I concentrate here on mothers' failure to protect their children from male violence in the home, grappling with two approaches to this problem. On the one hand, these maternal failures can only be assessed in the context of mothers' own experience of domestic violence, as well as the institutions that foster that violence and make it difficult for women to escape. Further, racist stereotypes about maternal unfitness and depravity help to determine the public and official perception of the severity of mothers' crimes. On the other hand, children are unable to protect themselves from family violence and depend on their mothers for care. Mothers sometimes sacrifice their children's interests for the sake of other concerns. How do we account for this dual liability for harm to children, both public and private? After considering both factors, I take a political stand on behalf of mothers.

Mothers' Duty to Protect Their Children

Numerous mothers have been convicted of serious crimes for failing to protect their children from another's abuse. Several states have recently passed laws that make it a crime for a child's custodian recklessly to permit the child to be injured or assaulted by another.[3] Courts, legislators, and social workers hold mothers responsible for violence in the family.

Even though men are at least as likely as women to abuse children, psychological theory generally attributes child abuse to maternal deficiency.

With respect to the failure of child abuse researchers to study the father's role, social work professor Judith Martin observes, "[T]he mother is not only expected to be most deeply and intimately concerned with child-rearing; she is also at fault should any mischance occur in that process. No matter who actually harms the child, mother has failed in her duty to create a safe environment for her young."[4] For example, an article on domestic sexual abuse argued that "[t]he mother is pivotal in establishing the father-daughter incestuous bond."[5] This researcher claimed that mothers not only passively condone their husbands' abusive conduct, but also actively "promote the incestuous behavior by frustrating their husbands sexually."

In her survey of literature on child abuse, Martin found that only 2 of 76 articles focused on men. Legal scholar Martha Fineman similarly discovered that in 125 articles, mothers were blamed for 72 types of psychological disorders in their children; no mother-child relationship was described as healthy.[6] Child protective services and court proceedings incorporate this stereotype by focusing their investigations and remedies on the mother.

While this exclusive blaming of mothers is unjustified, it is nevertheless true that mothers have some duty to protect their children. Mothers not only are "*expected* to be most deeply and intimately concerned with child-rearing," they usually *are* the person most involved in their children's welfare. They are the ones their children most often turn to to guide, nurture, and shield them. Even when mothers share childraising with others, the others are often women serving in mothering roles. Of course, women experience tremendous pressure, both systemic and ideological, to become mothers. Motherhood is virtually compulsory for women: No woman achieves her full position in society until she becomes a mother. Women should not be compelled to be mothers, but those who are mothers take on an obligation to care for their children. Children are the most vulnerable members of the family. And the mother may have contributed to that vulnerability by inviting an abusive partner into the child's life.

Besides, there are good reasons for entrusting some degree of child protection to mothers. We would not want the state constantly peering into homes to monitor the safety of children. Poor women, especially women of color, are already subjected to inordinate supervision by social workers, welfare bureaucrats, and other government agents. It preserves the autonomy of mothers and their communities to make mothers principal (although not exclusive) guardians of their children.

The maternal duty I have described is distinct from that imposed by courts that equate the harm inflicted on the child with the mother's failure to protect. The mother should not be held responsible for male violence in her home. But her failure to protect her child from that violence may give rise to a separate level of culpability and a separate type of harm. Terri Williquette's seven-year-old son and eight-year-old daughter reported over and over that their father did horrifying things to them while Terri was at work. The children told her that he beat them with a metal stick (which left numerous telltale bruises), put his "wienie" in their "butts" and their mouths, and forced them to scoop "poopy" out of the toilet and eat it. Their mother simply advised them "not to worry about it," promising to speak with their father. Once when Mr. Williquette left a lump on his daughter's head, Terri did no more than give the girl an ice pack. The Wisconsin Supreme Court upheld Williquette's conviction for child abuse, based on her knowing exposure of her children to cruel maltreatment.[7]

I usually present this case as an example of injustice: Terri Williquette should not have been held accountable for her husband's acts just because she was the victims' mother. It is unlikely that a man would have been punished for leaving his children in their abusive mother's care while he went to work. (The same court reversed the child abuse conviction of a man whose wife caused their little girl to suffer brain damage from "shaken baby syndrome.")[8] Certainly Terri was guilty of something different and less heinous than her husband. But should her refusal to heed her children's pleas by itself not subject her to some level of liability?

Indeed, some psychologists contend that the greatest harm to a child victim of sexual abuse "is caused not by the physical abuse itself, but rather by the mother's failure to acknowledge the abuse or to believe her child when the child confronts her with the abuse."[9] One author points to a victim of long-term incest whose severe depression stemmed less from her father's abuse than from the resentment she felt toward her mother for repeatedly witnessing the abuse and later denying in court that it had ever occurred. I doubt that the mother's inaction caused a *greater* harm than the sexual abuse itself. Nevertheless, I understand that children whose mothers ignore, deny, or respond with anger to the abuse suffer an additional sort of injury. It is the injury of being betrayed by the very person you placed your greatest trust in. In some sense, then, mothers who fail to protect their children may be derivatively liable for the harm inflicted by the blows or molestation, but also liable for the separate harm of betrayal.

The existence of a mother's duty to protect her child, however, does not tell us the extent of the duty or whether the mother has breached it. To answer those questions, we must examine the circumstances surrounding the harm to the child.

Maternal Failure in the Context of Family Violence

Overwhelming evidence of the connection between men's battering of women and the battering of children reveals that power relationships, rather than mothers' infirmities, are responsible for family violence. Women who fail to protect their children from violence are often victims of violence themselves. Numerous studies show that in most families in which the father batters the mother, the children are also battered.[10] One study reported that when women were severely injured, 77 percent of their children had also been abused.[11] Children whose mothers are battered are many times more likely to be battered than children whose mothers are not battered.[12] Although both partners in these violent homes are more likely to abuse their children than parents in homes where the mother is not battered, the woman's batterer is typically the one who is also beating the children. Evan Stark and Anne H. Flitchcraft conclude from their numerous studies on this association that "child abuse in these relationships represents an extension of ongoing violence and is an intermediary point in an unfolding history of battering."[13] They refute the view of abuse as a pathology that is transmitted intergenerationally, arguing instead that it results from the immediate power struggle within the home.

Courts, however, have not asked how this web of violence affects the mother's culpability. They presume that a woman's obligation to her children always takes precedence over her own interest in independence and physical safety. They presume that a woman's maternal instinct can always prevail over the harmful aspects of her children's lives. Feminists have criticized people who ask battered women "Why didn't you leave?" because this question fails to recognize the physical, social, and legal constraints that trap women in violent homes. Courts slowly are beginning to acknowledge these constraints in cases where battered women kill in self-defense.

These impediments do not seem to matter, however, when mothers have abused children. Judges assume that a mother's impulse to protect her children from harm can overcome any barrier to escape—even if her interest in self-preservation is insufficient. The law isolates each woman's maternal duties from other facets of her life, "requiring that pregnancy be a transcendent moment that can carry every woman outside the complexity of her particular history."[14] Motherhood is supposed to subsume a woman's identity and transcend her social situation.

I have no patience with judges who seem to think women enjoy living with violence, and are maliciously sacrificing their children when they stay. Or judges who become concerned about domestic violence only when children are at risk. Yet although we should reject the romantic and biased belief that maternal instinct can always overcome a battered mother's predicament, we still expect a mother's duty to her child to provide additional motivation to leave. Whatever the complicated reasons that keep a battered woman in the home, her interest in protecting her children is a countervailing force that supplements her interest in protecting herself. In fact, a battered woman's decision to leave is often governed more by concern for her children than by her assessment of personal harm.[15] While most battered mothers remain in violent relationships until their children are past infancy, they often leave when they believe that the violence also endangers their children.

In *The Woman Who Walked into Doors*, Roddy Doyle's heroine is an Irish woman, Paula Spencer, whose husband, Charlo, brutalizes her terribly beginning when she becomes pregnant with their first child. Paula stays with her husband not only because she is afraid of him, but also because she "never stopped loving him" and "was frightened of being without him." Although she thinks her husband is "destroying" her, she cannot bring herself to walk through the door. Instead Paula endures seventeen years of being punched, kicked, and burned, making up excuses to the doctors who mend her broken bones—that she fell down the stairs or "walked into doors." During the beatings, Paula takes steps to protect her frightened children, at least from physical injury:

> Having to keep my eyes on Charlo. Pleading with him, holding him back. Feeling Leanne's shivering. Keeping him back. Making sure I faced him. Making sure I didn't let her become a shield. Her hand gripping my jeans. Her heart beating. Keeping my eyes on Charlo's eyes.

It is only when Paula catches Charlo looking at their oldest daughter, Nicola, with a destructive gaze of "sheer hate" that she gathers the strength to hit him with a frying pan and kick him out of the house:

> I threw him out! I'll never forget that—the excitement and terror. It felt so good. It took years off me. God, it was terrifying, though—after I'd done it, after I'd walloped him. I didn't think. I couldn't have done it if I had. But when I saw him looking that way at Nicola, when I saw his eyes. I don't know what happened to me—the Bionic Woman—he was gone.[16]

Concern for her child is supposed to transform a beaten woman into the Bionic Woman. In Paula's case, it gives her the extra surge of strength she needs to do what she has been trying to do for years. As Mary Gordon wrote in a review entitled "The Good Mother," "She stops being a battered wife when she becomes a protective mother."[17]

This view of the protective mother, however, repeats the assumption that mothers' interests and children's interests are always complementary. There are also many mothers who, unlike Paula, ignore or paper over the child abuse they witness in order to maintain their relationship with the batterer. Although feminists have demolished false conflicts between mothers and children, the truth is that mothers' interests and children's interests often conflict. And mothers sometimes choose against their children in order to be safe, to pursue their own ambitions, to hold on to a man. Recognizing this conflict allows us to see that women have an identity apart from their children. Part of the quandary raised by maternal failures is determining how mothers may retain their own identity without violating their moral duty to protect their children from harm.

Punishing Mothers' Resistance

While some mothers who stay with their batterer sacrifice their children's interests for self-destructive reasons, others put their children at risk by *resisting* domination in the home. One approach that takes negligent mothers' situations into account argues that battered mothers are physically and emotionally incapable of controlling or escaping violence in their homes. Legal scholar Nancy Erickson, for example, proposes that a battered mother charged with failing to protect her child should be allowed to present expert testimony that "by reason of her battered condition, she was unable to prevent the battering of her children."[18] Several states provide an affirmative defense to a charge of allowing child abuse to defendants who feared that acting to prevent the abuse would risk greater harm to the child or to the defendant. This is an important legal strategy because it forces courts to consider the real limits on a mother's ability to guard her children from violence.

I believe that the law should go further to situate mothers' failure to protect their children in its *political* context. Rather than seeing battering as an excuse for mothers' failure to protect their children, we need to rethink the relationship between motherhood and family violence. Battering arises out of a struggle for power in the home—as law professor Martha Mahoney puts it, "the *batterer's quest for control* of the woman."[19] Many men respond to women's attempts to resist male privilege in the home by violently subjugating both women and children. The typical pattern of assault suggests that male violence is not random, but "is directed at a woman's gender identity."[20] For example, Lenore Walker, a leading authority on battered women, discovered that her battered clients encountered increased violence when they became more assertive and began to make their own decisions.[21] Battering typically is evoked by struggles around gender issues, such as sex, housework, child care, the woman's employment outside the home, and her involvement in family finances. Batterers often justify their assaults with complaints about the woman's inadequate performance of household chores. A batterer's violence is his attempt to control the boundaries of the woman's role in the family.

Battering often is directed particularly at a woman's identity as mother. Many women report that family violence began or intensified when they became pregnant.[22] Some commentators theorize that this intensified battering stems from the man's sense of competition with the child for the woman's attention. It may also be that battering pregnant women and new mothers is part of the man's continued quest to enforce the woman's compliance with her role as mother. For example, some men batter their pregnant wives and girlfriends in an effort to coerce them to carry the pregnancy to term.[23] Men sometimes also assault their children in an effort to enforce the woman's maternal role. A Detroit man, for example, cut off his sleeping daughter's pony tail and glued her eyes shut after fighting with his wife because she would not give him money.[24] Sometimes children are hit, thrown aside, or knocked down when they try to intervene in the beating of their mothers. Most abused children treated in emergency rooms are injured in the course of violence directed at their mothers.[25]

This may have been what happened in the case of Denise Maupin, who was convicted in 1991 by a Tennessee jury of aiding and abetting the first-degree murder of her two-year-old son, Michael.[26] The day her son died, Ms. Maupin left her two children at home in the care of her boyfriend, Thomas Hale, while she went to her first day of work at a local fast-food restaurant. When she returned home she found that Hale had beaten Michael until he was barely conscious for wetting his pants. Michael died that night at the hospital. The trial judge sentenced Maupin to life imprisonment.[27] It seems likely that Hale murdered Michael in retaliation for Maupin going to work and leaving him with the chore of caring for the boy.

If we understand child abuse as an extension of abuse experienced by their mothers, it is linked necessarily to women's resistance to their inferior status in the family. Male violence against children is often part of men's effort to control the mother and may intensify when the mother resists. When the criminal law punishes battered mothers for failing to fulfill their maternal role, then, it may be punishing women's resistance. Let me be clear: I am not arguing that permitting child abuse is a means of resisting a subjugating maternal role. Rather, I am arguing that child abuse for which mothers are punished is often triggered by the mothers' resistance in the home. These battered mothers are faced with the dilemma that their fight for greater power exacerbates the violence not only against themselves but also against their children.

Judges' decisions in child abuse cases support my proposition that the criminal law punishes mothers' resistance. Courts treat mothers who appear pathetically weak or deranged more leniently than mothers who were struggling to retain power in their homes. Perhaps the most well-known example is the case of Hedda Nussbaum, whose live-in companion, Joel Steinberg, killed their six-year-old illegally adopted daughter, Lisa Steinberg, in New York City in 1987.[28] Nussbaum must have been aware of the danger to Lisa for some time: At the time of her death, Lisa's hair was heavily matted, her skin was dirty and scaling, and her body was covered with bruises. Yet Nussbaum was never convicted for failing to protect Lisa. The press depicted Nussbaum as hunched over, demented, and totally subservient to Joel Steinberg's psychological spell. Prosecutors dropped manslaughter charges against Nussbaum after she underwent months of intensive, residential therapy at a psychiatric hospital.

The Louisiana Supreme Court similarly reversed Winifred Scott's conviction for her son's death from severe grease burns because the trial judge refused to compel production of health department records showing that Winifred did not participate in making family decisions, that she had received mental health counseling, and that she was "incompetent, weak, depressed and subservient to her husband."[29] It has been suggested that courts should place mothers who experience the unconscious defense mechanism called denial in mandatory psychiatric treatment and parenting classes instead of convicting them of a crime.[30]

By contrast, courts consider more rational mothers' experience of battering to support a finding of guilt because it evidenced their knowledge of their husbands' potential for violence. Anna Tsing makes an analogous observation about cases involving mothers who commit infanticide. Women who kill their newborns are sometimes excused because they suffer from postpartum psychosis, a mental disorder associated with hormonal changes during childbirth.[31] Women charged with killing their infants during an unassisted birth, on the other hand, are treated more harshly than these "psychotic" mothers because "the women's irresponsibility is associated with rationality, self-centeredness, and lack of emotional display."[32] Once again, courts are willing to mitigate mothers' liability based on their psychological weakness and irrationality, but not based on their deliberate attempts to gain greater control over their social circumstances.

The stereotype of battered women suffering from a psychological disability, such as "learned helplessness," that makes them weak and incapable of acting on their own also denies a defense to Black women who are battered. The dominant image of Black women as domineering, assertive, and hostile may make it difficult for juries to fit Black women's acts of self-defense or their failure to protect their children within current battered woman syndrome theory. This may explain why Lenore Walker found that courts are twice as likely to convict Black women of killing their abusive husbands as white women.[33] Hedda Nussbaum, a white book editor, was treated far more leniently than Black and Latina women charged with similar crimes in New York City around the time of Lisa Steinberg's death.[34]

Maternal Failure in the Context of Idealized Motherhood

Not only do courts ignore the context of family violence, but they judge mothers in relation to biased expectations. Courts often seem less concerned with protecting children from abuse than with imposing an idealized and racialized standard of selfless motherhood. A mother's liability for another's abuse of her child often depends on whether she is otherwise considered to be a good mother. In determining the mother's culpability for child abuse, courts look at further evidence of bad mothering, such as not wanting children, leaving the children in the care of another to go to work, and keeping a messy house. In the case of a Massachusetts mother convicted of manslaughter, for example, the court noted testimony that her "apartment was cluttered and dirty, with empty cans, beer cans, and dishes on the kitchen table."[35]

Newspaper coverage of children killed by men in the home also tends to focus on the mother's neglect of her domestic duties. Instead of investigating why the man was so violent, newspaper reporters ask why the mother was so neglectful. For example, a *New York Times* article concerning a twenty-four-year-old mother charged in the beating death of her daughter by the stepfather concentrated on the mother's history of problems caring for her four children.[36] The article reported that city welfare workers removed her children from her home two years prior to the beating because she left them unattended and because they were filthy and infected with lice and ringworms. It included a picture of the children's room littered with dirty clothes.

Judging mothers who fail to protect their children according to this standard tends to disadvantage Black women. Both the media and the criminal justice system have treated white, middle-class mothers, who fit the race- and class-based ideal of motherhood, more sympathetically. Black women are burdened with myths about their unfitness as mothers, which distort the public's view of their maternal failures. From the image of the lascivious Jezebel during the antebellum era to the contemporary mythical welfare queen, Black mothers are supposed to pass on a culture of depravity, dependency, and criminality to their children. It is easily assumed that they did not stop the violence in their homes because they are generally careless about raising their children.

In another front-page article reporting the death of a 5-month-old baby from burns inflicted by the mother's boyfriend, the *New York Times* devoted an entire page to exploring the cause of the tragedy. Although the mother claimed that the boyfriend had beaten her and the baby, the article focused solely on the failure of city welfare workers to supervise the Black mother adequately. Perhaps images of Black mothers' depravity influenced the reporter's obsession with maternal regulation. The article also appeared to chastise the mother for raising her children in a poor, inner-city neighborhood, noting that "[l]ater in 1990, Ms. Harden and her children moved into a crumbling, drug-infested building in Harlem, where young men peddled crack and most of the tenants were, like herself, formerly homeless families from city shelters. It was there that her son would be fatally burned."[37] In this way, blaming mothers for failure to protect their children becomes a way of justifying stepped-up state supervision of poor Black mothers. Indeed, I am convinced that some maternal crimes, such as exposing a fetus to drugs, are prosecuted for the very purpose of devaluing Black mothers.[38]

The ideal of mothers' exclusive responsibility for children also justifies punishing Black mothers in particular. Black women's style of mothering is often misinterpreted as child neglect precisely because it violates this standard. Black mothers have a long-standing cultural tradition of sharing childraising with other women in the community.[39] These cooperative networks include members of the extended family (grandmothers, sisters, aunts, and cousins), as well as nonblood kin and neighbors. Patricia Hill Collins uses the term "othermothers" to describe the women who help biological mothers by sharing mothering responsibilities.[40] Social workers and judges often believe that Black children raised in these arrangements are neglected because they do not have the constant, exclusive attention of their mother. This is yet another way in which the law punishes women's resistance to an oppressive maternal role, thwarting the potential of alternative visions of motherhood.

The Case of Julia Cardwell

Commonwealth v. *Cardwell* illustrates the complicated interweaving of these considerations of private and public responsibility.[41] Julia Cardwell was charged with failing to protect her daughter Alicia from sexual abuse by Clyde Cardwell, her husband and Alicia's stepfather. Clyde sexually abused Alicia for five years, beginning when Alicia was about eleven years old. Ten months passed between the time that Julia became aware of the danger to her child and the date Alicia finally ran away from home. Although Julia did nothing directly to hurt her daughter, she brought her in contact with Clyde and she was at least partly responsible for ensuring her child's safety. How could Julia not have noticed that Clyde was raping her daughter over the course of several years? And after Alicia told Julia about it, why did Julia not take effective action to stop the abuse?

During those ten months, Julia did take steps to try to escape with Alicia. Julia wrote two letters to Clyde, expressing her awareness of the abuse and her plan to leave him. She made an unsuccessful attempt to move to her parents' house, moving some of her and Alicia's clothing and applying for Alicia to transfer schools. The destruction of her parents' house by fire, killing her father, frustrated Julia's plans.

Were Julia's actions enough to relieve her of criminal or moral culpability? Clyde's violence, combined with the setbacks Julia encountered, might explain Julia's failure to do more to save Alicia. Alicia testified at the trial that she and her mother were afraid of Clyde. He had beaten Julia, smashed objects in the house, punched holes in the walls, and kept a pistol on the mantelpiece. Violence often escalates and becomes lethal when battered women attempt to leave the batterer. Martha Mahoney uses the name "separation assault" to identify "the particular assault on a woman's body and volition that seeks to block her from leaving, retaliate for her departure, or forcibly end the separation."[42] Unfortunately, women's appeals to the police and the courts often fail to prevent this deadly retaliation. The criminal justice system has a horrendous record of refusing to take these threats against women seriously enough.

Denise Solera kept silent for more than a year after her boyfriend beat her eight-year-old daughter, Justina Morales, to death because she was afraid that he would kill her and her other child, a six-year-old son.[43] One advocate for domestic violence victims explained why it might be safer to remain in the home: "We can better protect our children if we are there and can see the abuser than if we're on the run, and he has the opportunity and advantage of being able to track us down."[44] There was the possibility that Clyde even set the fire at Julia's father's house to block her escape. Perhaps Julia understood that continuing her attempt to leave Clyde would have been the most dangerous step she could take.

Julia may have also feared social workers as much as Clyde. The state often views a man's violence against his family as evidence of the *mother's* unfitness.[45] It blames the mother for being beaten, thereby creating a dangerous environment for her children. Instead of protecting the mother and child by ordering the batterer to leave the home, courts often remove the child from the mother's custody.[46] One judge even terminated a battered mother's parental rights based on a psychologist's prediction that the mother was at risk of entering into a relationship with another abusive man.[47]

A recent case in Brooklyn, New York, charging Patty G. with sexual abuse and neglect of her children, illustrates battered mothers' catch-22.[48] The case came to the attention of authorities when Patty went to the 68th police precinct for help after her husband violently assaulted her. After referral to the Victim Services Agency, she told a caseworker that her husband had been molesting the children, as well as beating her. At trial, Patty testified that her husband would threaten her, punch and kick her, and bang her head against the wall for trying to intervene when he abused the children. In 1987, Patty fled from her husband and moved in with her sister in Florida. Not long afterwards, Mr. G. located his wife through a private detective. He harassed Patty and her sister until she returned to him in New York. Two experts testified at trial that Patty suffered from battered woman's syndrome, which deprived her of the ability to protect herself and her children. Nevertheless, the family court judge entered a finding of neglect, reasoning that neglect was a strict liability crime. In other words, it did not matter whether or not Patty had made every reasonable effort to protect her children; it only mattered that she had failed to stop the abuse.

Reporting Clyde's criminal conduct, then, might have triggered an investigation of Julia, possibly leading a judge to remove Alicia from her care or even to terminate her parental rights. Facing the possible loss of her child, Julia may have decided to try to evade Clyde on her own.

For Black women, the stakes are heightened. Too often when police are summoned to a Black home, they end up injuring family members and even shooting someone to death. Too often social workers are especially quick to remove Black children from their parents. Given the history of racism in the administration of criminal justice and child protective services, Black women may be reluctant to utilize government agencies as a means of solving their domestic problems. Black legal scholar Kimberlé Crenshaw identifies this reluctance as "a community ethic against public intervention, the product of a desire to create a private world free from the diverse assaults on the public lives of racially subordinated people."[49] Of course, being beaten should not be the price of allegiance to one's community. It is a lie that Black women who defy a violent partner are disloyal to their race. But resistance to an oppressive legal system or the plain fear of police terror is yet another piece of the complicated puzzle a battered mother must put in place to protect her children.

Even without the threat of death or separation, the decision to leave may be difficult. Protecting the child from abuse is one of many factors the mother must consider in deciding what is best for her child. The abuse may be sporadic, and may seem less hazardous than the consequences of leaving home—losing the main source of income, moving into shoddy housing or a dangerous shelter, ripping the child from friends and family, finding child care, and depriving the child of the father's positive features. Taking all of these factors into account, then, transforms what first appeared as a mother's inaction into an intricate resistance strategy.

I can also imagine, on the other hand, that Julia ignored for years the signs that Alicia was being abused and could have tried harder to leave Clyde once she knew he was raping her daughter. There are usually clues even before the incest begins.[50] Before Clyde began having sex with Alicia, he bought her sexually suggestive clothing, photographed her in sexual positions, and wrote sexually explicit notes to Alicia nearly every day. Did Julia not ever come across the clothing, the photographs, the letters? Sexual abuse usually marks a child's behavior. Alicia became pregnant twice and had two abortions. I also wonder why Julia chose to write to Clyde to express her disapproval, suggesting a hope for reconciliation. Perhaps Julia's desire to maintain a relationship with her husband superseded her concern for her child. Perhaps her accommodation to patriarchal ideals, rather than resistance to them, caused her maternal failure.

It is impossible to explore these possibilities, however, unless the inquiry attends to the mother's social circumstances in failure to protect cases. The court in *Cardwell* did not even consider whether Clyde's terrorization of Julia and Alicia mitigated Julia's criminal liability. Ironically, the court only used Julia's efforts to challenge Clyde's abuse as evidence against her, finding that Julia's letters to Clyde established her awareness of the abuse and its endangerment of her daughter's welfare. Because courts are concerned only with a woman's compliance with an idealized standard of selfless, exclusive motherhood, they neglect to examine the power struggle typically underlying family violence. A political focus would enable courts to question the expectation that mothers alone are responsible for children and to recognize mothers' oppositional acts. Understanding how maternal failures originate in family power struggles, themselves embedded in structures of racism, sexism, and poverty, rather than in mothers' pathologies, will help us direct mothers' opposition toward more liberating forms of resistance and direct social resources toward creating better conditions for mothers.

Political Support for Mothers

I can only explain my position as a political stand on behalf of mothers. I have asked myself whether my reluctance to blame mothers stems from my own stereotypical belief in maternal love. Do I, too, hold fast to the myth that no mother would willingly allow her child to be harmed, and therefore look for some social explanation for any maternal failure? No: My reluctance is based not on a romantic faith in mothers, but on a realistic assessment of the conditions of mothering and a desire to make them more equitable. Although not all mothers are treated the same or treat their children the same, all mothers struggle, to various degrees, against oppressive social circumstances. The dominant culture and legal system place the bulk of childrearing on mothers' shoulders without the compensation, power, and support they need and deserve. And it is those very mothers who are most likely to be charged with crimes or to have their children taken away—poor women of color—who also face the greatest obstacles. They are the ones I identify with the most.

Mothers' culpability for children's problems is linked to the lack of social accountability for children's welfare. When the mother of a severely abused child brought a civil rights lawsuit against the child welfare department for failing to intervene, the United States Supreme Court ruled that the state is not required to "affirmatively protect citizens from the private actions of a third party."[51] Blaming mothers for harm to their children regardless of social context is a way of absolving society of liability. It ignores the ways in which institutions permit and support male domestic violence. It covers up mothers' resistance against brutal domination in the home, an effort that sometimes places their children at risk. It pretends that poor minority children's deprivation is caused by maternal neglegence and not by joblessness, deplorable housing, inadequate health care, and delapidated schools. It allows the state to focus its attention on regulating mothers rather than transforming the social order. And it cuts off support for alternative visions of mothers' relationships with their children.

My allegiance to mothers does not mean taking sides against children. I have not forgotten my image of the panelist as a frightened girl whose mother betrayed her. While there is a danger in ignoring the voice of the child, there is also a danger in viewing the problem solely from the child's perspective. Perhaps in her eyes, her mother alone had the ability to shield her from harm. The child is not entirely aware of the broader social forces that her mother must contend with or the possibilities for change. We must listen to the child's voice, but her voice is another reason to reexamine our expectations of mothers and to improve the conditions of mothers' lives. Protecting children depends far more on addressing social inequities by identifying with mothers than on pronouncing mothers' guilt.

1. *Commonwealth* v. *Howard*, 402 A.2d 674 (Pa.Super.Ct. 1979).

2. On feminist approaches to abusive mothers, see Marie Ashe and Naomi R. Cahn, "Child Abuse: A Problem for Feminist Theory," in *The Public Nature of Private Violence*, ed. Martha A. Fineman and Roxanne Mykitiuk (New York: Routledge, 1994), 166.

3. Linda Panko, "Legal Backlash: The Expanding Liability of Women Who Fail to Protect Their Children from Their Male Partner's Abuse," *Hastings Women's Law Journal* 6 (1995): 67.

4. Judith Martin, "Maternal and Paternal Abuse of Children: Theoretical and Research Perspectives," in *The Dark Side of Families: Current Family Violence Research*, ed. David Finkelhor et al. (Beverly Hills, Calif.: Sage, 1983), 293–294.

5. Ofra Ayalon, "The Daughter as a Sexual Victim in the Family," in *Child Abuse*, ed. Amnon Carmi and Hanita Zamrin (Berlin, N.Y.: Springer-Verlag, 1984), 136.

6. Martha A. Fineman, "Dominant Discourse, Professional Language, and Legal Change in Child Custody Decisionmaking," *Harvard Law Review* 101 (1988): 727, 767 n. 161.

7. *State* v. *Williquette*, 129 Wis.2d 239, 385 N.W.2d 145 (1986).

8. *State* v. *Rundle*, 176 Wis.2d 985, 500 N.W.2d 916 (1993).

9. Christine Adams, "Mothers Who Fail to Protect Their Children from Sexual Abuse: Addressing the Problem of Denial," *Yale Law and Policy Review* 12 (1994): 519, citing Karin C. Meiselman, *Resolving the Trauma of Incest* (San Francisco: Jossey-Bass, 1990), 139; Mark Everson et al., "Maternal Support Following Disclosure of Incest," *American Journal of Orthopsychiatry* (April 1989): 197.

10. Lee H. Bowker et al., "On the Relationship Between Wife Beating and Child Abuse," in *Feminist Perspectives on Wife Abuse*, ed. Kersti Yllo and Michele Bograd (Newbury Park, Calif.: Sage, 1988), 158; Naomi R. Cahn, "Civil Images of Battered Women: The Impact of Domestic Violence on Child Custody Decisions," *Vanderbilt Law Review* 44 (1991): 1041, 1056–1057.

11. Murray A. Straus et al., *Behind Closed Doors: Violence in the American Family* (Garden City, N.Y.: Anchor Books/Doubleday, 1980).

12. Evan Stark and Anne H. Flitchcraft, "Woman-Battering, Child Abuse and Social Heredity: What Is the Relationship?," in *Marital Violence*, ed. Norman Johnson (Boston: Routledge, 1985), 147, 165–166, and "Women and Children at Risk: A Feminist Perspective on Child Abuse," *International Journal of Health Services* 18 (1988): 97.

13. Stark and Flitchcraft, "Women and Children at Risk," 107.

14. Anna L. Tsing, "Monster Stories: Women Charged with Perinatal Endangerment," in *Uncertain Terms: Negotiating Gender in American Culture*, ed. Faye Ginsburg and Anna L. Tsing (Boston: Beacon Press, 1990), 282, 297.

15. Martha R. Mahoney, "Legal Images of Battered Women: Redefining the Issue of Separation," *Michigan Law Review* 90 (1991): 29.

16. Roddy Doyle, *The Woman Who Walked into Doors* (New York: Viking, 1996), 213.

17. Mary Gordon, "The Good Mother," *New York Times Book Review* (28 April 1996), 7, reviewing Doyle, *The Woman Who Walked into Doors*.

18. Nancy S. Erickson, "Battered Mothers of Battered Children: Using Our Knowledge of Battered Women to Defend Them Against Charges of Failure to Act," in *Current Perspectives in Psychological, Legal and Ethical Issues: Children and Families: Abuse and Endangerment,* ed. Sandra A. Garcia and Robert Batey (London: Kingsley, 1991), 197, 201.

19. Mahoney, "Legal Images of Battered Women," 1, 5.

20. Stark and Flitchcraft, "Women and Children at Risk," 100.

21. Lenore E. Walker, *The Battered Woman* (New York: Harper and Row, 1979), 202.

22. "Physical Violence During the 12 Months Preceding Childbirth," *Morbidity and Mortality Weekly Report* 43 (4 March 1994): 132, reporting that 4 to 17 percent of women are beaten during pregnancy.

23. This is one reason why the United States Supreme Court struck a state's spousal notification requirement as an undue burden on married women seeking abortions. *Planned Parenthood* v. *Casey*, 112 S.Ct. 2791, 2831 (1992). The Court recognized that "[f]or the great many women who are victims of abuse inflicted by their husbands, or whose children are the victims of such abuse, a spousal notice requirement enables the husbands to wield an effective veto over the wife's decision [to terminate her pregnancy]."

24. "A Father Is Accused of Gluing Eyes Shut," *New York Times* (20 August 1995), 19.

25. March of Dimes Report: Hearings Before Senate Committee on Judiciary, 101st Cong., 1st. Sess., pt. 2 (1990): 142.

26. *Tennessee* v. *Maupin*, No. 272 (Tenn.Crim.App. Oct. 7, 1991).

27. Although the Court of Criminal Appeals reversed *Maupin*'s conviction for first-degree murder for lack of sufficient evidence, it remanded the case for a new trial on lesser degrees of homicide. A Florida woman was recently sentenced to life imprisonment for standing by while her husband beat her daughter to death. The prosecutor had requested the death penalty. "Life Sentence in Girl's Death," *New York Times* (8 June 1995), A27.

28. *People* v. *Steinberg*, 573 N.Y.S.2d 965 (App.Div. 1991), aff'd, 79 N.Y.2d 673 (1992).

29. *State* v. *Scott*, 400 So.2d 627 (La. 1981).

30. Adams, "Mothers Who Fail to Protect Their Children from Sexual Abuse."

31. Laura E. Reece, "Mothers Who Kill: Postpartum Disorder and Criminal Infanticide," *UCLA Law Review* 38 (1991): 699.

32. Tsing, "Monster Stories," 297.

33. Lenore E. Walker, *Terrifying Love: Why Battered Women Kill and How Society Responds* (New York: Harper and Row, 1989), 206.

34. See, for example, Alexis Jetter, "Mom Given 5–15 Years in Tot Death," *Newsday* (27 February 1990), 4.

35. *Commonwealth* v. *Gallison*, 421 N.E.2d 757, 761 (Mass. 1981).

36. Jacques Steinberg, "Records Show Mother's Neglect Preceded a 3-Year-Old's Death," *New York Times* (5 March 1992), B3.

37. Celia W. Dugger, "Litany of Signals Overlooked in Child's Death" *New York Times* (29 December 1992), A1.

38. Dorothy Roberts, *Killing the Black Body: Race, Reproduction, and the Meaning of Liberty* (New York: Pantheon Books, 1997).

39. Carol Stack, *All Our Kin: Strategies for Survival in a Black Community* (New York: Harper and Row, 1974).

40. Patricia Hill Collins, *The Meaning of Motherhood in Black Culture and Black Mother / Daughter Relationships* (Newbury Park, Calif.: Sage, 1987), 3, 5.

41. *Commonwealth* v. *Cardwell*, 515 A.2d 311 (Pa.Super.Ct. 1986).

42. Mahoney, "Legal Images of Battered Women," 5–6, 61–71. See also Cynthia Gillespie, *Justifiable Homicide* (Columbus: Ohio State University Press, 1988), 150–152.

43. Lizette Alvarez, "Mother of Girl Missing a Year Won't Face Murder Charges," *New York Times* (24 February 1997), B3.

44. Quoted in Howard A. Davidson, "Child Abuse and Domestic Violence: Legal Connections and Controversies," *Family Law Quarterly* 29 (1995): 357, 362.

45. Kristian Miccio, "In the Name of Mothers and Children: Deconstructing the Myth of the Passive Battered Mother and the 'Protected Child,'" in Child Neglect Proceedings, *Albany Law Review* 58 (1995): 1087; Jill A. Phillips, "Re-Victimized Battered Women: Termination of Parental Rights for Failure to Protect Children from Child Abuse," *Wayne Law Review* 38 (1992): 1549.

46. Bernardine Dohrn, "Bad Mothers, Good Mothers, and the State: Children at the Margins," *University of Chicago Law School Roundtable* 2 (1995): 1, 7–8.

47. *In Re Farley*, 469 N.W.2d 295 (Mich. 1991).

48. *In Re Glenn G.*, 587 N.Y.S.2d 464 (Fam.Ct. 1992).

49. Kimberlé W. Crenshaw, "Mapping the Margins: Intersectionality, Identity Politics, and Violence Against Women of Color," in *The Public Nature of Private Violence*, ed. Martha A. Fineman and Roxanne Mykitiuk (New York: Routledge, 1994), 93, 103.

50. Adams, "Mothers Who Fail to Protect Their Children from Sexual Abuse," 522.

51. *DeShaney* v. *Winnebago County Dept. of Soc. Serv.*, 489 U.S. 189 (1989).

Martha Minow

Child Endangerment, Parental Sacrifice:
A Reading of the Binding of Isaac

What should I think about, when I think about the Binding of Isaac? The question, of course, arises each year during the Days of Awe. But it is a more persistent question for me as a teacher of law, as a woman, as a parent, and as a child. Should I respond with awe, horror, admiration, anger, relief? Any of these responses may be justifiable, but I worry that I mainly will feel a familiar perplexity. I wrestle for a fresher, deeper response. The knife Abraham uses almost to kill Isaac reminds me of the comment ascribed to Rabbi Moshe Leib: "The way in this world is like the edge of a blade. On this side is the netherworld, and on that side is the netherworld, and the way of life lies in between."[1] Can the Binding give us clues about how to live in this in-between?

As a teacher of law, I have often ended courses with stories and parables because that final moment feels like my last chance to remind budding lawyers both to question authority and to bear responsibility for the power they will wield. For these occasions, I used to use Woody Allen's version of the Binding of Isaac. In that version, Abraham, in his underwear, hears a deep, resonant voice directing him to sacrifice Isaac; Isaac asks why Abraham did not discuss the matter with God, and ultimately the angel of the Lord stops Abraham and admonishes him for having no sense of humor or ability to resist deep, resonant voices. I liked Allen's effort to remind us to be critical of authority and to resist even authoritative commands when they contravene fundamental values. But I do not use this story anymore. Since Allen faced charges of child abuse and then left his longtime companion for her adopted daughter—sacrificing his family relationships—his words are not the ones I want to leave with students.

The Binding of Isaac always resurfaces for me when I teach and write about parents who refuse medical treatment for their children because of religious conviction. These refusals sometimes turn into court disputes. Parents may be prosecuted for homicide or aggravated child abuse if their refusal of medical treatment leads to the child's death. For example, Ginger and David Twitchell were charged and tried for manslaughter after their two-and-a-half-year-old son, Robyn, died from a medically curable bowel obstruction. The Twitchells had turned to a Christian Science practitioner and to spiritual healing rather than taking Robyn to a doctor. The tenets of Christian Science do not forbid conventional medical treatment but view it as a weakness and as a failure to pursue the spiritual method of casting out the error in thought that is believed to have caused the problem. The jury convicted the Twitchells; the judge sentenced them to ten years' probation, conditioned upon their obtaining medical checkups for their other children and medical attention if any of them became seriously ill. Massachusetts' highest court later overturned the conviction because the jury was not permitted to view a Christian Science handbook used by the couple during the time that they decided that they lawfully could treat Robyn's illness without seeking medical care.[2]

Other cases go to court because parents invoke religious grounds to refuse particular medical treatment for a child already under a doctor's care.[3] Judges commonly authorize blood transfusions for a child over parental religious objections, such as those expressed by Jehovah's Witnesses, who believe that receiving blood prevents resurrection and everlasting life after death.[4] Or a court may consider ordering chemotherapy against religiously inspired views such as these: "We would love for [the child] to have a full and long life. But it is more important to us that his life be full instead of long, if that [is] the way it [has] to be."[5] A parent who deprives a child of food because of religiously inspired directions also risks state intervention.[6]

The director of a Massachusetts study that documents cases of children who died because their parents refused to seek medical treatment explained,

"It's just bloodcurdling how these kids suffered. There are kids with diabetes who got no insulin. They died slow, painful deaths. There are kids with operable cancer who went through suffering that was really unnecessary."[7]

Who could respond to these descriptions without wanting the state to protect vulnerable children against such harms? Yet I cannot help but worry about state power wielded with indifference or hostility to religious beliefs. What if my sincere religious beliefs pitted me against the intervening, intermeddling state? What if state officials decide that male circumcision is child abuse? Circumcision, practiced by Jews since Abraham circumcised Isaac, is a model of human obedience to God's will that reminds us of the Binding of Isaac.[8]

Courts can acknowledge the intensity of parents' religious beliefs and even declare respect for those beliefs while stepping in over the parents' objections to protect the child or punish the parents.[9] Judges may themselves feel torn between respecting parents who love their children and secular medical experts who say they know better. The almost universal result, however, is to prefer the medical experts.[10] When asking how much parents may impose their religious beliefs on their children, state officials tend to neglect how much the state imposes its secular beliefs on parents. When the legal question is what serves a child's best interests, religious conceptions of faith and redemption vie with secular notions of health and longevity. If I were a judge faced with charges of child neglect or homicide, I wonder how I would, and how I should, evaluate parental defenses based on religious belief or inspiration.

Perhaps it is ludicrous to take another step in imagination, but what would a contemporary secular court in the United States do if Abraham's attempt to sacrifice Isaac were brought before it? How would he defend himself?

Heat of passion could provide no excuse; Abraham had three days to think about it. Perhaps Abraham would testify, "The Master of Time and Space commanded me to take my son, the long-awaited child with my wife, to a mountaintop, to tie him with restraints, and offer him as a burnt-offering to the Almighty by sacrificing him mortally." To contemporary ears, this testimony is more likely to signal psychosis than religious devotion. Hearing voices increasingly falls in the psychiatric domain, while communication with the Divine is generally thought to be more subtle or indirect.[11] That Abraham never heard directly from the Almighty after this event might be of some help, at least in establishing Abraham's competency to stand trial.

With a lawyer's advice, he might then defend himself as follows: "I acted in my child's best interests because I demonstrated for him and all of his descendants what the love and fear of the Divine demands."[12] If Søren Kierkegaard, the philosopher, were the lawyer, Abraham might defend his action as a crucial moment of self-definition by having faith in the impossible, faith that despite his own act of killing his beloved son, Isaac would be restored to him. With Kierkegaard as counsel, Abraham might even acknowledge that no one can understand his act, which in its unique particularity becomes an absolute relation to the absolute.[13] Maybe Abraham, or his lawyer, would maintain that Abraham protected his child by testing the Almighty and revealing the All-Merciful, or by giving Isaac himself the chance to act heroically and to accept the role of sacrificial lamb.[14] Perhaps, Abraham would argue, Isaac not only survived, but became a different Isaac; no longer Abraham's, but the Lord's; or perhaps a stronger, more independent Isaac who could become a patriarch himself. Abraham might claim Isaac was not a child; at the age of thirty-seven (or sixteen?) he could have resisted the climb to Mount Moriah and what transpired there. Or the lawyer's investigation might reveal that it was not the Almighty, but Satan who inspired the test, and thus Abraham should be excused.[15] Even with hindsight, Abraham would have difficulty persuading a judge that he took his action in order to free humankind of child sacrifice. It was Abraham, after all, who cast his first son, Ishmael, out in the desert to die. Different modus of operation, but same intent, the prosecutor would argue.

In defending himself, Abraham might find it difficult to decide whether to claim that he acted without a hope of reward or fear of punishment.[16] He might argue, in the alternative, that he acted precisely because of hopes for his child's well-being or out of fears of greater harms. Would Abraham be better off indicating that he knew it was a test or an initiative rite for Isaac—implying confidence that the Master of the Universe would not let harm come to the precious child? Or might this reveal Abraham's own misunderstanding of the nature of the test, a test that had to terrify, not reassure? Isn't the point of belief to leap before there is confidence or proof? Lillian Smith, the acutely perceptive white Southern civil rights activist, once said, "To believe in something not yet proved and to underwrite it with our lives: it is the only way we can leave the future open."[17]

Perhaps only if Abraham knew with confidence that Isaac would emerge alive could he as the loving father wield the knife against his son. This would not be a powerful defense at a secular trial if somehow the son nonetheless died. Many religious parents evidence sincere shock when their children die without medical treatment. Yet this tends only to confirm the secular view that these parents failed in their duties to protect their children's best interests. God does not always come out well in tests of faith.[18] The extensive commentaries suggesting that Abraham did indeed slay Isaac may be evidence of this or may be evidence of the possibility of danger requisite for the test of faith.[19]

To imagine Abraham's defenses in a secular court is to expose anew the terrifying incomprehensibility of his action. The text's silences about Sarah underscore terror and incomprehension. Sarah, who already has sacrificed herself by arranging the liaison with Hagar to assure Abraham's progeny, and Sarah, who finally with joy has a son, Sarah is missing from the entire chapter on the Binding of Isaac. Abraham takes Sarah's long-wanted, beloved son to be sacrificed without any discussion; the next we hear of Sarah, she has died. No wonder the Rabbis tried to fill in the silences about Sarah. One commentary has Abraham lying and telling Sarah he will take Isaac to study the ways of the Lord. Sarah replies, "Thou hast spoken well. Go, my lord, and do unto him as thou hast said, but remove him not far from me, neither let him remain there too long, for my soul is bound within his soul."[20]

Another commentary shows Isaac concerned with Sarah just when Abraham is not. Isaac tells Abraham to take his ashes to Sarah so that she can keep them and weep for him.[21] Sarah's death, to the commentators, is entirely linked to the incident: Sarah dies while Abraham lifts the knife over Isaac or when she hears that Abraham did sacrifice Isaac.[22] Alternatively, Sarah dies of joy after learning that the Almighty had spared Isaac[23] or in response to the terrible truth that her son was all but killed.[24] If Sarah, the first observer to learn of the Binding of Isaac, dies upon hearing the story, is this a clue about how we should respond? Sarah would be unavailable to serve as a witness in court if Abraham were to face charges after the event. Perhaps he was estranged from her, as they lived apart before the incident. Some would say that the charges against Abraham should include causing Sarah's death.

Sarah's absence would not tell a secular court how to rule on Abraham's defenses. But perhaps Sarah's response tells me at least in part how I—yes a lawyer, but also a woman, a mother—should react to the Binding of Isaac. Whether she died of grief or joy, or instead screamed silently,[25] Sarah's response reminds me not to ignore the real, human connections and intense emotions implicated by the story of Abraham and Isaac, as well as by the stories of contemporary parents and children.

As a parent, I sympathize with the parents who face secular trials for adhering to religious beliefs that expose their children to harms. Despite my professional work defending rights for children, becoming a mother has given me pause about claims that children should have rights. It is not so much a vivid encounter with a totally dependent being that makes me question rights for children. We lawyers have not shied away from the language of rights for people who cannot speak—people who are comatose or severely disabled—just as we have not refrained from according rights to corporations and other artificial "persons." In these situations, and perhaps particularly in these situations, rights establish boundaries and bargaining chips where otherwise sheer power might prevail.

My doubts arise from the barely articulable but fierce resistance I have to anyone interfering with my care for my child. The idea that someone else—and, more worrisome, some stranger—could tell me how to raise my child is far more disturbing than all the strangers who dared to touch my pregnant belly. I do not trust those beyond my immediate sphere of family, friends, and tested teachers and physicians to know and understand my child, much less to cherish her and shield her from harm.

It is at these points in my reflections, though, that I hear echoes of a parent's shout aimed at me nearly two decades ago when I served as a court-appointed advocate for her child in a custody investigation. "Just wait until you have a child of your own," she leveled as if it were a curse. "Then you'll know how wrong it is for you to come in and stand between me and my child." The comment stung then, and it reverberates now that I have a child. Yes, it would be painful to have to deal with anyone else claiming to stand up for my child and, especially, to stand against me. If that someone else is a government official, a bureaucrat, or a social worker, my comfort level does not increase.

Yet some parents do abuse their children. Some adults, including public employees, inflict violence on children. Some parents expose their children to dangers with irreversible consequences. Denying medical care critical to the child's life may honor the parents' religious beliefs, but this permits parents to martyr a child without giving that child the chance to embrace or reject those beliefs.

So I do not disagree with the Supreme Court and state courts that have announced secular rights for children in judicial procedures, freedom of speech, education, and medical care. Rights for children necessarily involve

relationships between children and adults and depend on adults for assertion, enforcement, and responsibility. Children's rights represent not their
autonomy, but their connection with others; not their isolation, but their
membership in a community with others who care about them. If their
rights cut into parents' autonomy, perhaps that is because some parents, left
alone, hurt their children. That risk is threatening enough that we all should
embrace a system that checks parental power.

Even with my fierce resistance to interference with my child, I have come
to face this basic truth: My responsibilities to my child include living under
a system of laws that assure her more than me. If I fail her, the society—
through laws and customs—will step in. I must sacrifice some of my control
in order not to sacrifice my child.

If the fearsome story of the Binding of Isaac only reminded us not to
sacrifice our children for our own beliefs, crusades, needs, or wants, it would
be enough.[26]

I reread the Binding of Isaac as law teacher, as woman, as mother—and as
child. I feel a kind of helplessness in the face of the story that I associate with
childhood: a sense of overpowering events beyond my control, obedience
demanded without rationale; hope and endurance eked out because of a naive lack of alternatives rather than common sense.

I confess that I worry less about my own parents sacrificing their children than sacrificing themselves for their children. Maybe I should understand that not only Sarah, but also Abraham, or a crucial part of him, died
because of the events on Mount Moriah.[27] Maybe he was too willing to give
what he cared most about—his son—for the ironic promise of his descendants.

I am reminded of these thoughtful musings on sacrifice within families:
"The capacity to sacrifice, like any skill, always needs some fine-tuning. It is
one thing to sacrifice briefly one's sleep to comfort a child with a bad dream;
it is quite another for a mother to sacrifice her whole career for a child. It is
one thing for a father to sacrifice his desire to go fishing today because he
needs to go to work to feed the family; it is quite another to work for forty
years at a job he hates. Often such massive sacrifice, if not a result of cowardice, comes from an inability to discriminate between giving that is necessary
and life-giving and giving that brings death to the Martyr and hence to those
around him or her."[28]

Learning to fine-tune sacrifice seems contrary to Abraham's willingness to give the utmost. Yet the story gives us not only the model of Abraham's initial obedience, but also the concluding lesson: He need not sacrifice the utmost. The willingness to do it, but the recognition that it is not necessary: this, too, may be a lesson, especially in the complex negotiations between parents and children who have been in the habit of sacrificing for one another.

Sacrifices of parent for children are closely connected to the sacrifices of children by parents. I think about the extreme circumstances—Sethe, the tormented parent of Toni Morrison's novel *Beloved*, who kills her child rather than let her be recaptured into slavery and, in so doing, sacrifices part of herself;[29] the parent who must cast out one child in order to save others;[30] or the parent forced by war, economics, or terror to choose to live while a child dies or to die so a child may live.

Life is the edge of a blade. Elemental stories may horrify and terrify. But, like the Binding of Isaac, they may also remind us to try to see our worlds, our families, our beliefs—our very lives—anew.

Thanks to Jamie Wacks for imaginative research assistance and to Joe Singer and Avi Soifer for comments.

1. Martin Buber, *Tales of the Hasidim: Later Masters* 92 (Schocken Books: New York 1948).

2. Tom Coakley, "Christian Science Couple's Conviction in Death Overruled," *Boston Globe*, Aug. 12, 1993, p. 1; *Commonwealth v. Twitchell*, 617 N.E.2d 609 (Mass. 1993).

3. Judicial action may follow petitions of neglect brought by a state agency when parental refusals of medical treatment expose the child to serious harm even if those refusals are sincerely motivated by religious beliefs. See In the Interest of D.L.E., 645 P.2d 271 (Colo. 1982) (approving dependencing determination after parent failed to assure child with epilepsy followed prescribed medical treatment).

4. In the Matter of Elisha McCauley, 409 Mass. 134, 565 N.E.2d 411 (Mass. 1991); *Sampson v. Taylor*, 29 N.Y.2d 900, 278 N.E.2d 918, 328 N.Y.S.ed 686 (NY 1972); In re Pogue (No. M-18-74 Super. Ct. D.C. Nov. 11, 1974).

5. Custody of a Minor, 375 Mass. 733, 751, 379 N.E.2d 1053, 1064 (quoting mother).

6. *Nicholson v. Honda*, 600 So.2d 1101 (Fla. 1992) (mother convicted of felony-murder and aggravated child abuse after child died of starvation; mother had followed religious prophesies against gluttony).

7. Jetta Bernie, quoted in Bella English, "No Excuses for Child Abuse," *Boston Globe*, Nov. 30, 1992, p. 13.

8. See Avivah Gottlieb Zornberg, *Genesis: The Beginning of Desire* 106 (The Jewish Publication Society: Philadelphia, 1995).

9. See, e.g., *People v. Pierson*, 176 N.Y. 201, 211–212, 68 N.E. 243, 247–8 (NY Ct. Ap. 1903) ("We are aware that there are people who believe that the Divine power may be invoked to heal the sick and that faith is all that is required. There are others who believe that the Creator has supplied the earth, nature's storehouse, with everything that man may want for his support and maintenance, including the restoration and preservation of his health, and that he is left to work out his own salvation, under fixed natural laws. . . . But sitting as a court of law for the purpose of construing and determining the meaning of statutes, we have nothing to do with these variances in religious beliefs, and have no power to determine which is correct. We place no limitations upon the power of the mind over the body, the power of faith to dispel disease, or the power of the Supreme Being to heal the sick. We merely declare the law as given to us by the Legislature").

10. See, e.g., In re Willmann, 24 Ohio App.3d 191, 199, 493 N.E.2d 1380, 1390 (Ohio Ct. App. 1986) (Keefe, J. concurring). ("This matter has been for me an extremely difficult case mainly because of the troublesome conflicting authorities between loving parents on the one hand, and the juvenile court on the other.") Despite the difficulties, Judge Keefe concurred in the decision to substitute state judgment for parental judgment.

11. For a novelist's observation, see Louise Erdrich, *Love Medicine* (Harper-Perennial: New York, 1993, 1984): "Here God used to raineth bread from clouds, smite the Phillipines, sling fire down on red-light districts where people got stabbed. He even appeared in person every once in a while. God used to pay attention, is what I'm saying."

12. See Nehama Leibowitz, *New Studies in Bereshit (Genesis)* 189 (trans. Aryeh Newman, Eliner Library, Hemed Press, Jerusalem) (discussing Maimonides' commentary on the binding of Isaac).

13. See Søren Kierkegaard, *Fear and Trembling* 89–91 (trans. Alastair Hannay, Penguin Books: London, 1985); see Jerome I. Gellmann, *The Fear, the Trembling, and the Fire: Kierkegaard and Hasidic Masters on the Binding of Isaac* 18 (University Press of America, Inc.: Lanham, Mary., 1994).

14. Mishael Maswari Caspi and Sascha Benjamin Cohen, *The Binding [AQEDAH] and Its Transformations in Judaism and Islam: The Lamps of God* 28 (Mellen Biblical Press: Lewiston, 1995). If Isaac stoically accepted the role of the sacrificed, he prefigured the passion of Jesus. Id, at 50.

15. See Ellen Frankel, *The Classic Tales: 4,000 Years of Jewish Lore* 69 (Jason Aronson Inc.: Northvale, N.J., 1993).

16. Caspi and Cohen, at 23; Leibowitz, at 189.

17. Lillian Smith, *The Journey* (World Publishing Co.: Cleveland, 1954), 256; Women's Quotes 30.

18. See Virginia Woolf, *The Letters of Virginia Woolf*, vol. II 1912–1922, 585 (Harcourt Brace Jovanovich: New York, 1975) ("I read the book of Job last night—I don't think God comes well out of it").

19. Shalom Spiegel, *The Last Trial: On the Legends and Lore of the Command to Abraham to Offer Isaac as a Sacrifice: The Akedah*, 46–47 (trans. Judah Goldin, Jewish Lights: Woodstock, Vt., 1969); Jon D. Levenson, *The Death and Resurrection of the Beloved Son: The Transformation of Child Sacrifice in Judaism and Christianity* 198 (Yale University Press: New Haven, 1993).

20. Louis Ginzberg, *Legends of the Jews* 274–5 (Henrietta Szold, trans. The Jewish Publication Society of America: Philadelphia, 1938).

21. Caspi and Cohen, *supra*, at 31 (citing Midrash Bereshit Rabbati 955\90).

22. Caspi and Cohen, *supra* at 35 (citing ninth-cent. Midrash Tanhuma, Vayer. 81); id at 41 (citing Ginzberg, at 286).

23. Ellen Frankel, *supra* at 74–75.

24. Zornberg, *supra*, at 126–7 (discussing midrash).

25. See Caspi and Cohen, *supra* at 125–6 (describing Sarah's silent cry of anguish).

26. Ignaz Maybaym, "The Sacrifice of Isaac: A Jewish Commentary," Leo Baeck College Publication No. 1, London (1959).

27. Ellen Frankel, *supra*, at 72 (Abraham tells Isaac that Abraham and Sarah will survive but a few days before following Isaac to the grave).

28. Carol Pearson, *The Hero Within*, 105–6 (Harper & Row: San Francisco, 1989 (women's quotes, 279).

29. Toni Morrison, *Beloved* (Knopf: New York, 1987).

30. William Styron, *Sophie's Choice* (Random House: New York, 1979); Doris Lessing, *The Fifth Child* (Knopf: New York, 1988); Amy Tan, *The Joy Luck Club* (Putnam's: New York, 1989).

Lynn M. Paltrow

Punishment and Prejudice:
Judging Drug-Using Pregnant Women

Throughout the late 1980s and up until the current day, "crack moms" and "crack babies" have been the subject of vigorous public debate.[1] Much of this public discussion has been governed by speculation and medical misinformation reported as fact in both medical journals and the popular press and has been extremely judgmental and punitive in many instances. The harshest response has been the call for the arrest and prosecution of women who use cocaine during pregnancy.

In a country that has come to learn that certain drugs, such as thalidomide and DES, can cause serious damage to a child exposed to them prenatally, it is not surprising that people are concerned about the possible effects of prenatal exposure to cocaine. But a concern that could have become the basis for rational scientific inquiry as well as compassionate and constructive discussion quickly became a conclusion that all children exposed prenatally to cocaine would be damaged irrevocably and that their mother's selfish and irresponsible drug-taking behavior is to blame for a national health tragedy.

One key question is why there was such a "rush to judgment" both about the medical effects of cocaine and about the women who used it while pregnant.[2] While there is no one simple answer, it is clear that the issue of drugs and pregnancy touches on some of the most highly charged and deeply entrenched political concerns of our day. It involves America's long tradition of punishing drug use rather than providing treatment and education.[3] Because the problem of cocaine use in pregnancy has been presented predominantly as a problem of the African American community it is also deeply intertwined with issues of race, race discrimination, and the legacy of slavery:[4] while illicit substance abuse crosses all race and class lines, this particular debate has focused on low-income African American women, many of whom rely on welfare. Because it involves women and pregnancy, the issue of drugs and pregnancy is inseparable from issues concerning the status of all women as well as sex and sexuality.[5] Finally, the issue of pregnant women's drug use has been shaped by claims of fetal rights that are at the heart of today's abortion debate.[6]

It is not possible to address all of these influences here. But identifying them helps to explain why rational and compassionate discussion of the issue is so difficult. For example, if the issue of drug use does not trigger an emotional response, the issue of race or women's rights is bound to. As a result, there is little room for meaningful exploration of what the medical risks of cocaine use during pregnancy really are and what might actually help pregnant women and drug-exposed infants.

It also means that there is virtually no room to discuss complex ideas that take into account a range of human responses and possibilities. If I say cocaine may not be as damaging as once thought, people interpret that to mean that I am saying that it is perfectly fine to take cocaine.[7] If I oppose prosecution of pregnant women then I am heard to be saying that such women have no responsibility for their actions. If I say that fetuses should not be treated as persons under the law, I am accused of denying that they have any value at all. None of these assumptions or misinterpretations is correct.

The fact that cocaine may not be more damaging than cigarettes doesn't mean that pregnant women should now be urged to use it. Rather, it means that an unprecedented legal response to pregnant women who use cocaine can't be justified by claims of this particular drug's unparalleled or exceptional harm. Opposition to prosecution and other punitive responses does not mean that pregnant women lack responsibility for their actions. In our current political climate, however, prosecution and imprisonment appear to be the only mechanisms people recognize for holding people accountable for their actions. But they are not the only ways to encourage responsible behavior. In fact punishment in some circumstances can be the least effective social response.

Furthermore, to oppose the recognition of fetal personhood as a matter of law is not to deny the value and importance of potential life as a matter of religious belief, emotional conviction, or personal experience. Rather, by opposing such a new legal construct, we can avoid devastating consequences to women's health, prenatal health care, and women's hope for legal equality.

Exploring some of the real issues involving cocaine and pregnancy and how our discussion has been shaped or manipulated by the media coverage of these issues can help bring sensible and informed thought to the discussion. With luck it might also make room for compassion and understanding.

The Villain Cocaine

In the late 1980s and into the 1990s newspapers, magazines, and television were full of stories documenting the devastating effects of cocaine and predicting a lost generation irredeemably damaged by the effects of their mothers' cocaine use. For example, in 1991 *Time* magazine ran a cover story on the subject.[8] Bold yellow letters read "Crack Kids" followed by the headline: "Their mothers used drugs, and now it's the children who suffer." The face of a tearful child filled the page beneath the words.

Inside, on the table of contents, another photograph appears. This one is of a tiny infant's head, so small that a grown man's hand engulfs it almost completely. Next to the picture it reads: "A mother's sad legacy: Can the innocent legacies of drug use be rescued?" The inside story begins: "Innocent victims: Damaged by the drugs their mothers took, crack kids face social and educational hurdles and must count on society's compassion." This time a menacing picture of a distraught Black child accompanies the text. In fact, as the photographs become more sinister the subjects' skin color becomes darker.

The same year the *New York Times* ran a front page story entitled "Born on Crack and Coping with Kindergarten."[9] The story is accompanied by a photograph of a school teacher surrounded by young children. Underneath the caption reads: "I can't say for sure it's crack, said Ina R. Weisberg, a kindergarten teacher at P.S. 48 in the Bronx, but I can say that in all my years of teaching I've never seen so many functioning at low levels."

Throughout these years medical and popular journals, public school teachers and judges alike were willing to assume that if a child had a health or emotional problem and he or she had been exposed prenatally to cocaine, then cocaine and cocaine alone was the cause of the perceived medical or emotional problem. Rather than wait for careful research and evaluation of the drug's effect there was, as several researchers later criticized, a "rush to

judgment" that blamed cocaine for a host of problems that the research simply has not borne out.[10]

Indeed, an article in the medical journal *Lancet* in 1989 found that scientific studies that concluded that exposure to cocaine prenatally had adverse
effects on the fetus had a significantly higher chance of being published than
more careful research finding no adverse effects.[11] The published articles, de-
lineating the harmful effects on infants prenatally exposed to cocaine, reported brain damage, genito-urinary malformations, and fetal demise as
just a few of the dire results of a pregnant woman's cocaine use. Infants that
survived the exposure were described as inconsolable, unable to make eye
contact, emitting a strange high-pitched piercing wail, rigid and jittery.
These early studies, however, had numerous methodologic flaws that made
generalization from them completely inappropriate. For example, these
studies were based on individual case reports or on very small samples of
women who used more than one drug. Researchers often failed to control
for the other drugs and problems the mother might have, and/or failed to
follow up on the child's health.[12] The articles describing these studies were
nevertheless relied upon to show that cocaine alone was the cause of an array
of severe and costly health problems.

Like alcohol and cigarettes, using cocaine during pregnancy can pose
risks to the woman and the fetus. More carefully controlled studies, however,
are finding that cocaine is not uniquely or even inevitably harmful. For example, unlike the devastating and permanent effects of fetal alcohol syndrome, which causes permanent mental retardation, cocaine seems to act
more like cigarettes and marijuana, increasing certain risks like low birth
weight but only as one contributing factor and only in some pregnancies.[13]
Epidemiological studies find that statistically speaking many more children
are at risk of harm from prenatal exposure to cigarettes and alcohol. In fact,
one recent publication on women and substance abuse has created the label
"Fetal Tobacco Syndrome" to draw attention to the extraordinarily high
miscarriage and morbidity rates associated with prenatal exposure to cigarette smoke.[14]

By the late 1980s it was already becoming clear to researchers in the field
that the labels "crack babies" and "crack kids" were dangerous and counter-
productive.[15] If one read far enough in the *Time* article—past the pictures
of premature infants and deranged children—the story reported that

> [a]n increasing number of medical experts, however, vehemently challenge
> the notion that most crack kids are doomed. In fact, they detest the term

crack kids, charging that it unfairly brands the children and puts them all into a single dismal category. From this point of view, crack has become a convenient explanation for problems that are mainly caused by a bad environment. When a kindergartner from a broken home in the impoverished neighborhood misbehaves or seems slow, teachers may wrongly assume that crack is the chief reason, when other factors, like poor nutrition, are far more important.

Even the *New York Times* article about crack-exposed children in kindergarten eventually revealed that researchers "after extensive interviews [found] the problems in many cases were traced not to drug exposure but to some other traumatic event, death in the family, homelessness, or abuse, for example."[16] And despite the fact that school administrators "rarely know who the children are who have been exposed to crack . . . and the effects of crack are difficult to diagnose because they may mirror and be mixed up with symptoms of malnutrition, low birth-weight, lead poisoning, child abuse and many other ills that frequently afflict poor children," the article resorts to crack as the only reasonable explanation for an otherwise seemingly inexplicable phenomenon.

In fact, the outcry about cocaine and damaged children occurred at the end of eight years of Reagan-era budget cuts, many of them in social programs for poor women and children. As researchers Banks and Zerai noted,

> Resources for women and children were seriously affected. Between 1977 and 1984, maternal and child health block grants were reduced by one-third. As a result federally mandated comprehensive health clinics including well-baby, prenatal and immunization clinics were eliminated. Community and Migrant Health Centers were cut by one-third and the National Health Service Corp's budget was reduced by 64% (between 1981 and 1991). The WIC program did not sustain budget cuts, but by 1989 it still only served one-half of those eligible.[17]

Reports from the Children's Defense Fund for these years described the devastating consequences of increasing poverty, linking it to a dramatic decline in children's health and safety.[18]

When the headlines might more accurately have been "Born in Poverty and Coping with Kindergarten" and the real news was there is no such thing as a "crack kid," *Time*, the *New York Times*, and other leading news outlets continued to report pregnant women's use of cocaine as the primary threat to children's well-being. Even groups like the Center on Addiction and Substance Abuse at Columbia University, lead by Joseph Califano, in an otherwise tempered Annual Report that described their research on the cost of substance abuse to society, referred to newborns exposed to alcohol and especially cocaine as "a slaughter of innocents of biblical proportions."[19]

These stories and characterizations were not lost on the public officials looking at the question of substance abuse and pregnancy. One judge, assuming a knowledge of cocaine's effects that he simply did not have, and revealing his evident racial bias, admonished a woman accused of having a "cocaine baby":

> You know, we've got enough trouble with normal children. Now this little baby's born with crack. When he is seven years old, they have an attention span that long. [holding his thumb and index finger an inch apart]. They can't run. They just run around in class like a little rat. Not just black ones. White ones too.[20]

The Public Responds

The public response to the media and medical journal reports was largely one of outrage. The harshest reaction was the call for the arrest of the pregnant women and new mothers who used drugs. Numerous states considered legislation to make it a crime for a woman to be pregnant and addicted.[21] Although not a single state legislature passed a new law creating the crime of fetal abuse, individual prosecutors in more than thirty states arrested women whose infants tested positive for cocaine, heroin, or alcohol. Many of these women were arrested for child abuse, newly interpreted as "fetal" abuse. Others, like Jennifer Johnson in Florida, were charged with delivery of drugs to a minor.[22] In that case, the prosecutor argued that the drug delivery occurred through the umbilical cord after the baby was born but before the umbilical cord was cut. Still other women were charged with assault with a deadly weapon (the weapon being cocaine), or feticide (if the woman suffered a miscarriage), or homicide (if the infant, once born, died). Some women were charged with contributing to the delinquency of a minor.

While arrests were almost always the result of the action of an individual prosecutor, in the state of South Carolina there was unprecedented coordination between health care providers, the prosecutor's office, and the police.

In 1989, the city of Charleston, South Carolina, established a collaborative effort among the police department, the prosecutor's office, and a state hospital, the Medical University of South Carolina (MUSC), to punish pregnant women and new mothers who tested positive for cocaine. Under the policy, the hospital tested certain pregnant women for the presence of co-caine. Women were tested for the presence of cocaine to further criminal investigations, but the women never consented to these searches and search warrants were never obtained.

While the hospital refused to create a drug treatment program designed to meet the needs of pregnant addicts, or to put even a single trained drug counselor on its obstetrics staff, it did create a program for drug-testing cer-tain patients, their in-hospital arrest, and removal to jail (where there was neither drug treatment nor prenatal care); the ongoing provision of medical information to the police and prosecutor's office; and tracking for purposes of ensuring their arrest. Some women were taken to jail while still bleeding from having given birth. They were handcuffed and shackled while hospital staff watched with approval. All but one of the women arrested were African American. The program itself had been designed by and entrusted to a white nurse who admitted that she believed that the "mixing of races was against God's will."[23] She noted in the medical records of the one white woman ar-rested that she lived "with her boyfriend who is a Negro."[24]

While a civil suit in federal court challenging the Charleston practice failed at the trial level, it is now on appeal. However, the women who sued were successful in stopping the arrests. The National Institutes of Health found that research relating to the arrests violated federal law regarding re-search on human subjects; and the hospital agreed to stop facilitating the arrest of patients in a settlement agreement with the Office of Civil Rights which had been investigating it for race discrimination violations.[25]

As for other legal challenges, courts in twenty-four states have held that prosecutions of pregnant women are beyond the intent of the law, and in some cases beyond federal constitutional limits on state power. Only one court, the South Carolina Supreme Court, has upheld such prosecutions in a case called *Whitner* v. *State*.[26] This decision is now being challenged in the federal courts.

Who Are These Mothers?

As a report from the Southern Regional Project on Infant Mortality ob-served:

> Newspaper reports in the 1980s sensationalized the use of crack cocaine and created a new picture of the "typical" female addict; young, poor, black, urban, on welfare, the mother of many children and addicted to crack. In interviewing nearly 200 women for this study, a very different pic-

ture of the "typical" chemically dependent woman emerges. She is most likely white, divorced or never married, age 31, a high school graduate, on public assistance, the mother of two or three children, and addicted to alcohol and one other drug. It is clear from the women we interviewed that substance abuse among women is not a problem confined to those who are poor, black, or urban, but crosses racial, class, economic and geographic boundaries.[27]

African American women have been disproportionately targeted for arrest and punishment, not because they use more drugs or are worse mothers, but because, as Dorothy Roberts explains, "[t]hey are the least likely to obtain adequate prenatal care, the most vulnerable to government monitoring, and the least able to conform to the white middle-class standard of motherhood. They are therefore the primary targets of government control."[28]

Beyond the stock images and prejudicial stereotypes, the media has given the public little opportunity to meet or get to know the pregnant women on drugs. If we never learn who they are it is inevitable that their drug use will seem inexplicably selfish and irresponsible. Yet, if we could meet them and learn their history, we might be able to begin to understand them and the problems that need to be addressed.

Let me give an example. In the popular television show *NYPD Blue* we get to know the irascible Detective Sipowicz. While he is neither handsome nor charming, we come to care for him. We learn that he is an alcoholic who is able to stop drinking and improve his life. When he has a massive relapse and behaves outrageously, effectively abandoning his new wife and their newborn son, committing crimes of violence and countless violations of his responsibilities as a police officer, we nevertheless want to forgive him and give him another chance.

We are able to sympathize, at least in part because we have been given the information about why he has relapsed. His first son, whom he has finally reconnected with, is murdered, and Sipowicz, who can't handle it emotionally, turns back to the numbing, relief-giving effects of alcohol.

Sipowicz, in the end, is supported by his police colleagues who cover up for him and give him yet another chance. By contrast, when the same program did an episode involving a heroin-addicted pregnant woman, whose drug habit leads her two older sons to a life of crime, we never get to know why she has turned to drugs. We do not know as we did with Sipowicz what could have driven her to this behavior. The viewer can only assume that her drug use is purely selfish, stemming from a thoughtless hedonism. Thus, she is not entitled to understanding, sympathy, or the many second chances Sipowicz's character routinely gets.

But like Sipowicz, pregnant women who use drugs also have histories and complex lives that affect their behavior and their chances of recovery. We know that substance abuse in pregnancy is highly correlated with a history of violent sexual abuse.[29] In one study 70 percent of the pregnant addicted women were found to be in violent battering relationships. A hugely disproportionate number, compared to a control group, were raped as children. Drugs appear to be used as a means to numb the pain of a violent childhood and adulthood. Like Vietnam veterans who self-medicated with drugs for their post-traumatic stress disorders, at least some pregnant women also use drugs to numb the pain of violent and traumatic life experiences.[30]

Are their difficult childhoods or their experiences with violence an excuse for drug use? No. But the information begins to provide some idea of root causes that might need to be taken into consideration when trying to imagine the appropriate societal reaction. Will the threat of jail remove the trauma and pain that in many instances prompted the drug use and stands in the way of recovery? It is not that a woman who uses drugs is not responsible, but rather that we have to hold her responsible in a context that takes into account the obstacles, internal and external, that stand in the way of recovery.

Let me give a few examples. In the Jennifer Johnson case, Judge Eaton, who initially found Johnson guilty of delivery of drugs to a minor and sentenced her to eighteen years of probation and court supervision if she ever became pregnant again, said the following at her sentencing: "The choice to use or not to use cocaine is just that—a choice."[31] The judge ignored, as most people do, the physiologically addictive nature of cocaine. Despite the medical evidence as well as long-standing Supreme Court decisions recognizing that addiction is a chronic disease, marked by numerous relapses on the road to recovery, judges and the public continue to treat it as purely volitional behavior that is simply a matter of willpower.

Because addiction has both physiological and psychological components, achieving total abstinence or even successfully reducing the harms associated with drug use is difficult to do without help. Indeed the judge viewed Ms. Johnson's drug use alone as punishable under the law, despite the fact that the United States Supreme Court has recognized that addiction is a disease and that to punish someone for being an addict violates the Constitution's prohibition on cruel and unusual punishment.[32] Perhaps, however, the judge in the Jennifer Johnson case assumed that treatment was available for this disease. Unfortunately, then and now, pregnant women are routinely turned away from drug treatment programs. When Britta Smith, a woman in the state of Virginia, discovered that she was pregnant, she looked in the yellow pages for a drug treatment program that could help her with her cocaine problem. She was told none took women who depended on Medicaid for payment. Instead of being able to get the treatment she wanted, she was arrested on charges of child abuse.[33]

All pregnant women, not just poor ones, are routinely denied access to the limited drug treatment that exists in this country. In a landmark study in 1990, Dr. Wendy Chavkin surveyed drug treatment programs in New York City. She found that 54 percent flat out refused to take pregnant women.[34] Sixty-seven percent refused to take women who relied on Medicaid for payment, and 84 percent refused to take crack-addicted pregnant women.

One hospital in New York was sued for excluding women from drug treatment. The program argued that its exclusion of all women was justified and no different from its medical judgment to exclude all psychotics.[35] While New York State courts found that such exclusion violated state law, this did not automatically increase needed services. During the Dinkins' administration, however, new programs for women and children that proved cost effective and successful were created. When Mayor Guilliani took office, however, he promptly shut down the new programs.[36] Nationally, most of the new programs that have been developed for pregnant women and mothers are funded only as demonstration projects and primarily with federal dollars. Funding is unlikely to be renewed in the coming years. Most of the other existing programs, as numerous studies have shown, are not designed to meet the needs of women.[37] They are based on studies about male drug users and many rely on an extremely confrontational model that does not work for women, whose profiles generally include guilt and extremely low self-esteem. Furthermore, male-oriented programs do not take into account women's child care and family responsibilities. Many people, however, like Judge Eaton, think women should be punished for failing to get nonexistent treatment. Others disguise punitive policies of arrest as fair punishment for women who unreasonably refuse offers of voluntary treatment, when in fact, the "offer" is coerced under the threat of arrest and the treatment itself often inappropriate or inadequate to help the woman.

Other barriers also exist. Judge Eaton ruled that "the defendant also made a choice to become pregnant and to allow those pregnancies to come to term." The prosecutor argued that "[w]hen she delivered that baby she broke the law." By saying this, the judge makes clear that it was having a child that was against the law. If Ms. Johnson had had an abortion she would not have been arrested—even for possessing drugs.[38] But this statement not only reveals a willingness to punish certain women for becoming mothers, it also reflects a host of widely held beliefs and assumptions about access to reproductive health services for women.

For example, implicit in this statement is the assumption that Ms. Johnson had sex and became pregnant voluntarily. Given the pervasiveness of rape in our society, assuming voluntary sexual relations may not be justified. Perhaps, though, the judge, like many others, simply thought that addicts have no business becoming pregnant in the first place. A South Carolina judge put it bluntly: "I'm sick and tired of these girls having these bastard babies on crack cocaine." Apparently concerned about his candor, he later explained: "They say you're not supposed to call them that but that's what they are . . . when I was a little boy, that's what they called them."[39]

On call-in radio talk shows someone inevitably asks why these mothers can't just be sterilized or injected with Depo Provera until they can overcome their drug problems and, while they are at it, their low socioeconomic status. The consistency of this view should not be surprising given our country's history of eugenics and sterilization abuse. Indeed, the U.S. Supreme Court has declared sterilization of men unconstitutional, but has never overturned its decision upholding the sterilization of women perceived to be a threat to society.[40]

The suggestion of sterilization, however, is particularly attractive if there is no explanation about why a pregnant woman with a drug problem would want to become pregnant or to have a child in the first place. But drug-using pregnant women become pregnant and carry to term for the same range of reasons all women do. Because contraception failed. Because they fell in love again and hoped this time they could make their family work. Because they are "pro-life" and would never have an abortion. Because when they found out the beloved father of the baby was really already married, they thought it was too late to get a legal abortion. Because they do not know what their options might be. Because they have been abused and battered for so long they no longer believe they can really control any aspect of their lives including their reproductive lives. Because they wanted a child. Because their neighbors and friends, despite their drug use, had healthy babies and they believed their's would be healthy too.

The threat of sterilization is just another punitive response that denies the humanity of the women themselves. Although Judge Eaton did not propose sterilization as part of the sentence he imposed on Ms. Johnson, as some judges in related cases have,[41] he undoubtedly assumed that Ms. Johnson could decide, once pregnant, whether or not to continue that pregnancy to term. Since 1976, however, the United States government has refused to pay for poor women's abortions and few states have picked up the costs.[42] In Florida, like most other states, the "choice" Judge Eaton spoke of does not exist for low-income women.

It was in Florida, after all, where Dr. Gunn was hunted down and murdered for providing abortions to those women who could afford them. It was also where Kawana Ashley discovered she was pregnant. Ms. Ashley was already raising a child as a single parent and felt she could not responsibly have another one. Her boyfriend promised to help pay for the abortion. After waiting and waiting until weeks had passed, she realized he was not going to help her. She went to a clinic where she found out that she was already in the second trimester of her pregnancy. The abortion was prohibitively expensive and neither the state nor the clinic would provide one for free. Ms. Ashley, in an act of desperation, took a gun and shot herself in the stomach. She survived. The fetus, weighing two pounds, two ounces was delivered by cesarean section with a wound to its wrist. It lived briefly but did not survive. Ms. Ashley was charged with murder.[43] Even assuming that Ms. Johnson's religious and ethical beliefs would have allowed her to end her pregnancy, she, like Kawana Ashley, would have found that her "choices" were much more limited than Judge Eaton assumed.

Lack of access to abortion services is only one of the many barriers that exist for a drug-addicted pregnant woman who attempts to make responsible "choices." There are many other barriers that make it extremely difficult for pregnant women on drugs to get the kind of help and support they need. Access to services for drug-addicted women who are physically abused is also limited. For example, many battered women's shelters are set up to deal with women who have experienced violence, but are not equipped to support a woman who has become addicted to drugs as a way to numb the pain of the abuse.[44] Other barriers include lack of housing, employment, and access to prenatal care. As one of the few news stories to discuss these women's dilemmas explains:

> Soon after she learned she was pregnant, [Kimberly] Hardy [who was eventually prosecuted for delivery of drugs to a minor], convinced she had to get away from her crowd of crack users as well as her crumbling relationship with her [boyfriend] Ronald, took the kids home to Mississippi for

the duration of her pregnancy. But by moving, she lost her welfare benefits, including Medicaid. Unable to pay for clinic visits, she had to go without prenatal care.[45]

And what about the men in their lives? Their contributions to the problem, physiologically and socially, are ignored or deliberately erased. Rarely
in the media do we know what has happened to the potential fathers. Their
drug use, abandonment, and battering somehow miraculously disappear
from view.

Nevertheless, men often do play a significant role. For example, in California Pamela Rae Stewart was arrested after her newborn died. One of her
alleged crimes contributing to the child's ultimate demise was having sex
with her husband on the morning of the day of the delivery. Her husband,
with whom she had had intercourse, was never arrested for fetal abuse. Indeed, the prosecutor's court papers argued that Ms. Stewart had "subjected
herself to the rigors of intercourse," thereby totally nullifying the man's
involvement or culpability.[46]

Prosecutors in South Carolina have also managed to ignore male culpability, even when it is the father who is supplying the pregnant woman with
cocaine or other potentially harmful substances. Many women arrested in
this state were not identified as substance addicted until after they had given
birth, a point at which their drug use could not even arguably have a biological impact on the baby. Prosecutors argued that arrest was still justified because evidence of a woman's drug use during pregnancy is predictive of an
inability to parent effectively. But fathers identified as drug users are not automatically presumed to be incapable of parenting. Indeed, when a man who
happens to be a father is arrested for drunk driving, a crime that entails a
serious lack of judgment and the use of a drug, he is not automatically presumed to be incapable of parenting and reported to the child welfare authorities. Prosecutors nevertheless rely on biological differences between mothers and fathers. Arguing that a man's drug use could not have hurt the
developing baby in the first place. However, studies indicate that male drug
use can affect birth outcome: Studies on male alcohol use have demonstrated
a relationship between male drinking and low birth weight in their children
and a study of cocaine and men suggests that male drug use can also affect
birth outcome.[47]

We continue to live in a society with double standards and extremely
different expectations for men and women. Drug use by men is still glorified,
while drug use by women is shameful, and by pregnant women a crime. This

could not have been better demonstrated than by an advertising campaign by Absolut vodka. On Father's Day, as a promotional gimmick, Absolut sent 250,000 free ties to recipients of the *New York Times* Sunday edition. Scores of little sperm in the shape of Absolut vodka bottles swim happily on the tie's blue background. So while many call for arrest when a pregnant woman uses drugs or alcohol, fathers who drink are celebrated and, in effect, urged to "tie one on."

Of course, none of these arguments is made to suggest that women are not responsible for their actions or that they are unable to make choices that reflect free will. Rather, it is to say that popular expectations of what acting responsibly looks like and notions of "choice" have to be modified by an understanding of addiction as a chronic relapsing disease, of the degree to which our country has abandoned programs for poor women and children, and of the time, strength, and courage it takes for a drug-addicted woman to confront her history of drug use, violence, and abandonment. Compassion and significantly more access to coordinated and appropriate services will not guarantee that all of our mothers and children are healthy. But medical experts and both children's and women's rights advocates agree that such an approach is far more likely to improve health than are punishment and blame.

Some people argue, however, that a woman who "chooses" to become pregnant, and does not end that pregnancy, should be held legally accountable for her actions. Much of the problem with this argument has already been addressed above. How do we know that a woman chose to become pregnant? Or that she could have ended her pregnancy? Even assuming that at least some women's choices are completely free, totally conscious, and completely funded, the consequences of such a standard of accountability would result in a level of state surveillance and scrutiny of women's lives that is not only dangerous but also completely unprecedented under our system of law. As the Illinois Supreme Court explained in rejecting the argument that a child should be able to sue its mother for injuries caused by her behavior during pregnancy:

> It is the firmly held belief of some that a woman should subordinate her right to control her life when she decides to become pregnant or does become pregnant. Anything which might possibly harm the developing fetus should be prohibited and all things which might positively affect the developing fetus should be mandated under penalty of law, be it criminal or civil. Since anything which a pregnant woman does or does not do may

have an impact, either positive or negative, on her developing fetus, any act or omission on her part could render her liable to her subsequently born child. While such a view is consistent with the recognition of a fetus' having rights which are superior to those of its mother, such is not and cannot be the law of this state.

A legal right of a fetus to begin life with a sound mind and body assertable against a mother would make a pregnant woman the guarantor of the mind and body of her child at birth. A legal duty to guarantee the mental and physical health of another has never before been recognized in law. Any action which negatively impacted on fetal development would be a breach of the pregnant woman's duty to her developing fetus. Mother and child would be legal adversaries from the moment of conception until birth.

If a legally cognizable duty on the part of mothers were recognized, then a judicially defined standard of conduct would have to be met. It must be asked, by what judicially defined standard would a mother have her every act or omission while pregnant subjected to state scrutiny? By what objective standard should a jury be guided in determining whether a pregnant woman did all that was necessary in order not to breach a legal duty to not interfere with her fetus' separate and independent right to be born whole? In what way would prejudicial and stereotypical beliefs about the reproductive abilities of women be kept from interfering with a jury's determination of whether a particular woman was negligent at any point during her pregnancy?

As the court recognized, to hold women legally accountable would depend on the "legal fiction" that the fetus is "a separate person with rights hostile and assertable against its mother." As the court further explained:

The relationship between a pregnant woman and her fetus is unlike the relationship between any other plaintiff and defendant. No other plaintiff depends exclusively on any other defendant for everything necessary for life itself. No other defendant must go through biological changes of the most profound type possible at the risk of her own life, in order to bring forth an adversary into the world. It is after all, the whole life of the pregnant woman which impacts on the development of the fetus. As opposed to the third-party defendant, it is the mother's every waking and sleeping moment which for better or worse shapes the prenatal environment which forms the world for the developing fetus. That this is so is not a pregnant woman's fault: it is a fact of life.

The court concluded that it could not treat women as strangers to their own bodies, recognizing that "[j]udicial scrutiny into the day-to-day lives of pregnant women would involve an unprecedented intrusion into the privacy and autonomy of the citizens" of its state.[48]

But What about the Fetus?

Many, however, feel that protection of women's privacy and autonomy ignores the rights of the fetus. This argument has been borrowed from the rhetoric and legal grounds developed by the antiabortion movement in its efforts to gain legal recognition of fetal personhood and to outlaw abortion. Prosecutors trying women for their behavior during pregnancy borrow wholesale from the antichoice legal arguments made on behalf of the fetus.

These prosecutors assert that by promoting fetal rights and the view that a mother's drug use is the same as child abuse, they are somehow protecting fetuses and children. But just the opposite is true. As every leading health group has pointed out, threatening punishment of pregnant addicts will accomplish only one thing—deterring women from health care, including prenatal care, that can ameliorate problems of substance abuse even if a woman can't stop her drug use altogether.[49] It will also deter women from obtaining what little drug treatment is available. In fact, since the highly publicized Whitner decision, some drug treatment programs in South Carolina saw a drop of 80 percent in the number of pregnant women seeking drug treatment.[50] Punishment could have even more far-reaching deterrent effects: It might deter pregnant women from seeking the food they need during pregnancy. While low-income women can use the federal Women, Infant and Child (WIC) program that provides nutritional supplements to pregnant women, such programs are required to determine if a woman is using drugs. Public health workers including those employed by the WIC program are mandatory child abuse reporters under the South Carolina law. As a result, a pregnant woman using drugs in South Carolina might not even be able to get the food she needs without the risk of arrest.

The effect of treating a pregnant drug user as a child abuser will not help fetuses or children. It will, however, further an agenda to undermine women's rights. Few people realize that women are not yet recognized as full persons under the law: In a series of cases, the United States Supreme Court has recognized that the Constitution provides women with protection against certain forms of discrimination on the basis of sex. This protection, however, applies only in certain areas such as employment and education, and then only to a limited extent.[51] Significantly, the Supreme Court has held that the Constitution itself does not provide protection to women in many areas involving pregnancy and abortion.[52] For example, the Court found that it was not a constitutional violation to provide male state employees with health benefits for all of their health problems but to exclude coverage for women with health problems associated with pregnancy. The Supreme Court held that this was discrimination between pregnant persons and non-pregnant persons, not discrimination between men and women. The Court views a woman's capacity for pregnancy as something that makes her different from men, and extends constitutional protection against employment discrimination only where women are similarly situated to, or in fact, exactly like men. As long as the Supreme Court continues to hold that discrimination against pregnant women is not sex discrimination, women will not be equal under the law.[53]

The problem with treating the fetus as a person is that women will not simply continue to be less than equal, they will become nonpersons under the law. No matter how much value we place on a fetus's potential life, it is still inside the woman's body. To pretend that the pregnant woman is separate is to reduce her to nothing more than, as one radio talk show host asserted, a "delivery system" for drugs to the fetus.

It is only by treating the pregnant woman as a stranger to her own body that people can compare her drug use to a parent who feeds cocaine to her two-year-old child. It allows people to ignore the pregnant woman's mental and physical state and the physiological addiction that compels her to take drugs. As many authors have noted, pregnant women do not become pregnant and turn to drugs, but are already addicted when they become pregnant.[54]

Nevertheless, some argue that the drug-addicted pregnant woman should be treated as if her drug use is the same as child abuse and at least one state supreme court has apparently accepted that view. The Supreme Court of South Carolina, distinguishing itself from courts in twenty-four other states, has declared that at least inside the borders of South Carolina a viable fetus is a person and a pregnant woman who endangers its health can be found guilty of child abuse.[55]

The South Carolina court could not fathom the difference between a stranger who attacks a pregnant woman and the woman herself. The court argued if the fetus is not treated as a child under the law, then, "there would be no basis for prosecuting a mother who kills her viable fetus by stabbing it, by shooting it, or by other such means, yet a third party could be prosecuted for the very same acts."

But in order for a mother to "stab" or "shoot" the unborn child, she must first cut through her own flesh, rip apart her own body. Her actions thus have vastly different physiological and psychological implications than those of a third party who commits violence, not against his own body, but against that of another person.

Moreover, a parent addicted to drugs can avoid child abuse charges by providing for her child's needs and by ensuring that the child does not take drugs him or herself. Because the fetus is inside the woman's body, a drug-addicted pregnant woman may be a criminal no matter what she does. This is especially clear for a woman who is pregnant and addicted to heroin. If she stops using heroin, the ensuing effects of withdrawal could cause fetal death, in which case she would be guilty of murder. If she seeks late-term abortion she could be arrested either for having an illegal abortion or for committing murder. Alternatively, if she continues her pregnancy and gives life to a child despite her addiction problem, she could go to jail for ten years as a child abuser. Because the fetus is in her body, every option available to her is a crime.

If the fetus is a person, there are no limits on the state's power to police and punish pregnant women and on the power of husbands and putative fathers and even complete strangers to interfere with women's freedom.

Pregnant women could be prosecuted for drinking alcohol. It has already happened. Pregnant women could be prosecuted for failing to get sufficient bed rest or endangering the fetus by having sexual intercourse late in pregnancy. Remember, that too has already happened. Self-appointed guardians for the fetus could seek to prevent a pregnant woman with cancer from having chemotherapy that might endanger the fetus. It has already happened. Courts could order pregnant women to undergo cesarean section for the benefit of the life of the fetus, even when such surgery could cause the woman herself to die. Unfortunately, this has already happened as well.[56]

In 1987 Angela Carder, who was approximately twenty-five weeks pregnant, found out that she had a tumor the size of a football in her lungs. At thirteen she had been diagnosed with a rare form of bone cancer. She defied predictions of her death and lived despite chemotherapy and the removal of an entire leg and half her pelvis. Eventually she married and became pregnant.

When she realized she was having a recurrence of the cancer she made it clear to her doctors and family that above all she wanted to live. Her family felt the same way and her doctors did not believe they could do anything to save the pregnancy. A neonatologist at the hospital, however, decided that the fetus ought to be rescued from Angela's body. This doctor went to the hospital's lawyers, who in turn called a judge to decide what should be done in terms of the fetus.

A lawyer was appointed for the fetus, and she, along with another lawyer who appeared on behalf of the fetus, argued that what Angela wanted did not matter since the fetus had a right to life. Angela's doctors testified that the cesarean section could kill her and that none of them were willing to perform the surgery.

In the end the cesarean was ordered and performed. The decision rested entirely on the view that the fetus had a right to life. The fetus was so premature that it lived only for a few hours. Angela died two days later, with the cesarean section listed as a contributing factor in her death.

Although the order was eventually overturned, Angela's case is but one of many examples of distorted and inhumane health care resulting from the creation of fetal rights. A husband has sought a court order for visitation of his "child" to keep his estranged pregnant wife from leaving town. Juvenile courts have taken custody of the drug-exposed fetus and ordered "it" into drug treatment. In Colorado, state officials terminated a woman's parental rights to a child before it was even born, arguing that she was an "unfit" pregnant woman. Furthermore, in South Carolina, despite official claims that the purpose of prosecution is not to punish women who seek help and take care of their children, one woman, who had been able to stop using drugs, and who was working and home-raising three young, healthy children, was forced to serve a five-year jail sentence for child abuse based on a positive cocaine test at the birth of her son.

The possibilities for denying women's freedom are not the fantasies of lawyers engaged in slippery slope arguments, but rather current trends in the ever increasing effort to win legal recognition of the fetus and to undermine and ultimately abolish women's rights.

The truth is that we do not have to pit the woman against the fetus to promote healthy pregnancies or to value life. In fact, creating fetal personhood hurts both women and the possibilities for healthier pregnancies. We could treat addiction for what it is, a health problem. We could fund programs designed to meet women's needs not only during pregnancy, but throughout their lives, because we value them as whole persons. We could respect people's different values regarding fetuses without creating the legal fiction that fetuses are separate persons. We could commit to ending poverty, the greatest threat to children's health. We could attempt to develop a sane drug policy and ensure that health care and reproductive freedom are realities for all people.

Most people think these goals are too unrealistic to fight for. But it is exactly because we have given up these goals that there is now so much room for arguments for punishment, and for the protection not of life or health in general but of fetal life alone.

1. Lindesmith Center, *Cocaine and Pregnancy* (1997); Laura E. Gomez, *Misconceiving Mothers* (Philadelphia: Temple University Press, 1992).

2. Linda C. Mayes, R H. Granger, M. H. Bornstein, and B. Zuckerman, "The Problem of Cocaine Exposure, A Rush to Judgment," *Journal of the American Medical Association* 267 (1992): 406.

3. Stephan R. Kandall, *Substance and Shadow, Women and Addiction in the United States* (Cambridge, Mass.: Harvard University Press, 1996); Mike Grey, *Drug Crazy* (New York: Random House, 1998).

4. Dorothy Roberts, *Killing the Black Body: Race, Reproduction, and the Meaning of Liberty* (New York: Pantheon Books, 1997).

5. Sheila B. Blume, "Sexuality and Stigma: The Alcoholic Woman," *Alcohol Health and Research World* 15, no. 2 (1991): 139–146.

6. Katha Pollitt, "A New Assault on Feminism," *The Nation* (26 March 1990).

7. Lindesmith Center, *Cocaine and Pregnancy.*

8. *Time Magazine* (13 May 1991).

9. Suzanne Dale, "Born on Crack and Coping with Kindergarten," *New York Times* (7 February 1991), A1.

10. Mayes, "The Problem of Cocaine Exposure."

11. Gideon Koren, Karen Graham, Heather Shear, and Tom Einarson, "Bias Against the Null Hypothesis: The Reproductive Hazards of Cocaine," *Lancet* (1989): 1, 1440–1442.

12. Mayes, "The Problem of Cocaine Exposure"; B. Lutiger, K. Graham, T. R. Einarson, and G. Koren, "Relationship Between Gestational Cocaine Use and Pregnancy Outcome: A Meta-Analysis," *Teratology* (1991): 44, 405–414.

13. Barry Zuckerman et al., "Effect of Maternal Marijuana and Cocaine Use on Fetal Growth," *New England Journal of Medicine* 320, no. 12 (23 March 1990): 762–768; Deborah A. Frank and Barry S. Zuckerman, "Children Exposed to Cocaine Prenatally: Pieces of the Puzzle," *Neurotoxicology and Teratology* 15 (1993): 298–300; Deborah A. Frank, Karen Breshahn, and Barry Zuckerman, "Maternal Cocaine Use: Impact on Child Health and Development," *Advances in Pediatrics* 40 (1993): 65–99.

14. Center on Addiction and Substance Abuse at Columbia University, *Substance Abuse and the American Woman* (1997); Joseph R. DiFranza and Robert A. Lew, "Effect of Maternal Cigarette Smoking on Pregnancy Complications and Sudden Death Syndrome," *Journal of Family Practice* 40 (1995): 385. Cigarette smoking has been linked to as many as 141,000 miscarriages and 4,800 deaths resulting from perinatal disorders, as well as 2,200 deaths from sudden infant death syndrome, nationwide.

15. American Academy of Pediatrics, Committee on Substance Abuse, Drug Exposed Infants, *Pediatrics* 86 (1990): 639.

16. Dale, "Born on Crack."

17. Rae Banks and Assata Zerai, "Maternal Drug Abuse and Infant Health: A Proposal for a Multilevel Model," in *African-American and the Public Agenda: The Paradoxes of Public Policy*, ed. Sedrick Herring (Newbury Park, Calif.: Sage, 1997), 53–67.

18. Children's Defense Fund, 1994.

19. Center on Addiction and Substance Abuse at Columbia University, *Annual Report*, 1994.

20. *State* v. *Collins*, Transcript of Record (Pickens Cnty., S.C., Dec. 18, 1991).

21. Allison Marshall, 1992, 1993, 1994 Legislative Update, in *National Association for Families and Addiction Research and Education Update* (Chicago, 1993, 1994, 1995).

22. *Johnson* v. *State*, 602 So.2d 1288 (Fla. 1992).

23. Brown Trial Transcript, *Ferguson et al.* v. *City of Charleston et al.*, U.S. District Court for the District of South Carolina, Charleston Division, C/A No. 2:93-2624-1 at 5:18–21 (Dec. 10, 1996).

24. Plaintiffs' Exhibit 119, *Ferguson et al.* v. *City of Charleston et al.*, U.S. District Court for the District of South Carolina, Charleston Division, C/A No. 2:93-2624-1.

25. Philip H. Jos, Marshall Jos, and Martin Perlmutter, "The Charleston Policy on Cocaine Use During Pregnancy: A Cautionary Tale," *Journal of Law Medicine and Ethics* 23 (1995): 120–128.

26. *Whitner* v. *State*, 492 S.E.2d 777 (S. C. 1997).

27. Shelley Geshan, "A Step Toward Recovery, Improving Access to Substance Abuse Treatment for Pregnant and Parenting Women," *Southern Regional Project on Infant Mortality* (1993): 1.

28. Dorothy Roberts, "Punishing Drug Addicts Who Have Babies: Women of Color, Equality, and the Right of Privacy," *Harvard Law Review* 104, no. 7 (1991): 1419, 1422.

29. Dianne O. Regan, Saundra M. Ehrlich, and Loretta P. Finnegan, "Infants of Drug Addicts: At Risk for Child Abuse, Neglect, and Placement in Foster Care," *Neurotoxicology and Teratology* 9 (1987): 315–319.

30. Sheigla Murphy and Marsha Rosenbaum, *Pregnant Women on Drugs: Combating Stereotypes and Stigma* (New Brunswick, N.J.: Rutgers University Press, forthcoming).

31. *State* v. *Johnson* No. E89-890-CFA (Fla.Cir.Ct. July 13, 1989).

32. *Linder* v. *United States*, 268 U.S. 5, 18 (1925); *Robinson* v. *California*, 370 U.S. 660, 82 S.Ct. 1417 (1962).

33. Mike Hudson, "With Neglect Charge Behind Her, Mother Intent on Staying Clean," *Roanoke Times* (17 September 1991).

34. Wendy Chavkin, "Drug Addiction and Pregnancy: Policy Crossroads," *American Journal of Public Health* 80, no. 4 (April 1990): 483–487.

35. *Elaine W.* v. *Joint Diseases North General Hospital Inc.*, 613 N.E.2d 523 (N.Y. 1993).

36. Charisse Jones, "A Casualty of Deficit: Center for Addicts," *New York Times* (14 January 1996); Laura M. Lassor, "When Success Is Not Enough: The Family Rehabilitation Program and the Policies of Family Preservation in New York City," *Review of Law and Social Change* (forthcoming).

37. United States General Accounting Office Report to the Chairman, Committee on Finance, U.S. Senate, *Drug-Exposed Infants, A Generation at Risk*, GAO/HRD-90-138 (June 1990).

38. Lynn M. Paltrow, "When Becoming Pregnant Is a Crime," *Criminal Justice Ethics* 9, no. 1 (Winter–Spring 1990): 41–47.

39. *State* v. *Crawley*, Transcript of Record (Ct. Gen. Sess. Anderson Cnty., S.C., Oct. 17, 1994).

40. *Skinner* v. *Oklahoma*, 316 U.S. 535 (1942); *Buck* v. *Bell*, 274 U.S. 200 (1927); Stephen J. Gould, "Carrie Buck's Daughter," *Natural History* (July 1984).

41. *People* v. *Johnson*, No. 29390 (Cal.Super.Ct. Jan. 2, 1991).

42. *Harris* v. *McRae*, 448 U.S. 297 (1980).

43. *State* v. *Ashley* 1997, 701 So.2d 338 (Fla. 1997).

44. Amy Hill, "Applying Harm Reduction to Services for Substance Using Women in Violent Relationships," *Harm Reduction Coalition* 6 (Spring 1998): 7–8.

45. Jan Hoffman, "Pregnant, Addicted and Guilty?" *New York Times Magazine* (19 August 1990): 53.

46. Angela Bonavoglia, "The Ordeal of Pamela Rae Stewart," *Ms.* (August 1987).

47. Ricardo A. Yazigi, Randall Odem, and Kenneth L. Polakoski, "Demonstration of Specific Binding of Cocaine to Human Spermatozoa," *Journal of the American Medical Association* 266, no. 14 (9 October 1991).

48. *Stallman* v. *Youngquist*, 125 Ill.2d 267, 531 N.E.2d 355 (1988).

49. Lynn Paltrow, *Punishing Women for Their Behaviour During Pregnancy*, National Institute on Drug Abuse (1997).

50. Amicus brief of the National Association of Alcoholism and Drug Abuse Counselors et al., submitted in *Whitner* v. *State*, United States Supreme Court, No. 97-1562 (1998) at *www.lindesmith.org*.

51. Reva Siegel, "Reasoning from the Body: A Historical Perspective on Abortion Regulation and Questions of Equal Protection," *Stanford Law Review* 44 (1992): 261.

52. *Geduldig* v. *Aiello*, 417 U.S. 484 (1974); *Bray* v. *Alexandria Women's Health Clinic*, 114 S.Ct. 753 (1993).

53. Ibid.

54. NAPARE policy statement no. 1, "Criminalization of Prenatal Drug Use: Punitive Measures Will Be Counter-Productive," National Association on Prenatal Addiction Research (Chicago, 1990).

55. *Whitner* v. *State*, 328 S. C. 1, 492 S.E.2d 777 (1997); Ariela R. Dubler, "Monitoring Motherhood," *Yale Law Journal* 106 (1996): 935.

56. Terry E. Thornton and Lynn Paltrow, "The Rights of Pregnant Patients: Carder Case Brings Bold Policy Initiatives," *Healthspan* 8, no. 5 (May 1991): 10–16.

Nina Perales

Cultural Stereotype and the Legal Response to Pregnant Teens

In January 1996 newspapers and television stations around the nation reported that police and child welfare officials in Houston, Texas, were searching for a pregnant runaway, believed to be ten years old, and her twenty-two-year-old boyfriend. After the couple was found by authorities and the boyfriend charged with statutory rape, public interest shifted to his attorney's claim of a cultural defense. Several months later, Houston courts dismissed the statutory rape case based on a ruling that the girl, actually fourteen years old, was the common-law wife of her boyfriend.

This article will examine the events leading up to Adela Quintana's very public entry into motherhood and the response by the legal system to her pregnancy and relationship with an adult man. The article will contrast the case of Adela Quintana, and other Latina girls treated like her, with the national trend to discourage teen pregnancies by older men with stricter enforcement of statutory rape laws. The article will conclude with an analysis of the dangers inherent in using cultural stereotypes to create a distinct legal standard for Latina teens who become pregnant by adult men.

Adela Quintana

Adela Quintana was thirteen years old when she met Pedro Sotelo at a Christmas party in 1994 at which her brother was playing music. Shortly after, the couple began to date. In February 1995 two months after they met, Pedro and Adela moved in together with her father at her father's house on Cactus Street in Houston. They had their own bedroom. Pedro worked as an air-conditioning subcontractor and supported Adela. Adela became pregnant in March or April 1995 while still thirteen, and subsequently dropped out of school.

On January 12, 1996, eight months pregnant, Adela went to the welfare office to apply for welfare. To prove her identity, Adela gave the caseworker a birth certificate showing that her name was Cindy Garcia and she was born in Houston on September 13, 1985. According to the birth certificate, she was ten years old.[1] When the caseworker, who thought Adela was older, pressed the question, Adela insisted the birth certificate was correct. The caseworker then reported Adela as a possible case of child abuse to Harris County Child Protective Services (CPS). CPS immediately took Adela into custody and placed her in an emergency shelter for abused children. After Adela revealed Pedro's name in an interview, the District Attorney's Office charged him with aggravated sexual assault of a child, a first-degree felony carrying a maximum penalty of ninety-nine years imprisonment, and issued a warrant for his arrest.

On Sunday, January 21, 1996, Adela asked to go to church with her caseworker. When at church, Adela said she had to go to the bathroom and walked out of the church to meet Pedro, who had not yet been arrested on the sexual assault charge. They fled. Responsible for her welfare and fearing grave health risks if a ten-year-old gave birth outside the hospital, CPS publicly announced their search and the story was picked up by the national media.

For three days Pedro and Adela panhandled during the day and slept in a different place every night. On the night of Wednesday, January 24, a Houston woman saw Pedro and Adela looking cold and hungry on a street corner. She took them to her apartment and gave them dinner. After recognizing them, she called the police. Pedro and Adela were once again taken into custody.

On January 25, Pedro was placed in a maximum security jail and his bond was set at $200,000—an extraordinary amount usually reserved for drug dealers and murderers. The sexual assault charges against him were reduced to a second-degree felony which carries a maximum sentence of twenty years in prison and $10,000 fine. CPS placed Adela in a special foster home and required her to attend school. Adela gave birth to a son on February 3, 1996.

The Cultural Defense

Lawyers for Pedro in his criminal case invoked what has come to be known as a "cultural defense."[2] They declared that Pedro was not guilty of statutory rape because he was following the customs of his rural village in Mexico. "It was a cultural collision," stated Pedro's attorney, Dick Wheelan. "Where he comes from, this is not uncommon."[3] The *Austin American-Statesman* explained: "Sotelo's supporters have said he is the victim of cultural differences between the United States and his native country. In short, the argument goes, he simply was living by the rules of his native village."[4]

Pointing to the fact that Pedro had never denied his relationship with Adela, his attorneys argued that the relationship was legitimate in Pedro's eyes. Wheelan described Pedro as "bewildered" and said that Pedro didn't understand why he was being prosecuted.[5] "He was not exploiting and abandoning her. This was not a sexual hit-and-run. They were building a life together," elaborated Wheelan.[6]

Wheelan and others argued that in the area of rural Mexico from which Pedro and Adela came, it is common for girls as young as thirteen to marry older men. "It's not quite the same situation as if these two people were born and raised [in the United States]," argued Wheelan.[7]

Nancy Revelette, a lawyer hired by Pedro's family for civil court proceedings, described the cultural practice asserted by Pedro's lawyers in his defense:

> In this area of Mexico, and other areas, there is an elopement tradition as one way to get married. When a young woman and man are in love, he says "Yo te invito vivir conmigo" ["I invite you to live with me"]. The woman accepts and the couple sets a date to elope. On that day, the bride leaves her home with no belongings and stays away several days to consummate the marriage. The parents pretend to grieve and are plied with alcohol and consoled by friends of the groom. The young couple returns and the bride's family welcomes their new son.[8]

According to Revelette, CPS failed to understand that Adela and Pedro were married and treated the case as another instance in which a girl was living with her adult boyfriend. Revelette attributed this to a "culture gap" between Mexicans and Mexican Americans. Revelette says the Mexican American bilingual caseworkers who interviewed Adela were unfamiliar with Mexican culture and failed to understand that Adela was describing a marriage when she explained that she was living with Pedro but admitted that they weren't formally married. According to Revelette, Adela thought she was helping to explain a legitimate situation. The caseworkers interpreted it as "shacking up." "If you believe like I do that language reflects culture, there was a big linguistic misunderstanding from the start," declared Revelette.[9]

In their coverage of the events, newspapers and television shows elaborated on the lawyers' themes, in effect creating their own ethnography of Pedro and Adela. The national television program *Dateline* sent a reporter to Mexico to interview people in the streets of Pedro's village about their awareness of early marriage. The program referred to Pedro as "an innocent player in a big cultural misunderstanding."[10]

For the most part, the media portrayed Pedro and Adela as simple country peasants. "[T]hese two campesinos, or peasants, from the town of Ixcamilpa de Guerrero were in love and living in America—land of opportunity."[11] News reporters described Pedro as "naive," dazed, confused by what was happening to him, and childlike.[12]

While the media confidently reported their idea of Adela's and Pedro's "Mexican culture," they ignored distinctions between one Mexican and another. One newspaper reported that Adela and Pedro were from Totoapa, Hidalgo, several Mexican states away from their hometown in Guerrero.[13] *Dateline* contrasted pictures of the Houston skyline with pictures of the rural, undeveloped town of Ixcamilpa de Guerrero, announcing: "This is Mexico!"

The Court Cases

In February 1996, before Pedro's statutory rape trial was scheduled to start, Pedro's family hired Houston attorney Nancy Revelette. Revelette, an Anglo who speaks fluent Spanish and lived some years in Mexico, would try to declare Pedro's and Adela's relationship a marriage and thus avoid the statutory rape charge. According to Revelette, CPS would not let her see Adela.[14] Revelette finally got a court order to interview Adela in her law office and took an affidavit from Adela explaining that Pedro and Adela intended to live as husband and wife and held themselves out as a married couple since February 1995.

Revelette submitted one affidavit each from Pedro and Adela to the family court judge in charge of Adela's case. On June 14, 1996, in family court, State District Judge Mary Craft ruled that Pedro and Adela had a valid common-law marriage. Judge Craft held no hearing on the issue; she accepted the affidavits without further testimony. Revelette said that Judge Craft was familiar with the case and the media coverage because she had been overseeing Adela's child protective case since January.[15]

What Revelette asserted, and Judge Craft accepted, was that Adela and Pedro had fulfilled the requirements of a common-law marriage under Texas law. Texas recognizes informal, or common-law marriages in addition to formal marriage, which requires a marriage license and ceremony.[16] An informal marriage is created when a couple agrees to be married and after the agreement they live together as husband and wife and hold themselves out as married in Texas.[17]

Critical to the outcome in this case, the Texas statute defining common-law marriage in 1996 included no minimum age.[18] The common-law marriage statute focused on the three elements of behavior required to create such a marriage but did not address the qualifications of the bride and groom. Although Texas courts have stated that in order to establish a valid marriage the parties must possess the capacity to marry (*Esparza* v. *Esparza*, [Civ.App. 1965] 382 S.W.2d 162 [common-law marriage not formed when one spouse is already married]), there is no case since the statute was recodified in 1970 that voids a common-law marriage because of young age.[19]

In Adela's case, because her parents knew she was living with Pedro and did not seek to void the marriage in court within the statutory deadline, the marriage could not be voided afterward, under a provision of Texas law that provides a child's parent, guardian, or next friend can void the child's marriage through a lawsuit.[20]

Three days later, after the family court ruling on common-law marriage, the statutory rape case against Pedro was dismissed by the Harris County District Attorney's Office. Prosecutors were no longer able to prove statutory rape because as Pedro's wife, Adela could legally consent to sex.[21]

Adela's status as wife invoked an exception to the Texas statutory rape law. In Texas children under the age of fourteen are legally incapable of giving consent to sexual intercourse.[22] However, the statutory rape law defines a "child" as "a person younger than 17 years of age *who is not the spouse of the actor*." The statute defines a "spouse" as "a person who is legally married to another."[23]

The family court ruling that Adela and Pedro had a valid marriage was the catalyst that resolved the criminal case against Pedro. Although Adela was still under the age of fourteen when she had sex with Pedro, because Adela was considered Pedro's wife she was no longer a child as defined by the statutory rape law.

Culture and the Legal Outcome

Ultimately it was Texas law that provided the basis for ruling that Adela and Pedro were married and he did not commit statutory rape. In effect, it was Texas culture (embodied in statute), not Mexican culture, that resolved the case. Texas permits early marriage because early marriage is socially acceptable in the state. The early marriage provisions in the Texas Code are not simply remnants of a distant, frontier past. At least one amendment of the Family Code since 1970 has made it easier for young people to marry. In 1975 the Texas Legislature reduced the age for marriage with parental consent from sixteen to fourteen.[24]

The Mexican cultural defense was unnecessary to the legal disposition of Pedro's case. Nevertheless, it played a key role in the outcome. Cultural arguments made by Pedro's lawyers, and expanded upon in the media, persuaded child welfare officials, a family court judge, and county prosecutors that it was appropriate to recognize a marriage in this case.

Although declaring a common-law marriage between a thirteen-year-old and her adult lover was legally novel to say the least, Judge Craft made her ruling on the scantiest of records: two affidavits. In thanking the judge publicly after her ruling, lawyer Nancy Revelette stated, "The judge was helpful, because this was uncharted waters."[25] CPS did not petition the family court to appoint a guardian for Adela and seek to void the marriage once they learned of the ruling because child welfare officials apparently concurred with the judge. Rock Owens, the chief of the Houston County Attorney's Child Protective Division, conceded that "I don't think the result of this is bad for Pedro and Adela."[26] When presented with the family court order, county prosecutors dropped their criminal charges the following court day and did not investigate further whether Adela and Pedro had sex before moving in together.

In accepting lawyers' arguments that Adela's marriage was appropriate according to traditional Mexican culture, the legal system changed Adela from a child in need of protection to a wife and mother fulfilling her proper role within a traditional family. The cultural information advanced by Pedro's lawyers went beyond the argument that Pedro believed he had an actual marriage with Adela because they followed the elopement ritual. The descriptions of very young girls who marry older men and have many children were meant to construct Adela at thirteen as a mature, capable wife and mother. Once no longer a child, Adela could be treated differently from other thirteen-year-old girls for whom mandatory schooling, agency supervision, and the protections of statutory rape law are appropriate.

A great deal of the cultural information advanced in the public debate over Adela related her early sexual maturity and that of other Mexican women. These comments expanded on descriptions of rural Mexican life to invoke the stereotype of the young Latina as full-bodied and oversexed. Nancy Revelette described Adela as physically mature and a "buxom lass." Revelette stated that in rural Mexico, "once a girl hits puberty she is fair game."[27] Regarding relationships between young teenage girls and older men, John Hart, a professor of Mexican history at Rice University, commented, "These people are doing what they're taught to do." Hart added for support that his wife, who is Mexican American, has a mother who wed, at thirteen, a thirty-year-old.

Images of Adela as the "foreign," undocumented immigrant served to further distance her from mainstream girlhood. "Police also discovered that the girl they knew as Cindy Garcia is actually an illegal immigrant from Mexico."[28] Press reports characterized Adela as a Mexican child-bride, a girl mature beyond her years and happy in the traditional role of wife and mother. In describing their life together in 1995, *USA Today* stated: "[Adela and Pedro] seemed to live harmoniously. Quintana cooked and cleaned and Pedro supported them. They held barbecues and offered guacamole, tortillas and beef to the neighbors."[29] The *Houston Chronicle* reported: "The small, shy Quintana was quiet and hesitant Monday when asked about the ruling clearing her husband. 'I'm happy,' she said. 'I'm glad they recognize that we're married and I hope they will now leave us alone so we can be happy with our baby.' "[30]

These images and stereotypes make Adela and other young Latina girls unexploitable by definition. Antonio Zavaleta, Dean of the College of Liberal Arts at the University of Texas in Brownsville, adopted the view that girls like Adela are not vulnerable children despite their age: "They come from an area . . . where what they have done is perfectly normal. There's absolutely nothing wrong with a man of his age taking a woman of that age. . . . Isn't the state of Texas big enough to say: 'OK, we now understand this isn't so bad, this guy isn't a child molester?' "[31]

Latina Teen Mothers: A Backward Trend
in Statutory Rape Prosecutions?

The use of "culture" to sanction Latina teen mothers marrying their adult partners is not unique to Adela Quintana or to Texas. In Orange County, California, from 1994 to 1996 approximately fifteen girls under the protection of the county Social Services Agency were helped by the agency to marry the men who had fathered their children. All but one of the girls were Latina. In July 1996 a pregnant thirteen-year-old named Isabel Gomez was given permission to marry her twenty-year-old boyfriend, Juan Piñeda, with whom she'd been living.[32] Some social workers who approved the marriages suggested that there is a cultural difference between the way the United States and Mexico view the marriages of young girls.[33]

In most cases, the agency's assistance came in the form of a recommendation to the Juvenile Court that the girl be permitted to marry or ruled no longer a dependent of the court so she would be free to marry. Although two thirds of California's teenage pregnancies involve adult men, Orange County was the only county in the state facilitating marriages of teen mothers.

The Orange County agency head, Larry Leaman, insisted that each case was based on an individual evaluation. At the same time, however, he admitted that he believed the age of consent for marriage in Mexico to be twelve; in fact, it is eighteen.[34] One social worker wrote to Leaman, "The whole thing, I'm sorry to say, smacks of racism and sexism. . . . I would venture to say . . . the justification for allowing [the girls] to continue to be abused is that it is 'cultural.'"[35]

In California births to unmarried Latina teens more than doubled from 1985 to 1994 and now constitute more than 62 percent of the state's unwed births. The *Los Angeles Times* in 1996 noted that the marriages facilitated by Orange County Social Services Agency appeared in sharp contrast to the campaign by then Governor Pete Wilson to reduce teen pregnancies by prosecuting more statutory rape cases.[36] Within weeks of press reports of the Orange County teen marriages, the state welfare director had called on the county to cease its practice, stating, "Something is going on down there that I just don't understand."[37]

The Orange County marriages and the case of Adela Quintana are exceptions to the national legal trend with respect to teen pregnancies. In the wake of studies showing that about 60 percent of the babies born to unwed teen girls are fathered by adult men, many states have stepped up statutory rape prosecutions in the hopes of deterring adult men from having sexual relationships with teenage girls.[38]

Delaware passed the Sexual Predator Act of 1996, which provides a penalty of twenty years imprisonment for having sex with a girl under age sixteen. Also in 1996 the Gem County, Idaho, prosecutor began to file criminal charges against pregnant teens and their boyfriends under a 1921 law banning sex by unmarried people.[39] California has allocated $8.4 million to prosecute statutory rape cases in recent years and Georgia raised its statutory age of consent from fourteen to sixteen and strengthened criminal penalties for sex with underage children.[40]

Although many advocates are skeptical about states' ability to reduce teen pregnancies through enforcement of statutory rape laws, these prosecutions are a sign that most states want to stop, not assist, unions between young teen girls and older men. The philosophy maintained by these states and supporters of statutory rape laws is that these teen–adult relationships should be prevented in every instance.

These advocates protested vigorously the outcome in Adela's case. Howard Davidson, Director of the American Bar Association Center for Children and the Law, has stated, "There is no good reason for a man in his 20s to have sex with a girl in junior high."[41] Kathleen Sylvester, vice-president of the Progressive Policy Institute, which studies teen issues, explains: "This has been a problem for years and years, but no one has wanted to talk about it. This is a case of men meeting junior high girls at the school gate. She is not mature enough emotionally to consent. They are involved in inherently exploited relationships."[42]

Adela Quintana and the Mis-use of Culture

As feminists, how do we respond to claims that some thirteen-year-old girls are mature and capable enough to marry the adult men with whom they became pregnant? If we can agree that a pregnant thirteen-year-old requires a legal response different from that of sanctioning marriage, at what age do we draw the line between "too young" and "not too young"? Is there any age at which we refuse to recognize these girls as mothers in any more than the biological sense, choosing instead to view them as exploited children?

Most teen mothers, no matter how young, have a strong connection to their babies and want to care for them. Refusing to acknowledge their motherhood beyond the biological function of giving birth (such as automatically removing the babies from their care) would be destructive and also unresponsive to many of the reasons the girls became pregnant in the first place. However, that does not mean that we should ignore the teen mother's need for vast amounts of support and preparation for the roles of adult, worker, and parent. In no other part of society do we assume that young teens have skills, experience, patience, maturity, and judgment equal to an adult and we should not do it in the area of parenting. The commitment of marriage from an adult man, or even today's welfare rules requiring the teen mother to live with her parents, does not approach the level of parenting support and education needed by young teen mothers.

The resolution of these larger questions is beyond the scope of this article and will depend on further debate among feminists and others. It is the goal of this article, however limited, to serve as a warning on the dangers of inserting "culture" into the discussion on young teen mothers whose children are fathered by adult men.

There can be no question that every young woman is influenced by her culture in the decisions she makes or that each girl's culture plays a strong role in her sexual behavior and childbearing. But analyzing the cultural influences, among a host of influences, in a girl's life requires more than reference to her country of origin or unspecific and uncorroborated descriptions of cultural practices. We cannot allow our consideration of the individual characteristics of girls to become cultural essentialism or to allow ideas of culture to slip into stereotype.

At the outset of cases like Adela's it is important to ask: "For what purpose is cultural information being used?" Although cultural information was used by Pedro's lawyers to inform the court about the state of mind of Pedro Sotelo, much of it related to Adela, the person who needed no cultural defense.

Nevertheless, the court's declaration that Adela was married to Pedro had several very serious results for her. First, Adela was removed from the supervision of CPS. Adela's baby was also removed from CPS supervision, absent a separate proceeding filed by CPS on the baby's behalf. Adela's marriage emancipated her from her parents. Finally, it affected her immigration status. Once she was married, Adela could no longer seek permanent legal status through her mother, a resident immigrant. Because Pedro was undocumented, and because the baby cannot serve as the basis of his parent status until he is an adult, Adela's marriage left her an undocumented immigrant with no sponsor.[43]

It is similarly important to ask whether cultural information is presented in an individualized way. In her article on the cultural defense, Leti Volpp argues:

> Information about the defendant's culture should never be reduced to stereotypes about a community but rather should concretely address the individual defendant's location in her community, her location in the diaspora and her history. The information should be provided so as to give insight into an individual's thoughts, and should not be used for purposes of explaining how an individual fits into stereotypes of group behavior.[44]

In Adela's case, the cultural information was not individualized to Adela. Instead, the experiences of other girls living in Mexico were projected onto Adela. Nancy Revelette stated, "The girls from Mexico live a very different life from the girls here. . . . By age 13, they know how to take care of babies." She stated further that children in this region get a third-grade education and then go to work.[45] These assertions do not describe Adela's life in Houston. Adela was attending school until she got pregnant and there was no evidence that her family was actively looking to marry her off. Even the traditional elopement asserted by Pedro's attorneys did not fit the actions of Pedro and Adela. Statements by Pedro indicated he had sex with Adela before they moved in together. The couple went to live in Adela's father's house and did not establish a separate home of their own.

Adela's life, like everyone else's, was complex. Despite the efforts of Pedro's lawyers and the media, her experience cannot be contained within their framework of "traditional rural Mexican culture." Although born in the rural town of Ixcamilpa de Guerrero, Adela was brought by her mother to Houston when she was seven years old. Her parents were divorced and she had a chaotic family life in her mother's house; Francisca Quintana was neglectful of her children and cared very little what Adela did with herself. Adela's fifteen-year-old sister had also left the home to go live with her boyfriend. Adela was English-speaking and attended school until she became pregnant.

It seems clear that almost everyone failed Adela. Her mother took so little care of her that CPS considered pressing child neglect charges against the mother.[46] School teachers, although they suspected Adela was in the wrong grade, did not move her to the right one. Pedro, who by all accounts truly cares for Adela, had sex with her within a month of the couple's beginning to date. Adela's father let her live in his house with Pedro. In the end, both CPS and Adela's court-appointed therapist concluded Adela was better off with Pedro than anywhere else.[47]

Adela was characterized by her mother as headstrong; her mother complained that she tried to keep Adela away from Pedro but Adela kept running away to see him.[48] Nancy Revelette described Adela as "street smart" and said that she was far less naive than Pedro.[49] Adela ran away from her foster care placement and the only public statement she made was that she wanted to live with Pedro and their baby.[50] When she moved in with Pedro, it may be that Adela was directing her own life and choosing among the only options she could see.

All of Adela's complexities and needs were packaged in the court proceedings as "culture." Adela's insecurities, any fear or reluctance she may have felt about her choice, remained locked inside the image of satisfied mother created for her by the media and legal system. The result of this essentialism, for Adela and other Latinas, is to dismiss what could be a real need on the part of a pregnant teen for safe housing, counseling, and education. For this reason, when cultural information is offered in an attempt to deflect us from a close scrutiny of the best interests of a pregnant teen, we should question both the cultural information offered and the resolution to which it points.

In Adela's case, no cultural information was presented to the court by anyone who could remotely be characterized as an expert on Mexican cultural practices. Given the generalized nature of the information, the factual disparities and lack of expert guidance, Judge Craft should have demanded more and better information before rendering her decision with respect to Adela.

We should be equally suspicious of the resolution urged on the court in Adela's case. As a child in the custody of CPS, concern for Adela's well-being included considerations of a safe place to live, continued schooling, emotional support, and help with the baby. Pedro's lawyers contended that her well-being was best addressed in a traditional marital arrangement. This argument was summed up by Pedro himself: "All there is to it are two people in love. . . . I didn't deserve this because I didn't abandon her."[51] In the resolution urged by Pedro's lawyers, Adela's best interests are met as long as she is supported financially by Pedro. It does not answer the question whether she can be "taken care of" and harmed at the same time.

Declaring Adela a traditional wife and mother because of "culture" does not only change the nature of her best interests. It removes consideration of gender oppression inherent in the marriage of a thirteen-year-old girl to a twenty-two-year-old man. By invoking culture and the stereotype of Latinas as traditionally exploited and self-sacrificing wives and mothers, Pedro's lawyers de-emphasized the gender issue confronting the court in the case.[52]

Conclusion

The pregnancy of young teens too often is ignored or dismissed for a variety of reasons, including "culture." As a *Houston Chronicle* staff editorial stated, "For Adela and all the thousands of Houston teens who will have babies before they are prepared, school will probably fall by the wayside, and all the years they might have spent learning about life and preparing for a productive future will be irrevocably lost. It's horrifying if we as a community have seen it so many times before that we cannot even work up a little shock."[53]

The legal response to such pregnancies, including statutory rape prosecutions, have proven to be awkward and ultimately ineffective in addressing the real needs of these young mothers. However, as feminists consider legal responses to young teen motherhood, it would be wrong to retreat from intervening in these young women's lives because of cultural essentialism.

A father of two daughters, Leonard Pitts, columnist for the *Miami Herald*, writes of the struggles of young teenage girls:

> [W]hat has gone wrong with our girls? . . . I'm talking about serious trouble [including] babies. . . . Girls run away a lot, so many girls trying to escape their own lives. I spoke with a psychologist and he, too, said girls are a special problem. Many, he said, live by wishes, making major decisions on the basis of what they want to be true rather than what really is. They behave as if consequences deferred are consequences escaped; their choices are not informed by anything we would recognize as logic or even self-preservation. And many, said the doctor, suffer an acute lack of self-esteem. . . . I've known too many girls who were unable to be complete within themselves, who needed the validation of a boy—any boy—more desperately than a boy would ever need them.[54]

In our effort to see these girls as both children in need of protection and mothers who deserve our respect, we must incorporate all parts of their lives, and remember that "culture" can be misused to discard a girl as often as it can provide an insight into her life.

I wish to dedicate this essay to my son, Javier Agustín Maldonado. Much of the information regarding Adela and Pedro before January 1996 is from a telephone interview with Nancy Revelette, Houston attorney, 26 September 1997.

1. Francisca Quintana, Adela's mother, had obtained this birth certificate for her daughter because Adela was undocumented. Her mother explained that she obtained the birth certificate so her daughter could go to school. The U.S. Supreme Court, in *Plyler* v. *Doe* 457 U.S. 202 (1982), declared that undocumented children cannot be barred from public education because of their immigration status. However, some Texas school districts continue improperly to demand proof of citizenship of enrolling students and many immigrants believe they must produce citizenship documents in order for their children to attend school. As a result of her inaccurate birth certificate, Adela was enrolled in the fifth grade at the time she dropped out.

2. Although in this article I use the term *culture* and quote others describing "culture," especially "Mexican culture," I want to note at the outset that Mexican culture is not an objective or rigid concept. "Culture" changes with geographic place, generation, and individual. In this article I do not attempt to define "Mexican culture" but merely discuss how "culture" was presented by others in the case of Adela Quintana.

Pedro Sotelo's use of the cultural defense in a statutory rape case is not unique. In another nationally publicized case from Lincoln, Nebraska, an Iraqi man was jailed on child abuse charges and held on $10,000 bail for forcing his thirteen- and fourteen-year-old daughters to marry adult men aged twenty-eight and thirty-four. The two grooms were also arrested and held on $50,000 bail each and charged with rape. "It is a clash between cultural mores and U.S. law," said Terry Cannon, a lawyer for the alleged husbands. An Iraqi university professor said the three men were following Islamic tradition and did not intend to violate state law. See "Iraqi Accused of Forcing Teen Daughters to Marry," *San Antonio Express-News* (11 November 1996), 5A.

3. "Charges Dismissed Against Dad of 14-Year-Old's Son," *Austin American-Statesman* (18 June 1996), B3.

4. Ibid.

5. Jennifer Liebrum and Jerry Urban, "'He Is bewildered'; Man Does Not Understand Illegality of Relationship with Girl," *Houston Chronicle* (27 January 1996), 30.

6. "Case of Culture Clash; Actions of Mexican Couple Under Fire in U.S.," *Austin American-Statesman* (19 February 1996), B2.

7. Liebrum and Urban, "'He Is Bewildered.'"

8. Telephone interview with Nancy Revelette, 26 September 1997.

9. "Texas Judge Drops Charges Against Mexican Migrant," *Reuters*, North American Wire (17 June 1996).

10. *Dateline* (NBC television broadcast, February 1996).

11. Sandra Sanchez, "In Texas, Worlds Collide: Expectant Couple Caught in Clash of Two Cultures," *USA Today* (29 January 1996), 1D.

12. "Sotelo, flanked by an interpreter, nervously tugged at his jail-issued pants and complained of a headache while State District Judge Jim Barr read him his rights Friday." Liebrum and Urban, "'He Is Bewildered.'" "Throughout the interview, he appears dazed and confused, uncertain of U.S. law and unaware of the way he's being reviled in many circles." Sanchez, "In Texas, Worlds Collide." *Dateline* NBC referred to Pedro as "naive."

13. "Case of Culture Clash."

14. Revelette interview (26 Sept. 1997).

15. Telephone interview with Nancy Revelette, 17 October 1997.

16. Tex. Family Code Ann. §2.001 (1998).

17. Tex. Family Code Ann. §2.401 (1998).

18. Tex. Family Code Ann. §1.91(a)(2) (1997). With respect to formal marriage, in order to obtain a marriage license, both bride and groom must be at least eighteen years old. Tex. Family Code Ann. §2.101 (1998). Persons under age eighteen may obtain a marriage license with parental consent or with a court order. Tex. Family Code Ann. §2.003 (1998).

19. In 1997 the Texas Legislature passed a new law providing that a person under age eighteen may not be party to an informal marriage. From 1970 to 1997 Texas law provided no minimum age for informal marriage. Prior to 1970 the Texas Family Code prohibited all marriage by persons under age fourteen. Vernon's Ann. Civ. St. Art. 4603. Two court decisions made under that old statute refused to recognize common-law marriage as a defense to a charge of statutory rape of a girl under fourteen. In *Carson* v. *State* 94 Cr.R. 159

(1923) the court held that no common-law marriage existed between the defendant and a thirteen-year-old girl who ran away with him because Texas law banned marriage by persons under fourteen. *Carson* cited an earlier decision in which the court refused to recognize a common-law marriage between the defendant and a ten-year-old girl. *Hardy* v. *State*, 38 S.W. 615 (1897).

20. If the lawsuit is filed by a parent or legal guardian, it must be filed within ninety days after the date of the marriage. Tex. Family Code Ann. §6.102(c) (1998).

21. After the criminal charges were dismissed, Pedro was immediately detained by the Immigration and Naturalization Service (INS) and transferred to the Corrections Corp. of America detention facility.

22. *May* v. *State*, 919 S.W.2d 422 (Cr.App. 1996). Because statutory rape in Texas is a strict liability crime, a defendant charged with this crime cannot use a defense that the child consented, that the defendant believed the child to be over the age of consent, or that the defendant was ignorant of the law. *Morman* v. *State*, 248 S.W.2d 932 (1952); *Hohn* v. *State*, 538 S.W.2d 619 (1976 Cr.App.). The statutory rape provisions apply equally to men and women. *Finley* v. *State*, 527 S.W.2d 553 (1975 Cr.App.).

23. Tex. Penal Code Ann. §22.011(c)(1) and (2) (1994 & Supp. 1999) (emphasis added). The Texas statutory rape law, codified in the Penal Code under Assaultive Offenses, provides that the unrestricted age of consent for sex is seventeen. Sex with a person under the age of seventeen is categorized as sexual assault. Tex. Penal Code Ann. §22.011 (1994 & Supp. 1999). It is a defense to prosecution under this provision of the statutory rape law that the actor was not more than three years older than the victim and the victim was over the age of fourteen. Tex. Penal Code Ann. §22.011(e) (1994 & Supp. 1999). Sex with a child under the age of fourteen is categorized as aggravated sexual assault. Tex. Penal Code Ann. §22.021 (1994 & Supp. 1999).

24. Acts 1975, 64th Leg. p. 620, ch. 254, §4, eff. Sept. 1, 1975.

25. Jennifer Liebrum, "Crime Story Winds Up as Matrimony; Judge Rules Girl, 13, Married to Man, 22," *Houston Chronicle* (17 June 1996), A1.

26. Ibid.

27. Revelette interview (17 Oct. 1997).

28. "Pregnant Runaway May Be 14 Rather Than 10; Girl Is in U.S. Illegally," *Memphis Commercial Appeal* (26 January 1996), 4A.

29. Sanchez, "In Texas, Worlds Collide."

30. Jennifer Liebrum and Jo Ann Zuniga, "Deportation Possible for Girl and Husband," *Houston Chronicle* (18 June 1996), A11.

31. Sanchez, "In Texas, Worlds Collide."

32. Matt Lait, "Teen-Adult Weddings Draw More Criticism," *Los Angeles Times*, Orange County Edition (11 September 1996), A1.

33. Matt Lait, "Agency Helps Some Girls Wed Men Who Impregnated Them," *Los Angeles Times*, Orange County Edition (1 September 1996), A1.

34. Ibid.

35. Ibid.

36. Ibid.

37. Lait, "Teen-Adult Weddings Draw More Criticism."

38. Patricia Donovan, "Can Statutory Rape Laws Be Effective in Preventing Adolescent Pregnancy?" *Family Planning Perspectives* 29, no. 1 (January/February 1997).

39. Brenda Rodriguez, "Bills Target Men, Girls Having Sex; Teen Pregnancies Alarm Lawmakers," *Dallas Morning News* (11 August 1996), 1J.

40. Donovan, "Can Statutory Rape Laws Be Effective?," 32.

41. Rodriguez, "Bills Target Men."

42. Ibid.

43. Because they were both undocumented immigrants, Adela and Pedro were subject to deportation. In March 1997, after a deportation hearing, an immigration judge ruled that Adela may remain in the country. Pedro, however, was not allowed to remain. Today, he is appealing this ruling while working and living with Adela and their baby. Telephone interview with Pablo Rodriguez, Houston attorney, 26 September 1997.

44. Leti Volpp, "(Mis)Identifying Culture: Asian Women and the 'Cultural Defense,'" *Harvard Women's Law Journal* 17 (1994): 57. Volpp argues against creation of a formalized cultural defense and suggests that "[c]ultural information should be allowed only as an informal factor to be considered in deliberations." She contends that appropriate use of cultural information must acknowledge the fluid nature of culture and that

users of cultural information must be aware of when cultural information is really necessary to show intent versus when the information merely promotes stereotype.

45. Revelette interview (26 Sept. 1997).

46. Liebrum and Urban, "'He Is Bewildered.'"

47. Revelette interview (26 Sept. 1997).

48. Sanchez, "In Texas, Worlds Collide."

49. Revelette interview (26 Sept. 1997).

50. Jennifer Liebrum and Jo Ann Zuniga, "Deportation Possible for Girl and Husband," *Houston Chronicle* (18 June 1996), A11.

51. Sanchez, "In Texas, Worlds Collide"; Rodriguez, "Bills Target Men."

52. Volpp, "(Mis)Identifying Culture."

53. Liebrum and Urban, "'He Is Bewildered.'" "CPS Spokeswoman Judy Hay said the agency would never have gotten involved had Quintana admitted up front she was 14." Liebrum and Zuniga, "Deportation Possible for Girl and Husband."

54. Leonard Pitts, "Plight of Teenage Girls Cries Out for New Lessons in Self-Worth," *Miami Herald* (27 July 1997).

Carol Sanger

Leaving Children for Work

I.

In the winter of 1746, Jean-Jacques Rousseau delivered the first of his five children to the Paris Foundling Hospital. The child's mother was Therese Levasseur, Rousseau's lifetime mistress. Rousseau described his behavior as follows: "From this liaison were born five children, who were all sent to the Foundling Hospital and with so little precaution for ever recognizing them afterwards, that I have not even kept the dates of their births."[1] Years later, when accused of heartlessness by a former patron, the now famous Rousseau responded: "You know my situation: I earn my living from one day to the next with some difficulty; so how could I feed a family as well? And if I were compelled to resort to the trade of a writer, how could I find the peace of mind necessary to do profitable work in an attic surrounded by domestic cares and the noise of children?[2]

Rousseau was right: Children complicate the progress of work. They make it necessary for parents to work in the first place: Feeding a family requires a steady income. Second, as Rousseau explained—and centuries before Tillie Olsen's *Silences*—it is difficult to accomplish much of anything with children around, let alone the sustained quiet that writing requires. Substitute caretakers were and still are often hard to find, so that working undisturbed by the noise of children becomes an impossibility. For any or all of these reasons, giving children away makes some sense.

And this is exactly what parents *have* done historically. Studies of Western parenting practices reveal that separations between parents and their children were common. From antiquity until the mid-nineteenth century, children were exposed in forests and market places, sold into slavery or servitude, given to monasteries, left with churches, deposited in foundling homes, sent to wet nurses, and placed out as apprentices.[3]

While the *forms* of these separations may seem drastic and unfamiliar, the *reasons* for separating from children are not. Children were commonly given away to relieve family poverty, as is often the case today when children are put into foster care. Children were given up to avoid the burdens and stigma of single motherhood, a factor still at play in adoption and in the regularly reported cases of newborns left for discovery in public places—no longer in ancient Rome but in public toilets and gas stations around the United States. In the eighteenth and nineteenth centuries, parents regularly sent children away to improve their future prospects by placing them out as apprentices, much as urban parents today send sons and daughters away to distant relatives or boarding schools to spare them the dangers of city life or to better prepare them for further study and adult life.[4] And some parents, like Rousseau, give children away for a combination of reasons: to protect their mother's honor (but *five times?*); as a kind of triage against impending poverty; *and* in order to take their own adult needs and preferences seriously.

In this essay I want to reconsider Rousseau's conclusions about work and children by applying them to the position of working mothers today. When does a mother's self-proclaimed situation permit her, like Rousseau, to leave her children in order to provide them a livelihood or in order to pursue and perhaps achieve some goal of her own? How are maternal decisions to separate from children on account of work regarded by mothers themselves, by their families and communities, and by the state?

The enterprise requires some adaptation: Background conditions regarding children's worth and mothers' authority have changed considerably since 1750. Children, both illegitimate and legitimate, are now regarded as intrinsically more valuable than in earlier times.[5] Mothers now have the authority, both legal and moral, to make custodial decisions regarding their children.[6] In addition, the forms of separation have changed. Unlike Rousseau, mothers today rarely give their children away *permanently* in order to work. They do, however, leave children on temporary bases all the time. They leave them at home with nannies or with latchkeys. They leave them in licensed child care centers and unlicensed family homes. They leave them with relatives they know well and with neighbors they don't. Almost all working mothers leave children for at least some part of a day, although separations are sometimes more sustained. Consider mothers who come to the United States as migrant workers or as nannies, leaving their own children behind in Mexico or the Caribbean for a season or even for a period of years. While there is no one script, it seems that working mothers separate from their children for whatever periods of time getting to, performing, or excelling at a job may require.

An early example of what we might now call an "employment-related separation" is found in the European practice of sending nursing infants to rural wet nurses.[7] Until the invention of pasteurization in the 1880s, most infants required breast milk in order to survive. This presented a predicament for the working-class mothers, married and single, of Europe's developing cities. A seamstress or domestic servant who chose to nurse her own child would lose her wages for nearly two years, the usual period required before weaning. Dispatching the baby to the countryside was therefore a matter of family economy: The costs of transportation and wet-nursing were less than the wages earned. By the mid-nineteenth century, nearly 20,000 infants were sent out each year to rural wet nurses from Paris alone. Wet-nursing had become a major industry, complete with commercial placement offices, transportation networks, and paid baby collectors.

Not surprisingly, the care that nurslings received was frequently indifferent and often fatal. Many newborns failed to survive the trip and others died while in the care of wet nurses who were often overburdened and sometimes inattentive, especially when awaiting payment from parents. In the eighteenth century only one in three babies sent out from Paris returned home. National regulatory reform in the 1870s—such as requiring wet nurses to have cradles and fire screens—improved conditions somewhat, but even so, a quarter of all nurslings died.[8] Nonetheless, until bottle feeding became safe at the end of the nineteenth century, urban working-class mothers had little choice but to send their babies away.[9] Their predicament was understood and little social or legal censure attached to the practice. The state intervened not to punish the mothers, but to improve the circumstances of the babies: stipends to the poorest mothers so they could nurse their own infants and regulatory efforts to monitor the wet-nursing industry itself.

To our modern sensibilities, the emotional and developmental consequences of such lengthy, risky, and deliberate separations between mother and infant might seem irreparable, a fruitful topic for years of subsequent therapy. But George Sussman usefully historicizes the matter:

> Our present-day psychological theories concerning the impact of maternal deprivation on infantile development may not be applicable to these circumstances, where wet-nursing was so normal a part of the life cycle that it required an independent mind, a strong will, and even courage on the part of a mother to keep her newborn baby and nurse it herself.[10]

That notion of maternal fortitude has since been thrown into reverse. Today it is a mother's decision to *leave* her children that requires an independent mind, strong will, and courage.

Indeed, something more than just the form and duration of mother–child separations has changed. There has also been a massive shift in attitude toward the very idea of separating from children on account of work, especially when *mothers*, as opposed to fathers, are the ones leaving. In his time, Rousseau was in good and substantial company; some 3,300 other children were sent by married and unmarried parents to the Foundling Hospital the same year as Rousseau sent his first child. But this more casual conception of parental obligation no longer holds, or at least it no longer holds for mothers. Separating from one's children—even in forms far more benign than dispatch into a foundling home or to a distant wet nurse—is now commonly regarded as a sign of maternal neglect, a selfish if not unnatural act. Linda Gordon makes the comparison with regard to earlier apprenticeships: "In the nineteenth century a mother's attempt to place out her children was often encouraged and even applauded as evidence of an appropriate and rational commitment to the child's good. By mid-twentieth century, a mother making such a request would almost certainly be viewed as unloving, unmotherly, forfeiting her future credibility as a mother."[11]

An influential mid-century source of this shift in attitude was the work of British psychiatrist John Bowlby. Drawing from his wartime studies of juvenile delinquents and institutionalized children, Bowlby explained that a mother's sustained absence is devastating to her young child's emotional development. Maternal deprivation, to use his term, "may have grave and far-reaching effects . . . on the whole future of [the child's] life."[12] As maternal deprivation theory took hold, separation itself rather than the circumstances surrounding or occasioning it was regarded as a sufficient cause of injury to children. Maternal absence of any kind or duration, including employment, substituted for the more sustained and traumatic absences on which the original research was based.[13] Thus Rousseau's explanation that his children were better off elsewhere carries little weight when applied to working mothers today. By modern definition, children cannot be better off if they are not with their mothers.

II.

How did this dramatic change in the meaning and practice of mother-hood—presence as the primary measure of good mothering—come about? Our present notions of maternal virtue derive from a nineteenth-century romantic-religious image of (at least) white motherhood as distinctively pure and from a twentieth-century Freudian culture that made the all-powerful mother determinative of her children's every attribute. I have provided a more detailed history of that transformation elsewhere.[14] For now, however, we can accept, if not as historians then perhaps as participant-observers, that mothers who choose to leave children for any but the most compelling reasons are understood to have elevated their own needs and desires above those of their children and that the children are understood to pay whatever price is due for such maternal self-interest.

At the same time, we also know that mothers today leave children for work *all the time* and they do so long before their children enter kindergar-ten, the once traditional moment for mothers to enter or reenter the labor market. Yet despite the *fact* of mothers working, the ideology that they *shouldn't* work—or at least that they remain responsible for the negative consequences to children of anything that can be attributed to their working if they do—persists with a surprising vengeance.

To demonstrate the power and pervasiveness of public sentiments on this matter, I invoke a cautionary tale from 1997. Readers may remember the sad and much publicized case of a ten-month-old Boston baby, Matthew Eappen, who died while under the care of a nineteen-year-old British au pair, Louise Woodward. Woodward was initially convicted of second-degree murder and much of the subsequent debate was legal in tone: Was murder or manslaughter the proper charge for a baby-sitter who may have been reck-less in handling the baby but for whom there was no evidence of an intention to kill?

Swirling alongside this debate was another, also focused on standards of culpability. The object of this second controversy, however, was not the nanny, but the mom. Wasn't she, Dr. Deborah Eappen, a practicing ophthal-mologist, *really* responsible for her baby's death? Hadn't she chosen to leave him at home to be cared for (ha!) by some inexperienced teenager? Wasn't the mother really the reckless one here? The ferocious buzz around the case revealed a barely forgiving tolerance for working mothers, especially mothers for whom work is not a matter of family survival. Discussions about the case in print, on the air, and in chatrooms made clear that a mother who leaves her child with someone else risks nothing less than the child's death.

Judgments about working mothers also arise in the context of custody cases. Mothers who put children in day care while they work may lose custody of them in a subsequent divorce, as maternal employment increasingly creeps into the calculation of trial courts. Consider the 1995 case of Jennifer Ireland, a full-time college student who lost custody of her three-year-old daughter after putting her in day care while the mother attended class, despite the fact the child had lived with the mother since birth in what the court acknowledged was "an established custodial environment."[15] In awarding the child to the father, the trial court noted that "there is no way that a single parent attending an academic program at an institution as prestigious as the University of Michigan can do justice to their studies and the raising of an infant child." I suspect that the decision, later reversed on appeal, had more to do with the judge's view that a mother should be doing justice to her child, not her studies. Both parents, after all, were full-time students; both had arranged for someone else to mind their daughter while they were at school. Nonetheless, the trial court's decision is not surprising; working is almost always held more stringently against mothers than against fathers, for whom there has been little expectation of a caretaking presence.

III.

Suppose one were to restructure the existing scheme of regulation in which maternal decisions to leave children are marked almost automatically as evidence of self-interest and as antithetical to the welfare of children. Where would one begin? I propose to start from a more neutral premise: one that assumes mothers are no more selfish or selfless than other adults and that regards leaving children for work as a reasonable maternal practice. The premise is not widely shared. Despite the fact that most mothers work, accusations accompanied by a strange sense of vindication quickly emerge when harm to a child can be linked to his mother working. Of course, only in the rarest cases does the harm take the form of death; more often the injury anticipated is emotional or behavioral, even though studies continue to show that the quality of substitute care, not child care per se, determines how well children do.[16]

And here the rules about work and mothers become curiouser and curiouser. The problem is not simply that the ideology of separation—mothers harm children if they leave them to work—has little to do with actual maternal practices or with what is now known about developmental outcomes for children in child care. It is also that this ideology is selectively applied. The view that mothers should stay home, take care of their own children, and never leave them with inexperienced caretakers has never applied to all mothers in the culture. Poor women have always worked—as servants, maids, laundresses, field hands, factory workers—with little concern from employers or anyone else about how or where their children fared. Even the much heralded Progressive Era mothers' pensions, aimed at enabling poor mothers to stay home, were largely symbolic: The actual stipends were too small to keep most mothers out of the labor force and they excluded women of color from the start.[17] This class-based conception of how much of their mothers poor children are entitled to has not changed much. There is a general consensus, as reflected in recent welfare legislation at state and federal levels, that poor mothers should—indeed must—leave their children to work and that the question of where or with whom these mothers leave their children is a matter for them to solve on their own. It simply matters less what becomes of poor children than that their mothers work.

This contradiction creates—or ought to create—a problem for those concerned with the welfare of children or with the integrity of law. For if we are serious about what we take to be the harmful effects of mother–child separations, then we must ask just as seriously why that concern is suspended for certain mothers and their children, as in recent workfare legislation. On the other hand, if it turns out that children are *not* automatically at risk just because their mothers work, then it may be time to abandon the scare tactics still used to influence, demoralize, and sometimes punish working mothers and instead direct public attention and resources to improving the conditions of substitute care.

What explains the current split screen where some mothers are vilified for leaving their children to work, and others are condemned if they do *not?* Why are some employment-related separations welcomed—even required—and others disparaged? And why are *all* working mothers, no matter what their actual preferences about working outside the home, held responsible for whatever befalls their children along the way? How are these contradictions sustained?

The answer for many is that there are no contradictions. That is because although there are in fact great disparities in attitudes toward working mothers, there is also a pretense that such disparities are principled, or at least sufficiently principled to justify differences in treatment among categories of mothers and their children. The pretense is sustained by a seemingly neutral question applied to all employment-related separations: What are the mother's motives for working?

The "right" answer to this question is not hard to work out. If a mother works because it is in her family's basic economic interest to do so, her departure is more acceptable. At least on this score, the poor working mother is less likely to have to defend herself against charges of negligent or bad mothering. If, on the other hand, a mother works for her own satisfaction, all bets are off. The selflessness equated with proper motherhood is then lost and whatever social sympathy or public support that existed is quickly withdrawn. Leaving one's child to pursue self-fulfillment doesn't look like much of a maternal sacrifice. Who does the mother think she is, Rousseau?

That question guides the remainder of this essay. I want to pursue the matter of why mothers work and ask how their answers stack up when compared to Rousseau's. My conclusion on this point is that with regard to their *motives* for chosen work, modern mothers are increasingly like Rousseau. This is a good thing. Women, like army recruits, also aspire to Be All That They Can Be. Leaving children, even temporarily, is often a crucial aspect of discovering for oneself the meaning of that popular slogan. The argument is not that working is a necessary condition for "finding oneself." As Patricia Hill Collins reminds us, any theorizing about mothers must recognize that not all mothers can afford "to see themselves primarily as individuals in search of personal autonomy."[18] Yet it is important to recognize that for women of all classes, work may be both chosen and rewarding.

But it is in this regard that the comparison between working mothers and Rousseau comes to a complete halt. Let us review Rousseau's repeated decisions to give up child after child, as summarized by his biographer: "The most plausible explanation . . . is that when he gave them up, he knew he could not both earn a decent living for a family as a music copyist and write the books he had to write, so rather than watch his children grow up hungry, he let them find better luck elsewhere."[19] No one disputed his decision and the Foundling Home took the children. Rousseau then wrote the books that stirred within him, and his children, in all likelihood, found rather bad luck and died.[20]

And are modern mothers able to work well by virtue of their children being out of sight? I suspect that until recently even the most talented mother would be unlikely to finish writing *Emile* under Rousseau's arrangement. In the first instance, she is less likely to have been able to leave her young children or to send them away. Tillie Olsen first published at age fifty not because she had nothing to say before then, but because, as she explains in *Silences*, writing does not come easily to those "consumed in the hard, everyday essential work of maintaining human life."[21] But even when mothers are able to break away, they need something more than physical distance from their children in order to work well. They need to know (and not to pretend, as Rousseau seems to have done) that their children are properly cared for. Elizabeth Badintur has recognized the irony. She attributes to none other than Rousseau the inculcation of total devotion to children in French mothers of the later eighteenth century; "Every woman who wanted to appear 'enlightened' wanted to be Rousseau's dream mother."[22] Inattention to children and their needs was inexcusable and maternal presence quite central to the dream.

That view of maternal obligation has persisted with amazing vitality into the present. As Susan Chira notes in her study of working mothers in the late twentieth century, there is still a steady drumbeat directing mothers back into the home or at least pounding out the message that their absence can only result in damaged children.[23] But mothers—all kinds of mothers—now work. I therefore want to turn our attention to what we know about why they do, and what it might take to remove the anxiety that presently accompanies so many mothers to their jobs each day. What would provide working mothers today with the peace of mind Rousseau was able to secure simply by sending his children away?

IV.

Recall that Rousseau scattered his children for two reasons: They were expensive, and they were distracting. He saw them as little walking opportunity costs, preventing him from the "profitable work" he wanted to do. Until recently, mothers were thought neither to desire nor to be capable of profitable work outside of motherhood. It was accepted as a tenet of middle-class life that when a woman married—or certainly no later than her first pregnancy—she would quit her job.[24] For mothers who slipped past the social prohibitions against working, a firmer hand was in place: Restrictions against mothers working were legal until well into the twentieth century. Exclusionary policies and practices were justified by a variety of concerns: support for the family wage, the protection of maternal reproductive health, and solicitude for feminine sensibilities and vulnerabilities (no bartending, no mail delivery).

Happily, it is now recognized that neither maternal physiology nor lack of interest satisfactorily explains why for most of this century at least middle-class mothers did not work, or, to use Tillie Olsen's striking example, why only one writer in twelve was a woman with children.[25] But although most legal restrictions against mothers working have now been removed, as a *cultural* matter working mothers are still regarded differently than are working fathers. We have not quite shaken off the idea, or the preference, that at least some children are better off when their mothers are home. As I suggested earlier, the acceptability of mothers leaving children for work is often linked to determinations about why they are leaving: Is the mother's decision in some sense necessary and therefore *in*voluntary, or has she chosen to leave when she could have stayed home? The characterization of some work as voluntary has regulatory as well as rhetorical and social significance. If leaving children is understood—however mistakenly—from a developmental perspective to put them at risk, then separating from them unnecessarily must be worse. Policies that discourage *that* behavior—skimpy and unpaid maternity leaves, no public support for child care, penalizing mothers in custody disputes—then make sense.

Working mothers are not unaware of the distinction between voluntary and involuntary separations and at times try to fit themselves into the more advantageous category of compulsion. For example, during the 1990 Persian Gulf War, some mother-reservists in the National Guard who volunteered for service softened the blow at home by telling their husbands they had been called up involuntarily. One such husband explained how he had to "wrestl[e] with feelings of 'How could you do this to me?' once he realized that his wife had volunteered. 'It's my selfish heart, but inside it hurts to know she had a choice.' "[26] By removing their decisions to leave from the category of voluntariness, these military mothers suppressed overt self-interest—an odd characterization for professional contribution in times of war—to make their departures more acceptable to those left behind with the kids.

Conscription is not, however, available as a cover for most mothers who like their work. Of course, whether a mother "has" to work is rarely clear-cut. In most cases I suspect that the decision is less a clear-cut matter of compulsion versus free choice than a mix of competing motives. At present, the acceptability of maternal employment is often sorted out by family income; the meaning of compulsion tied to low income. Certainly many mothers *must* work to satisfy the immediate needs—income, health care coverage—

of themselves and their children. In 1991, 22 percent of American children lived in families headed by single mothers.[27] Many of these head-of-household mothers are already in the workforce, and durational limits on public assistance means that *all* poor mothers will eventually be at work whether they would rather be caring for their children at home or not.

But many middle-class mothers, even those in two-parent families, also work to provide or to supplement family income. At times, the mother's income makes the difference between receiving public assistance or not. At other times, the difference is of a different qualitative order: between a vacation or no vacation, private school or public school, a fancy computer or an old Mac. In these latter cases, mothers' salaries are less a matter of economic necessity than what demographers call a "standard of living preference."[28] Even here, however, categorizing maternal work motives gets complicated, as research (and common sense) show that mothers often choose to work when it is *not* absolutely necessary as a hedge against the possibility of a subsequent divorce.

Mothers with professional careers, especially those also married to professionals, are most often seen as working unnecessarily and therefore as the most selfishly motivated. Kathleen Jamieson notes that "high salaried women in positions of power are presumed to be working for self-satisfaction or luxuries, not to meet basic family needs. . . . [W]hen they purchase child care, they are, as a result regarded as negligent mothers. [In contrast] the low wage mother . . . is assumed to be working for her children."[29] Of course, if professional mothers are subject to greater social disapproval, they are also more able to afford good substitute care and even to leave work altogether, if they choose.

In addition to providing for their families financially, mothers in all ranks of the labor force also work to satisfy themselves, however mixed with (or camouflaged under) more altruistic, child-directed motives that motive may be. Consider the former First Mother, Virginia Clinton Kelly, who as a young widow, "took control of her life in a manner that was unusual for women of her time, leaving 2-year-old Bill with his grandparents [in Arkansas] until she had completed her education [in New Orleans]."[30] Kelly's description of the decision reveals a jumbled (and wonderfully candid) mix of motives: "I had abandoned my old goal of becoming a nurse anesthetist because I knew I couldn't take my baby with me. . . . But I decided it was in his best interests that I go. . . . It almost killed me to be away from Bill, and yet I'm convinced that my second stint in New Orleans ultimately saved my life. . . . [I]n a year we would all be out in the real world in business for ourselves. This appealed to my independent spirit."[31] President Clinton's mother acted on the principle that his and her best interests did not automatically conflict, and on conventional measures of professional accomplishment, her son has done all right. (I have little doubt, however, that explanations for President Clinton's moral failings will eventually lead to Mrs. Kelly's doorstep.)

What *is* the relationship between maternal employment and children's well-being? Research has identified three factors that mediate between work-related separations and developmental outcomes for children: the quality of substitute care, the quality of the child's home life, and the mother's attitude toward work. Each makes sense. With regard to child care, small groups, fewer children per adult, and low turnover in staff not surprisingly correlate with positive outcomes for children.[32] With regard to the second factor, home life, it is also no surprise to learn that children from poorer homes are, in the absence of governmental subsidies, more often in lower quality child care. In addition, a mother who works long hours, with long travel times to work, and at lower pay, may well be more tired and less patient at the end of her work day.

I want to focus, however, on the third factor, the mother's attitude toward her work. Studies show that whether mothers work or stay home, children are developmentally better off when the mother's preferred status matches what she is actually doing. That is, when mothers want to work, that preference positively affects their attitudes toward leaving their children which in turn positively affects developmental outcomes for children.[33] These findings demonstrate yet again that maternal behavior that might be characterized as self-interested (mother wants to work) is not at odds with the interests of her children.

And why do some mothers want to work? The independence of spirit that sparked Virginia Clinton Kelly is often linked to the satisfactions of economic independence. A recent study of working Chicano mothers found that the mothers enjoy having their "own" money, even if most of it goes for family expenditures.[34] Again, the mothers justified money spent on themselves ("make-up and going out with the girls") in terms of family welfare: Such purchases improve their emotional well-being, which in turn helps them to be better wives and mothers.[35] In addition to financial benefits, work offers other meaningful satisfactions: those of adult company, intellectual stimulation, and nondomestic accomplishment. As Sara Ruddick and Pamela Daniels explain in discussing the place of "chosen work" in the lives of women writers and scientists, there is a human need—at long last extended to women—"to make a difference, to make one's mark in the world by pro-ducing something with dignity."[36] Not only artists and scholars find personal satisfaction in work. Surveys of working-class mothers—waitresses, factory workers, and domestics—report that they too are committed to their jobs and work not for income alone.[37]

It seems then that mothers leave children for work both as an aspect of good mothering—to benefit their children, whether financially or by virtue of the mother's increased emotional well-being—*and* to satisfy preferences unconnected to parenting. This second category includes the kind of self-affirming reasons that are no big deal, respected, and encouraged when made by fathers—such desires as achieving a sense of self-worth or financial independence, accomplishing a goal in a chosen area of work, and experi-encing the pleasures of power, creativity, and contact. Mothers, too, like Rousseau and other dads, want to engage in what Rousseau identified as "profitable work."

Yet a crucial difference in the circumstances between fathers and moth-ers remains as they decide whether, for whom, how long, and how hard they will work. Mothers are still assigned and still accept the primary obligation for raising the children. When mothers work, even in two-parent homes, they remain responsible for arranging and supervising, paying and answer-ing for whatever substitute care they put into place. And it is here that Rous-seau and modern mothers again part company.

V.

Rousseau explained that getting rid of his children ("brats") was necessary to provide "the necessary peace of mind." Once they were gone, he could concentrate. He did not dwell further on the children's fate—"I made up my mind cheerfully [to send the child to the Foundling Hospital] and without the least scruple"—and was able to ignore, repress, or accept the whopping mortality rate of the babies so consigned.[38] This is not proof that fathers, then or now, are heartless. Rather, they are simply not in the habit of think-ing about the well-being of their children as a day-to-day, hour-to-hour con-cern; that duty lies elsewhere.

Mothers, in contrast, are always on duty and rarely lose the habit of con-cerned responsibility. As a result, separation from "the noise" does not by itself provide the tranquility required for productive work. Leaving children does not sufficiently assure a mother's peace of mind. As one working mother put it, "Always worrying about a sick child. . . . Managers tell you to leave personal problems at home, but you can never separate child from mind."[39]

There are at least two reasons why mothers have trouble separating "child from mind": guilt and concern. Guilt first. As I have described more fully elsewhere, we live in a culture that has conflated the notion of separating from a child and abandoning it.[40] The logic is easy. If abandonment (leaving a child who needs it without substitute care) is bad, and leaving a child (even with proper care) is merged with abandonment, then mothers who leave children have a lot to answer for. Many mothers have internalized this view. For them, guilt sits as an overlay on the daily experience of work, expressing itself in a variety of ways.[41] Mothers who can afford to sometimes stop working. Others avoid the problem by engaging in "homework"—phone calling, baby-sitting, and garment assembly, for example—labor done (or attempted) in one's home. Still others, like professors and house cleaners, choose their work in part to have control over their schedules and be home when their children finish school for the day or for the summer.[42] Another working-mother strategy for dealing with guilt is to spend no time away from the children when the mother is not at work. A study of elementary school teachers revealed that despite the intense desire for adult conversation after a day at school, teacher-mothers "rarely spend any of their time at home away from their families because they feel guilty about leaving their children with baby-sitters."[43] Readers will likely supply additional examples of guilt accommodation.

Of course, not all working mothers feel guilty about leaving their children. Some mothers work precisely to escape or curtail the experience of full-time motherhood. Others have the good fortune to know that their children are well cared for in their absence. But variations in guilt levels are not wholly a matter of luck or personality. Class makes a tremendous difference in how women view and are able to view their maternal obligations. Poor mothers, for whom work has never been optional, have always had to leave their children, often to take care of other children in wealthier, often whiter homes. Thus in some communities leaving children for work is an accepted part of what good mothers do. Mexicanas, for example, "raised in a world where economic and household work often merged, . . . appear to view employment as one workable domain of motherhood."[44] Linda Gordon offers the historical example of Black clubwomen in the 1920s. Because most Blacks worked for wages regardless of class, staying home with children was for them much less a part of personal or community expectations than it was for white mothers.[45] Black women reformers therefore directed their political efforts at urging state assistance for child care, and at organizing their own when no such help was forthcoming.

The distractions for mothers with few resources and little job flexibility are simply of a different order than for mothers whose options include the comfortable unemployment afforded by a well-paid spouse as well as a range of satisfactory choices about where to place the kids if work appeals. In contrast, genuine *worry* rather than guilt may blanket the concerns of poorer mothers. There is the initial problem of finding child care in the first place. Consider the following description:

> I'd waitress in the restaurant and then go to work in the bar until two in the morning. So I would need somebody from four thirty in the afternoon till two in the morning and you just can't get sitters for those hours, there's no way. . . . You try to prearrange it y'know as early as you can in the week to get a sitter. . . . But the majority of people I knew worked days, so they didn't want to be tied down to my kid in the evenings. . . . [My employer] offered me suggestions like—well, maybe you can have so and so watch your kid on her off days—well, I don't know so and so, and . . . I didn't want to leave my kid with anybody I didn't know.[46]

The lack of decent care can itself result in more drastic forms of separation. As one working-class mother in New York explained, "I sent my children back to Jamaica and many mothers here still do. With family back home, there can be structure and safety. I always missed my children, but I always said goodbye gladly."[47]

Mothers with no family back home and none nearby take what child care they can find. There is not enough subsidized licensed care for the children of mothers receiving welfare, and there is even less for the children of the working poor. The result is that mothers who well know what their children need in terms of nightly sleep and daily stimulation cannot provide it to them. Take just the case of Yvonne Garret, a young married Florida mother who withdrew her children from church-sponsored day care because she could not manage the $180 a week for three children charged by the Holy Temple Christian Academy. "My children are bright," she explained, dropping them off before dawn at a clean but stark family day care where for $50 a week they will watch television for ten hours a day. "[At the church] they teach them, they train them. You would be amazed at what they would acquire in a year. . . . [This] is temporary. I am doing what I have to do."[48]

Yvonne Garret's predicament, her distraction and her fortitude, should take center stage as governments and private companies propose policies for working mothers and their children. This is not to deny certain commonalities among all mothers as they negotiate the dilemmas of children and work. But it is one thing to dwell on whether one's nanny is really good enough (and quit work if the guilt pangs become unmanageable) and quite another to lock a nine-year-old boy in a hot New York City apartment because there are no affordable activities for him to attend while his mother has to work.[49] It is one thing to ponder whether one's baby is becoming too attached to the sitter and another to observe children "congregating by the thousands after school in the lobbies and on the lawn of numerous factories while their parents, usually their mothers, are working the day shift."[50] It is wonderful for a mother to observe her child at play in his day care center via video camera from her computer hook-up but something quite different to have no access to a phone during one's shift so that the mother cannot call home to see if the children have arrived safely after school.[51]

If we continue to tolerate such massive differences in the care that children receive, we will have returned (perhaps) unwittingly to the days of Rousseau, who believed that deliberate custodial negligence benefited certain kinds of children, including his own: "I know that these children are not delicately reared, and so much the better for them that they are not; they become more robust, they receive what is necessary and nothing superfluous; they are brought up to be not gentlemen, but workers and peasants— I see nothing in such an education I would not choose for [them] even if I were master of the situation."[52]

Rousseau had definite notions about how children should be raised. We, however, do not believe that children thrive if their care is limited to the basics; we do not think that deprivation of the commodities of civilized life is an advantage. We certainly do not believe that for our own children, whatever we may think about the children of the poor. Instead, guided by common sense, affection, and early childhood specialists, we establish standards for the care of our children: low adult-child ratios (sometimes a nanny per child), proper equipment and sufficient space, and caretakers paid well enough to prevent the constant turnover that creates instability in young children's lives. By tolerating a different, lower set of standards for the children of the poor, we subscribe *sub silentio* to eighteenth-century ideas that children have predetermined destinies based on their parents' class and that the working classes should be cared for accordingly. We subscribe in effect to a model we profess to have abandoned.

At some level, we know that all mothers—upper, middle, and lower class—need assistance in raising children. We simply dress up the labels that attach to the forms of help that enable wealthier mothers to leave their children: preschool, not subsidized child care centers; nannies, not a patched-together network of friends and relatives; enrichment activities, not latch-keys. The terms mask the conundrum: Poor mothers whose children are at greatest risk in inferior care must leave them and mothers whose children are well cared for (the occasional rogue nanny aside) are subject to social disapproval for taking off. There is but one commonality: an active indifference to the quality of all women's lives as they manage the often incompatible demands of raising children, earning income, and seeking the personal satisfactions of various kinds at work.

It is now time to facilitate rather than presuppose the work that mothers do as mothers and as working mothers. In this regard the United States straggles far behind Canada and most of Western Europe, where maternal stipends to enable new mothers to care for their babies themselves are an ordinary component of social legislation and where mothers do not work in order to obtain such crucial services for their children as medical coverage.[53] With regard to working mothers, the United States has begun to gesture at governmental solutions. The president's 1998 State of the Union Address included proposals for increased funding for subsidized care, tax credits to businesses that provide child care, and larger tax deductions for parents for child care expenses.[54] This is a positive move, even if slanted toward the middle class and even if motivated by election considerations rather than a principled commitment to improve the lives of working mothers and their children.

The project of reform would advance significantly, however, if we could put into place a social consensus that recognizes separating from children as a respectable, responsible choice for mothers to make. My argument is not that all mothers *must* work. I suspect that even under a regime where mothers could leave children for work as freely and with the same kinds of encouragement as fathers, many women would choose to mother away with the same intensity and devotion as they do today. Having, caring for, and loving children is for many an incomparable source of satisfaction. Yet other mothers—mothers who also love their children—may find a regime in which work is regarded as an acceptable activity for mothers liberating. They may choose to work *and* to mother. What matters under the revised scheme is less which way women decide than the relocation of motherhood and the practice of its practices from the fixed category of imposition to something closer to choice. (I therefore appreciate but reject Simone de Beauvoir's position that women should *not* be given the choice to stay home and raise children "precisely because if there is such a choice, too many women will make that one.")[55]

To assist working mothers and their children under this new regime, we might well invoke twentieth-century versions of at least certain Enlightenment theories. I have in mind the notion of governmental responsibility, relied upon by the French and Russian governments in conceiving a heightened duty to their most vulnerable citizens, nursing infants and foundlings, as they built and staffed foundling homes to care for children and experimented with payments to mothers so they could care for the children themselves. Of course, a few changes are in order. We no longer subscribe to the exact methods of caring for children used 200 years ago. We must substitute pre-school children for nurslings and well-run child care centers for massive foundling homes, and of course, fathers too must enter the ranks of those who physically care for children. The goal of such policies is to update Rousseau's sentiments—not about the selfless duties of mothers extolled in *Emile* but about securing *for mothers* the harmony between profitable work and peace of mind that Rousseau enjoyed. This requires nothing more than expanding responsibility for the care of children so that their well-being is no longer an exclusively maternal assignment. Mothers too may then achieve the complex satisfactions of children and of work.

1. Maurice Cranston, *Jean-Jacques: The Early Life and Work of Jean-Jacques Rousseau, 1712–1754* (Chicago: University of Chicago Press, 1982), 246.

2. Ibid., 244.

3. The most comprehensive work is John Boswell, *The Kindness of Strangers: The Abandonment of Children in Western Europe from Late Antiquity to the Renaissance* (New York: Pantheon Books, 1988). Other careful discussions include Rachel G. Fuchs, *Abandoned Children: Foundlings and Child Welfare in Nineteenth-Century France* (Albany: State University of New York Press, 1984); David I. Kertzer, *Sacrificed for Honor: Italian Infant Abandonment and the Politics of Reproductive Control* (Boston: Beacon Press, 1993); David L. Ransel, *Mothers of Misery: Child Abandonment in Russia* (Princeton, N.J.: Princeton University Press, 1988); Joan Sherwood, *Poverty in Eighteenth-Century Spain: The Women and Children of the Inclusa* (Toronto: University of Toronto Press, 1988).

4. Marita Golden, "Why I Sent Him Away," *Washingtonian* (December 1993): 31, 33.

5. Viviana Zelizer, *Pricing the Priceless Child: The Changing Social Value of Children* (New York: Basic Books, 1985).

6. Mary Anne Mason, *From Father's Property to Children's Rights* (New York: Columbia University Press, 1994).

7. See generally George D. Sussman, *Selling Mothers' Milk: The Wetnursing Business in France, 1715–1914* (Urbana: University of Illinois Press, 1982); Rachel G. Fuchs, *Poor and Pregnant in Paris: Strategies for Survival in the Nineteenth Century* (New Brunswick, N.J.: Rutgers University Press, 1992).

8. Sussman, *Selling Mother's Milk*, 143.

9. Elisabeth Badinter has pointed out that upper-class mothers quite free from financial pressure also sent their babies to wet nurses. She used this pattern of behavior to suggest that children in the late eighteenth century had not yet become devotional objects entitled to their mothers' constant attentions. Indeed, Badintur argues that mothers were permitted to be (and perhaps were in fact) indifferent to their children, much as Rousseau appears to have been. Elisabeth Badinter, *Mother-Love Myth and Reality: Motherhood in Modern History* (New York: Macmillan, 1981).

10. Sussman, *Selling Mothers' Milk*, 67.

11. Linda Gordon, *Heroes of Their Own Lives: The Politics and History of Family Violence, Boston 1880–1960* (New York: Viking, 1988), 162.

12. John Bowlby, *Maternal Care and Mental Health* (New York: Schocken Books, 1966), 46.

13. Diane E. Eyer, *Mother–Infant Bonding: A Scientific Fiction* (New Haven, Conn.: Yale University Press, 1992).

14. See Carol Sanger, "Separating from Children," *Columbia Law Review* (1996): 375, 399–409; see also Peggy Cooper Davis, this volume.

15. *Ireland* v. *Smith*, 1995 WL 662889 (Mich.Ct.App. Nov. 7, 1995).

16. See the National Institute of Child Health and Human Development (NICHD) Study of Early Child Care. The study is available at *http://nih.gov./nichd/html/news/early-child/Early Child Care.htm*; for a summary, see Barbara Vobejda, "Better Behavior in Day Care; Federal Study Finds Groups Beneficial," *Washington Post* (3 April 1998), A1.

17. Joanne L. Goodwin, *Gender and the Politics of Welfare Reform: Mothers' Pensions in Chicago, 1911–1929* (Chicago and London: University of Chicago Press, 1997), 129, 162–164.

18. Patricia Hill Collins, "Shifting the Center: Race, Class, and Feminist Theorizing About Motherhood," in *Mothering: Ideology, Experience, and Agency* (New York: Routledge, 1994), 45, 48.

19. Maurice Cranston, *The Solitary Self: Jean-Jacques Rousseau in Exile and Adversity, 1763–1778* (Chicago: University of Chicago Press, 1997), 183.

20. Cranston, *The Early Life*, 245. "An enormous proportion" of children taken to the Paris orphanages died; in 1741, the year Rousseau brought his first-born child, 68 percent of the foundlings died in infancy.

21. Tillie Olsen, *Silences* (New York: Seymour Lawrence/Delacorte Press, 1978), xx.

22. Badintur, *Mother-Love*, 181.

23. Susan Chira, *A Mother's Place: Taking the Debate About Working Mothers Beyond Guilt and Blame* (New York: HarperCollins, 1998).

24. Lynn Y. Weiner, *From Working Girl to Working Mother: The Female Labor Force in the United States, 1820–1980* (Chapel Hill: University of North Carolina Press, 1985), 98–99.

25. Tillie Olsen, "One Writer in Twelve: Women Who Are Writers in Our Century," in *Working It Out: 23 Women Writers, Artists, Scientists, and Scholars Talk About Their Lives and Work*, ed. Sara Ruddick and Pamela Daniels (New York: Pantheon Books, 1977), 323.

26. Jane Gross, "Confrontation in the Gulf: New Home Front Developing as Women Hear Call to Arms," *New York Times* (18 September 1990), A1.

27. Marital Status and Living Arrangements: U.S. Dept. of Commerce, Series P-20, no. 461 (March 1991).

28. See David Eggebeen and Alan J. Hawkins, "Economic Need and Wives' Employment," *Journal of Family Issues* 11 (1990): 48–49.

29. Kathleen H. Jamieson, *Beyond the Double Bind: Women and Leadership* (New York: Oxford University Press, 1995), 63.

30. Gwen Ifill, "Tenacity and Change in a Son of the South: William Jefferson Clinton," *New York Times* (16 July 1992), A1, A14.

31. Virginia Kelly, *Leading with My Heart* (New York: Simon and Schuster, 1994), 70, 78.

32. National Research Council, *Who Cares for America's Children: Child Care Policy for the 1990s*, ed. Cheryl D. Nayes et al. (1990), 92–97.

33. See National Research Council, 76.

34. See Denise A. Segura, "Working at Motherhood: Chicana and Mexican Immigrant Mothers and Employment," in *Mothering: Ideology, Experience, and Agency*, ed. Evelyn Nakano Glenn et al. (New York and London: Routledge, 1994), 211, 221.

35. Ibid.

36. Sara Ruddick and Pamela Daniels, eds., *Working It Out: 23 Women Writers, Artists, Scientists, and Scholars Talk About Their Lives and Work* (1977), xxvi.

37. Rena L. Repetti et al., "Employment and Women's Health: Effects of Paid Employment on Women's Mental and Physical Health," *American Psychology* 44 (1989): 1394; Eggebeen and Hawkins, "Economic Need and Wives' Employment," 58, citing 1984 study showing many wives say they would keep working even if their husbands' incomes increased.

38. Cranston, *Jean-Jacques*, 208. The only stumbling block for Rousseau was the children's mother: "The only scruples I had to overcome were those of Therese; I had all the difficulty in the world in making her adopt this one means of saving her honour. Her mother, who has a different fear—that of another brat to feed—came to my aid and finally Therese gave in." Only in his later years did Rousseau indicate any remorse for his decisions, and then in deference to the feelings of Therese and out of concern for his then increased reputation.

39. John P. Fernandez, *Child Care and Corporate Productivity: Resolving Family / Work Conflicts* (Lexington, Mass.: Lexington Books, 1986), 57.

40. Carol Sanger, "Separation and Abandonment," in *Mothers in Law: Feminist Theory and the Legal Regulation of Motherhood*, ed. Martha Fineman and Isabel Karkin (New York: Columbia University Press, 1995).

41. Diane E. Eyer, *Motherguilt: How Our Culture Blames Mothers for What's Wrong in Society* (New York: Times Books/Random House, 1996); see also Elsa Walsh, *Divided Lives: The Public and Private Struggles of Three Accomplished Women* (New York: Simon and Schuster, 1995), especially "Meredith's Story," 29–121, recounting baby/job trials of former CBS *60 Minutes* reporter Meredith Vieira; Constance Belfiore, "The Case for Becoming a Full-time Parent," *Washington Lawyer* (May/June 1988): 46; Ronnie Caplane, "Choosing Domesticity over Depositions," *Legal Times* (3 April 1995): 54; Patricia A. Mairs, "Bringing Up Baby: Attorney / Mothers Are Increasingly Leaving Their Jobs, Saying Motherhood and Law Don't Mix," *National Law Journal* (March 1988): 1.

42. See Mary Romero, "Day Work in the Suburbs: The Work Experience of Chicana Private House Keepers," in *The Worth of Women's Work*, ed. Anne Statham et al. (Albany: State University of New York Press, 1988), 77, 83–84. A few businesses now pitch employee recruitment campaigns around this kind of flexibility.

43. Dee Spencer, "Public Schoolteaching: A Suitable Job for Women?" in *The Worth of Women's Work* [1880], ed. Anne Statham et al. (1988), 167.

44. Segura, "Working at Motherhood," 211, 212.

45. Linda Gordon, *Pitied But Not Entitled* (New York: Free Press, 1994), 135–140.

46. Valerie Polakow, *Lives on the Edge: Single Mothers and Their Children in the Other America* (Chicago and London: University of Chicago Press, 1993), 85.

47. Joe Sexton, "Poor Parents' Summertime Blues; Choices for Children: Enforced Boredom or Street Roulette," *New York Times* (25 June 1995).

48. Sara Rimer, "Children of Working Poor Are Day Care's Forgotten," *New York Times* (25 November 1997), A1.

49. Sexton, "Poor Parents' Summertime Blues," 27, 30.

50. Louis Uchitelle, "Lacking Child Care, Parents Take Their Children to Work," *New York Times* (23 December 1994), A1, reporting that most parents bring children to work not because they cannot bear to separate from them but because they have no other safe place to leave them.

51. Kathryn Edin and Laura Lein, "Work, Welfare and Single Mothers' Economic Strategies," *American Sociological Review* 62 (1997): 253–263.

52. Cranston, *Jean-Jacques*, 245.

53. See Sheila Kamerman and Alfred J. Kahn, *Starting Right: How America Neglects Its Youngest Children and What We Can Do About It* (New York: Oxford University Press, 1995).

54. Robert Pear, "Clinton to Offer a Child Care Plan, White House Says," *New York Times* (14 December 1997), A1.

55. Simone de Beauvoir, "Sex, Society, and the Female Dilemma," *Saturday Review* (14 June 1975), 18.

Hilde Lindemann Nelson

Always Connect:
Toward a Parental Ethics of Divorce

The U.S. divorce rate, which had been rising at a rate of 3 percent per decade since the time of the Civil War, hit a high of 5.3 per thousand per year in 1981, producing projections that 50 percent of recent marriages would end in divorce. After fluctuating a little in the 1980s, the number of divorces settled down to a steady 4.6 per thousand per year, which works out to a 48 percent chance that a given marriage will not last.[1] The debate over what these statistics mean and what should be done about them has recently taken a new turn. Voices on the Left have joined the chorus on the Right in calling for greater restrictions on divorce in families where there are young children.[2] The liberal argument for why parents of dependent children should stay married has largely been an economic one. In *Liberal Purposes*, for example, William A. Galston cites David Ellwood's report that only 2 percent of children in two-parent families in 1988 experienced poverty of seven years' duration or longer, as compared to the 22 percent of children in single-parent households who "literally grow up poor."[3]

The threat to children's economic well-being is thus posed as a threat to "the family as we know it." But there is a difficulty here. The family as we know it, while it has many features to recommend it, is not without serious moral flaws of its own. A picture holds us captive: We cleave to a patriarchal, middle-class ideal of the family which came into fashion in the United States in the 1830s, and which consists of a committed father who works outside the household but is its head, a loving mother who runs the household and nurtures her children, and the young children themselves, who are incompetent and around whom the household revolves. The household is private, sharply marked off from the public sphere.[4] This family structure, sometimes called the sentimental family, is supposed to meet its members' emotional, physical, and social needs. Divorce "breaks" or "ruptures" it.

To be sure, we may distinguish between the ideal and the real. An actual family, even if it consists of father, mother, and dependent children all under one roof, is unlikely to resemble the sentimental model in every respect. For one thing, over 50 percent of married women now work for pay outside the home.[5] In fact, those on both the Right and the Left who call for restrictions on divorce as a means to keep children out of poverty are counting on mothers' working for pay: Their point is precisely that two wage earners are better than one. I have no quarrel with this point, but it does not follow that stricter divorce laws are the best or only way to secure children's economic wellbeing. I think that the two-wage-earner family is often the contemporary variation on the sentimental theme, leaving all the characteristic features of that model save the financial division of labor essentially unchanged. And there is reason to think that sentimental families, whether of the mother-at-home or mother-in-the-workforce variety, are good for neither the women nor the children who live in them.

Women in sentimental families are expected to defer to the interests and desires of their husbands, which means they must perform the brunt of the domestic labor, including taking responsibility for child care and the care of the elderly, despite the measure of independence they may have achieved by working for pay outside the home.[6] Sometimes this deference is purely logistical, required by a corporate climate that demands too much of the father to permit his sharing equally in the life of the household. Often, however, one or both spouses have internalized the norms of deference to the male head of the household which they learned from their own parents and culture. In this case, even when the woman earns as much as her husband, her economic viability does not meliorate her deference to her spouse.

Children in sentimental families are unlikely to learn gender justice from their parents' example, nor will they find it easy later to refrain from dividing labor along gender lines as they form new families of their own. And because the sentimental family is child centered, its children are not expected to exercise much self-reliance. While they are encouraged to think of themselves as consumers, they are neither asked nor encouraged to fulfill any other socially useful roles.

These points regarding children, divorce, and the sentimental family have been developed elsewhere,[7] and I shall not pursue them further here. Instead, I shall argue that what children require of their parents is not that a particular familial *structure* be maintained, but that children's intimate *relationships* be safeguarded, as it is within these relationships that the familial functions of protection, nurture, and identity formation are carried on.[8]

I begin by providing an account of parental obligations as arising from relationships that include but also extend beyond the parent-child relationship, showing that many of these are crucial to the child's well-being. I then explain why the cluster of relationships surrounding parent and child can sometimes generate conflicting duties that result in the parents' doing wrong no matter what they do, and that their feelings of inescapable moral wrongdoing should be taken seriously. I consider several cases of what I take to be genuine moral dilemmas of this sort, arguing that parents have a responsibility to try to mend relationships they should have protected, but could not. Next I show how parents' participation in the formation of their children's moral agency can be made to play a central role in fostering the ties that are necessary to children when their families are reconfigured. Finally, I take up the problem of serial domestic partnerships, examining whether the duty to safeguard children's existing relationships precludes involving them in new ones.

Parental Obligations

Many obligations arise because persons voluntarily undertake them: If I promise to do something that is morally permissible, then I ought to do it. What installs the obligation is my free consent; if the promise was extracted by force or fraud, I am not morally required to keep it.[9] Some parental obligations seem to arise in this way, as for example when a woman seeks to adopt a child or purposefully becomes pregnant; in initiating a relationship with a vulnerable child, a parent implicitly promises to take on special duties to meet the child's needs.

It is not clear to me, however, that parental obligations are grounded *solely* in the parent's consent. It is tempting to think that they ought to be, when one considers the evils brought about by coerced sex, rape, forced childbearing, and forced childrearing, all of which have contributed greatly at every time and in all cultures to the suffering of women. I do not for a moment wish to condone any of these practices, but rather to suggest that even where the parent-child relationship began with the parent's consent, not all of what is owed the child is exhausted by a contractual account of obligation. Parents who look after brain-damaged or schizophrenic children have seldom bargained for this; it's not typically a promise that keeps the mother of a teenage drug addict from relinquishing all responsibility for her child. The contractarian account is unsatisfactory. Something important seems to have been left out.

Moral theories other than contractarian ones have offered their own explanations of where parental duties come from. In various utilitarian accounts, for example, parents ought to care for their own children because this produces greater happiness, on the whole, than other arrangements; deontological theories bid parents to do right by their children out of respect for the moral law. But here again something important seems to have been left out. As Michael Stocker puts it:

> What is lacking in these theories is simply—or not so simply—the person. For love, friendship, affection, fellow feeling, and community all require that the other person be an essential part of what is valued. The person— not merely the person's general values nor even the person-qua-producer- or-possessor-of-general-values—must be valued. The defect of these theories in regard to love, to take one case, is not that they do not value love (which often, they do not) but that they do not value the beloved.[10]

While some part of morality may consist in allegiance to the values of consent, maximizing happiness, or duty for its own sake, a great deal of it surely consists in how we prize *persons*. And as the connections among persons not only contribute to persons' sense of who they are, but are themselves the ground of many moral obligations, interpersonal relationships too must be valued. The ways in which persons become connected to one another are diverse and only some are chosen freely, but regardless of how the relationship comes about, if it is allowed to grow it creates responsibilities. These responsibilities then become constitutive of the relationship, as well as having arisen from it.[11]

I am supposing for purposes of this essay that a parent-child relationship has already come into existence by one of the various ways in which this happens, and that the parent is concerned to know not *whether* he has special responsibilities to his children, but *what* these are. Children's vulnerabilities elicit many of the duties owed them: They must be protected, fed, clothed, and sheltered or they will die; if they are not loved and socialized they cannot live well. So much is fairly clear.

Less obvious, however, are responsibilities arising from the way in which the parent-child relationship contributes to the formation of the child's identity. It is within the highly particularistic context of the parent-child relationship that the child learns to think of herself as *this* kind of person rather than *that* one. Her parents are her first and most powerful influences, the ground of many of the identities she will retain into adulthood. Her social class, her religion, her attitude toward learning or the fine arts or certain groups of people, the moral meanings she attaches to her gender— all these things and many others are likely to become central features of who she is because her parents have passed them on to her in one way or another. The identity-forming function of the parent-child relationship thus gives rise to an added responsibility: that of offering children a richly detailed vision of life that expresses the parents' best judgment of how to be and behave in the world. In other words, parents have an obligation to teach their children their own "thick" conception of the good life.

It is not parents alone, of course, who bear these various responsibilities. So, arguably, do others closely connected to the child—as for example a day care worker, teacher, neighbor, or older sibling in a position to know the child's needs and meet them. All things being equal, these others do not have the same degree of obligation to the child as its parents do. In a society organized as ours is, her mother and father are assigned primary responsibility for the child's well-being; parents are open to blame and sometimes legally punished if they neglect their children. Nevertheless, a child's vulnerability exerts a moral pull on others as well, particularly when parents do not or cannot meet their own responsibilities to the child.

I bring these others into my account of parental obligations because the parent-child dyad does not typically exist in isolation from other relationships. It is generally but one configuration in a cluster of overlapping relationships of partiality, each of which gives rise to its own set of responsibilities. For most young children, these relationships form the context in which they live and grow. They watch their mom and dad being loving (or spiteful) to one another; see or are involved in quarrels and games with siblings; worry because their playmate's mother gets sloppy-loving when she drinks too much; love their day care giver but hate her children. The relationships are overlapping because children are generally on intimate terms with at least some of the people inside the parents' circle of intimacy—particularly those who form the child's household. These other intimates, whether family members or nonrelatives, play a role in forming children's identities second only to that of the parents. They too set the possibilities not only for what children can do and what they can know, but who they can be.[12] How parents, siblings, day care workers, and others carry out their responsibilities to the child is thus a matter of crucial moral importance.

Many of the people in this cluster of relationships are also of moral significance to the *parent*. Men and women generally trust that they will be parents within the context of their intimate relations, not only because they rely on these intimate others to help them fulfill their obligations to their children, but also because these people too are dear to them, loved in their own right. The function by which intimates forge children's identities has its analogue in maintaining and affirming the identities of adults, and the parent both performs this function for others and is a recipient of it herself. She may have filial duties to her own parents, spousal responsibilities to her husband, obligations to help a coworker who is down on her luck or a neighbor who is elderly and frail, duties of hospitality to an old friend from out of town. And these people in turn have responsibilities—sometimes but not always the same ones—to her.

In general, then, parents are obliged to protect, nurture, and socialize their children, and are further obliged to participate wisely in their children's identity-formation by sharing with them their own rich and detailed conception of what it is to live well. To these responsibilities, however, must be added the responsibility for loving their children, as children not only require this love for self-formation and self-esteem, but also learn how to love others by being loved themselves.

Now, it might be objected that love is a feeling and thus cannot be summoned at will, and since a necessary condition for doing one's duty is that it be possible to do it, there can be no parental duty to love. There are two responses to this objection. One is that the Kantian principle that ought implies can is not always true. "For example," observes Christopher Gowans, "I may have a responsibility to make my car payment but be unable to do so because I have been laid off from work."[13] Similarly, one may have a duty to love one's young child but be unable to do so because, for example, one is mentally ill. The second response is that morally competent adults are capable of working on their feelings and learning new habits. If, for instance, I feel repulsion when an African American enters the room, I have a duty to examine my emotions, acknowledge their injustice and viciousness, and discard the false beliefs about racial inferiority and the like that seem to be fueling them. In the same vein, if a parent finds himself continually hostile or indifferent toward his young child, he is obliged to find out why he harbors these feelings, what beliefs underlie them, and what he can do to change his ways.

This brings us to a final responsibility—one that takes on a particular significance in the context of divorce, as we shall see shortly. Because a

parent-child relationship typically exists within the cluster of intimate relationships through which the functions of protection, nurture, and identity-
formation are carried on, and since these relationships are crucially important to the child, the parent has a duty to foster them. In teaching her
children to refrain from bullying one another, for example, a mother does
not merely cut down on the amounts of whining and bickering she will have
to endure, but cultivates and strengthens the ties of intimacy binding child
to child. In taking his children to buy a birthday gift for a favorite neighbor,
a father promotes an important connection between the children and their
adult friend.

Responsibilities arising from intimate relationships are so crucial that
we may take them to be paradigmatic of morality. It is within the context
of such relationships that we receive the nurture and protection necessary
for survival, that we first learn what love is and how to love, that we acquire
much of the stuff of which selves are made. How could the responsibilities
to provide these essential goods not be central to any conception of the
moral life? Moreover, if a child is going to come to recognize obligations,
she is going to have to value the relationships in which they arise. There is
thus an additional reason why intimate relationships are crucial to a child:
Her moral development cannot take place without them. For all these reasons, then, the responsibility to protect these relationships can be seen as a
meta-responsibility—the one on which all the others depend.

Parental Dilemmas

My parental ethics of divorce thus begins with an account of responsibilities
to children. As I am concerned here to understand how these responsibilities
play themselves out in the aftermath of a divorce, I will not explore the ethics
of a given decision to end a marriage, but will concentrate instead on the
parent's postdivorce moral deliberations as they affect his or her children.

Suppose a father negotiating the terms of divorce with his estranged
wife is faced with either selling her his interest in their house and moving
to the town where his parents live, or keeping the house but forgoing the
logistical help his parents are prepared to give him. Suppose too that he can
continue in his present job or find a new one with equal ease. The house—
the only one his daughter has ever lived in—is only three doors away from
the daughter's longtime best friend. The father, who has physical custody of
his daughter, knows how important this relationship is, but also knows there
is some possibility that the friend's family may soon move to another city.

The father faces a practical dilemma, where he must judge under conditions of uncertainty whether the consequences of moving are likely to be worse for his child than staying where they are.

Sometimes a parent's dilemma is not merely practical, but moral. Because divorcing parents have responsibilities to a number of persons, including themselves,[14] it is possible for their responsibilities to conflict. As Gowans argues,

> Though deliberation can determine that one of these responsibilities is more compelling than the other, meaning that that responsibility is the one to be acted on, it does not thereby eliminate altogether the fact that there is another, conflicting responsibility. . . . Each of them is fundamental, meaning that its moral demand does not simply disappear every time a more compelling moral consideration comes into conflict with it.[15]

In an approach to morality based on responsibilities to persons, genuine moral dilemmas arise because the chief concern of moral deliberation is to respond appropriately to the persons with whom we are connected in various ways. Even when the moral reason for one action clearly overrides the moral reason for the other, one may, in performing that action, fail in one's responsibilities to some person. One then wrongs that person.

A divorcing parent may in this way do wrong no matter what she does. Suppose her husband is a good enough father to their young son, but a bad spouse: He has repeatedly been unfaithful to her and repeatedly lied about what he was doing. She no longer trusts him, but because she still loves him, his infidelities make her deeply miserable. She knows she is beginning to lose her self-respect and she finds it hard to get through the day without crying. If she stays in this marriage, she fails to honor her own dignity and worth; if she divorces, she makes it much harder for her son to get the good of his relationship with his father[16]—a relationship that is crucially important to him and one she ought, for his sake, to protect.

We will suppose that after much careful reflection, this mother concludes that her reasons for divorcing heavily outweigh her reasons for remaining married. This conclusion, Gowans argues, leaves a "moral remainder"—namely, the genuine moral value of her son's relationship with his father. In unavoidably undermining this, she has done wrong. The feelings of distress that are generally elicited by the knowledge that one is guilty of wrongdoing may in her case be undercut by feelings of outrage at her former husband for having put her in this position—indeed, if she is angry enough with this man she may be unable to acknowledge her responsibility to promote their child's relationship with him at all. In her more dispassionate moments, however, she might well reflect that what he is and does is of great moral value to the boy, and that this value does not decrease just because there has been a divorce. While she could not help but infringe on this relationship, she now owes it to her son to affirm its goodness.

Dilemmas can also arise as families are reconfigured after divorce. Consider a mother whose daughters are four and fourteen years of age at the time of the divorce. Both mother and father agree that the mother should be awarded full physical custody of the children, as the father's job requires him to be out of town overnight several times a month. A year passes. Although the father is scrupulous about paying child support, he is less scrupulous about seeing the children. For the past six months, despite the mother's remonstrating with him, he has not seen or communicated with his daughters at all—an estrangement that was recently compounded when he took a job in a distant city. The older daughter, fearing she will lose every connection with her father, feels strongly that she needs to live with him. Her doing so will be very hard on the five-year-old, who loves her sister dearly and is dependent on her in many ways. If the mother allows her older daughter to rejoin her father, her younger daughter will lose something of great moral value; if she forbids the move, the older daughter loses.

The moral distress this mother feels ought to be taken seriously, as it is an acknowledgment that she cannot avoid doing something morally wrong, no matter what she does. Nor is it irrational for her to feel she ought in some way to apologize to or compensate the daughter she wrongs. She might, for example, attempt to compensate the five-year-old for her older sister's absence by insisting that the older daughter spend summers with her and the younger child. Or, if she has not allowed the older daughter to move, she might renew her efforts to involve the father in the children's lives. She certainly ought to enlist her daughters' help in deliberating about how best to fulfill her responsibilities to them both. What she must not do, however, is to dismiss the moral remainders as nonexistent or unimportant.

Children as Moral Agents

One of the most pressing reasons for safeguarding children's intimate relationships during and after divorce is that these crucial relationships are more fragile at this time than before. After a divorce, the child no longer has daily access to both parents, and while parental relationships are the most significant ones to undergo upheaval, other intimate relationships are at risk of harm as well: Children may be forced to move out of their old school districts or neighborhoods; important family friends may no longer be speaking to one or the other of the parents; depression, anger, and misery may make the custodial parent unavailable emotionally even though he or she is present physically.

For a parent who is struggling to keep his child's supportive relationships intact as he negotiates the circumstances of postdivorce life for himself and his children, the idea that the children are to be consulted about how to do this might seem to be an abdication of responsibility. As the parent feels the weight of having to decide how and with whom his children will live, he might well be tempted to protect them from this burden by excluding them from his deliberations. The temptation to protect, however, may make it harder for the parent to see that his children have their own moral perspective from which to view these matters, and that their opinions deserve his respectful hearing. If he does not recognize that his children are moral agents in their own right, albeit perhaps limited ones, he may fail to take seriously their interest in contributing to his thinking about arrangements that will deeply affect their future.

The child's intimate relationships, I have suggested, are the primary site where children's moral agency is formed. Children learn to love by being loved; they learn to respect others when their parents, siblings, and other intimates respect them; when these people are reliable, they learn to trust. In addition, however, these relationships are the context in which children's exercise of their moral agency is most free.

In support of this claim, let me turn to Paul Benson, who has argued that even a five-year-old is a moral agent, in that he is capable of controlling his conduct by reflecting on and making choices about what he will do. Nevertheless, Benson says, the child's agency is not free. The reason is that children's actions lack "normative self-disclosure": They do not reveal who the child is as a person, morally speaking. A five-year-old's teasing of his younger sister does not warrant onlookers to infer that the child is a nasty person; a four-year-old's greediness at table does not warrant her dinner companions to infer that the child is greedy. These inferences are unreliable, Benson believes, because the child lacks normative competence. He does not yet conceive of his actions as open to evaluation in the terms in which they are likely to be evaluated, nor does he have much basis for judging the applicability and worth of the standards used in this evaluation. "At the heart of free agency," Benson argues, "is the power of our actions to reveal who we are, both to ourselves and to others, in the context of potential normative assessments of what we do."[17]

Now, in the case of adults, Benson thinks, moral agency can be restricted not merely because the person is morally undeveloped, but because others in her community refuse to *recognize* her as a morally developed person. How a community constructs a moral subject's identity is a function of the community's own history, the kinds of identities that are available in the community, and the understandings that guide the community's moral practices. The process is a complex one, and the actions of the moral subject play only one role in it. Whether the moral agency of the person can be exercised freely depends largely on the outcome of that process—some identities make for free subjects and others do not. When Native Americans are stereotyped by the wider society as shiftless and immoral, for example, or the disabled in body are taken to be mentally disabled as well, these people are not free no matter how morally developed they really are.[18]

At best, normative self-disclosure requires more than that the agent act in ways that *reveal* who she is; it also requires that others *recognize* these actions as self-disclosing. Benson's observer who is unable to infer from someone's actions what those actions say morally about that person might have trouble doing this, not because the person is morally sub- or abnormal, but because the observer's community has constructed an identity for the person that entails her being morally inept. She cannot act freely. She will be discounted, ignored, or, in extreme cases, physically restrained. Benson acknowledges that women in a sexist society face special difficulties in the task of becoming fully free agents because mainstream perceptions trivialize or suppress their contributions and experience. To this observation I wish to add a friendly amendment: The same can be said of children.

What is interesting about children in this regard is that the child's intimate relationships form a special moral context that differs in significant respects from the ordinary moral context of the wider community. For one thing, intimates who care for the child have a special responsibility for teaching the child the standards of morality that are applicable in the wider community. They have a duty, in other words, to foster the child's moral development. Children receive moral *lessons* from any number of sources, including the playground bully, television, or a teacher who plays favorites. But moral *training* is done by parents, other members of the child's household(s), schoolteachers, the neighbor who baby-sits, day care workers. Not all these trainers have the same status, however. Members of the child's household, and in particular her parents, are especially obligated to help her attain moral maturity. Their love for the child and hers for them, along with their ongoing presence in the child's life, permit this training to be more intensive and enduring than that given in less intimate settings.

Another way in which the relationships of intimacy form a moral context different from the ordinary context of the wider community is that those who stand in a loving and ongoing relationship with the child ought to and often do possess a close and detailed knowledge of the child which can be used to interpret her actions. That is, parents are in a better position than members of the wider community to understand what the child's action says about who she is morally.

Sometimes recognizing a child's act as morally self-disclosing requires an active imagination. I know of a three-year-old whose horrified mother found her one day rubbing her infant sister's face with a wadded-up piece of aluminum foil. An effort of interpretation was necessary before the mother understood that the three-year-old was distressed because the baby had been crying and was trying to help by drying the baby's tears. The action that members of the normal moral community might carelessly misinterpret as a sign that the child was too undeveloped morally to be trusted near her baby sister could, in the special moral community of loving relationships that parents owe their children, be seen more clearly as a sign of sisterly devotion carried out with the wrong equipment.

With luck, the child will occasionally cross paths with skillful, caring strangers or people specially trained to deal with children who recognize that she can be taken as a moral agent and interpret her actions accordingly. Those who have a special responsibility for the child's well-being are, however, morally obliged to practice this kind of imaginative interpretation, because this is what is required if they are to do a good job of loving and socializing her. They should draw on the detailed knowledge of the child that is available within the special moral context of the family to interpret her actions as these take place against the moral backdrop the family itself has provided. By using their special knowledge of and engagement with the child to break the code that misleads ordinary adults, the child's intimates supply the context for the normative self-disclosure that makes the child's agency free.

The special moral community of the family, then, is one in which people can and should acknowledge the child's steadily forming moral agency and bestow on the child's acts the normative meaning the child only imperfectly conveys. The two features of the special context that I have just isolated each contribute to this task in their own way: The moral training is a crucial ingredient in developing the capacities that allow the child's action to *reveal* who she is, while knowledge of the child makes possible the *recognition* of the child's act as self-disclosing. Together, parental training and knowledge free up the child's moral agency.

The task of fostering and recognizing a child's moral agency can be specially difficult as a parent negotiates with a former spouse how she, he, and their children will live after a divorce. Not only might the parent feel she ought to shield her children from the responsibility of involvement in the negotiation, she may also be tempted because of her own new needs to dismiss her children's desires as irrational wants rather than as expressions of moral values. She might, for example, see a child's plea that her father be invited to her birthday party as a part of a story about the child's unreasonable desire to reintegrate the father into the household, when what the child is actually doing is organizing a family party—the family in question being the child's, not the mother's. This child is dealing in her own way with the new complexity of her intimate context, but the mother might have difficulty in recognizing this if she does not take her child's moral agency seriously.

Or, to take another example, if the child runs away from the father's house, the father may weave this into a story about the child's unwillingness to accept discipline, when in fact the child is rejecting the frequent verbal abuse she receives from her father's new girlfriend. Here, the newly intense conflicts between the father's needs for intimacy and his child's needs for respect can only be exacerbated if the father fails to see the child's actions as those of a moral agent. In both cases, the children are standing for something that has moral value—in the first instance, for the goodness of the child's family; in the second, for her own dignity and worth.

These children's actions do possess the normative self-disclosure that is necessary for the free exercise of moral agency, but only to those who have eyes to see. Whereas a person with an insensitive, arrogant, or blind eye is apt to tell a story about the child's actions that justifies excluding the child from the normal moral community, those who see the child with the eye of love owe it to her to make use of their loving perception to construct a story about the child's acts that counters the blind interpretation that creates for her an identity of moral incompetence.[19] This counterstory allows the child entry into the moral community because it acknowledges the legitimacy of the child's identity as a member of that community: It confers on the child the recognition that is just as essential to the free exercise of agency as is knowing the moral rules. That parents should cultivate a faculty for counterstories on behalf of their children would seem to follow from their obligation to foster their children's moral development, but as it turns out, telling counterstories that allow the parents to take their children's moral perspective seriously also allows children to exercise their own initiative in protecting the relationships that are of central importance to them.

This is not to say, of course, that a ten-year-old child should call all the postdivorce shots. Young children are harmed when they are given power that properly belongs to their parents, and besides, as I have been at some pains to point out, parents also have responsibilities to people other than their children. Moreover, a child's moral agency is still under construction, and even when she exercises it freely, what she expresses about herself isn't always admirable. Her cognitive ability is under construction as well: Young children are not capable of the abstract thought that is required for forming judgments about what is best for them in the long run. But the fact that children are not yet fully competent does not mean that they should be shielded from the moral deliberations that concern their interests and well-being. Even young children can offer their parents insights and perspectives about people who are valuable to them that allow the parents to see more clearly what they ought to do.

Dangerous Liaisons

The final question I want to take up is whether parents' responsibility to protect the important relationships that already support a child entails that they not encumber the child with new relationships. To answer this question, I look once more to the account of morality that forms the basis for my parental ethics of divorce.

Because this account is based on responsibilities to persons with whom one stands in relationships of intimacy, it is dogged by the same difficulties that attach themselves to any partialist ethics, whether this one or, for example, the feminine ethic of care.[20] I am thinking in particular of the "options" problem. Although it has been most famously advanced as a criticism of utilitarianism,[21] both the ethic of care and an ethics of interpersonal responsibility are likewise open to the charge that they generate theoretically unlimited responsibilities, and so do not permit moral agents the option of pursuing the personal projects or intimate relationships that make life worth living in the first place.

If I, a divorced mother, am bidden by the responsibility ethic to fulfill all my obligations not only to my children but also to all the other people with whom I am connected in various ways, how can I possibly make new friends, take a lover, or remarry? And aren't matters made worse when I consider the extra responsibilities I have toward those to whom I am bound by ties of love or friendship? It would seem that a responsibilities to persons account does not merely produce occasional instances of genuine moral dilemmas—it generates them constantly. There will always be people to whom I have failed in my responsibilities, always those whom I cannot avoid wronging, no matter what I do.

One response to this criticism is to suggest that one's responsibilities to others are neither so numerous nor so stringent as the "options" problem supposes. This response puts the burden of proof on the critic, who must then show how and why morality requires so much more of us than seems intuitively plausible.[22] Another response is to invoke the methodology of wide reflective equilibrium to balance our sense that our responsibilities to others are limited against theoretical accounts that insist otherwise.[23]

There is also a third response—one that grants the criticism a certain validity while at the same time suggesting a way to avoid incurring it. It is this: Because one's relationships to others—and especially to friends and family—generate responsibilities, we might have a duty to enter into no more of them than we can responsibly accommodate. If we would limit our responsibilities, so this line of reasoning goes, then we must limit our relationships. Doing otherwise not only leaves us with no moral option to pursue our own projects, it also makes it impossible for us to escape moral wrongdoing, as we will find ourselves in a continual crossfire of conflicting responsibilities that cannot all be met.

This response has a particular salience for a parental ethics of divorce, because it suggests that entering new relationships after divorce is morally risky, as these put undue pressure on relationships that already exist. While its proponents might acknowledge that introducing a stepmother or other new family members into a child's life can be a blessing for the child as well as the father, they would argue that if these people then exit the child's life as the father moves on to yet another partner, the child may be worse off than if she had never known them. None of us can flourish in a continually unstable environment, they would point out; it is surely no business of a parent to visit constant instability on his child.

In any case, they might go on to observe, new family members aren't always a blessing. It takes a long time for even a loving stepparent to feel the same deep affection toward her partner's children that she feels toward her own, and not all stepparents—or stepsiblings—are loving. Familial relationships are the very ones over which the child has least control, while at the same time they often have the greatest impact on the child's well-being. For all these reasons, then, isn't a parent obliged to forgo new relationships— at least until the children are old enough to leave home?

Well, no. The trouble with this solution to the "options" problem is two-fold: It rests on too narrow a conception of the moral life and it also offers an impoverished view of what familial reconfigurations can and should be like. If we try to play it safe by refusing to enter relationships as a means of carving out space for our personal projects and avoiding situations in which we cannot escape wrongdoing, we turn our backs on the very entities that are most valuable in an account of morality based on responsibilities to persons—namely, persons themselves.

The morally good life "crucially involves numerous, deep, and complex relationships with others,"[24] and this is true, it seems, even if having these relationships means that we cannot avoid doing wrong to those others. As we can maintain our own innocence only by cutting ourselves off from people, it is the hope of innocence, not the presence of people in our lives, that must be given up. This is not to say, of course, that we should be either careless or promiscuous about the liaisons we form; our responsibilities to others are real and should never be assumed lightly. Severely curtailing our relationships, however, cannot secure a morally good life for any of us.

Moreover, if we think we must refrain from new relationships after divorce because they will be hard on our children, we probably need to expand our vision of what familial relationships can be. There is no reason, for example, why a stepmother should have to love her stepchildren as deeply and devotedly as she loves children of her own. She *may* love them in the same way, of course, or she may come to do this in good time, but such love is only one of many goods that might inhere in a stepmother-stepchild relationship. From the child's perspective, a stepmother's deep maternal devotion might be neither necessary nor sought, particularly if the child already has a perfectly good enough mother to give her this kind of love. Like adults, children thrive on all sorts of connections to others, including those to a stepmother whom they think of as a grown-up friend, an "othermother,"[25] or an affectionate person who has lived in their house for a time.

The picture continues to hold us captive. So long as we cleave to the idea that postdivorce families ought to resemble as closely as they can the predivorce ideal of the sentimental family, we will limit ourselves unnecessarily to the very few familial roles that the sentimental ideal allows. Freed of that ideal, parents will certainly find themselves adrift, with no real guidance as to what their new relationships ought to look like. Rather than allowing that prospect to terrify them, however, they might take it as an invitation to let a new richness and complexity into their lives, welcoming the fluidity of their reconfigured families, prizing any relationships that are a source of joy to them and their children, and teaching the children to do the same.

What I have offered here is little more than a rough sketch of what a part of a parental ethics of divorce might be. I do not know of other attempts at such an ethics, nor why moral philosophers have seemingly had little professional interest in a phenomenon that touches many of us so nearly. Perhaps there has been an assumption that each divorce is different, each cluttered with such a number of particulars that nothing general can be said about them. If so, then I hope to have shown that this assumption is untrue, and that there are resources available within moral philosophy for thinking carefully about one's responsibilities both during a divorce and in its aftermath.

Thanks to Jeffrey Blustein, Mary English, Christopher Gowans, John Hardwig, Bill Morgan, James Lindemann Nelson, Betsy Postow, Elise Robinson, and, most especially, Sara Ruddick and Margaret Urban Walker for their many useful comments and suggestions.

1. National Center for Health Statistics, report of most recent figures released in 1994, in conversation on September 24, 1997.

2. On the Left, see Hillary Rodham Clinton, *It Takes a Village: And Other Lessons Children Teach Us* (New York: Simon and Schuster, 1996); and William A. Galston, *Liberal Purposes: Goods, Virtues, and Diversity in the Liberal State* (New York: Cambridge University Press, 1991), 283–287. See also William A. Galston, "Needed: A Not-So-Fast Divorce Law," *New York Times* (27 December 1995). On the Right, a recent argument against divorce on the grounds that it is bad for children has been that of Barbara Dafoe Whitehead, *The Divorce Culture* (New York: Alfred A. Knopf, 1997).

3. Galston, *Liberal Purposes*, 284, citing David Ellwood, *Poor Support* (New York: Basic Books, 1988), 83–84.

4. For an excellent history of American families, see Steven Mintz and Susan Kellogg, *Domestic Revolutions: A Social History of American Family Life* (New York: Free Press, 1988).

5. In 1890 only 4.6 percent of married women were in the paid labor force. By 1985 it was 54.2 percent. See Kingsley Davis, "Wives and Work: A Theory of the Sex-Role Revolution and Its Consequences," in *Feminism, Children, and the New Families*, ed. Sanford M. Dornbusch and Myra H. Strober (New York: Guilford Press, 1988), 67.

6. See in particular Susan Moller Okin, *Justice, Gender, and the Family* (New York: Basic Books, 1989), chapter 7.

7. For a feminist critique of the sentimental family and an alternative view of what families are about, see Elise L. E. Robinson, Hilde Lindemann Nelson, and James Lindemann Nelson, "Fluid Families: The Role of Children in Custody Arrangements," in *Feminism and Families*, ed. Hilde Lindemann Nelson (New York: Routledge, 1996), as well as other essays in that volume. See also Barrie Thorne and Marilyn Yalom, eds., *Rethinking the Family: Some Feminist Questions* (New York: Longman, 1992); and Linda J. Nicholson, *Gender and History: The Limits of Social Theory in the Age of the Family* (New York: Columbia University Press, 1988).

8. Although I agree with Sara Ruddick that women are lost sight of when the work of tending children, which has traditionally been done primarily by women, is referred to as "parenting," I also agree that maternal work can and should be done by men. Since, as far as I can see, the responsibilities that fathers have to their children after divorce are the same as those of mothers, I shall speak throughout this essay of parental responsibilities. See Sara Ruddick, *Maternal Thinking: Toward a Politics of Peace*, 2d ed. (Boston: Beacon Press, 1995), and "The Idea of Fatherhood," in *Feminism and Families*, ed. Hilde Lindemann Nelson (New York: Routledge, 1997).

9. For an argument that forced promises might under certain circumstances still be binding, see Betsy Postow, "Coercion and the Moral Bindingness of Contracts," *Social Theory and Practice* 4, no. 1 (1976): 75–92.

10. Michael Stocker, "The Schizophrenia of Modern Ethical Theories," in *The Virtues: Contemporary Essays on Moral Character*, ed. Robert B. Kruschwitz and Robert C. Roberts (Belmont, Calif.: Wadsworth, 1987), 40.

11. Christopher Gowans writes, "Moral responsibilities have a twofold origin: first, in the belief that . . . persons are intrinsically and uniquely valuable . . . and as such are beings for whom we can have responsibilities; and second, in the diverse ways in which particular persons come to be connected with one another . . . and thereby establish a relationship of which specific responsibilities are a constitutive part" (*Innocence Lost: An Examination of Inescapable Moral Wrongdoing* [New York: Oxford University Press, 1994], 128).

12. For a particularly lucid explanation of how families form children's identities, see Salvador Minuchin, *Families and Family Therapy* (Cambridge, Mass.: Harvard University Press, 1974), 47–48.

13. Gowans, *Innocence Lost*, 140.

14. On valuing oneself, see Stocker, "The Schizophrenia of Modern Ethical Theories," 41.

15. Gowans, *Innocence Lost*, 18.

16. I am assuming that this family's postdivorce arrangements will conform to the national norm, whereby most dependent children live with their mothers. In a recent large-scale California study, six months after divorce, only 9.6 percent of children lived with their fathers on a daily basis; three years after divorce this figure was still only 11.7 percent. By comparison, 67 percent of children lived with their mothers only. About 15 percent lived in dual residence. See Eleanor E. Maccoby and Robert H. Mnookin, *Dividing the Child: Social and Legal Dilemmas of Custody* (Cambridge, Mass.: Harvard University Press, 1992).

17. See Paul Benson, "Feminist Second Thoughts About Free Agency," *Hypatia* 5, no. 3 (Fall 1990): 55.

18. I am indebted for these ideas to Margaret Urban Walker. See her *Moral Understandings* (New York: Routledge, 1998).

19. For a fuller explanation of how counterstories permit someone who has second-class citizenship in a community to gain full access to the goods on offer in it, see Hilde Lindemann Nelson, "Resistance and Insubordination," *Hypatia* 10, no. 2 (Spring 1995): 23–40.

20. One difference between the feminine ethic of care and the responsibility to persons account of morality advocated by Gowans is that the axiology of the care ethic valorizes care, where Gowans' approach does not; neither does my use of Gowans' approach to develop a parental ethics of divorce. For criticisms of the ethic of care that apply equally to the responsibility to persons account, see Claudia Card, "Caring and Evil," *Hypatia* 5, no. 1 (1990): 101–108; and in the same issue of *Hypatia*, Sarah Hoagland, "Some Concerns About Nel Noddings' *Caring*" (109–114). Suggestions for developing the care ethic in response to these criticisms are found in Alisa L. Carse and Hilde Lindemann Nelson, "Rehabilitating Care," *Kennedy Institute of Ethics Journal* 6, no. 1 (1996): 19–35.

21. By Bernard Williams. See his "Persons, Character, and Morality," in *Moral Luck* (Cambridge: Cambridge University Press, 1981).

22. A relentless demonstration of precisely how stringent these duties are has been offered in defense of consequentialism by Shelly Kagan, *The Limits of Morality* (Oxford: Clarendon Press, 1989).

23. This is Gowans's response; see *Innocence Lost*, 94.

24. James Lindemann Nelson, "Is It Ever Right to Do Wrong?," review of Gowans's *Innocence Lost, Hastings Center Report* 25, no. 3 (1995): 48–49.

25. This useful word was added to the language by Patricia Hill Collins. See her *Black Feminist Thought* (New York: Routledge, 1990).

PART

Mothers, Families, and
the State: Reexamining the Old,
Reinventing the New

Martha Albertson Fineman

Law of the Father

Introductory Caveat

In this essay, I refer to "mother" and "father" as terms representing complementary and differentiated ways of assuming responsibility for and rights over children. I realize that these terms are "loaded" in cultural significance—it is for that reason that I use them. Mother is used as shorthand for a practice of nurturing and caretaking; father, to indicate an authoritative and economically supportive set of responsibilities. The tendency in progressive and policy circles has been to reject such stereotypical divisions and treat parents as fungible. While some may be in practice, as cultural categories they remain distinct. I do realize (and even applaud) that men can "mother" children just as women can economically support them. What I also assert, however, is that those crossover patterns are difficult to maintain in this society and fairly atypical in practice.

Law is an imperfect instrument with which to try to either effect significant social change or capture and accommodate nuanced and complicated social practices. Yet we resort to law for these purposes all the time. When an institution as complex and fraught with symbolism as the family with its gendered roles of mother and father becomes highly politicized, the law is a site for a war between idealistic and pragmatic objectives. We now find ourselves at the end of a protracted struggle over the significance of transformative trends in the family and it is time for an assessment of what has been won and lost in the arena of the law.

Contemporary policy discourses on motherhood and fatherhood continue to implicitly recognize that these parental roles are distinct and complementary cultural and social categories. This is so even though the legal rhetoric applied to family law issues is formally gender neutral. This discourse prioritizes sameness of treatment and formal equality. As social practices, however, motherhood and fatherhood are far more than simple legal terms. They are expressions of relationships that define not only expectations about parental interactions with children, but also spouses' expectations for themselves and each other as both parents and representatives of the broader categories of women and men. Each social category or role occupied by women and men, whether located in the "private" family or in the "public sphere," reflects an interactive and gendered status with an idealized set of expectations and obligations enscripted upon it. In other words, the rhetoric may be gender neutral, but the underlying assumptions and direction of regulation reflect the old model of family organization.

There are two areas in which recent legal reforms and revisions have been the occasion for attempts to articulate anew (and in gender-neutral terms) the obligations attached to the categories of mother and father: the evolution of rules for custody decision making at divorce and the federal revision of Aid to Families with Dependent Children (AFDC). In both these areas, historic perceptions about the distinct and complementary natures of motherhood and fatherhood ultimately prove central to the policy and rules developed. In this regard, both custody and poverty discourses continue to reflect the intractability of the traditional role divisions between mothers and fathers. This division is exemplified in the historic hierarchical, patriarchal common-law family with the male "head" of the household assuming legal, social, and economic responsibility for dependent and subservient wives and children. This formal and stylized chain of command and authority may now be more obscure, but the fundamental assumptions regarding the inevitability and necessity of male economic responsibility for and supervision of family members continues to shape policies today.

While the language of family roles in policy and in the courts is recast in gender-neutral egalitarian modes, the direction of reform reflects gender differentiation historically built up to reinforce and normalize the patriarchal organization of the reproductive family. Gendered expectations continue to influence the ways in which we think about motherhood and fatherhood and shape our expectations for women and men acting outside of their family roles. They also profoundly influence the direction and nature of legal reforms.

Law and Transition

The transformation in social behavior most often posited as provoking legal reform in family law is the changed nature of women's roles in society—the "equality revolution" of the latter part of the twentieth century. Feminist legal theorists have been primarily focused on the gendered nature of public institutions. They have addressed the implications of altered perceptions about sexuality and reproductive rights as a result of women's participation in the public sphere and have generated public concern about sexual harassment in the workplace and domestic (and other gendered) violence. But the major theoretical emphasis has been placed on situations of domination, subordination, and discrimination; and feminist theory has focused largely on public institutions and not specifically on the family as an independent social institution. The family was treated as subsidiary to the market or as a bastion of male prerogative and privilege. Many feminists tended to perceive it either as another obstacle, a burden, hindering full participation in the public sphere, or as an arrangement subjecting women to domination and victimization. In this formulation, women's traditional gendered roles within the family were considered problematic primarily because they impede realization of their role as equal participants in the economic and political aspects of life. Family and family roles, particularly that of mother, were often analyzed as oppressive and impeding individual growth and independence. The family itself was alleged to be often violent and dangerous.

One particularly pernicious consequence of the undertheorizing of the family has been that traditional family roles are typically perceived as malleable and easily recast and reformed in order to facilitate women's equality in the public sphere. Reforms in the public sphere mandate employers treat women equally, but the family remains gendered and the workplace untransformed. What this means in practice is that mothers and other caretakers now are free to compete with unencumbered women and men in a workplace basically unchanged. We remain relatively unresponsive to the contradictory and conflicting demands placed on caretakers within families who also are in the paid workforce.

There is an additional problem in this regard as many people share the perception that the gender revolution has been accomplished. For many, the workplace is conceived of as successfully "reformed" and the problems of caretaking are hidden within the family. If some see a problem, the solution is to complement and facilitate women's movement into the market with male movement into the nursery, substituting androgynous individuality for differentiated, complementary roles within the traditional family. There are problems with this set of assumptions for women and the workforce, but my focus in this chapter is the effect that such perceptions have in the so-called private sphere of family law.

What we see in family law is that the imposition of an equality model on an existing unequal distribution of labor and sacrifice actually results in equality operating to further disadvantage women (and ill serve children). The imposition of equality furthers inequality.

Certainly, one casualty of the equality revolution has been the relatively recent recognition given to the institution of motherhood in law. Recognition of mothering or nurturing as something warranting "special" treatment or consideration has been attacked by liberal legal feminists as well as by policymakers, politicians, and father's rights groups. Some policymakers, politicians, and father's advocates condemn special treatment because they wish to "restore" the authority of the father in the family and fear that women are raising children without appropriate paternal supervision and economic support. For this group of equality advocates, the real goal is restoration of historic inequality.

For feminists, however, the distrust of special treatment for motherhood often springs from their overarching commitment to equality for women. Although feminists' reform suggestions are seldom punitive in motive, they still seem explicitly concerned with prospective social engineering in the direction of equality. For example, the suggestion is that we not respond to "need" at divorce by structuring property division rules or granting alimony to address the social problem of economically dependant wives and mothers. Equal treatment is equated with equal economic responsibility, considered to be so important a goal that it should be the focus of legal reform even if it produces harsh results for poor women at divorce. Another example of this equality fetish in family law is the endorsement by many feminists of a presumption of joint custody. For these feminists it is imperative that the law reflect society's *aspirations* for equality rather than remedy hardships caused by existing (gendered) allocations of household labor. The rationale is that "for their own good," all women must be directed to paid work and economic self-sufficiency. Of course, men are to be nudged into assuming their share of domestic tasks. The belief was that by refusing to compensate or reward women for choosing traditional domestic tasks over market work, women and, correspondingly, men would change their priorities and behavior. The motivation of these actors is not punitive, but social engineering in the interests of gender equality is clearly a paramount concern.

Liberal feminist equality motivations aside, a great deal of political discussion about legal reforms *is* explicitly punitive in nature. There is much interest in finding ways to structure into policy reforms incentives against single motherhood, whether single motherhood results from divorce or from women having children outside of marriage. Some of the proposals for driving women back into the institution of marriage or preventing them from leaving it seem overtly vindictive as well as punitive. For example, politicians have suggested that children be taken from single mothers and placed in orphanages. Some are more subtly coercive, however, such as recent attempts to repeal no-fault divorce, thus impeding the ability to exit from marital relationships. Harsh proposals directed at single mothers have received surprising general approval as the recent gutting of programs designed to aid poor families with children indicates.

Whatever the motivation of reformers, the high divorce rates and the statistics on reproductive, workplace, and family behavior show that wide-sweeping and general punitive measures enacted into law seem unlikely to cause significant change in behavior. Cultural and social forces that are more powerful and compelling on a day-to-day basis than the law drive the evolving changes in norms concerning sexuality, reproduction, and family formation at the end of this millennium. Law seems a feeble and inadequate tool for those who wish to challenge these emerging forms of family and norms of individual behavior.

More realistic and pragmatic (therefore more likely to have some measurable effect) are reforms that, while seemingly changing expectations, nonetheless ensure that old patterns prevail: that paternal "right" and "responsibility" will continue in a world in which the form of many families otherwise may not be traditional. For example, joint custody and other "shared parenting" measures that are designed to equalize biological fathers' rights to children regardless of their marital status or demonstrated commitment to parenting can be (and have been) justified as means to establish male ties to children that increase the assumption of male responsibility for those children. Increased efforts and the introduction of more invasive schemes to collect child support, along with broadened use of paternity proceedings for linking men to their nonmarital children, are other examples of measures explicitly invoked to implement male responsibility toward children.

Note that the concept of "responsibility" that informs the debates and discussions of these and other efforts reflects the gendered norms of the traditional patriarchal family—the male is clearly viewed as the economic provider and as the disciplinarian for the family. Male ties to children are biological, legal, and economic. Also important to note is the link between arguments about ensuring paternal responsibility in the reconfigured family and arguments that it is essential to reestablish paternal control over children. The flip side of paternal responsibility is paternal "right" and authority. What is fascinating is that the inherently patriarchal project is accomplished within the framework of equality. In fact, the proponents of the new manifestation of patriarchal power use equality as the logic driving their reforms.

Family Law Reform—Purging Mother

The objective of reconstituting paternal responsibility and its corollary paternal right outside of the traditional marital context has flourished in the context of equality rhetoric in family law reform. This rhetoric has its roots in the midcentury women's movement for legal or civil equality.[1] One significant feminist law reform effort sought to discourage formal gender classifications and different treatment for women and men in the workplace and the political arena as well as in families. This movement was successful and family law is now formally "gender neutral." In custody cases, this means that reference to or explicit use of a preference for maternal custody for younger children is no longer acceptable. Neither parent is to be advantaged (or disadvantaged) as a result of her or his gender.

In and of itself, a reform that removes explicit gender designations from statutes and decision making is not objectionable. In fact, it can be viewed as desirable on a symbolic level, particularly if removal of gender has no negative effect in terms of ultimate results in actual cases. In fact, it might be beneficial to be clear about social policy in this important area—laws could specifically reiterate the desirability of adhering to and supporting those caretaking and nurturing norms that historically underlie the maternal preference, yet express them in contemporary, gender-neutral terms. For example, we could consider the paramount factor in custody determinations to be not the *maternal* preference, but a preference for the parent who has undertaken responsibility for the ongoing day-to-day care of the child or has demonstrated that she or he is most likely to put the child's interests ahead of individual career demands.[2]

The articulation of caretaking expectations outside of the cultural shorthand of "mother" might have been productive and encouraged genuine reform. Yet the course of reform has been quite different. The quest for gender neutrality in custody decision making has proven to be too ambitious and too singularly focused on equality to be satisfied with the mere imposition of gender-neutral language. In custody decision making in particular, the search has also been for standards or decisional factors that are neutral in *result* as well as expression. Of particular concern are those factors that are deemed to favor mothers disproportionately, such as a preference for custody with the "primary caretaker."

The argument is that the fact that mothers are typically primary caretakers makes a preference for primary caretakers unacceptably gender biased in favor of women in practice. This is a classic "disparate impact" legal argument: The primary caretaker standard would be said to have an adverse disparate impact on the custody prospects of men. Thus, a nurturing standard cannot be used. In its place are what are deemed more "neutral" considerations, such as the quality of the respective school districts of the parents or general assessments about which parent is more likely to facilitate and support visitation by the other post divorce. As one court succinctly stated, "custody determinations must be born of gender-neutral precepts in both result and expression."[3]

A fetish for gender neutrality, particularly one that imports disparate impact concepts from wholly unrelated areas of discrimination law to assess the appropriateness of otherwise neutral rules, is inappropriate in the family area. More is at stake in custody rules than an objective assessment of the relationship and roles of women and men. Custody decision making occurs within the context of a legal system that has as its stated object custody determinations that are in "the best interest of the child." Given this mandate, it seems clear that the need and welfare of the child, not the equality of the parents, should be the central inquiry, the measure with which to judge general rules and specific cases. It seems that gender neutrality as it is implemented as nurturing neutrality is likely to actually prove harmful to children.

The obvious question is, "How can we apply the best interest test without considering and heavily valuing those things that mothers specifically and overwhelmingly (even if stereotypically) do with and for children?"

Nurturing and caretaking—practices that are of primary importance to the rearing of children—are heavily identified in our society with the practice of responsible mothering. This cultural judgment is distinguishable from the economic expectations that primarily define responsible fathering. What is the logic or the justice in the position that women who live up to the expectations of motherhood (as well as the men who "mother") should be denied the "reward" (as well as the responsibility) of continued custody and care of their children?

Why this obsession with gender neutrality? Many feminists paradoxically justify the tendency to devalue the identification of women with mothering by pointing to the need to use gender neutrality to secure women's equality with men in areas of life outside the family. Gender neutrality in one area is considered to mandate it in all others. The demands of equality outside the family are not only a backdrop but a driving impulse for the legal system's reassessment of the "fairness" or "justice" of rules favoring mothers and maternal behavior in determining custody for children.

It is not considered problematic that alongside feminist legal reform in the direction of gender neutrality, the reestablishment of paternal right in the absence of changed paternal behavior has also resulted in the devaluing of the practice and the legally recognizable category of mothering. In fact, contemporary discussions about the unfairness of rules that favor mothering often assume that there have been extensive changes in parenting patterns that make fathering and mothering more alike. There is little empirical evidence to support this assumption (and some to refute it). The rhetoric of equality in this regard is a rhetoric of assertion, aspiration, and accusation.

According to this idealized notion of the new, egalitarian family, mothers no longer formally assigned to separate spheres must be considered as equal to men in their inclination and capacity to earn money and fathers must be considered equal to women in their desire and ability to provide nurturance. If this ideal can be made real, it follows that the law should facilitate and institutionalize egalitarian social transformations by insisting on the gender-neutral ideal—an ungendered "parenthood" standard. This argument concludes with a basic appeal to justice based upon the erroneous perception that fathers, as a group, are unjustly discriminated against in the family court system.

Offered as proof of this claim are the statistics that indicate that only a small percentage of fathers get custody of their children at divorce. These statistics have been fleshed out by harrowing horror stories—accounts of men excluded, prevented from seeing their children and unjustly treated by courts, lawyers, and vindictive custodial mothers. Testimonials to the unfairness of the entire process, some more scholarly in nature and ambition than others, are offered by the extensive and prolific father's rights network. The message is that men have lived up to their paternal responsibilities, even changed their parenting behavior, yet are unjustly treated as second-class parents. They deserve equal status with mothers and protection from the excesses historically perpetuated by the custody and control monopoly over children that courts have given to mothers.

Such anecdotal and undocumented assertions have changed the way fatherhood is approached and articulated in the rules governing custody at divorce. Fathers are increasingly seen as victims of an outmoded system of stereotypes, justifying a call for restructuring of the custodial process in the direction of conferring full equality upon fathers. Equality is best encouraged through the implementation of a "shared parenting" of children model after divorce and men are now more likely to get custody if they engage in a real contest. The real gain for fathers, however, is in their ability to maintain significant post-divorce control over day-to-day decisions regarding their children even when they do not have primary responsibility for those children and can, therefore, evade the consequences of such decisions. What happens is that fathers are given an "option": the right to intercede and require that primary caretakers consult and negotiate with them, but they are not required to participate.

In an interesting rhetorical maneuver, this restructuring on behalf of fathers is justified as being in the "best interest of the child." It is argued that extensive contact with both parents post-divorce is essential to child development. As a result, the rights of the noncustodian are aligned with the needs of the child, and thus given ascendency. The rules reflect a preference for custody not in the most nurturing parent, but the "most generous parent"—the one who is most likely to facilitate extensive contact with the other parent post-divorce. Further, generosity is accomplished and ensured by extensive monitoring and supervision of the primary caretaking parent. For many advocates of paternal equality, the new ideal can only be realized in a preference for joint custody.

Rather than justice and egalitarianism, the degendered custody rules represent a perverse affirmative action scheme in which men are excused from nurturing and caretaking norms and are permitted to continue to devote their major energy and attention to their careers and extrafamilial activities without risking adverse consequences when they decide they want to assert claims to control their children post divorce. A basic biological connection is a sufficient tie to the child in making a claim for shared custody and control rights equalizing the post-divorce relationships between both parents and their child. Nurturing is devalued, ignored, and unrewarded in such a scheme.

Of course, part of the logic behind this approach to custody is that fathers contribute in different ways to the well-being of their children. They provide economically. Some argue that men should not be penalized post divorce merely because they were the prime economic provider for their children rather than the primary caretaker or nurturer. And, the argument proceeds, the assumption of the wage earner role of necessity decreases the time and energy available for caretaking. To value the time and energy expended in caretaking in assigning post-divorce responsibility and authority would provide an inequitable windfall for the caretaker, unfairly advantaging her in the custody determination.

The basic asymmetry of this logic should be clear (though it is not apparent to those making the argument). Any system disregarding caretaking because of a desire to avoid "penalizing" the primary wage earner (equalizing his chances to gain custody and/or retain control over children) risks ignoring the penalties already suffered by the parent who has been the primary caretaker. Time and energy devoted to caretaking does in fact decrease and detract from opportunities to invest in individual market skills and participate in market activity. This argument, used by father's rights proponents to argue that it thus would be unfair to privilege caretaking, concedes the sacrifice to individual development caretaking mandates. Should our laws further deprive the caretaker, denying her the benefits of her nonmarket work by denying her custody and control over her children? We further burden the primary caretaker by forcing her in the future to negotiate, cajole, and console the noncaretaking parent because she continues to be tied to him in a shared parenting scheme after divorce?

My point is that provision of economic benefits to the family does not have the same implications and consequences in the post-divorce world as does the provision of caretaking. A caretaker may compromise or forgo altogether skill development that will add to their resumes and culminate in enhanced marketable skills and improved economic position. Economic contribution to children's welfare, by contrast, results from market activity that improves one's skills and stature in the market; this self-investment is not the equivalent of the investment in others involved in caretaking.

The investment in children in the form of caretaking has adverse effects on development of market skills. Even if a mother does work, by assuming primary responsibility for her children, she compromises her market position. There are risks associated with everyday events like illness or failures in child-care arrangements that necessitate missing work or establishing more flexible (therefore more tangential) connections with the workplace. These responsibilities are typically assigned within a family to only one parent (usually the one with the lowest wage-earning potential). And, lest the anti-essentialist rhetoric totally obscure appreciation for elementary biology, we must take into account that pregnancy and childbirth as well as breast-feeding are female functions that may temporarily affect the physical and emotional resources available for other endeavors. These are gendered factors that have serious economic implications. Nonetheless, custody debates do not explicitly address these implications and, through the imposition of the equality model, treat caretaking and economic support as equivalent sacrifices and contributions to the family.

In addition to this basic justice point, there is a social engineering argument that also should be made. Equating care and economic contribution perpetuates the very behavior that equality advocates seek to change. If, as a result of the devaluation of caretaking, men can leave the marriage relationship with the future benefits gained by their investment in themselves intact as well as realize the benefits of their wife's investment in the marital children, why should they change their behavior? They are not penalized for failing to sacrifice personal development or advancement to care for children. Through the assertion of neutrality and equality, they are free to continue the traditional male preoccupation with the workplace and marketplace, someone else's labor making it possible for them to also have children, without risking loss of control or paternal authority should divorce occur.

Justifying Paternal Irresponsibility

Why have the arguments evolved in this way? Certainly, as already argued, the power of equality ideology is central, but it is certainly not typical that policymakers and legislators adopt feminist perspectives. Less symbolic justifications also have been at work. One very effective argument for increasing the rights and control of noncustodial fathers has been that this will ensure compliance with child support orders. The fact that child support enters into the picture as an influential factor in the context of divorce is not unexpected in a society in which payment of child support is the exception and not the norm. But the nature and source of these arguments are curious. Economic irresponsibility is excused and justified by father's rights groups who argue that men's widespread failure to pay child support is attributable to the frustration and pain they experience as a result of their unjust treatment as second-class parents. Overwhelmingly male legislatures and judiciaries have accepted this argument and assumed that divorced fathers have basic goodwill and the "natural" inclination toward responsible behavior. This assumption prevails in spite of substantial statistical evidence that this is not how many divorced fathers respond.

What has been missing from policy and reform discussions thus far is a debate about the nature of fatherhood and the transformation of the role of the father in response to changing expectations, norms, and practices. How does the desire for gender neutrality and the ideal of egalitarianism play a role in the creation of a new set of norms for fatherhood? Men should be engaged in this type of rhetorical and conceptual exercise, following the consciousness-raising and conversational models of the last few decades through which women successfully transformed their roles. Much contemporary father's rights discourse, however, has concentrated almost exclusively on perceived failings of mothers and their alleged vindictiveness and irresponsibility. The strategy is successful and fathers' failures are turned back on mothers. Male foibles are cast as merely responsive or understandably defensive.

A sense of crisis for fathers has been generated concerning visitation rights, for example. The assertion of father's rights groups is that mothers typically persist in interfering with fathers' access to children. There are suggestions that in retaliation these mothers should be subject to fines and/or imprisonment or lose custody of the children. It is also alleged that mothers are at fault for misuse of child support payments. Father's rights advocates speculate that mothers use their meager and sporadic child support awards to support vile habits or indulge new lovers. These undocumented accusations receive media and legislative attention and have prompted suggestions for invasive reforms such as mandatory yearly accounting. A substantial amount of father's rights discourse characterizes mothers in negative and malicious stereotypes, arguing for monitoring, punishment, containment, and control over mothers. Such rhetoric is premised on the assumption that mothers can exercise "rights" in regard to their children only at the expense of others. Every step to benefit custodial mothers is perceived as causing potential harm to someone else, fathers in particular, but often also to those same children.

There is another strain of father's rights rhetoric, not as overtly hostile to mothers, that is associated with the historical exclusion of some men from many of society's rewards and privileges because of their race, class, or ethnicity. While this discourse does not conceptualize the problem as a loss of men's traditional privileged position in the family, it still indulges in the assumption that it is imperative to restore fathers to their mythic position as "head" of the household. In this discourse, fatherhood represents a window into the "real" or hard issues of unemployment. Fathers must have access to jobs and training programs, it is argued, in order to be fathers. Once again, here the essential nature of fatherhood is not found in caretaking, but rather in economic provision. These arguments resort to images of traditional patriarchy in an attempt to persuade the dominant culture of the need for economic justice for this class of fathers. In fact, it is considered problematic if mothers are economically independent of fathers through provision of state resources to single mothers or because the mothers earn wages themselves. Economically independent women are seen as taking over the male role. Some of the rhetoric of civil rights organizations has gone so far as to suggest that Black women, particularly as single mothers, emasculate Black men, and that women in general are incapable of raising sons. Even when sympathetic to women, the discourse is paternalistic and patriarchal.

Both strains of father's rights discourse are based on notions of traditional father right and position. Neither has any conceptual difficulty with the reactionary assertion that the welfare of children is primarily and largely dependent upon society treating men better and reining in women who have exceeded their family authority. The emerging social reality of single mother and child units is either ignored or provokes punitive measures that are justified as necessary so that men can assume their appropriate roles and actually perform as the heads of families.

Welfare and Responsibility

Many of the arguments about paternal rights and responsibility in regard to children that are made concerning custody determinations are also made in the nonmarital context. In recent years unwed fathers' claims to custody and visitation have strengthened significantly. In contrast to the patina of parental equality in the discourse concerning divorce, however, fatherhood in the welfare context is almost exclusively and most explicitly about how to enforce male economic responsibility.

Paternal responsibility, the argument goes, can be manifested either by marriage to and subsequent support of the mother of one's children (considered the preferable method) or through admission of paternity and subsequent payment of child support to the single mother-child unit. There is no prolonged discussion of the nurturing father in the welfare context. In fact the rhetoric indulges in the viability of traditional family role differentiations—the assumption is that the women can adequately take care of children only within the context of marriage, with men providing economically.

The welfare debates also contain a powerful attack on mothers. Single mothers at divorce and in the welfare context are cast as incompetent and potentially dangerous to their children and to society at large. Divorcing mothers, however, are not demonized to the same degree as are the stereotypical unwed mothers of welfare discourse. In debates concerning welfare, many commentators have explicitly condemned women who are single mothers and insisted that these women, in deviating from the ideal family form, are responsible for social ills and the poverty afflicting their children. According to this logic, it is the fundamental deviation from the norm of the traditional or marital family and not the ultimate economic deprivation that is responsible for the problems single mothers face. This is a convenient position for those who want to avoid the necessity of providing real welfare provisions and guaranteeing a minimal standard of living for children in this society.

As exemplified in 1990 by Senator Daniel Moynihan's designation of "broken" single-mother families as the source of social pathologies,[4] welfare policy reformers equate the "crisis" in the family with the disintegration of society. This view has dominated policy discussions. Moynihan astonishingly displaced the economic crises with a moral one, asserting that the dilemma in which poor families found themselves was not "fundamentally economic," but rather attributable to the "behavior" (or, more accurately, the misbehavior or irresponsibilities) of parents who reproduce outside of the institution of marriage. An even more strident example of the misplacement of responsibility for economic and social inequality on the individual is found in the work of Charles Murray, who casts "illegitimacy" as the "single most important social problem of our time—more important than crime, drugs, poverty, illiteracy, welfare or homelessness, because it drives everything else."[5] The proposed solution for these evils he argues is marriage—the provision of male economic and disciplinary responsibility and control to supplement and save the single-mother family.

The desire to ensure the dominance of marriage and the belief in the essential incompleteness and, hence, necessary complementariness of the distinct social roles of mother and father is also prevalent in the work of more liberal commentators. Political theorist Iris Marion Young astutely identified the patriarchal dimensions in the policy arguments of William Galston, an influential advisor to President Clinton. Galston has asserted that the state should not be value-neutral but rather should pursue policies that validate and strengthen traditional marriage.[6] Young admonished Galston that society's interest in the raising of good citizens can be accomplished in a variety of family forms. Galston's suggestion that the state create incentives to strengthen marriage wrongly opines that only one family form can provide a strong society. Galston makes his assertions on the basis of ambiguous and inconclusive studies that children in divorced families tend to suffer economic and psychological damage that reduces their capacity to become independent and contributing members of society.[7] As Young points out, Galston equates poverty with single-parent status (although many of the poor are married) and recommends marriage as the cure for poverty.[8] She addresses and refutes these assertions in part by pointing out that Galston ignores the fact that stable marriage means that women are often dependent on men and often suffer power inequality and various degrees of domination by men both in and outside the home.

Father or State: Family or Market?

Perhaps the most interesting features of the liberal and conservative arguments against single motherhood and for the reestablishment of a marriage-based family ethic in the welfare context is the conflation of family form with economic consequences. The likelihood of any family, traditional or not, successfully escaping poverty and raising law-abiding citizens is related to the economic, social, and community resources it has available. To refute the idea that only the traditional family provides mechanisms for avoiding poverty and other social ills, one need only examine the example of other countries where there are viable social goods provided by the state, such as health care, day care, child allowances, housing, and a guarantee of a basic income. In this country we ignore the fact that European countries that provide such guarantees, even if they have high rates of nonmarital births, have far less crime and poverty than we have in the United States. In Sweden, for example, where the typical child is born in a nonmarital family, social status and economic destiny are not overdetermined by the marital status of one's mother.

We have never had a "real" welfare state, a structure in which the collective national community ensures basic entitlements for all its members as individual citizens, independent of the form of family in which they live.

In the United States it is the "private family," not the "public state," that is primarily responsible for the dependency of children, the ill, and the elderly, eclipsing the need for consideration of collective responsibility. Ideally, this private family is assumed to operate independently of the state and of the market in fulfilling its caretaking responsibilities. This independence, however, is impossible unless the family is able to produce both economic support and caretaking labor. Typically these tasks are allocated among family members and are historically distributed along gendered lines. Men have not begun to seriously revise the fatherhood ideal in part because it still serves an important ideological and policy function for a society in which dependency is privatized.

As this last insight indicates, changing the historic division of labor within the family will necessitate recasting our societal expectations for fatherhood so that it is more than just an economic relationship with the family. It will also require transformation of the workplace and a revisioning of the role of government in ensuring family-friendly public institutions. We cannot think of important areas of activity that profoundly affect the family as differentiated, "public" spheres (market or government), with little or no responsibility for dependency.

The fact that there has been so little adjustment of market or governmental structures to facilitate and foster attempts to make the family more egalitarian is a major impediment to change. If one were interested in real reform, there are a few areas in which substantial reassessment and reevaluation might be undertaken. First and foremost, it seems necessary to consider the roles of men as husbands and fathers in an egalitarian world. In doing so, there will of course be substantial implications for the roles they now occupy within the public sphere.

Bringing men into the debate in this way will make it obvious that it is necessary to tear down the walls erected between family, state, and market and realize that all are mutually contingent. As our current policy rhetoric proceeds to construct independent spheres, we limit and confine the obligation, responsibility, operation, and authority of others. What is needed is integration. If we recognize that people have a right to work, but also recognize that workers are also family members and that we want families to be the primary location to handle dependency—care for children and others incapable of caring for themselves—it seems clear that as a society we have to develop policies directing workplaces to facilitate that caregiving.

It is naive to think that transformation in the family will not necessitate some complementary restructuring of workplace and increased participation on the part of government. Government and market in combination must remove the obstacles and burdens associated with combining caretaking and paid work that an antiquated, unrealistic model of the family in which there is a caretaker who complements the wage earner has caused.

The new workplace norm should be that of the "dually responsible" worker. The question would become, "How can we ensure the caretaker's right to work—her right to earn and not sacrifice the well-being of her children or other dependents by doing so?" The market must be transformed. If it does not do so on its own, the government must structure family-friendly policies into the workplace. This can be accomplished through regulation or through incentives offered through the tax system. The list of proposals may be long and details will be vexing, but paid family leave for all workers, flexible workweeks, and subsidized child-care facilities in which the workers are decently paid would be a minimum foundation.

The point is that in making the facilitation of nurturing and caretaking a central responsibility of the nonfamily arenas of life, we structure an equal opportunity to engage in nurturing and caretaking. Under these circumstances, men may actually be more likely to take time and energy from their market careers to invest in nurturing families. And, if they don't, at least it will be clear that they have made a free choice to forgo nurturing—a choice unfettered by institutional constraints. And they can justly be held to the consequences of that choice when it comes time to decide who has earned the custody of children or the right to demand social subsidy for caretaking work. In this way, establishment of a dually responsible norm will have the advantage of lessening the cases where women are punished in the market for caretaking responsibilities in the home.

Women's roles within families and relation to the marketplace have undergone tremendous changes over the past several decades. The expectation is that women will work in the market and continue to perform in the home and this is enforced through gender-neutral family laws and an accompanying explicit set of expectations that women are responsible for their own and their children's economic well-being either post divorce or if they do not marry.

Expectations about men have not been so transformed. In part this is because we value the economic over the nurturing. There are no corresponding sets of individually applicable rules mandating that men be responsible for nurturing to complement our expectations that women be economically sufficient. Furthermore, families bear the burdens of dependency while market institutions are free to operate as though domestic tasks that reproduce the society were some other institution's responsibility. Instead of making more and more concessions to the unequal state of affairs that has resulted from this explicit ordering of priorities, my suggestion is that we forgo attempts to coax men into caretaking and require all social institutions to assume some responsibility for the needs of caretakers.

Instead of structuring in incentives for men to act responsibly, we should worry about the double burdens that have been foisted on mothers and seek to make it possible for them to meet the conflicting demands society is extracting. This will require substantial societal reordering, but when caretakers have the means to meet the demands of those for whom they have assumed responsibility, the entire society, including our children, will benefit.

1. At the turn of the century, family law reform was also related to women's push for equality. Ironically, in attacking the rule of father custody feminists of that era privileged motherhood by casting caretaking as gendered work that is deserving of recognition in custody determinations. The success of our foremothers in displacing father right and fostering maternal preferences for young children were explicit targets of contemporary feminists seeking to enshrine a system of gender neutrality and equality primarily focused on women's participation in the public sphere.

2. It should be obvious that even in situations where both parents work, typically one assumes primary responsibility for securing, organizing, and supervising alternative care and is the one to step in if glitches or crises disrupt such arrangements.

3. *Linda R. v. Richard E.*, 162 A.D.2d 48, 561 N.Y.S.2d 29 (1990).

4. 136 Congressional Record S14416-11417 (daily ed. October 3, 1990).

5. Charles Murray, "The Coming White Underclass," *Wall Street Journal* (29 October 1993), A14.

6. Iris Marion Young, critiquing Galston's *Liberal Purposes* in "Mothers, Citizenship and Independence: A Critique of Pure Family Values," *Ethics* (1995).

7. Ibid., 280.

8. Ibid., 285.

Lisa C. Ikemoto

Lessons from the *Titanic*:
Start with the People in Steerage, Women and Children First

I. Introduction

The purportedly unsinkable *Titanic* departed on its first voyage with 1,320 passengers, 907 crew members, and only 20 lifeboats. The ship sank in the early hours of April 15, 1912, leaving only 705 survivors and becoming a well-known metaphor for disaster.[1] Many have lauded the gallantry of the male passengers and crew who used a "women and children first" policy when loading the lifeboats. Some have made unwarranted attacks on the men in steerage for being less gallant than the men from the upper decks.[2] A few have noted the higher death rate among passengers in steerage compared to that for passengers in first and second class, suggesting that class may have asserted its privileges when it came to allocating lifeboats.[3]

It may not have been only class privilege operating. Those on the upper decks sailed as vacationers, on a ship advertised to be a home away from home for those who lived in luxury. Most of those in steerage were immigrating from Europe.[4] When they boarded the ship, in a sense, they became foreigners relative to the other passengers and foreigners by virtue of their destination. They were bound for the United States where nativism was then and is again at high tide, on a ship that, despite its end, carried all the ingredients for current law and policy.

In the next section, Part II, I look at motherhood and the social contract, two normative frameworks deployed in national policy discourse to assign and limit responsibilities in the relationship between the individual and society. I sketch a shift in emphasis from valuing liberty to valuing responsibility, and the resulting shift in priorities from equality concerns to citizen obligations. I argue that the result is a notion of Americanism that operates by racist and nativist citizen-typing, as expressed in recent national law and policy on poverty and immigration.

Through consideration of what I call living-room political discourse, I trace how the dominant images of the immigrant shifted during the period of re-formation, and the resulting emergence of the immigrant mother and immigrant family as significant figures in mainstream print media. I then return to the story of the *Titanic* to suggest what might follow from current law and policy.

II. Immigrants and the Ship of State

The recent welfare and immigration law revisions have placed immigrants, particularly poor immigrants of color, in the crosshairs of Republican-led national policy "reform." One of the most effective moves that conservatives have made has been to link immigration and welfare. Anti-immigration forces have at different times used racist notions of nativism to justify restrictions on immigration from particular regions or countries. Antiwelfare forces have consistently used racist notions of citizenship to justify laws reducing assistance and privacy for those with low incomes. The immigration–welfare linkage has put noncitizen immigrants of color and welfare recipients of color on the same target. The archetype being raised again to embody that link is that of the immigrant mother—a type highly visible in 1912.

According to those who forged the link, the ship that is our nation is about to sink under the economic and social burdens that past liberality has created. What they say sounds like free-market individualism with some behavioral psychology thrown in. Conservative analysts' claims—that welfare undermines individual initiative and personal responsibility by creating disincentive to work—frame the problem as one of failed choice. By marking a failed work ethic as the cause of so many social problems, conservatives justify the use of coercive tactics, such as "workfare," as means necessary to change harmful behavior.[5] At the same time, the continuing use of racial and marital status to distinguish between deserving and undeserving poor in welfare law and discourse indicates that welfare and immigration reform are more about social control than social change.

The linkage has made the immigrant mother prominent as a type, and has had at least two normative effects. First, it has refigured the immigrant from man to mother; and second, it has shifted the understood role of non-white immigrants from that of inexpensive shadow workforce to an obvious and self-perpetuating presence. The second shift has occurred, in large part, because the immigrant mother figure serves to make the immigrant family obvious. The immigrant family as a sign of stability, permanence, and population growth has made nativist fears about the changing racial identity of the nation concrete.

The material effects of welfare and immigration reform are hitting immigrants very hard. The Personal Responsibility and Work Opportunity Reconciliation Act of 1996 disproportionately affects immigrants. Before "welfare reform," noncitizen immigrants constituted 5 percent of welfare recipients. The 1996 "welfare reform" law made 40 percent of its cuts from benefits for this group. While Congress, in August 1997, reversed one of the harshest aspects of the welfare reform by restoring Supplemental Security Income for some elderly and disabled legal noncitizen immigrants, immigrants still take the heaviest blow. Immigrants who have the least access to opportunity, financial stability, and the American version of independence will experience the greatest deprivations. In simplistic terms, since employers use gender, race, ethnicity, and immigration status to structure the labor sectors, and since welfare reform is part of a larger economic restructuring that has a disproportionately negative impact on women, women of color, and immigrant women of color in increasing measures, immigrant Latinas and Asian women are among those who are taking the heaviest blows.

By virtue of their gender, race, immigration status, economic status, and citizenship status, poor noncitizen immigrant women, largely from Latin American and Asian countries, are being assigned much of the blame for sinking the ship. The policies implemented by recent reforms sound like a satirical lyric about the *Titanic*: Start with the people in steerage, women and children first, then throw them into the sea, to save the ship for the rest. What conservatives are in fact implementing is uncannily like a badly learned lesson from the *Titanic*.

III. The Frameworks of "Responsibility"

Conservative critics of the welfare system have used the image of the "welfare mother" to illustrate problems with welfare—problems they describe and offer as reasons for substantially changing the premises, requirements, and the amount of government assistance provided to poor people. The welfare–immigration linkage has added the figure of the immigrant mother to arguments for reducing public assistance and restricting immigration. Recent policy reform debates place these troubling mother figures at the center of a constellation of social problems to call for the re-formation of the relationship between the state and its residents.

Motherhood

The mother, in a wide variety of race- and class-specific forms, has served as a cultural reference point or framework for particular sets of norms. These norms operate on three overlapping levels. At each level, patriarchy, white supremacy, white nativism, and middle-class privilege interlock into a matrix of standards and presumptions that appear to be part of the "natural order." This matrix most directly affects women's lives, but also reflects social patterns and ways of knowing, and the tensions among the patterns and ways, that implicate each of us.

At one level, there are norms that operate directly on women by expressing assumptions, expectations, and standards for women who are pregnant or who have children. Motherhood at this level is about mothering. Biological essentialism has shaped those assumptions, expectations, and standards. For example, the claims that women are inherently more nurturing, selfless, and intuitive are based directly or indirectly on the fact that women have the biological capacity to bear children. Racism and class bias also mediate the assumptions, expectations, and standards set for pregnant women and women with children. Ways of thinking structured by white supremacy and middle-class privilege have created negative presumptions about the parenting abilities of poor women, especially poor women of color.

At a second level, there are a set of norms that operate on women (and men) with respect to the roles, priorities, behavior, appearance, and responsibilities they assume or are given in society. The first set of norms addresses a woman's responsibilities to her family, even while these norms provide a basis for social pressure and government intervention into the family. This second set of norms addresses woman's place in society, and operates in part by predicating normal womanhood on mothering. Many have commented on how motherhood, as a collection of norms and images, serves as a means of social control that is patriarchal, racist, and classist in nature.[6] For example, explanations given for infertility among middle-class couples speak of career women and delayed motherhood in subtly critical terms. These accounts offer "lessons" that indirectly support early childbearing, discourage women from choosing careers over childbearing, and identify white middle-class women as those who should, for the sake of society, be mothers. On the other hand, stories about welfare mothers with too many children have put many women of color in the position of having to defend the decision to have children. Racial stereotypes make mothering by women of color seem naturally and socially undesirable.

At a third level, motherhood serves as a social repository for values and norms deemed core to a moral culture that is, in turn, cast as uniquely "American" and the basis for claims to moral superiority in the international arena. The American flag, Mom, and apple pie fit together in our iconography because they represent the (male) soldier's longing for home and the America for which he fights. In part, motherhood is represented as an artifact of American culture that proves its superiority. The American mother as a type is understood to be different from mothers in other societies. What she produces—American citizens and American moral culture—are claimed to express the values of individualism, equality, and independence that support the moral high ground the U.S. claims.

This use of motherhood is part of a prevailing metaphor that portrays the nation as family. This metaphor can be used to express various longings—from unity, tolerance, and inclusion to uniformity and closed ranks. What is interesting is that this metaphor does not describe the nation as mother. Patriarchal figures remain dominant in this notion of family—the "father" of our country, our "founding fathers." At the same time, many of the values and virtues attributed to the national culture are represented as feminine figures—justice and liberty. What is becoming clear in welfare and immigration policy is that the private/public distinction has an effect on national policy that is similar to its effect on domestic life and policy. The feminine values and protections are reserved for those recognized as "family." A power-based logic governs relations between the "family" and others. The nation as family must protect itself against those who would subvert that which bonds the "family."

Personal Responsibility

In political theory terms, that which bonds the nation is the social contract. Both Democrats and Republicans have tapped into this metaphor in recent years. As a presidential candidate, Clinton invoked communitarian rhetoric to describe the relationship between individual and state. Republicans introduced the Contract with America when they took control of Congress in 1994. Clinton's use of communitarian rhetoric intimated and the Republicans' Contract with America proclaimed a new agenda for U.S. government. Both Democrats and Republicans have used the familiar theme of individual liberty, but the prevailing message has been that of personal responsibility. Just as the recently enacted welfare "reform" law is entitled the "Personal Responsibility and Work Opportunity Act of 1996," the new immigration law is entitled the "Illegal Immigration Reform and Immigrant Responsibility Act of 1996." Both describe a notion of personal responsibility that emphasizes the individual's side of the contract as it has not been emphasized in peacetime before.

The message seems to be that asking what one can do for one's country is no longer sufficient; one must do what one's country asks. Not that the new agenda is for servitude, but it does assume that authoritarian measures are necessary for those defying the social compact. Thus, Democrats and Republicans pushed for workfare by characterizing the failure of poor women with children to work their way out of welfare as a failure necessitating the use of state sanctions.[7] The immigration "reform" law's expressly punitive measures are explained as necessary to deter those who come here "illegally" solely to exploit government benefits. The prevalence of racial stereotypes in the welfare reform campaign shows that, in large part, the failure being sanctioned was that of being poor, female, and Black or Latina, or, that being poor, female, and Black or Latina was equated with being unwilling to work. Immigration law echoes this conclusion.

The new emphasis on the individual's side of the social contract has shifted the focus of the individual–state relationship from liberty to citizenship. Citizenship, in this context, is mostly about the expectations expressed and the judgments made about a person's or a group's contributions to society. Any focus on legal citizenship is a by-product of social citizenship. So the shift in focus is from the state's obligation to the individual to the individual's obligation to the state and society. When the focus is on the state's obligation to the individual, equality is an important standard for measuring the state's use of power. But when the focus is on the individual's obligation, the measure drawn is between those deserving and those undeserving of the state's benefits.

Citizen-Types

The focus on citizenship may have opened the door for the immigration–welfare linkage or vice versa, but their synchrony could not have been a coincidence. The racism used to call for welfare reform and the racism used to justify immigration restrictions are both about being undeserving. Once the immigration–welfare linkage was made, that linkage became a line used to distinguish between those deserving and those undeserving of welfare.

What has emerged, implicitly, is the notion of citizen-types which are ranked as more or less desirable, based on how deserving they are perceived to be. The emerging citizen-types do not necessarily redraw the lines of race, gender, class, and nativism that form familiar stereotypes, although the lines drawn by white nativism have become more prominent in recent years. Citizen-type are stereotypes—types that express two messages. The first is that the state's obligations have been redefined and are now contingent on reciprocity. The second is about who should be precluded from receiving state benefits, and who may not be entitled to the state's protections.

The state's side of the contract, then, is owed to those who contribute to society's economic and moral well-being. The standards for measuring those contributions are largely set by marital status and immigration status. Both the marital family and legal resident status have been accepted prerequisites for many state-conferred benefits.[8] Neither the labor market nor the welfare system adequately accommodates women with children in defining work. Joan Williams has shown that the ability of women with children to do work recognized as contributing is largely predicated on middle-class status and the accompanying ability to pay others to perform domestic work, and on the presence of a female, largely immigrant, population to perform the domestic work.[9] Poor women, especially single mothers of color and immigrant mothers, are by these measures unable to contribute to society.

The prevailing assumption undergirding the emphasis on personal responsibility is that individual will and behavior govern the individual's side of the contract. Within this view, the fact that employment and marriage rates differ along race, immigration, and class lines results from differences in choice and behavior. That is, those choices might evidence a culture of poverty, an unwillingness to work, a weakness in family commitment that is particular to certain racial, immigrant, and class groups. But employment and marital status do not, given the prevailing assumption, reflect the fact that racism, nativism, class bias, and patriarchy might structure the labor market and the desirability of marriage.

The failure, then, to "take responsibility," to fulfull one's side of the contract, is a breach that identifies one as undeserving. The patriarchy inherent in motherhood, the race/class subordination that mediates motherhood at all levels, and the racist nature of nativism has determined that women of color are most likely to be found undeserving of state benefits and to be labelled undeserving citizen-types.

IV. Immigrant + Mother in Living-Room Politics

In the mainstream media's articulation of the welfare–immigration linkage, adding "mother" to immigrant signals significant shifts in the welfare and immigration debates. I trace these shifts by comparing the gendered images of immigrants before and during the immigration–welfare linkage. While the immigrant mother is largely derived from preexisting archetypes, the immigration–welfare linkage has reshaped both immigration and welfare in public discussion. According to anti-immigration/antiwelfare forces, the welfare state has become a safe harbor for the alien nation, resulting in the feminization of immigration. Accordingly, the representative of the immigrant problem has shifted from that of immigrant worker to immigrant mother.

The words and pictures that the media presents do not stand on their own. We each participate in the formation of these types by reading our own assumptions into the words in ways that confirm, enhance, question, resist, or even counteract their persuasive power. Critical readers bring a split focus, so to speak, to this analysis. We use our own mainstreamed consciousness to see the "normal," accepting readings of the images. At the same time, we take a critical stance to identify the normative, standard-setting messages contained in the depictions, and, hopefully, to counteract them.

Before the Immigration–Welfare Linkage:
Immigrant Women as Substitute Mothers

Before the immigration–welfare linkage was made in full, the newspaper articles addressing the immigration debate consistently used the now familiar distinction between "legal" and "illegal," or more accurately "documented" and "undocumented" immigrants. Most of the stories focused on Latina(o)s. A few mentioned Asian immigrants. Fewer still commented on immigrants from the former Soviet Union, Canada, or Ireland. Those calling for immigration restrictions have proposed (and largely implemented) a wide variety of mechanisms—stronger border patrol, speedy deportation process, increased criminal penalties, greater employer penalties, educational and financial criteria, higher sponsorship requirements, smaller quotas for legal immigration, and so forth. Clearly, some of these proposals are aimed solely at immigration by those who enter the country without official U.S. government approval, and other proposals are aimed solely at reducing the number of documented immigrants. But the ultimate message sent about these laws has been one that equates the need for regulation with immigration from Latin America and Asia, and with Latinos, in particular, as a group.

Typically the prelinkage articles focused on immigrants as workers, and in particular on the problem of "illegal" immigrant workers. Karen Hossfeld, Mary Romero, and others have shown how race, ethnicity, gender, and immigration status structure the labor markets in which immigrant women are typically employed.[10] In fact working-class immigrant women who are Latina and Asian are often employed in the same labor sectors, although race and ethnicity are often used to stratify the women.[11] Domestic work, high-tech assembly, and the garment industry are three of the major labor sectors for these women. Yet, newspaper accounts seem to rest on the premise that immigrant women are somehow drawn to certain labor sectors or that the hiring of immigrant women in specific employment areas simply results from a coincidence of supply and need.

What I find particularly interesting is that in the prelinkage newspaper accounts of undocumented immigrants, immigrant men are sometimes described as fathers, but stories describing immigrant women in family roles do so only to describe their work outside their homes. Accounts of both immigrant men and immigrant women describe them as workers first, family members incidentally. Stories that purport to explain why men immigrate without required documents often describe the practice of remitting wages to families in the country of origin. So while immigrant men may be motivated by concern for family, they function as workers while on U.S. soil. Many of the stories that place women immigrants in family roles are stories about women who work as domestics. In the context of these stories, the women who work as nannies and maids become substitute mothers to the children placed in their care and pseudo-sisters and mothers to their employers. This transformation occurs in the descriptions given by employers and journalists. The stories do not mention the genuine (as opposed to attributed) family relationships, obligations, and needs of the women.[12]

Creating the Immigration–Welfare Linkage: Emergence of the Immigrant Mother

The period from 1993 to the present is the period in which conservatives made the immigration–welfare linkage. This period includes the 1994 election in which Republicans took control of Congress and announced the Contract with America as the new agenda for government, the 1994 California elections that resulted in a majority vote for the anti-immigrant ballot initiative, Proposition 187, the 1996 enactment of federal welfare "reform," and the initial efforts to implement the Personal Responsibility Act at the state and local levels.

During this period, newspaper stories that describe immigrant women as mothers, not substitute mothers, have become as common as articles that describe immigrant men as fathers. However, the types of stories about immigrant mothers and immigrant fathers differ. Certainly, the articles continue to deploy the legal/illegal dichotomy, but that line cuts differently across "immigrant mothers" than it has across "immigrant workers." With respect to "immigrant workers," anti-immigration proponents primarily use nativistic arguments about the economy and fairness to American workers and taxpayers. The addition of the "illegal, immigrant welfare mother" by anti-immigration proponents has enabled them to argue that immigration poses the threat of a permanent and expanding moral and cultural underclass.

Most of the newspaper articles that describe immigrant men as fathers during this period fall into three groups: (1) stories that profile a person in a way that makes that person's immigrant father part of background biographical information; (2) stories about how immigrant fathers are coping with their struggles; and (3) immigrant success stories. A relatively small number of stories addressed immigration restrictions and/or welfare restrictions. While the overall tenor of articles describing immigrant men as fathers is positive, the stories do not identify or establish "immigrant father" as a type or a label that carries much attached meaning.

The news articles about "immigrant mothers" and immigrants identified as women with children as stories fall into five groups: (1) stories about recent or proposed changes in welfare law; (2) stories about recent or proposed immigration restrictions; (3) stories about social problems identified with immigrant mothers; (4) stories in which an immigrant mother is part of the subject's biographical information; and (5) stories about how immigrant mothers are coping with their struggles. In the first three groups of articles, the immigrant mother figure is almost always a negative one, or is strongly associated with a problem. In the last two groups, the immigrant mother figure is not directly identified as a problem, but is described using narratives that reinforce assumptions stated in the immigrant mother as problem stories. The vast majority of the articles fall into the first two groups—stories about changes in welfare law and stories about changes in immigration law. These stories do express and establish that "immigrant mother" is a type, a label that has already acquired multiple attached meanings.

The starting point for this type is the layering of the welfare mother image on the immigrant image. The layering occurs first in the articles recounting the debates over immigration and welfare restrictions. Explanations borrowed from long-standing welfare debates appear as the argument that immigrants from Mexico, Central America, and Asia come to collect benefits from the U.S. government, just as citizen welfare mothers stay home (and unemployed) to collect benefits. In the prelinkage stories, the most prevalent claim was that immigrants came to take jobs from U.S. citizens. During recent years, the claim about taking jobs remains tacitly in place with respect to immigrant men. But the welfare linkage has made women's attributed motives more complex and more clearly related to motherhood. According to the (conservative) claims, immigrant women come to collect undeserved benefits for themselves and for their children. They may work outside the home, but like the standard welfare mother, they do so under the table. While the standard welfare mother fails to report earned income to prevent the loss of government assistance and therefore "double dip," the immigrant welfare mother fails to report earned income because she is undocumented. This does not make the immigrant mother less culpable than the standard welfare mother. According to the claims, the activities of both types of welfare mothers are "illegal." But it is the immigrant woman who is expressly labeled as such.

The immigrant mother figure is not wholly composed of preexisting parts. The stereotype sets up presumptions that are particular to immigrant motherhood. Normatively, mothers are assigned responsibility for inculcating their children with appropriate cultural and moral values. Anti-immigrant proponents during each period of extreme nativism have claimed that immigrant women from marginalized ethnic and racial groups are culturally or innately incapable of shaping their children into productive American citizens. During the mid-1990s, even the most positive groups of articles—those that identify the subject's mother as an immigrant and those about immigrant mothers coping with their struggles—suggest these claims. Most of the articles that identify a subject's mother as an immigrant are profiles of a successful or powerful person. Typically, the profile describes the subject as having achieved success *despite* the fact that his mother was an immigrant. The articles about immigrant mothers overcoming obstacles usually imply that if she succeeds, she will be atypical, and she will achieve success in spite of herself.

The standard welfare mother stereotype may say that welfare mothers are an obstacle to their children becoming productive adults, but immigrant mothers are obstacles to Americanness. The message is that neither immigrant mothers nor their children will ever fit into the national identity. The message does not reflect a shift away from the stated ideal of America as melting pot; the message, in fact, reinforces that ideal. However, the message may be that some immigrants will always be foreign. Efforts to legislate this message have reinforced the permanent foreigner presumption. In a follow-up to Proposition 187, anti-immigrant proponents tried to qualify a California ballot initiative that would deny birthright citizenship to U.S.-born children whose parents had immigrated without government authorization. The initiative failed to garner sufficient signatures to qualify for the 1996 ballot in California. Congress debated a similar Republican-sponsored bill in June 1997. That bill stalled, but the message has been sent.

In the third set of articles, immigrant mothers are simply lumped together with other representations of issues that have achieved the status of social problem. For example, during 1996 and 1997, the media provided extensive coverage of suspected maternal infanticide and baby abandonment cases.[13] Newspaper stories about these cases often describe infanticide and baby abandonment as an emerging problem linked to teenage pregnancy, "illegal" immigrants, and welfare.[14] In part, the lumping of problems reflects the linkage made between immigration and welfare. But the accumulation of "bad mother" types and their cumulative use indicates something more, perhaps a heightened intensity in the demonization of poor women of color. At the same time, the ease with which authorities invoke these images speaks of their persuasiveness. The complete failure of the media and law enforcement to look for explanations beyond the types, to ask what kind of desperation might motivate an infanticide, shows how powerful those stereotypes have become. These identities have become the unholy trinity of mother-hood.

Archetypes serve multiple purposes. Negative archetypes or stereotypes often place blame for particular problems on the labelled group. They also signal particular anxieties. The targeting of immigrants of color whose first language is not English speaks of racist, nativist anxieties. As mentioned, motherhood often serves as a repository for values and norms deemed uniquely "American." In contrast, all that is threatening to national identity and social stability has been attributed to the immigrant mother, and in particular to her foreignness, her poverty, her race, and her reproductive capacity.

Compare how the type of the immigrant worker is used. The operative assumption is that the United States' position as a "first world" nation has been secured by its white, English-speaking so-called native stock. In that light, the complaints about the harmful influx of immigrant workers expresses, on the one hand, anxiety about the accuracy of the assumption, and on the other hand, anxiety about the United States' ability to compete. Both anxieties are normatively masculine. They speak to public sphere concerns and they are about competition. The immigrant mother, by comparison, expresses domestically located anxieties about our ship of state. Patriarchy, in other words, segregates and ranks the concerns signalled by the immigrant mother and immigrant worker types.

Those anxieties are having a real effect on the lives of immigrant women. Take, for example, former California governor Pete Wilson's efforts to eliminate subsidized prenatal care for undocumented immigrant women. While Governor Wilson targeted all benefits to undocumented immigrants, the focus was on prenatal services. In other words, the focus has been on immigrant women who are pregnant.

Wilson made his first attempt to cut prenatal care as one of his first and most public responses to the majority vote in favor of anti-immigrant initiative, Proposition 187, in the 1994 state election. A federal district court declared much of Proposition 187 invalid, and with that decision went Wilson's initial efforts to cut prenatal care. In 1996, Congress enacted the Personal Responsibility Act, also known as "welfare reform." The "welfare reform," as mentioned above, derives most of its so-called welfare savings by eliminating benefits for documented noncitizen immigrants. The "welfare reform" eliminates virtually all social and health benefits for undocumented immigrants, and makes substantial cuts in benefits for noncitizen-documented immigrants. In effect and not coincidentally, the "welfare reform" law implements many of the provisions declared invalid in the Proposition 187 litigation.[15]

The welfare law at issue provides that state and local governments can continue most forms of government assistance to undocumented immigrants if the state enacts law that specifically authorizes such assistance. When President Clinton signed the "welfare reform" law, Wilson proposed emergency regulations that directed all state departments to prepare means of barring assistance, including prenatal services, to undocumented immigrants. In August 1997 the state legislature passed a budget that authorized limited funding for benefits, including prenatal care, to undocumented immigrants, and Wilson vetoed those plans. In September 1997 a federal court held that Wilson could use the welfare law to make undocumented immigrants ineligible for state-assisted prenatal care.

Wilson has acknowledged the efficacy of prenatal care, but argued that such aid acts as incentive for immigration. Eliminating incentives has been the main argument in favor of all efforts to enact restrictive welfare and immigration laws. But why target pregnant immigrant women? Pregnancy arguably makes the immigrant woman's position more sympathetic. On the other hand, the fact that she is pregnant makes her reproductive capacity obvious and inevitable. In addition, the pregnant immigrant woman and the immigrant mother make family visible. She is not only a worker. She has children, and often, a spouse. Sometimes, she has extended family as well. Family typically represents permanence and settlement. The "illegal immigrant," drawn largely in racial terms, as a permanent and reproducing presence in the United States, threatens the stability of the existing racial order. The immigration–welfare linkage has deemed the immigrant mother to be both representation and agent of this threat.

V. Start with the People in Steerage

The "welfare reform" and recently enacted immigration restrictions contain some interesting contradictions. Despite the rhetorical line drawn between "legal" and "illegal" immigrants, "welfare reform" diminished the significance of that line and underscored the distinction between citizen and noncitizen. In immigration law, the legal/illegal distinction remains significant for purposes of determining who should leave. But one of the most significant new directions in immigration law does not rest on that distinction. It is aimed at families.

Citizen/Noncitizen

As mentioned above, Congress made 40 percent of the cuts in "welfare reform" from assistance given to noncitizen immigrants. Undocumented immigrants received a very small percentage of government assistance before August 1996. As a result of 1996 changes, states have the authority to ban undocumented immigrants from virtually all but emergency services. This ban extends even to those in temporary legal status. So while little of the welfare savings comes from cuts in benefits to undocumented immigrants, for low-income undocumented immigrants the harm is significant.

Most of the cuts came from assistance to documented immigrants. For example, noncitizen immigrants no longer receive federally subsidized food stamps. Congress recently restored Supplemental Security Income (SSI) to low-income blind, elderly, and disabled documented immigrants, but that "fix" contains serious limitations. Only those who were in the U.S. as of August 22, 1996, may ever qualify for SSI. Even though documented noncitizen immigrants contribute toward SSI, those in the U.S. as of August 22, 1996, who qualify for SSI in the future may only do so based on blindness or disability, and not age, as citizens can.[16] In effect, the "legals" have been treated as "illegals."

The relocation of the line from legal/illegal to citizen/noncitizen may in part illustrate the point that the immigrant figure has become so perniciously negative that all immigrants are perceived as "illegal." Or to take it a step further, normatively, immigrants are illegal. The elimination of most benefits for documented immigrants may also follow from the re-formation of the relationship between individual and state and the requirement of reciprocity. But the issue is not whether noncitizen immigrants are deserving or undeserving. The decision seems to be made that noncitizens cannot even enter the social contract.

Protecting "Our Own People"

Recent immigration restrictions seemed to be aimed either at undocumented immigrants or at immigrant families, whether members are documented or not. Supporters of both types of restrictions speak, in various ways, of protecting "our own people."

The primary justification for targeting undocumented immigrants is that they "steal" jobs and benefits from "our own people." The criminalization of immigrant status that this justification suggests is not coincidence. The penalties are measured in years. For example, a 1996 law bars immigrants who lived in the United States for six months without government authorization from reentering the country for three years. If they lived here for twelve months without authorization, the law bars them from reentering for ten years. For many who have established homes, families, jobs, and community ties here, the law has many of the effects of a penal sentence.

The possible expiration of 245(i) of the Immigration and Nationality Act has created the potential for exacerbating the potential penalties that immigrants face. This law, enacted three years ago, has allowed immigrants with pending green card applications to pay a $1,000 fine and remain in the United States while finishing the paperwork necessary to gain "legal" status. The provision initially expired in September 1997, but Congress issued a short-term extension until proposals for a permanent extension could be considered. Those calling for the end of 245(i) have argued, "We're supposed to be caring for the citizens of the United States and people who have come here legally."[17] The arguments restate the premises of the re-formation— that liberty and justice, the feminine virtues, are limited to family members only. Supporters of the extension, on the other hand, invoke the now older notion of social contract that emphasizes the state's obligation to the individual and the accompanying presumption that individual contributions will follow. As one official stated, "To me, it is atrocious to separate a healthy, loving, law-abiding, self-sufficient couple who have realized their American dream."[18]

Other recently enacted immigration restrictions aim more directly at family unity. The 1996 immigration law, for the first time, requires that U.S. residents who sponsor new immigrants meet specific financial requirements. Generally, sponsors must have household incomes at least 25 percent above the federal poverty level. Sponsors will be legally and financially liable for an immigrant until the immigrant becomes a U.S. citizen or until the immigrant has paid taxes for ten years. This would substantially reduce the number of sponsors and hence employer- and family-sponsored immigrants. This type of legislation, along with legislation like the bars on reentry, operates without regard for family ties. The pending sponsorship requirements would prevent low-income documented immigrants from having spouses, children, parents, and other loved ones join them in the United States. Supporters of these restrictions use the same logic that supports the targeting of immigrants in "welfare reform"—these cuts reduce incentives to immigrate. And like the restrictions contained in the "welfare reform," the recent immigration restrictions express the same unease about the effect of family immigration on the color of national identity.

Public Servants

We generally think of family as the basis and framework for our private lives. The immigration–welfare linkage expresses different expectations for noncitizen immigrants, particularly those with low incomes. Feminists have criticized the public/private distinction as a means of protecting patriarchy within the family and home and as a means of sheltering harms such as domestic violence. Others, including feminists, have pointed to the private sphere as a source of rights, a buffer against state interference. I want to use the standard public/private line as a point of comparison to show how differently the lines of protection are drawn for noncitizens.

Martha Fineman has noted that "[o]ccupying either the category of poverty or that of single motherhood places women (along with their children) into the realm of 'public' families."[19] Welfare law provides services that families usually provide—assistance for food, shelter, and health care. It is a public law that serves personal needs. But it is administered in a way that removes privacy from the recipient's life by extracting compliance and imposing judgment on decisions most middle-class families consider to be personal. In contrast, immigration law in the past seemed anomalous. It is public sphere law, governing entry and legal status in the U.S., yet it provided for (relatively) easy family reunification. That is, it contained (relatively) extensive means of enhancing and protecting the basis of private life, the family. The recent immigration restrictions have narrowed protections for family life. The low-income noncitizen immigrant is now clearly in the public/public world described by Aida Hurtado, social identity and feminist theory scholar.

The material effects of this shift may be substantial for some. State surveillance of noncitizen immigrants has increased. Since the state and federal laws now bar even documented immigrants from so many government services, the state and federal governments must do a lot more gatekeeping. The fact that the immigrant mother type has made immigrant women and immigrant families visible means that those who apparently fit the type will (and do) trigger surveillance, both by the state and by the citizen public.[20]

The secondary effects of shifting the expected place of family in the lives of immigrants flow from the stated goal of reducing incentives to immigrate. As noted, if prior laws did provide incentives to immigrate, they did so with families, and it seems to be families that anti-immigration proponents are targeting. Recent proposals support my conclusion that families and the private sphere of immigrants are the targets. Current bills would further shift the focus away from family reunification and toward attracting skilled workers. If combined with heightened sponsorship requirements, the result might be a primarily means-tested, class-based immigration. The emerging message is that noncitizens owe their first duty to the state, not to their families, and immigration is for the nation, not the immigrant.

VI. A Night to Remember[21]

In 1912 a New York minister characterized the losses aboard the *Titanic* in these terms: "There were men lost that the city and the country needed, and there are widows surviving who speak no language that you or I can understand, and who will inevitably become public charges."[22] Newspaper accounts stated the same conclusions. "While the lowly immigrants and their offspring were being borne to safety, Americans and Englishmen of fame and wealth . . . from the deck of the *Titanic* watched the last lifeboat disappear, and went to heroes' graves marked by the depthless sea."[23]

Today we are hearing echoes of the many messages contained in these few words—the distinction between deserving, American (men) and the "lowly" immigrant (mothers), the equation of wealth and whiteness on the one side and deserved privilege and national interest on the other, the equation of cultural difference and foreign birth on the one side and societal burden on the other, and the use of the immigrant mother as the reference point for these messages.

The particulars of the welfare–immigration linkage may be recent, but clearly the use of the immigrant mother figure to synchronize the ideologies framed as motherhood with standards for citizenship molded on a white nativist vision of America is well established. The objectives have not changed all that much either. Five days after the *Titanic* sank, the U.S. Senate passed a bill that would have required a literacy test for all new immigrants.[24] Senator William Dillingham supported the legislation by distinguishing between the "old" immigrants from northern and western Europe and the "new" immigrants from southern and eastern Europe. Others who supported the bill expressly denied having any race-based motivations, even while explaining that a literacy test would exclude immigrants who were "the least intelligent, the least capable of being manufactured into good American citizens, the most dangerous as a new and unassimilated element in our body politic."[25]

Those who supported the Personal Responsibility and Work Opportunity Act of 1996 and the Illegal Immigration Reform and Immigrant Responsibility Act of 1996 may claim that economic common sense and neutral moral standards guided their votes. But the persistent use of the immigrant mother figure and the disproportionate material effects of these laws belie that claim.

The welfare "savings" made by cuts in benefits to low-income immigrants too often translates directly into financial deprivation, hunger, illness, and homelessness. The immigrant mother figure was used to call for these "savings." Immigrant women and their families are, in a sense, paying for these savings with their well-being and their privacy. For immigrant women the effects of being perceived as a type are real. For those who live in poverty the struggle has been made harder. The "reforms" have further limited access to food, shelter, and even basic health care. The so-called welfare savings means fewer social, educational, income, and wealth opportunities for low-income immigrants. This will, in turn, make them more vulnerable to the traps of labor sectors premised on the assumption that female, foreign, and Latina or Asian are justifications for failing to pay a livable wage. The risk of becoming part of a permanent underclass and a source of "cheap" labor has increased for low-income immigrants, and women in particular. At the same time, the change in immigration policy from promoting family unity to means-testing makes the class status of the desired citizen type concrete. The prediction of higher impact on immigration from certain Latin American and Asian countries makes the nonwhiteness of the undesirable citizen types obvious.

Making the normative and material effects of social and legal policy visible is a small part of the work needed to support immigrant women and others who are currently being pushed away. The alliances necessary to respond to the exclusions that the welfare–immigration linkage have created are difficult to form and even harder to maintain. Some of this work has been done by advocates for welfare rights, immigrant rights, labor, and women's rights. Analyses that challenge the individualist logic of current law and policy do and will continue to reveal points of coalition and possible strategies for further resistance and a new re-formation.

1. John P. Eaton and Charles A. Haas, *Titanic: Destination Disaster, The Legends and the Reality* (New York: W. W. Norton, 1996), 24.

2. Steven Biel, *Down with the Old Canoe: A Cultural History of the Titanic Disaster* (New York: W. W. Norton, 1996), 23–27.

3. Ibid., 38.

4. Eaton and Haas, *Titanic: Destination Disaster*, 78.

5. I am focusing on the period immediately preceding and following the "welfare reform" of 1996, but Nancy A. Naples has argued that a revised "social contract" emerged in the 1987–1988 U.S. Congressional Hearings on Welfare Reform which privileged individualist and coercive behavioralist strategies. Nancy A. Naples, "The 'New Consensus' on the Gendered 'Social Contract.'" The 1987–88 U.S. Congressional Hearings on Welfare Reform. *Signs* 22 (1997): 908–909.

6. Patricia Hill Collins, *Black Feminist Thought* (New York: Routledge, 1990), 67–90; Carol Sanger, "M Is for the Many Things," *Southern California Review of Law and Women's Studies* 1 (1992): 15–67; Lisa Ikemoto, "The Code of Perfect Pregnancy: At the Intersection of the Ideology of Motherhood, the Practice of Defaulting to Science, and the Interventionist Mindset of Law," *Ohio State Law Journal* 53 (1992): 1206–1306; Dorothy Roberts, "Racism and Patriarchy in the Meaning of Motherhood," *American University Journal of Gender and the Law* 1 (1993): 1–38.

7. Naples, "The 'New Consensus' on the Gendered 'Social Contract,'" 909.

8. Martha Fineman, *The Neutered Mother, The Sexual Family and Other Twentieth Century Tragedies* (New York: Routledge, 1995), 189; Mimi Abramovitz, *Regulating the Lives of Women* (Boston: South End Press, 1988), 2.

9. Joan C. Williams, "Restructuring Work and Family Entitlements Around Family Values," *Harvard Journal of Law and Public Policy* 19 (1996): 753.

10. Karen J. Hossfeld, "Hiring Immigrant Women: Silicon Valley's 'Simple Formula,'" in *Women of Color in U.S. Society*, ed. Maxine Baca Zinn and Bonnie Thornton Dill (Philadelphia: Temple University Press, 1994), 65–93; Mary Romero, *Maid in the U.S.A.* (New York: Routledge, 1992); Paul Ong, Edna Bonacich, and Lucie Cheng, "The Political Economy of Capitalist Restructuring and the New Asian Immigration," in *The New Asian Immigration in Los Angeles and Global Restructuring*, ed. Paul Ong, Edna Bonacich, and Lucie Cheng (Philadelphia: Temple University Press, 1994), 3–35.

11. Edna Bonacich, "Asians in the Los Angeles Garment Industry," in *The New Asian Immigration in Los Angeles and Global Restructuring*, ed. Paul Ong, Edna Bonacich, and Lucie Cheng (Philadelphia: Temple University Press, 1994), 137–163; Hossfeld, "Hiring Immigrant Women."

12. See Evelyn Nakano Glenn, *Issei, Nisei, War Bride: Three Generations of Japanese American Women in Domestic Service* (Philadelphia: Temple University Press, 1986).

13. See Anna L. Tsing, "Monster Stories: Women Charged with Perinatal Endangerment," in *Uncertain Terms: Negotiating Gender in American Culture*, ed. Faye Ginsburg and Anna L. Tsing (Boston: Beacon Press, 1990), 282–299.

14. See, for example, *Los Angeles Times*, 15 August 1997.

15. Proposition 187 provisions banning public elementary and high school education for undocumented immigrants were declared invalid because they interfered with federal authority in immigration law. The district court left provisions banning access to social and health benefits, and college education undecided until state attorneys provided procedures for implementing these bans. The "welfare reform" law is federal law, and is therefore considered to be a legitimate exercise of federal authority. On January 10, 1997, California state attorneys asked the federal district court to reconsider the Proposition 187 case in light of the new federal legislation. After the judge denied the request, Governor Wilson asked the federal appellate court to order the district court judge to act.

16. "APALC Responds to Welfare Changes," *Asian Pacific American Legal Center News* 14, no. 4 (Winter 1997): 1, 5.

17. Jodi Wilgoren, "Challenge to Green Card Reprieve Fails," *Los Angeles Times* (30 October 1997), A3.

18. Ibid.

19. Fineman, *The Neutered Mother*, 189.

20. The irony is that some of those same citizens use their privacy to cloak the fact that the domestic worker in their home is an immigrant woman. She may or may not be documented, but is probably being paid "under the table" so her citizen employers do not have to pay social security and other taxes.

21. *A Night to Remember* is the title of one of the most popular and best-selling books about the *Titanic* disaster. It was initially published in 1955. The author acknowledged the class and race/ethnic biases that governed the era in which the *Titanic* sank. See Walter Lord, *A Night to Remember* (New York: Bantam Books, 1997).

22. Biel, *Down with the Old Canoe*, 43.

23. "Why Many May Not Hope That Loved Ones' Lives Are Spared," *Washington Post* (18 April 1912), in Biel, *Down with the Old Canoe*, 39.

24. Shortly after this vote, the House also voted to approve the bill. President Taft vetoed the bill. The Senate then voted to override his veto, but the House voted to sustain it. Accordingly, the bill was never enacted.

25. Biel, *Down with the Old Canoe*, 20.

Mary Lyndon Shanley

Lesbian Families:
Dilemmas in Grounding Legal Recognition of Parenthood

The past twenty-five years have witnessed dramatic changes in the ways in which people choose to live and define themselves as family, and in the possibilities of disjoining genetic and social family ties. Rising divorce rates have increased the number both of single-parent households and of "blended families" following remarriage; extramarital cohabitation (of both heterosexual and same-sex couples) has become common; and active extended kinship networks including "fictive kin" have developed to allow a pooling of resources particularly among urban poor and working-class households.[1] As Cheshire Calhoun has observed, "Increasingly sophisticated birth control methods and technologically assisted reproduction . . . undermine cultural understandings of the marital couple as a naturally reproductive unit, introduce nonrelated others into the reproductive process, and make it possible for women and men to have children without a heterosexual partner."[2] Lesbian families in which the partners decide together to have a child through the use of alternative insemination challenge both the notion of family as beginning with a heterosexual couple and the notion that every child has two (and only two) parents of different sexes to both of whom the child is biologically related. Children in these lesbian families have two female parents, and a male progenitor. To date, obtaining legal recognition and protection for the relationships that constitute such families has only occasionally been successful. In addition to the lack of recognition of same-sex marriage, it has proven very difficult for lesbian co-mothers to obtain legal recognition of their parental status, while the issue of whether a known sperm donor should have any parental rights has on occasion been sharply contested.

Two prominent cases in which courts considered the parental status of lesbian co-mothers, *Alison D.* v. *Virginia M.*[3] and *Thomas S.* v. *Robin Y.*,[4] provided concrete examples of the kinds of issues that arise under current law, and elicited very different responses about the grounding of parental rights. I examine what both the courts and various scholars have said should be the basis for granting parental rights to adults seeking recognition as the legal parents of a child born to a lesbian couple through alternative insemination. Even among those who support legal recognition for lesbian families, and in particular protection for the relationship between lesbian co-mothers and their children, there is no consensus about how to justify the legal recognition of parental status for such mothers. Nor is there agreement about whether known sperm donors of the offspring of lesbian partners should have any kind of parental or quasi-parental rights.

A number of perspectives emerge from the literature on how to decide who should be recognized as a legal parent in cases of "collaborative procreation," that is, when the donors of genetic material, the gestational mother, and the social parents may be different people. What I call proprietary theories of parenthood regard individuals as owners of their genetic material; individuals are to be regarded as parents of their genetic offspring, and they may agree to donate or sell sperm or ova to others. Intentional theories of parenthood look to what the participants in collaborative reproduction intend and agree to do with respect to relinquishing or assuming parental status. Some theories of intentional parenthood are closely related to proprietary theories, since they assume that parental rights can be transferred by contract; others infer intent from what people do or how they act, thus tending in the direction of functional theories of parenthood. Functional theories, for their part, look at what people actually do in order to decide whom the law should designate a legal parent. Child-centered theories look at the best interests of the child or needs of the child to decide who should exercise parental rights.

I argue here that child-centered theories are the most satisfactory because they emphasize the fact that the primary purpose of establishing legal parenthood is not to gratify adults but to provide a necessary condition for the protection and nurture of children. I suggest that although many people have criticized "rights talk" for its tendency to focus too much on the individual and to pay insufficient attention to the social and interdependent nature of human life, the language of children's rights may be useful in helping us think about who should be granted parental status in lesbian families. Because children are ineluctably dependent on adults for their survival and ability to thrive, one of the rights every child has is to have at least one responsible adult designated as his or her parent(s). Another is to have the legal relationship between parent and child protected and sustained whenever possible. Children's rights, in other words, do not necessarily imply atomistic individualism, but may encompass among other things rights to be in relationships.

Because they raise fundamental questions about the proper grounding of the legal recognition of the parent–child relationship, the controversies in *Alison D. v. Virginia M.* and *Thomas S. v. Robin Y.* are relevant not only to lesbian families but to gay, heterosexual, and single-parent families as well; both changing social practices and reproductive technology have made the two-parent family in which the social and genetic parents are the same people only one of many different kinds of families. The struggles of lesbian families to gain legal protection for the relationship between parents and child and the uncertainty about how to ground parental rights reveal the difficulties in answering the question, "Whom should the law recognize as a legal parent?" for a wide variety of families in contemporary America.

I. Case Histories: *Alison D. v. Virginia M.* and *Thomas S. v. Robin Y.*

The issue in *Alison D. v. Virginia M.* was whether a lesbian co-mother had standing to seek visitation rights with a child after she and the child's biological mother separated. The New York State Court of Appeals, in a six-to-one decision, held that she did not, saying that "although plaintiff apparently nurtured a close and loving relationship with the child, she is not a parent within the meaning of Domestic Relations Law §70."[5]

Alison D. and Virginia M. began living together in 1978, and two years later decided to have a child. They agreed that Virginia would use alternative insemination to become pregnant, and that they would share all the responsibilities of childrearing. In July 1981 Virginia gave birth to a baby boy, A.D.M., who was given Alison's last name as his middle name and his birth-mother's last name as his last name. Alison shared in all birthing expenses and after birth continued to support him financially, and during the first two years of his life she and Virginia shared childrearing equally. In November 1983, when A.D.M. was a bit over two years old, Alison and Virginia ended their relationship and Alison moved out of their jointly owned home.

They agreed that Alison would continue to pay half of the mortgage and major household expenses, and that she would visit with A.D.M. several times a week. This arrangement continued for three years, at which time Virginia bought out Alison's interest in the mortgage and then began to restrict Alison's visits with A.D.M. Alison moved to Ireland to pursue career opportunities, but continued to try to keep in touch with A.D.M. Virginia, however, terminated all contact between Alison and A.D.M. and began returning all the gifts and letters Alison sent to A.D.M. Alison then sued for visitation; Virginia was found to be a fit parent, and the issue before the court was whether Alison had standing to seek visitation.

The Court of Appeals of New York State (the state's highest court) affirmed the finding of both the trial court and the Appellate Division that Alison did not have standing to seek visitation under Domestic Relations Law §70. The relevant statute declared that "either parent may apply to the Supreme Court for a writ of habeas corpus to have such minor child brought before such court; and [the court] may award the natural guardianship, charge and custody of such child to either parent . . . as the case may require." The courts found that Alison "is not a 'parent' within the meaning of section 70," because she was neither A.D.M.'s biological mother nor his legal mother by adoption. The court noted that New York had not adopted language similar to that of Oregon, whose law declares that "any person including but not limited to a foster parent, parent, stepparent, grandparent . . . who has established emotional ties creating a parent-child relationship with a child" may seek "visitation or other right of custody."[6] Because New York had not created such an expansive category, the courts construed "parent" to refer only to biological or adoptive parents.

The only dissenter to this opinion was Judge Judith Kaye, who argued that the court had the authority to define "parent" as it saw fit, since the term was not in fact defined in the statute. The proper course for the Court of Appeals, Judge Kaye insisted, was to remand the case to the trial court to determine whether Alison "stands in loco parentis to A.D.M. and, if so, whether it is in the child's best interest to allow her the visitation rights she claims."[7]

For those who want to secure legal recognition of gay and lesbian family relationships and protections for children of gay and lesbian families, *Alison D. v. Virginia M.* was a severe disappointment. Here was a couple who planned together to have a child, lived together with the child for two years, and shared responsibility for and care of the child until the child was over five years old. A.D.M. had a strong attachment to Alison and called her "mom," and called her parents Grammy and Granddad.[8] Even among Alison D.'s supporters, however, views about what exactly should have grounded or justified a decision to give Alison standing to seek visitation differed, as I discuss below.

Where *Alison D.* concerned a dispute between mothers, *Thomas S.* v. *Robin Y.* concerned lesbian parents who were united in their opposition to a biological father's efforts to establish parental rights over a child conceived with his sperm, and their determination to maintain what they saw as the integrity of their family against disruption by a man they portrayed in court papers as an "outsider."

The mothers, Robin Y. and Sandra R., met in 1979 and established an exclusive lesbian relationship. Early in their relationship they decided to have children, and chose a known sperm donor, Jack K. Robin, Sandra, and Jack agreed that Jack would not have parental rights or obligations, and that Jack would allow himself to be known to the child if she ever asked about her biological origin. Cade R.-Y. was born in May 1980 as a result of Sandra's alternative insemination with Jack's sperm. Sandra and Robin then decided that Robin should bear a child. They enlisted Thomas S., like Jack a gay man, to be the sperm donor. Again, all three adults agreed that any resulting child would be raised by Robin and Sandra as co-parents; that Thomas would have no parental rights or obligations; and that he would make himself known as the biological father if the child asked about her biological origins. Robin was successfully inseminated, and Ry was born in November 1981. Like Cade, she was given Sandra's and Robin's last names.

In early 1985 Cade, who was almost five, began to ask about her biological origins. Sandra and Robin contacted Jack and Thomas, and asked whether they would meet the children. Both agreed, and Sandra, Robin, Cade, and Ry traveled from New York to San Francisco to meet both men. The meeting was by all accounts successful and pleasant for everyone. Subsequently, Jack developed a drinking problem and could not give much attention to Cade. Sandra and Robin asked Thomas to treat both Cade and Ry equally, and he agreed. Between 1985 and 1991 Thomas visited with Robin, Sandra, and the girls several times a year.

Initially, all contacts between Thomas and the girls were at the discretion of their mothers, and this seemed to cause no difficulty. In late 1990 or early 1991, however, Thomas asked that Ry visit him and his biological relatives in California by herself, without Robin and Sandra. Robin and Sandra felt that Thomas's request to have the girl visit him and meet his biological family undermined the understanding that the two women were equally mothers to both girls, and that the girls were fully sisters, regardless of biological relationship. The mothers also worried that were Robin to die, Thomas or his biological family might seek custody of Ry. They refused Thomas's request to have Ry visit him without them. Thomas commenced a proceeding for an order of filiation (that is, a legal determination that he was Ry's father) and visitation rights.

Judge Kaufmann of the Family Court in New York County denied Thomas's petition for an order of filiation, and said that were it granted, he would deny Thomas's application for visitation. In making his ruling, Judge Kaufmann invoked the doctrine of equitable estoppel, which says that a person may not ask for enforcement of a legal right where his or her action or inaction has induced reliance by another which would be to the latter's detriment were the right enforced. Thomas's actions, Judge Kaufmann held, had consistently indicated that he had no intention of seeking recognition as Ry's father.[9] The Appellate Court reversed in a 3-to-2 decision. The majority ruled that Robin could not seek "to deny [Thomas's] right to legal recognition of [his parental] relationship," granted filiation, and remanded the case to Family Court for a hearing on visitation. The dissenters, however, would have affirmed the trial court's decision denying Thomas's petition for an order of filiation on the grounds that equitable estoppel of Thomas's action would serve "the best interests of this child."[10]

Robin announced her intention to appeal, and the New York Court of Appeals stayed the Appellate Division ruling, pending the outcome of the appeal. Thomas, stating that his health was deteriorating (he had AIDS), declined to oppose the appeal.[11] This ended the litigation without his being granted an order of filiation, but with the Appellate Division ruling the declared law of New York. Litigation concerning Ry's legal parents ceased, but the issues raised by the case were scarcely resolved.

II. Proposed Rationales for Assigning Legal Parenthood in *Alison D.* and *Thomas S.*

I find four major positions arising from statutes, court decisions, and legal commentators concerning the question, "What should give someone a claim to be recognized as a legal parent?" For some people, the actual genetic link between adult and offspring is fundamental; in their eyes, the genetic tie makes it reasonable to give parental rights to a biological lesbian mother while denying them to her partner, and to allow sperm donors to seek legal recognition of their paternity. Others believe that people should be able to

use contract or indications of intent to control the disposition of their genetic material and that nongenetic caregivers should be able to assume parental status by agreement or contract. A closely related position with respect
to those assuming parental status looks at actions, and would grant parental
rights to those adults who actually perform the functions of parents. Proponents of this view would give scant regard to the genetic tie unless it were
accompanied by caregiving activity, and would recognize the parental claims
of nonbiological caregivers like lesbian co-mothers. A fourth set of criteria
for grounding parental rights focuses not on adults but on the child, asking
variously what is in the child's "best interest," what meets a child's needs,
and to what kind of care do children have a right. Such a viewpoint tries to
adopt the perspective articulated by or attributable to the child. In the next
section I examine how each of these perspective appeared in the various judicial decisions and scholarly discussions about *Alison D.* v. *Virginia M.* and
Thomas S. v. *Robin Y.* In the final section I evaluate the strengths and weak-
nesses of each perspective, and conclude that the child-centered rationale is
the most persuasive of the four. I believe that placing the child at the center
of analysis would work tremendous change in the law which would have implications for the way we think not only about families, but also about the
nature of individualism and individual rights in a humane and liberal social order.

A. Genetic Bases of Parental Status

In both *Alison D.* and *Thomas S.* the courts laid heavy emphasis on the presence or absence of a genetic tie between adults and child. Perhaps the most
prevalent view of the proper grounding of parental rights is that genetic donors should be the legal parents of a child created from their sperm and
ovum. Indeed, this seems to many people to be the "natural" position, from
which thinking about parental status must begin. From this perspective,
granting parental status to persons other than the genetic donors requires
explanation and justification; the burden of proof rests on anyone who
would ground parental rights in something other than genetic ties.

One of the best known proponents of this position is law professor John
Robertson, who has taken the position that being the source of genetic material used in procreation should bestow parental rights in the absence of an
explicit divestment of such rights. In his eyes the right to control the disposition of one's genetic material is part of what it means to be a self-possessing

individual: "Although the bundle of property rights attached to one's own-ership of an embryo may be more circumscribed than for other things, it is an ownership or property interest nonetheless. . . . [T]he persons who pro-vide the egg and sperm have the strongest claim to ownership of the em-bryo."[12]

Several of the judicial opinions in both *Alison D.* and *Thomas S.* re-flected the view that egg and sperm donors are to be regarded as the legal parents of a child. In declaring that Alison did not have standing as a parent and so was not entitled to a hearing concerning visitation with A.D.M., the majority of the Court of Appeals relied on a biologically based understand-ing of the parent–child relationship. The court did not pay attention to Ali-son's and Virginia's joint decision to procure sperm and inseminate Virginia, nor to Alison's childrearing activities and her role as a functional parent to A.D.M. The only relevant fact, the court contended, was that Virginia was A.D.M.'s genetic and gestational mother and was therefore a parent, while Alison, a genetic and biological stranger to him, was not.

The dispute in *Alison D.* was between lesbian ex-partners, while *Thomas S. v. Robin Y.* pitted a biological mother in an intact lesbian relationship against a sperm donor seeking an order of filiation. Thomas's brief relied on genetic arguments and spoke of Robin's position as analogous to that of an unwed mother. His brief stated that nothing stood in the way of declaring him to be Ry's father because "a known donor of a child conceived by an unmarried woman as the result of artificial insemination is the legal father of the child."[13] An order of estoppel such as Robin was seeking, he argued, can defeat a claim of paternity only where the mother is married and the paternity order would make the child "illegitimate." The Appellate Court followed Thomas's lead. It rejected the trial court's assertion that the case involved a threat to an "established family unit." Instead the court treated the case as analogous to disputes concerning visitation between an unwed father and an unwed mother; at issue, it contended, was whether it could "cut off the parental rights of a . . . biological father" without complying with due process procedures of New York's Social Services Law.[14] Like the Court of Appeals decision in *Alison D.*, the Appellate Court in *Thomas S.* held that while a genetic parent has a *prima facie* claim to be declared the legal parent, a person who assumes a parental role in the absence of a genetic tie does not. This grounding of legal parenthood has been criticized by those who assert that the *intention* to become a parent, more than the contribution of genetic material, is the proper foundation of parental rights.

B. Intentional or Contractual Bases of Parental Status

Legal scholar Marjorie Shultz has proposed that when more than two persons are involved in the process of procreation, the law "should recognize the importance and legitimacy of individual efforts to project intentions and decisions into the future." Spurred primarily by her dissatisfaction with the uncertainty surrounding the legal status of "surrogate motherhood" contracts, Shultz argued that when procreative agreements are "deliberate, explicit and bargained for, where they are the catalyst for reliance and expectations, as they are in technologically-assisted reproductive arrangements, they should be honored." Enforcing such contracts would "enhance individual freedom, fulfillment and responsibility."[15] For one thing, the respect for individual autonomy and sense of self just mentioned would suggest that people planning collaborative procreation should be able to decide themselves what to do with their sperm or ova. For another, individuals planning for collaborative procreation are already assuming some responsibility for the child even prior to conception. As a sperm or ovum donor can relinquish with forethought any claims to be considered a legal parent, so nonbiological and biological lesbian co-mothers can assume financial responsibility for procuring sperm, the insemination procedure, and prenatal care. Furthermore, because contractual provisions could reflect whatever division of labor and household responsibilities the parties chose, such contracts might encourage greater flexibility of gender roles than statutory provisions have traditionally done.

Although often used to support parental status for nongenetic parents like Alison D. or Sandra R., as well as to bolster the parental claims of commissioning parents in surrogacy arrangements, intention-based theories of parental rights are related to genetic-based theories because they presuppose the right of individuals to control the disposition of their genetic material. Beginning with a view that the right to control the use of one's genetic material underlies the right to procreate, John Robertson developed an intention-based theory of parental rights: "[P]reconception rearing intentions should count as much as or more than biologic connection" in establishing legal parenthood. Someone with a right of ownership or control can alienate or transfer that right to another; positive agreement among persons who collaborate in procreative activity should determine whom the law recognizes as a legal parent. Robertson argued that "there are compelling reasons for recognizing the preconception intentions of the parties as the presumptive arbiter of rearing rights and duties, as long as the welfare of the offspring will not be severely damaged by honoring these intentions."[16] Indeed, pregnancies by alternative insemination do not occur inadvertently, but are carefully planned.

Certainly many supporters of Alison D. and of the custodial rights of lesbian co-mothers in general argue that they should be recognized as parents because they planned the pregnancy of their partner, supported her through the pregnancy, and cared for the child after birth. Robertson found that the human relationships recounted in *Alison D.* v. *Virginia M.* "directly challenge the importance of bloodline in determining parenting relations, and require us to rethink whether a nonbiologic party should always be barred from a prearranged rearing role when the biologic parent insists." And although Alison's interest in maintaining her relationship with A.D.M. was not recognized because she was not a biological parent, Robertson thought that interest might independently be worth protecting, as it would be in the case of adoptive parents.[17]

Defenses of enforceable contracts for human reproduction would apply in disputes between known sperm donors and lesbian co-mothers as well as in disputes between co-mothers. Contracts would stipulate in advance the extent of involvement of a known sperm donor. If insemination were contingent on the donor renouncing any parental rights and agreeing to assume a limited role in the child's life, then contract could preclude both his seeking more extensive rights *and* the mothers' excluding him altogether from the child's life. When parties who had previously acted in concert changed their minds and disagreed, a pre-conception contract would settle any subsequent disputes involving surrogacy, lesbian and gay co-parenting, alternative insemination, and frozen embryos. As Robertson put it, "[I]f the parties who have contracted to rear are adequate child rearers, their preconception agreement should trump the claims of donors or surrogates who later insist on a different rearing role than they had agreed upon."[18] A pre-conception contract would make the parties' expectations explicit and could be used to settle any subsequent disagreements.

Interestingly, despite this scholarly literature arguing that intent or contract should provide the basis upon which to adjudicate disputes over parental status, none of the court decisions in either *Alison D.* or *Thomas S.* looked to the pre-conception understandings of the parties to resolve the conflicting claims over who was to be considered a legal "parent." Instead, those who wished to argue against the genetic link as dispositive of parental status either considered which parties had acted as functional parents or invoked the best interest of the child or the child's need. Each of these rationales shifts attention from the proprietary understanding of parental rights found in genetic-based and intention-based theories, but does so in rather different ways.

C. Functional Grounding of Parental Status

A number of legal theorists have insisted that a person's *actions*, not simply their stated intentions, should establish the right to be recognized as the legal parents of a child. This position supported arguments that if the gestational mother in a surrogacy arrangement changed her mind about relinquishing the child, she should not be bound by her pre-conception contract; her action in carrying the fetus to term created a right to be heard in a custody dispute with the individual(s) who commissioned the pregnancy. It also supported parental status for lesbian co-mothers who plan for and take care of a child, and for gay men who jointly raise a child. A functional theory of parental rights lies behind the proposal that in divorce proceedings custody should be awarded to the "primary caretaker," determined by the amount of time spent in physical care of the child, rather than by an equal division of time or agreement between the parents, or judicial determination of what placement would be in the child's future "best interest."[19]

In her dissent in *Alison D.* v. *Virginia M.*, Judge Kaye's view that the trial court should find Alison to be a "parent" rested on her understanding of theories of functional parenting. Judge Kaye cited Katharine Bartlett's argument that the law should grant certain rights to people who can demonstrate that they have actually assumed a parental role and discharged parental responsibilities over a significant period of time.[20] Bartlett contended that to do this those who are neither biological nor adoptive parents must demonstrate that they have had physical custody of the child for at least six months; that their motive for seeking parental status is "genuine care and concern for the child" and if the child is old enough to express herself that this also be the perception of the child; and that the relationship with the child began with the consent of the child's legal parent or under court order.[21] In a similar vein, Nancy Polikoff has proposed "expanding the definition of parenthood to include anyone who maintains a functional parental relationship with a child when a legally recognized parent created that relationship with the intent that the relationship be parental in nature."[22] The gestational mother is to be considered a parent unless shown to be unfit, and another person can properly be recognized as a parent if he or she has assumed care for the child with the consent of the biological parent. Nancy Polikoff contended that Alison and Virginia "are like divorcing parents." Alison D. should have had standing to be heard in court and probably should have been granted visitation because she performed the functions of a parent with the consent of the legally recognized parent. Courts should preserve the bonds of parenthood when a family dissolves because they "consider it critical to a child's well-being to protect the child from the traumatic and painful loss of a parent."[23]

Polikoff's and Bartlett's criteria for designating someone to be a "functional parent" would give parental status to Sandra R., Robin Y.'s partner, since Sandra planned for Ry's conception and provided her physical care, all with the consent of Robin, Ry's legal mother. Even some commentators who felt that Thomas's genetic relationship to Ry, combined with the social ties he had established with her, entitled him to seek visitation, found Thomas's effort to portray himself and Robin as Ry's (only) two "parents" troubling. They saw Thomas's effort to make his situation analogous to that of an unwed father seeking visitation against the wishes of the unwed mother as an unwarranted dismissal of Sandra's role in both Robin's and Ry's lives and, by extension, a threat to all lesbian co-mothers.[24] The notion of "functional parent" would make it clear that Sandra could not be excluded from membership in Ry's legal family, any more than Robin could be denied recognition as Cade's co-mother.

There has been considerable dispute among commentators, however, over the question of whether Thomas himself had any claim to be considered as some kind of "functional parent." The Appellate Court, while relying mainly on Thomas's genetic relationship with Ry in granting him standing to seek an order of filiation, mentioned that Thomas also had established some social relationship with Ry. "[T]he 'nature, duration and constancy' of Thomas' relationship with Ry during the six years prior to his petition seeking an order of filiation demonstrate his "interest and concern for his child."[25] Several commentators argued that Robin and Sandra had themselves initiated and encouraged Thomas's relationship with Ry, and subsequently with Cade, and were wrong to seek to cut him off and sever an existing bond.[26] Even those sympathetic to Thomas were not certain, however, that he should be designated Ry's legal "parent" with all its attendant rights and responsibilities. Some proposed a new category called "limited parenthood" to deal with situations such as Thomas's, a proposal I discuss in section III.

D. Child-Centered Groundings of Parental Status
1. The "Best Interest of the Child" Standard

The "best interest of the child" standard is a well-established and frequently invoked element of family law. When disputes about custody arise, judges often justify their order placing the child in the custody of one or another parent or with someone else by saying that such placement is in the "best interest of the child." The strength of the best-interest standard is that it places the child at the center of the analysis, and allows (indeed invites) a particularized ruling in the light of the specific facts of a given child's situation. It distinguishes the grievances adults have with one another from their respective abilities to provide for and nurture a child. The best-interest standard directs attention not to adults and what should follow from the premise of adult self-ownership, intent, or action, but to how best to provide a particular child with physical sustenance and psychological nurture.

Given the long history of the courts invoking the best-interest standard for settling disputes over child custody, placement, and visitation, it is not surprising that in her dissenting opinion in *Alison D.* v. *Virginia M.*, Judge Kaye used the "best interest of the child" standard to argue that Alison D. should be given standing to argue her case for visitation. Judge Kaye cited precedent that held that "the best interest of the child has always been regarded as superior to the right of parental custody," a reflection of the principle that "a child is a person, and not a subperson over whom the parent has an absolute possessory interest."[27] She asserted that the majority's refusal to exercise the power to define "parent" in applying the New York Social Service statute "close[d] the door on all consideration of the child's best interest in visitation proceedings ... unless petitioner is a biological parent," and needed to be interpreted more broadly. She argued that the case should be returned to the trial court with instructions that the court begin to develop some more inclusive definition of "parent" in order to prevent situations in which a consideration of the child's best interest would be altogether precluded.[28]

The dissenters on the Appeals Court hearing *Thomas S.* v. *Robin Y.* similarly argued that Ry's "best interest" would be served by dismissal of Thomas's petition for an order of filiation. The dissenting justices focused their analysis on the *consequences* that would stem from "a dramatic abrogation" of Ry's understanding of her family: "While the child has always known that petitioner is her biological progenitor, it had consistently been demonstrated by petitioner himself that this factor did not confer upon him any authority or power over her life, that it did not mean that Sandra R. was less her mother than Robin Y., and that it did not mean that her sister was not her full sister." The order of filiation, the dissent believed, would lead to further litigation concerning visitation and possibly custody, if not by Thomas then by his parents or other relatives. Even if no other legal action transpired, "the constant, frightening potential for it is a burden that the child ... should not have to bear."[29]

Like Judge Kaye, the dissenters on the Appeals Court hearing *Thomas S. v. Robin Y.* said that "[i]f the child's best interests are to be the touchstone of the analysis, the attempts by both parties to argue the equities of their own respective personal positions are not germane."[30] Rather, the relevant consideration was what configuration of parental rights and responsibilities would be best for Ry. Since her mothers were well able to support Ry financially, the dissenters looked to the emotional repercussions of giving Thomas legal status as Ry's father, and concluded that those repercussions would be negative and not in her best interest.

2. The Child's Need

While sympathetic to looking at a child's best interest when adjudicating family disputes, Barbara Woodhouse has observed that the ideal can fall short of its promise. It does so either because judges substitute their own beliefs and prejudices for a child's needs and wants, or because children are voiceless and powerless in defining their needs. Woodhouse would replace or supplement the best-interest standard with what she calls "a generist perspective." That perspective "affirm[s] the centrality of children to family and society" and "define[s] parenting as the meeting of children's needs." The term *generist* is meant to evoke words "like 'generation' and 'regeneration,' 'genius' (guardian spirit), 'genus' (ours is *homo* as in *homo sapiens*), and 'generous' (willing to share, unselfish), all of which derive from the Latin *generare* and *genere* (to beget) and the Greek *gignesthai* (to be born, to become)." Generism would view parenthood "as stewardship, not ownership," and would value "highly concrete service" to meeting children's needs.[31] Woodhouse's generist theory rejected not only genetic and intentional models of parental rights, but also functionalist approaches that assume that adults can "earn" the right to custody of children. Woodhouse's generist approach did not confer parental status on the basis of genetic tie, intention, or the performance of certain actions, but started with a consideration of children's needs, and bestowed parental status on those who can—and should—fulfill those needs.

In the dispute between Alison D. and Virginia M., Woodhouse saw little ambiguity in assessing whether A.D.M. had regarded Alison as his parent. Unlike the trial court, Woodhouse believed that the biological connection between Virginia and A.D.M. gave Virginia no superior custodial claim if Alison provided emotional, physical, and financial prenatal care to Virginia (which was in effect to provide support to A.D.M. as well). From A.D.M.'s perspective, the two mothers who held and cuddled him after birth give similar care (even if Virginia breast-fed A.D.M., this did not make her so much more involved with his care as to justify excluding Alison). Moreover, Woodhouse sharply criticized the legal approach that suggested that Virginia might bar Alison from future contact with A.D.M. She insisted that "[o]ur focus on individual rights and dyadic relationships masks the fact that children need us to care not only for them but for one another. A truly child-centered family law recognizes and sustains the child's network of care."[32] While Woodhouse would not expect Virginia and Alison to reunite, she would regard them as having a mutual responsibility to protect the network of A.D.M.'s relationships, including his relationship with Alison.

The same emphasis on sustaining "the child's network of care" that led Woodhouse to support Alison D.'s claim led her to reject Thomas's claim. She agreed with Judge Kaufmann's reasoning that "[t]o Ry, Thomas S. is an outsider attacking her family, refusing to give it respect, and seeking to force her to spend time with him and his biological relatives, who are all complete strangers to her." Woodhouse remarked that Judge Kaufmann's decision was unusual, and correct, in taking Ry's perceptions as the proper starting point for assessing the adults' claims. "[T]he child's network of care . . . and not traditional parent's rights, is the reason for protecting a functioning unitary family from destructive intrusion and for seeking ways to minimize conflict and stress when families do separate."[33] Similarly, Woodhouse applauded the dissenters on the Appeals Court who looked at Ry's understanding of her family in rejecting Thomas's request for an order of filiation.

III. Reflections on the Groundings of Legal Parenthood

Both Thomas S.'s effort to present his situation as analogous to that of an unwed father seeking visitation with his offspring and Virginia M.'s effort to exclude Alison D. from visitation suggested that the genetic relationship they had to the child gave them a stronger claim to parental rights and status than the child's co-mother who had planned for the conception, partnered the biological mother throughout her pregnancy, and resided with and cared for the child after birth. As we have seen, the New York State Court of Appeals in *Alison D.* and the Appellate Court in *Thomas S.* seemed to recognize the claims of the genetic parent and reject or ignore the claims of the nonbiological lesbian co-mother. But for many people, including me, this elevation of genetic tie over actual caregiving and assumption of responsibility for a child's welfare is the wrong foundation for establishing legal parenthood. One of the disturbing aspects of the controlling decisions in both *Alison D.* and *Thomas S.* was that they "read down the role of the non-biological mother, to a point where she is not even the functional equivalent of one member of the heterosexual couple." Rather than stand in a privileged position as a member of a parenting couple, she stood as an outsider, "[akin to] child care workers, baby-sitters, and housekeepers," a dismissal both of her status and of the integrity of the family unit of which she was a part.[34]

There is, of course, a sense in which the genetic tie *should* be relevant to the establishment of legal parenthood—the custody of a child is not up for grabs at birth. Notions of self-ownership, generational ties, and the right to control the disposition of something so central to one's sense of self as genetic material should prohibit the government or anyone else from appropriating a person's ova, sperm, or offspring without carefully constructed and rigorously enforced procedures, including the consent of the genetic donor. Where heterosexual couples living together are concerned, absent a strong showing of cause or voluntary relinquishment, it is proper to presume that the biological parents are the custodial parents. But it does not follow from principles of self-ownership and autonomy that society is well served by conceptualizing an individual's relationship to his or her genetic material as proprietary.

In instances of "collaborative procreation," when the genetic progenitors and the caregivers or social parents are not (all) the same people, it is tempting to argue (as John Robertson, Marjorie Shultz, and others have done) that we should look not to genetic link but to the *intentions* of those involved to decide disputes over custody. Lesbians and sperm donors have described the kinds of considerations and negotiations that often accompany the decision to engage in (or not to engage in) collaborative procreation.[35] Intention-based theories of parental rights look at explicit statements of intent such as contracts or verbal agreements or signs of tacit agreement to ascertain what the parties intended and their states of mind and their wills. In neither *Alison D.* nor *Thomas S.* were there formal written agreements, but there were indications of the mothers' intentions to raise a child together. Judge Kaye said that Alison should have had standing to seek visitation because she had fulfilled the function of parent over a considerable period of time, and that it was clear that both Alison and Virginia had intended that Alison function as A.D.M.'s parent. To some extent the arguments over whether equitable estoppel provided a tool by which the dispute between Thomas S. and Robin Y. might be adjudicated assumed that the parties' actions either signaled what they each understood their own and one another's parenting roles to be, or might reasonably have been thought to signal those understandings and intentions. Ruling in favor of Thomas S., the Appellate Court reasoned that equitable estoppel might as justifiably be exercised against Robin as against Thomas: "If respondent [Robin] now finds petitioner's involvement in his daughter's life to be inconvenient she cannot deny that her predicament is the result of her own action." The "nature, duration and constancy" of Thomas's relationship with Ry during the six years prior to his petition seeking an order of filiation, in turn, demonstrated his "interest and concern for his child."[36] As Kate Harrison put it, "since Thomas S. relied on the mothers' encouragement of his relationship with Ry, changing his position as a result and becoming actively involved with the child, the mothers should not subsequently be able to deny him visitation with the child" since his emotional involvement grew initially from actions he undertook at their request.[37]

When intentions are set forth in pre-conception agreements between genetic donors and intended social parents, there is no bright line between an intention-based and a proprietary model of parental rights. When intentions are inferred from actions rather than verbal agreements, there similarly is no bright line distinguishing theories grounding parental status in intention from those grounding such status in the performance of parental roles or functional parenthood. For this reason Nancy Polikoff and Katharine Bartlett both insisted that for someone to be legally recognized as a parent using the notion of functional parenthood, the legal parent must explicitly agree to extend parental rights to the co-parent.[38] Otherwise it might be possible for someone like a full-time nanny or a grandparent to take care of a child and then argue that she or he had custodial or visitation rights. For Polikoff, simply performing a parentlike function is not enough to create a claim to be considered a functional parent in the absence of the explicit agreement of the legally recognized parent. That requirement clearly would have defeated Thomas's claim. Other commentators argued that Polikoff's contention that one either is or is not a legally recognized parent perpetuates overly rigid and dichotomous categories. They contended that while existing legal rules required that the courts had to exclude Thomas altogether from parental status or declare him to be one of Ry's two (and only two) parents, this state of the law was unacceptable. In their view the law should be changed to accommodate persons who have a relationship to a child somewhere *between* that of "parent" and "stranger." Such commentators made the case for the creation of a category of "limited father" for known sperm donors who are known to and involved in the lives of their offspring.[39]

Kate Harrison argued that all-or-nothing grants of parental rights "fail to grasp the mid-point reality of a limited father's position. For Thomas S., recognizing the reality of his position would mean acknowledging both the validity and the limitations of his claim."[40] Others agreed that people like Thomas who have played a limited but significant role in a child's life may have limited but significant claims to continued visitation. Obviously not every caregiver should be able to insist on continued access to a child. Advocates of some legal recognition for "limited fathers" identified a conjunction of factors, all or some of which might be necessary for someone to claim such status. These included genetic tie, repeated contact between adult and child and mutual acknowledgment of the nature of their relationship, and a pre-conception agreement among co-mothers and limited father that he will assume that role. In other words, most defenders of legal recognition of limited fatherhood seemed to draw on a mixture of genetic, intentional, and functional understandings of parenthood. Of these, however, the primary rationales were genetic and contractual.

Not to recognize limited father status, said advocates, not only causes harm to an individual adult and/or child, but also reinscribes the model of the two-parent nuclear family and in doing so may thwart efforts to secure protection for gay and lesbian family relationships. Thomas S.'s effort to be declared Ry's father elicited two quite different responses from advocates of gay and lesbian rights. On the one hand, Fred Bernstein argued that despite the fact that Thomas was himself gay, his effort to make his situation analogous to that of an unwed father seeking visitation with his biological offspring who is being raised by an unwed mother was an "offhand, even cynical, dismissal of gay/lesbian concerns" that treated lesbian couples as if they had no autonomy interests equivalent to those of heterosexual couples.[41] On the other hand, Harrison argued that the summary exclusion of Thomas and other involved sperm donors worked to deny "the most radical aspect of many lesbian and gay families: that children do have ongoing relationships with multiple 'parents,' some biologically related and some not, who live both inside and beyond their household, with differing levels of responsibility for them and different types of relationships with them." Instead of reinscribing the model of the two-parent nuclear family against efforts to reconfigure and expand responsibility for childrearing, "[m]any lesbian families have been successfully constructed around men who have agreed to, and are acting as, limited fathers." Harrison contended that Judge Kaufmann's reliance on Ry's understanding of who was a parent "drew a line around the adults who were directly involved in her day-to-day care; this analysis would exclude anyone in a noncustodial parental position, including someone who was acting as a 'limited father.'" In fact, the decision "sets a high performance threshold for someone trying to establish they are a functional parent, almost assuming that only daily carers, living with the child, will qualify."[42] But if both the mothers and the sperm donor agree that he should play a role in the child's life, it makes sense to guarantee him continuing access to the child, and to create legal recognition for a "limited parent" status.[43]

The radical aspect of proposals for limited parent status is that they would expand the number of adults who could claim some right of access to and be assigned some responsibility for a child. Acceptance of limited parent status could legitimate diverse family forms and so undermine the hegemony of the dyadic, heterosexual couple and their offspring as the normative (because "natural") model of family. Despite these desirable efforts, however, the idea of looking to the intentions of adults engaged in collaborative procreation (whether expressed in pre- or post-conception, explicit or implied contracts) in order to determine parenting roles and rights in cases where there are different genetic, biological, and social parents gives me pause.

Introduction of the practice and the language of contract into procreative relationships would both create greater opportunity to establish a range of family relationships and risk introducing market concepts into the regulation of family life and suggesting that children are objects of trade. Contract in this context is derived from market relationships, and resistance to the incursion of market concepts into the regulation of family relationships has led some feminists (myself among them) to argue against the enforceability of pregnancy contracts against the wishes of the gestational mother.[44] Pregnancy contracts and limited parent contracts mark the ascendancy of the language of the market in the realm of interpersonal affairs. Even Harrison, who has favored limited father contracts, noted that "[p]arenting contracts . . . embrace a concept of the child as the object of negotiated rights, suggesting that parents have an inherent 'ownership' right with respect to their children, which can properly and ethically be varied between the parties or contracted away."[45] There need not be an exchange of money for the language and conceptual terms of the market to invade the realm of intimate human relationships.

Imagining all the various configurations to which adults engaged in collaborative procreation might agree alerts us to the fact that pre-conception parenting contracts rest on "a concept of the child fulfilling the needs and desires of parents rather than on the parents fulfilling the needs and desires of the child."[46] An adequate theory of parental rights, however, should begin not with adults but with children, and not with volition but with need. While we may use mechanisms of consent or agreement, or look at what the adults have in fact done (or have not done) to care for the child, as evidence that adults have assumed or relinquished parental rights and responsibilities, we should not regard it as adults' acts of will that create those rights and responsibilities, but the needs of the child. Even theories of functional parenting, while a huge step forward from the proprietary roots of genetic and some intention-based models, retain a focus on adult volition and activity both on the part of the adults who relinquish or decide to share authority and on the part of those who assume parental responsibilities.

By contrast, the traditional "best interest of the child" standard based parental rights and responsibilities not on what adults will or do, but on the imperatives of providing a child with care. Asking what and who fulfills a child's needs rather than who has the right to a specific child shifts the focus from adult claims to a child's present and future well-being. Especially since adults sometimes advance their claims not simply out of solicitude for their child, but also out of anger with and a desire to defeat the claims of another adult, refocusing the inquiry on the child is appealing. In their classic book *Beyond the Best Interests of the Child* Joseph Goldstein, Anna Freud, and Albert Solnit argued that when the child had two caring and attentive parents who could not get along with one another, trying to determine the "best interest" of a child was often difficult and led the noncustodial parent to argue that his or her changed ability to serve the child's best interest should reopen the question of which parent(s) should have custody.[47] Such lack of finality often had very detrimental effects on a child. Many feminists have also criticized the best-interest standard, arguing that it often opened the door to judgments based on cultural preferences or prejudices, favoring the party with greater financial resources (usually men), and inviting repeated visits to court. Thus while the best-interest standard properly focused on the child as the most relevant person in any effort to determine who should exercise parental rights, the term itself may have exaggerated the degree to which a court can discern and help to bring about conditions conducive to a child's future well-being.

In place of the best-interest standard, Barbara Woodhouse's "generist" approach "would place children, not adults, firmly at the center and take as its central values not adult individualism, possession and autonomy, as embodied in parental rights, nor even the dyadic intimacy of parent/child relationships,"[48] but the needs of the child him- or herself (which often may include, of course, protecting "dyadic intimacy"). Woodhouse's generist approach demanded consideration of broader relationships than the parent–child dyad, and might be thought to be more likely than other approaches to seek to maintain the involvement of multiple adults in a child's life.

Beginning with the perceptions of the child emphasizes that the foremost claim in cases involving children is not adult entitlement but a child's need for the conditions (both material and psychological) that will allow her or him to thrive and become a self-governing adult. But, as with the best-interest standard, it can be difficult to know in advance what will enable a child to thrive. Where commentators Katharine Bartlett, Brad Sears, and Fred Bernstein all argued that legal recognition of nonexclusive parenting status or some visitation rights for "limited" parents like Thomas S. would acknowledge a child's interest in maintaining relationships with important adults, Woodhouse rejected Thomas S.'s effort to be awarded visitation with Ry on the grounds that it would undermine Ry's own understanding of who constituted her family.[49] Like function-based theories, Woodhouse's generism looked at actual relationships as central to the question of assigning parental rights and responsibilities, but she contended that analysis of whether someone has acted as a "functional parent" should begin with the child's perception rather than with an assessment of the adult's actions per se.

Asking a child to define who is in his or her family, however, may produce various answers depending on when the question is asked, and could place a tremendous burden on the child. For the first three years of her life, Ry did not think of herself as having a known father. Thereafter, she entered a social relationship with Thomas which began because her mothers introduced him to her as her genetic father, and she regarded him as an adult who cared for her, her mothers, and her sister. Not surprisingly, Ry's perception of Thomas's role in her family changed once he and her mothers disagreed about visitation. Undisputed testimony makes it clear that Ry understood the complexity and unconventionality of her family relationships. Prior to the litigation she understood her family to be composed of two mothers and a sister who were "family" despite the asymmetry of their genetic ties to one another, and she knew that she had a biological father whom she had been encouraged to regard as someone more than a "stranger." But once litigation commenced, she regarded Thomas as a threat. While Woodhouse was right that it was important to protect Ry from emotional distress once litigation began, it is also clear that the inability of her mothers and Thomas to reach agreement about the conditions under which the girls might visit him and his parents destroyed existing bonds of affection that all had a responsibility to try to preserve. Clearly the present state of the law exacerbated the dispute between Robin and Sandra on one side and Thomas on the other. Had it been clear from the start that Thomas was a "limited parent" with only limited rights of visitation, and no legal grounds on which to bring action for an order of filiation, he would probably not have seemed a threatening figure to Robin, Sandra, Cade, and Ry, and their relationships might have been sustained.

Those who have advocated creation of limited parent status have done so by referring to adults' rights to enter contractual agreements for collaborative procreation. While I think a pre-conception agreement may be the *mechanism* by which to establish someone's willingness to be a known sperm donor and a limited father, the *justification* for accepting pre-conception agreements for limited father status should not be deference to adults' alleged freedom to do with their bodies and genetic material what they will, but the well-being of children. Thinking about the relationships among interested parties does suggest that the existence of a legally recognized status of "limited parent" might enhance children's interests by stabilizing and protecting relationships between some children and adults. In cases of alternative insemination, it might foster such relationships by encouraging a shift away from anonymous sperm donors to known sperm donors, a shift that I believe would benefit those born through collaborative procreation.

Stability in their relationships with the adults they love is important to children's welfare. There is a tension, however, between achieving such stability by protecting the authority of the primary caregivers and the autonomy of the family unit they have created on the one hand, and protecting the child's relationships with adults other than primary caregivers on the other.[50] Thinking about limited parenthood raises the question of how exclusive the exercise of parental rights and responsibilities should be. On the one hand, it is not always in a child's interest to maintain active ties with adults outside the household. On the other hand, adults should have to adjust to enable their children to maintain ties with those who have functioned as parents. As Woodhouse noted, the bestowal of legal parenthood means "not only the right to give children our love but the power to give and withhold children's love from others. Parental autonomy becomes the freedom to deploy and redeploy children . . . as enhancements to shifting adult relationships."[51] Adults who cut others off from access to a child not for the child's well-being but for their own perceived interest, shift consideration from the child's need to the adult's volition.

Legal recognition of limited parent status for sperm donors might also help children (when young or when they reach adulthood) by leading more women to use known rather than anonymous sperm donors. Current law that makes parenthood an all-or-nothing status, and decisions like that of the Appellate Court in *Thomas S.* v. *Robin Y.*, understandably deter women using alternative insemination from using sperm from an identifiable donor. Genetic fathers seeking legal recognition as parents can cause devastating hardship and harm to both children (like Cade and Ry) and their parents. But were such disruption precluded by law, it would probably be desirable from the child's perspective that the identity of the genetic father be known (or at least knowable), whether such knowledge led to a social relationship or not. Fred Bernstein makes an argument along these lines that I do not find persuasive. He says that the fact that "Ry understood the importance of father in our culture, and then developed a relationship with the man she knew to be her father, is the key fact of the case," and suggests that the creation of legal recognition of "limited fathers" is in a child's interest.[52] But the argument that it is in a child's interest that she know her genetic father because genetic fatherhood is almost universally regarded as important in our society (even if its importance is a social construct) is not persuasive if the point is to change the cultural construct of "father" (say, from progenitor to daily caregiver). More significant, in my view, are reflections on the role played by each person's sense of a biological connection both to progenitors and to offspring in the construction of the sense of self, and on one's place in the ongoing unfolding of human life.[53] More concretely, I am influenced by considerations arising from the efforts of some adult adoptees to open adoption records and to promote "open adoptions" in which the identities of the birth parents are known to the adoptive parents and their child. The desire to know one's origins (not simply to have access to such matters as the medical history of one's genetic forebears), and to be able to construct a narrative of who one is by knowing how one came to be in the world, seems to be very strong for many people.[54] The construction of a coherent and complete life story seems so central to a sense of self and to psychological well-being that access to knowledge of one's genetic progenitors might be regarded as a right, as something that the state should guarantee for every citizen.

Despite my conviction that family law should be grounded in a consideration of a child's need, not an adult's desert (whether due to tradition, genetics, contracts, or performance of parental functions), utilization of such an approach is difficult. The traditional "best interest of the child" standard is a powerful counterweight to adult-centered theories, but risks the interjection of class, gender, racial, and cultural biases and perhaps promises greater predictability than the world allows. Woodhouse's generist approach is very appealing, although its language is unfamiliar and like all theories leaves room for debate about what in fact best meets a child's need (and what the needs of that particular child may be). In addition to these approaches, the shift from an adult-centered to a child-centered legal approach might be facilitated by the language of children's rights. Some people may object that the language of children's rights would exacerbate the individualistic tendencies of American law and would therefore be inadequate for generating principles to govern relationships and interdependencies. I cannot do more here than suggest ways in which turning "rights talk" on its head to focus on children's rights rather than adults' rights might make it easier to advance the notion of relational rights (or the right to be in relationship), and so strengthen rather than disaggregate family ties.

Certainly the use of "rights talk" has traditionally posed significant difficulties in family law. Martha Minow has observed that in the past "[r]ights rhetoric has failed to afford a language supple enough to speak about relationships, affiliations, attachments, and care," and so has not yet proven itself adequate to articulate relations among individuals, families, groups, and the state in a fully satisfactory manner.[55] There is a long history of ambiguity and tension between recognizing the individual rights of family members and preserving the privacy of the family itself. As Hendrick Hartog has noted, "The influence of [Lockean] possessive individualism . . . helps explain the relative unavailability of constitutional language for litigants asserting the collective rights of families. Either family rights became the individualistic, libertarian rights of individuals within a family, or they were equated with the property rights of a patriarchal head of household."[56] *Thomas S.* v. *Robin Y.* illustrated the hold of the patriarchal assumption that a genetic father had a right to legal recognition of his paternity, as well as the tension between the individual and the family unit. Thomas asserted his right as an individual to be declared Ry's father, while Robin and Sandra asked the state to defend the integrity and autonomy of their two-parent family.

A child-centered approach to the question of whether the law should recognize a "limited parent" status for some persons engaged in collaborative procreation would change the focus of discourse concerning family privacy. The authority given to parents by invocations of family privacy has traditionally been justified as the right of adults to fend off intrusions into the private realm of the family by the state. The realm of privacy has been a realm of adult autonomy. The shift of emphasis to the need of the child for stability gives adults authority over children and exclusionary rights against the state and other adults neither because it follows from their right to control their bodies, their genetic material, or their children, nor because the caretaking adults have earned that right, but because children need parents to have such authority in order that they (the children) may thrive. One might bring to the discussion of whether or not the law should recognize "limited parents" questions concerning a child's right to know the identity of her or his forebears (at least upon reaching his or her majority) and a child's right to the protection of her or his affective ties.

The rubric of parental rights not only carries echoes of possession or proprietary rights but also focuses on each parent's relationship with his or her child and obscures or downplays the way in which a child's well-being may depend not simply on those dyadic relationships but on the relationship of the parents with one another. Attention to a child's rights to relationship and care draws attention to the fact that such rights cannot pertain simply to individuals—they reflect children's utter dependence on others, and on specific others, for their well-being.[57] Talk of parental rights also downplays the responsibility of the larger community for children's welfare as well as a community's collective stake in how well children grow into adulthood. The kinds of children's rights encompassed in Woodhouse's notion of generism emphasizes the role of those outside the family itself—such as schools, community organizations, and social service agencies—in supporting children. Taking children's needs seriously might also lead to an articulation of children's rights that included the right to food, shelter, and education, and that guaranteed that no child would be removed from a family because of poverty, or lack of services that if supplied would allow the parents to continue caring for their child. Using claims arising from children's needs to generate social rights would help children and would also strengthen the weak tradition of social rights in the political and legal culture of the United States.[58]

Related to concerns about the adequacy of rights talk to encompass the complexities and interdependencies of family relationships, a significant number of theorists regard "rights talk" as an obstacle to the transformations necessary to reclaim American jurisprudence and social life in general from atomistic and selfish individualism. Part of this criticism stems from a broader skepticism about the ability of liberal political theory and jurisprudence to articulate the normative values and shared purposes that must underlie any viable civic life. Some of these critics come from what has come to be called a "communitarian" perspective which opposes what it sees as the undue deference given to individualism and proceduralism in current political life.[59] Other critics of liberal theory with respect to family life are part of those working to develop the implications of an "ethic of care" for social and political relations.[60] Such theorists might move toward a child-centered jurisprudence and justification of lesbian motherhood that would speak of children's *needs* rather than children's *rights*.

What might a child-centered theory like that proposed here have suggested to the courts deciding *Alison D.* v. *Virginia M.* and *Thomas S.* v. *Robin Y.*? A child's right to relationship with his or her parents would have greatly strengthened Alison D.'s case. Although she was not related to A.D.M. genetically, she planned his conception, supported his gestational mother during pregnancy, and functioned—and was recognized by him—as one of his parents. From A.D.M.'s perspective, Alison was his "mother" until Virginia cut back their visitation. In A.D.M.'s experience they were no different from divorced parents who had once been legally married. The dispute between Thomas S. and Robin Y. might have been prevented had there been a recognition of relational rights through "limited parent" status. Were one to think about limited parent status from a child's perspective, one might consider whether the law should recognize a person's interest in knowing the identity of his or her genetic forebears. If there is such a legally cognizable interest, pre-conception agreements might not only record the identity of a genetic donor but also stipulate the intentions of the parties for contact (or lack of contact) between a known sperm donor and his offspring, and between a known sperm donor and the custodial parent(s). Limited parent status might facilitate recognition of genetic ties and clarify the responsibility of the custodial parents to sustain a child's relationship to limited parents. By strictly limiting the claims that could be put forward by limited parents, it might also ward off challenges to the authority of custodial parents and the integrity of their family unit.

Providing children with stability and care is a pressing need of contemporary American society. One important source (although not the only one) of such stability and care comes from a child's family. It is clear, however, that current law is inadequate to the task of identifying who are a child's "parents" in a variety of nontraditional family situations, including stepfamilies or blended-families, heterosexual families using gamete donation or gestational services, families formed by open adoption, and gay and lesbian families. This article suggests that thinking about the issues posed by disputes over who is a legal parent may lead to greater justice both for members of lesbian families and for other parents and children, and may also produce a reconceptualization of parenthood that will enrich not only family law but liberal political theory as well.

1. On trends in household composition, including extended kinship ties with former spouses and their relatives, see Judith Stacey, *Brave New Families: Stories of Domestic Upheaval in Late Twentieth Century America* (New York: Basic Books, 1990). On the development of "families of choice" among gays and lesbians in the San Francisco area see Kath Weston, *Families We Choose: Lesbians, Gays, Kinship* (New York: Columbia University Press, 1991). On extended kin networks among poor urban Black households see Carol Stack, *All Our Kin: Strategies for Survival in a Black Community* (New York: Harper & Row, 1974).

2. Cheshire Calhoun, "Family's Outlaws: Rethinking the Connections Between Feminism, Lesbianism, and the Family," in *Feminism and Families*, ed. Hilde Lindemann Nelson (New York: Routledge, 1997): 143. Calhoun discusses various ways in which lesbian families are constructed as "outlaws" rather than as legitimate families.

3. *In the matter of Alison D. v. Virginia M.*, 77 N.Y.2d 651, 572 N.E.2d 27, 569 N.Y.S.2d 586 (1991).

4. *In the Matter of a Proceeding for Paternity Under Article 5 of the Family Court Act Thomas S. v. Robin Y.*, 157 Misc.2d 858, 599 N.Y.S.2d 377 (April 13, 1993); *In re Thomas S. v. Robin Y.*, Sup.C.App.Div. 209 A.D.2d 298, 618 N.Y.S.2d 356 (November 17, 1994); *Matter of Thomas S. v. Robin Y.*, C.App.N.Y., 86 N.Y.2d 779, 655 N.E.2d 708, 631 N.Y.S.2d 611 (July 26, 1995).

5. *Alison D. v. Virginia M.*, at 654. For an account of a nonbiological lesbian comother's commitment to remaining a parent to her daughter even after she and the biological comother separated see Toni Tortorilla, "On a Creative Edge," in *Politics of the Heart: A Lesbian Parenting Anthology*, ed. Sandra Pollack and Jeanne Vaughn (Ithaca, N.Y.: Firebrand Books, 1987), 168–174.

6. Oregon Rev Statutes §109.19 [1] (1985, amended 1988) (1989), quoted in *Alison D. v. Virginia M.*, at 657.

7. *Alison D. v. Virginia M.*, at 662.

8. Jane Levine, David Chambers, and Martha Minow, *Brief for Amici Curiae*, Eleven Concerned Academics, Court of Appeals, State of New York, Index no. 000692–88 (1990), 5.

9. *Thomas S. v. Robin Y.*, 599 N.Y.S. 2d 377 (Family Court, 1993).

10. *Thomas S. v. Robin Y.*, 618 N.Y.S. 2d 356 (Appellate Division, 1994), 362 and 363.

11. *Thomas S. v. Robin Y.*, 631 N.Y.S. 2d 611 (Court of Appeals, 1995).

12. John A. Robertson, *Children of Choice: Freedom and the New Reproductive Technologies* (Princeton, N.J.: Princeton University Press, 1994), 104–105. This proprietary view informed Robertson's understanding of a number of issues that arise from new reproductive technologies. For example, he argued that posthumous procreation with frozen sperm with the offspring having rights of inheritance from the sperm donor was acceptable if it was clearly the intent of the deceased that someone should use his genetic material for this purpose. He also held that a person might prohibit the use of his or her genetic material in procreation; he views the right *not* to procreate as a corollary of the right to procreate.

Robertson's emphasis on an individual's relationship to his or her genetic material led him to conflate the work of social reproduction (which involves the rearing of a child over many years) and biological procreation (which brings together sperm and egg): "In a sense, reproduction is always genetic. . . . Thus, a woman who has provided the egg that is carried by another has reproduced, even if she has not gestated and does not rear resulting offspring" (Robertson, *Children of Choice*, 22). I would say that she has donated materials used in procreation, not that she has "reproduced." Barbara Katz Rothman makes this distinction between procreative and reproductive activity in *Recreating Motherhood: Ideology and Technology in a Patriarchal Society* (New York: W. W. Norton, 1989).

13. Brief for Petitioner-Appellant at 28, quoted in Fred A. Bernstein, "This Child Does Have Two Mothers . . . and a Sperm Donor with Visitation," *New York University Review of Law and Social Change* 22 (1996): 30.

14. *Thomas S. v. Robin Y.*, 618 N.Y.S. 2d at 358, citing N.Y. Social Service Law section 384.

15. Marjorie Maguire Shultz, "Reproductive Technology and Intent-Based Parenthood: An Opportunity for Gender Neutrality," *Wisconsin Law Review* 1990 (1990): 300, 302–303.

16. Robertson, *Children of Choice*, 125, 143.

17. Robertson, *Children of Choice*, 135.

18. Robertson, *Children of Choice*, 127.

19. Martha A. Fineman, *The Illusion of Equality* (Chicago: University of Chicago Press, 1991); Katharine Bartlett, "Re-Expressing Parenthood: *Yale Law Journal* 98 (1988): 293, and "Rethinking Parenthood as an Exclusive Status: The Need for Legal Alternatives When the Premise of the Nuclear Family Has Failed," *Virginia Law Review* 17 (1984): 879.

20. *Alison D. v. Virginia M.*, Judge Kaye dissenting at 662.

21. Bartlett, "Rethinking Parenthood as an Exclusive Status," 946–947.

22. Nancy Polikoff, "This Child Does Have Two Mothers: Redefining Parenthood to Meet the Needs of Children in Lesbian-Mother and Other Nontraditional Families," *Georgetown Law Journal* 78 (1990): 459, 464.

23. Polikoff, "This Child Does Have Two Mothers," 542.

24. Bernstein, "This Child Does Have Two Mothers . . . and a Sperm Donor," 30.

25. *Thomas S. v. Robin Y.*, 618 N.Y.S. 2d 356 (Appellate Division, 1994), 362.

26. Bernstein, "This Child Does Have Two Mothers . . . and a Sperm Donor"; Brad Sears, "Winning Arguments/Losing Themselves: The (Dys)functional Approach in *Thomas S. v. Robin Y.*, *Harvard Civil Rights–Civil Liberties Law Review* 29 (1994): 559–580; Kate Harrison, "Fresh or Frozen: Lesbian Mothers, Sperm Donors, and Limited Fathers," in *Mothers in Law: Feminist Theory and the Legal Regulation of Motherhood*, ed. Martha A. Fineman and Isabel Karpin (New York: Columbia University Press, 1995).

27. *Alison D. v. Virginia M.*, Judge Kaye dissenting at 660, quoting *Matter of Bennett v. Jeffreys*, 40 NY2d 543, 546.

28. *Alison D. v. Virginia M.*, Judge Kaye dissenting.

29. *Thomas S. v. Robin Y.*, 618 N.Y.S. 2d 356 (App.Div., 1994), 367, 368.

30. Ibid., 367.

31. Barbara Bennett Woodhouse, "Hatching the Egg: A Child-Centered Perspective on Parents' Rights," *Cardozo Law Review* 14 (May, 1993): 1754–1755, 1756.

32. Woodhouse, "Hatching the Egg," 1864.

33. Ibid.

34. Harrison, "Fresh or Frozen," 187.

35. See, for example, Philip Gambone, "The Kid I Already Have: On Considering Fathering a Child with a Lesbian," in *Sister and Brother: Lesbians and Gay Men Write About Their Lives Together*, ed. Joan Nestle and John Preston (New York: HarperSanFrancisco, 1994), 251–264; see also Kate Hill, "Mothers by Insemination: Interviews," Sandra Pollack, "Two Moms, Two Kids: An Interview," and Carolyn Kott Washburne, "Happy Birthday from Your Other Mom," all in *Politics of the Heart: A Lesbian Parenting Anthology*, ed. Sandra Pollack and Jeanne Vaughn (Ithaca, N.Y.: Firebrand Books, 1987), 111–119, 120–124, and 142–145, respectively.

36. *Thomas S. v. Robin Y.*, 618 N.Y.S.2d 356 (App.Div., 1994), 362.

37. Harrison, "Fresh or Frozen," 192.

38. Bartlett, "Rethinking Parenthood as an Exclusive Status," 946–947; and Polikoff, "This Child Does Have Two Mothers," 489–490.

39. Harrison, "Fresh or Frozen"; Sears, "Winning Arguments/Losing Themselves"; Bernstein, "This Child Does Have Two Mothers . . . and a Sperm Donor." Others have suggested that grandparents, stepparents, and siblings might also be recognized as persons who have a right to maintain an established relationship with a child.

40. Harrison, "Fresh or Frozen," 192.

41. Bernstein, "This Child Does Have Two Mothers . . . and a Sperm Donor," 30.

42. Harrison, "Fresh or Frozen," 190–191.

43. Katharine Bartlett, Brad Sears, and Fred Bernstein all argued that recognition of the child's interest in maintaining relationships with important adults may make it advisable to recognize nonexclusive parenting status or some visitation rights for "limited" parents. And while the appeals court majority that granted Thomas' appeal to petition for an order of filiation made no mention of "limited fatherhood," their decision made it clear that at most Thomas had a claim to visitation, not custody; they might have preferred to declare Thomas a limited parent rather than Ry's legal "father," had such a category been available.

44. Mary Lyndon Shanley, " 'Surrogate Mothering' and Women's Freedom: A Critique of Contracts for Human Reproduction," *Signs: Journal of Women in Culture and Society* 18 (1993): 618–639. Arguments against enforcing surrogacy agreements include considerations of women's economic vulnerability, the inherent commodification of the human body of the gestational mother and of the child, and the dismissal of the relevance of the possible intense experience of pregnancy and birth.

Unlike a surrogate mother who by carrying a fetus to term might claim to have some kind of experiential relationship with the newborn child, neither sperm nor ovum donor has that kind of sustained contact with the developing life. On the implications for law and public policy of the differences between men's and women's relationship to a fetus during pregnancy, see Mary Lyndon Shanley, "Fathers' Rights, Mothers' Wrongs? Reflections on Unwed Fathers' Rights and Sex Equality," *Hypatia* 10, no. 1 (1995): 74–103.

45. Harrison, "Fresh or Frozen, 199.

46. Ibid.

47. Joseph Goldstein, Anna Freud, and Albert Solnit, *Beyond the Best Interests of the Child* (New York: Free Press, 1973).

48. Woodhouse, "Hatching the Egg," 1815.

49. Barbara Bennett Woodhouse, " 'Out of Children's Needs, Children's Rights: The Child's Voice in Defining the Family," *BYU Journal of Public Law* 8 (1994): 333–335.

50. The situation in *Thomas S. v. Robin Y.* raises this tension, as did the action by a biological father seeking a hearing to obtain an order of filiation in *Michael H. v. Gerald D.* (491 U.S. 110 1989). Michael H., a biological father, who had lived intermittently with and provided care to his biological daughter and her mother, even though the mother was married to and intermittently lived with her husband as well, argued that he had a right to a hearing to establish his paternity when the husband and wife sought to cut off his contact with the child. Like Thomas S., Michael H. had developed ties with and feelings for his daughter because of actions taken by the child's mother, who had at one point sought to include him in the child's life. Although the child's guardian *ad litem* advised that continued visitation with Michael would be in her best interest, the Supreme Court rejected Michael's claim, stating that the state had an interest in preserving the "unitary family" and that neither Michael nor his genetic daughter had a constitutionally protected liberty interest in maintaining their relationship (410 U.S. 110 at 227–228).

Commenting on *Michael H.*, Nancy Polikoff argued that " 'Third parties' who have functioned as parents to a child . . . should be able to obtain visitation under the standard applicable to parents. Thus, even jurisdictions in which nonparents can be awarded visitation have not gone far enough. In these jurisdictions the grant of visitation is discretionary with the court or requires [proof] that visitation is in the best interests of the child. . . . [Instead, d]enying visitation should be predicated on the same grounds as it is between legally recognized parents—only upon proof of detriment to the child" (Polikoff, "This Child Does Have Two Mothers," 521). What the law guardian and Polikoff saw as a way to maintain affective ties with an occasional "limited father," however, Barbara Woodhouse saw as an invitation to disruption and tension in Victoria's primary family relationships (Woodhouse, "Hatching the Egg," 1856–1858).

51. Woodhouse, "Hatching the Egg," 1811.

52. Bernstein, "This Child Does Have Two Mothers . . . and a Sperm Donor," 48.

53. Sidney Callahan, "Gays, Lesbians, and the Use of Alternative Reproductive Technologies," in Hilde Lindemann Nelson, *Feminism and Families* (New York: Routledge, 1997), 188–202, questions the ethical bases of the use of collaborative procreation by heterosexuals as well as by gay men and lesbians because of the importance of the "particular, specific, unique, and most important, irreversible connections" created by the "biological links in a family" (191). Although I disagree with her conclusion that third-party collaborative procreation is "harmful to the common good and to individuals who are involved—the gestational mothers, egg donors, sperm donors, recipient families, and the children so conceived" in all instances, I do think that third-party collaborative procreation can harm the individuals involved, and that certain kinds of justifications for use of third-party collaborative procreation (partciularly those based on notions of unrestricted individual choice and freedom of contract) are misguided and harmful to the development of a proper social ethic.

54. See Barbara Yngvesson, "Negotiating Motherhood: Identity and Difference in 'Open' Adoptions," *Law and Society Review* 31, no. 1 (1997): 31–80.

55. Martha Minow, "We, the Family: Constitutional Rights and American Families," *Journal of American History* 74, no. 3 (December 1987): 983.

56. Hendrick Hartog, "The Constitution of Aspiration and the Rights That Belong to Us All," *Journal of American History* 74, no. 3 (December 1987): 1027.

57. With respect to the notion of a right to relationship and care see Kenneth Karst, "The Freedom of Intimate Association," *Yale Law Journal* 89, no. 4 (1980): 624–693, and Martha Minow and Mary Lyndon Shanley, "Revisioning the Family: Relational Rights and Responsibilities," in *Reconstructing Political Theory: Feminist Perspectives*, ed. Mary Lyndon Shanley and Uma Narayan (University Park: Pennsylvania State University, 1997), 84–108.

58. On the relationship of discourses about needs and rights see Nancy Fraser, "Talking About Needs: Interpretive Contests as Political Conflicts in Welfare-State Societies," *Ethics* 99, no. 1 (January 1989): 312–313. See also Linda Gordon and Nancy Fraser, "Decoding 'Dependency': Inscriptions of Power in a Keyword of the U.S. Welfare State," in *Reconstructing Political Theory*, 25–47.

The U.N. Convention on the Rights of the Child has articulated some very important autonomy rights for children that would greatly improve the treatment of children in the United States as well as abroad. U.N. Convention on the Rights of the Child, U.N. Dec.A/Res/44/25 concluded November 20, 1989. See also Cynthia P. Cohen and Howard A. Davidson, eds., *Children's Rights in America: U.N. Convention on the Rights of the Child Compared with United States Law* (Chicago: American Bar Association Center on Children and the Law, 1990).

59. See, for example, Jean Bethke Elshtain et al., "A Communitarian Position on the Family," *National Civic Review* 82, no. 1 (Winter 1993): 25–35; Amitai Etzioni, *The Spirit of Community: Rights, Responsibilities, and the Communitarian Agenda* (New York: Crown, 1993); William A. Galston, *Liberal Purposes: Goods, Virtues, and Diversity in the Liberal State* (Cambridge: Cambridge University Press, 1991); Mary Ann Glendon, *Rights Talk: The Impoverishment of Politics* (Cambridge: Harvard University Press, 1991); Michael Sandel, *Democracy's Discontent* (Cambridge: Harvard University Press, 1996).

60. See, for example, Joan Tronto, *Moral Boundaries: A Political Argument for an Ethic of Care* (New York: Routledge, 1993) and Selma Sevenhuijsen, various articles. Milton C. Regan, *Family Law and the Pursuit of Intimacy* (New York: New York University Press, 1993) incorporates both communitarian and ethics of care perspectives into his nuanced study of family law.

Drucilla Cornell

Reimagining Adoption and Family Law

I. Introduction

Why have feminists been reluctant participants in the politics of adoption? Today the law in most states pits two mothers against one another and the media dramatizes the purportedly hostile relationship between them. Think of the "heart-tugging" pictures of baby Jessica as she is removed from her adoptive parents to be given back to her birth mother and father. The press in general has never shown much sympathy for birth mothers. Nor has the feminist press, in which members of the various birth mothers' associations have tried to publish for years without success. These organizations have accused feminists of favoring adopting mothers, either because they are adopting mothers themselves or because, like the public in general, they have disdain for the birth mother who gave up her baby.

This reluctance may not spring from conscious attitudes about birth mothers. Custody battles between birth and adoptive mothers challenge one of our culture's deepest fantasies—that there can only be one mother and therefore we have to pick the "real" one. Picking one mother over another is a harsh judgment not easily reconciled with feminist solidarity. Feminist solidarity supposedly grew out of the shared experience of our oppression as women that was uncovered when through consciousness-raising new meaning was given to what women have had to endure under male domination.[1] At first glance the so-called "birth mother" and the adopting mother do not recall a shared experience upon which solidarity can be based.

Adoption is fraught with issues of race, class, and imperialist domination that have persistently caused divisions in the second wave of feminism. The woman who is picked by law as the "real" mother is usually the one privileged by class and race. In international adoption the politics of imperialist domination and the struggle of postcolonial nations to constitute themselves as independent nations are inevitably implicated. Hence it is not surprising that one of the first steps in the constitution of nationhood is to end international adoptions in the courts.[2]

Nor is it surprising to find that the language of adoption is the language of war. In most states the "birth mother" "surrenders" her child to the state which then transfers the child to the adopting, predominantly white, middle-class, heterosexual parents. According to current law, what the "birth mother" surrenders is not just primary custodial responsibility of her child, but her entitlement to any kind of relationship with him or her in the future. She is denied even the most primitive kind of information as to the child's well-being. In states where records are closed, adopted children have to "show cause," make some claim that they will be or have been physically or emotionally damaged if they are not allowed to get information about their heredity or the whereabouts of their "birth mother" and/or their biological father. Lorraine Dusky eloquently writes:

> They call me "biological mother." I hate those words. They make me
> sound like a baby machine, a conduit, without emotions. They want me to
> forget and go out and make a new life. I had a baby and gave her away. But
> I am a mother.[3]

We can see all the contradictions wrought by this demand for absolute surrender in recent lesbian co-parent adoptions. In such adoptions, the last thing the "birth" mother wants to give up is all access to her child. She wants to share joint custody with her lover. Yet it is still the exception to the rule that a lesbian can adopt her lover's "birth" child, ascending to the status of a legally recognized parent. There are almost no states in the United States that allow a gay or lesbian couple to openly adopt a baby as a couple. Single or coupled, gay men are almost entirely excluded from access to legally recognized parenthood. Due to the narrow heterosexist definition of the family embodied in our law as the norm, lesbian and gay couples are not given the right to adopt the children of their partners, a right that traditional heterosexual stepparents can take for granted and easily exercise. My own sketch of the fair conditions of family law reform expands the potential reach of para-parenting beyond traditional couple arrangements. It is only recently that single mothers are allowed to adopt because they, too, were not thought to meet the norm of the "normal heterosexual couple." The corrective I advocate to the unfair treatment of people who do not fit the heterosexist norm is not simply that gays and lesbians be given the right to parenthood if they can successfully show that they mimic the "normal" heterosexual couple. To adequately address the relationship of adopting mothers to birth mothers, and their children to both, we need to rethink our current conception of the legal family from the ground up.

For decades now, birth mothers' organizations have militantly protested against the surrender of their entitlement to the status of mother even if they chose or were forced by circumstances to forsake primary custodial responsibility of their child. Now adopted children are also in the process of challenging as unconstitutional their unequal treatment at the hands of the legal system. After all, nonadopted children have access to information about themselves and their genealogy. It seems obvious that adopted children are indeed being treated differently from other children. Could there be a compelling state interest that would legitimate such unequal treatment?

A feminist answer to that question has to be that there could be no compelling state interest that could legitimate the relinquishment of the birth mother's entitlement to access to her child or to the child's access to her. Why has adoption come to be understood as demanding the complete relinquishment of all access or even information about the child? We need a deeper analysis of why that relinquishment has historically been enforced and felt by many to be so necessary to the protection of "family values." Without this analysis we will continue to establish victors and vanquished in a war that is usually portrayed as being one between women.

Modern legal adoptions are only one form of adoption and are a recent historical event.[4] Long before lesbian adoptions became possible to the limited degree they are now, informal "adoptions" in African American communities kept families together by extending them, rather than shutting out the birth mother.[5] In these communities there are often two mothers, which avoids the demand to pick one as the "real" mother.[6] What legal interests are at stake in the requirement that adoption demand total surrender both of the child and of all information about her? Why not identify adoption as only the signing away of primary custody?

Feminists have a strong political interest in insisting that the right to build families and to foster our own intimate lives be privileged over the

state enforcement of any *ideal* of the good family. My own proposed guidelines for family law reform would change the very meaning of adoption as
it is now legally and culturally understood.

II. Patriarchy and Its Legal Effects

For my purposes, the word patriarchy indicates the manner in which a
woman's legal identity remains bound up with her duties to the state as wife
and mother within the traditional heterosexual family. Our feminist demand must be for the full release of women from this legal identity which
is wholly inconsistent with the recognition of each one of us as a free and
equal person. Only on the basis of this recognition should we willingly subject ourselves to the law as an arm of the state.

We cannot demand release from a legal identity that defines and limits
what it means to be a woman through state-imposed duties without challenging the legal institution of the monogamous heterosexual family. The
duties that now define woman in her social identity, as in herself, rather than
for herself, are inseparable from the conjugal institution of the heterosexual
family. Therefore the redefinition of "woman" is inseparable from the demands of gays and lesbians to be free to create their own persons.

If we understand that women's legal identity in both family life and civil
society remains bound up with an externally imposed set of duties we can
at least make sense of why it is that the so-called birth mother is considered
to have given up all entitlement to any kind of relationship with her child
when she yields her duty to be the child's caretaker. Under the patriarchal
scheme, a woman is entitled to protection by the state because she takes up
her duties as caretaker of her family. If she forsakes those duties she is denied
any of the protection given to mothers. Since she has no independent standing in civil society there is nothing left of her social life. Let me put it as
clearly as possible: It is only in the context of a system of duties that remain
bound up with women's legal identity in the heterosexual family that we can
even begin to understand the unequal treatment of birth mothers and
adopted children.

The relationship among legal identity in civil society, "social life,"[7] and
the system of duties in the heterosexual family can help us understand the
driving anxiety about infertility which has haunted the history of modern
adoptions. If a woman's social worth is inseparable from the fulfillment of
her duty as a mother, then, if she cannot live up to that duty, she is confronted with the loss of her only social status. Of course, the obsession with

genetic ties is also tied into unconscious fantasies about the meaning of masculinity and racial superiority.[8]

To protect from public exposure the adopting mother's failure to be a woman because she has failed to meet the symbolic meaning of womanhood demands the erasure of the birth mother. It is not entitlement but rather the terror before the loss of identity that explains so much of the secrecy that surrounds adoption.

III. Donning a Citizen Identity

The scene of adoption is ensnared in imposed roles associated with women's legal identity within the heterosexual family. The first step in untangling ourselves from these imposed roles is to don our identity as citizens and to demand a full civil identity as persons. Simply put, as feminists we must insist that we are entitled to rights, not because we are mothers, but because we are citizens and persons.

The Argentinean movie *The Official Story* illustrates some of these points. An adoptive mother has blinded herself to the reality of her daughter's tragic circumstances of adoption. During the course of the film she discovers that her daughter is a child of one of the missing persons, probably murdered by the government. Gradually she comes to heed the call made to her by her daughter's grandmother. What relationship the two women will have to one another is left open, but it is clear that there can be no going back once the grandmother is accepted and embraced.

It is only by slowly freeing herself from the imprisonment of imposed familial duties that the adoptive mother can see her way to her responsibility as a citizen of Argentina. She sheds her exteriorized feminine identity, and in a profound sense becomes her own person, when she dons the identity of a citizen responsible for the fate of her country as well as for the destiny of her adopted daughter. Before, she left the world of politics to men. She dons her identity as citizen by taking her place in a demonstration beside the grandmother of her daughter. Her prior life in the conjugal institution of the heterosexual family does not survive her insistence on her political responsibility as citizen and her ethical responsibility to her daughter's grandmother. The woman's eventual embrace of the grandmother as someone entitled to a relationship to her daughter ended her life in the traditional family.

The Official Story presents in an extreme form the continuing presence of kidnapping disguised as an economic transaction in an adoption. *The*

Official Story also graphically demonstrates the ability of the rich and powerful in many of the world's nations to steal children of the poor or the politically dispossessed. This phenomenon is well documented in heart-wrenching stories of the mothers of "the disappeared." The dictatorship in Argentina that allowed babies to be stolen for adoption is not an isolated event. Indeed, the open stealing of a person's children is part of the enactment of psychic as well as physical torture.[9] The message of *The Official Story* is clear: Disappeared persons do not have children because they are socially dead, and their social death is a preliminary obliteration foreshadowing their actual murder.

IV. Feminist Responsibility and International Adoptions

In my own case, as an adoptive mother, I also feel ethically compelled to recognize the rights of the other mother and of my own daughter's right to her person. In any adoption there are always two mothers as well as a biological sperm donor who may or may not deserve or wish to be designated as the father. When the two mothers, or mother and grandmother, are from different countries and linguistic traditions, the responsibility of the adopting mother to the birth mother does not go away. Indeed, it can be accentuated. We are inescapably confronted with a scene of adoption that is far from ideal given the unjust world we live in. The history of the child's adoption may not be as dramatically wrought with tragedy as that of the young girl in *The Official Story*. Still, at least in international adoptions, the adopting parents are confronted with the history of imperialism and economic devastation, which may be at least the partial explanation for why the child is being put up for adoption in the first place.

As I will argue shortly, we can certainly reimagine a different scene, one in which adoption does not carry with it the same burdens and responsibilities that are imposed by the reality that it is injustice that often makes one of the mothers give up her baby and all access to her. But given that we do live in an unjust world we have to confront the responsibilities that come with it. One way of trying to meet that responsibility is to demand the birth mother's right to access to the child she bore. In any world we can also demand that the child's freedom to know her mother be protected.

There is another responsibility to the adopted child, and one that cannot easily be imposed by law because it involves extensive affirmative duties. What are the responsibilities of an adopting mother who takes a child from a South American country, for example, and brings her to the United States?

Is she simply to be assimilated to the adopting mother's or parents' country and culture? Assimilation comes at a cost to the child's freedom. The mother, mothers, or parents consciously or unconsciously cut the child from a past she will ultimately have to integrate as part of herself. If she is to be recognized as the ultimate source of her own representations of who she is, then certain decisions to keep her options open must be maintained by the parent.

If the child is from South America, for example, the meaning of her roots in Hispanic culture can only be kept alive for her if Spanish is maintained and/or taught and access to her country of origin is kept available.[10] A number of South American nations have now stopped international adoptions to the United States. Fierce opposition to the United States and bitter accusations against adopting parents have been made by many countries. This history should not be "white-washed." Nor, of course, is the proper response guilt. But if the child's freedom is to be maintained, the adopting parents must face their responsibility for their daughter's or son's freedom. Obviously only a small part of that responsibility is met by demanding legal rights for birth mothers and adopted children, but doing so is at least a first step.

For many parents it may feel scary or even unnatural that their child has access to a language, a country, and a culture they cannot share. One of our most foundational and commonsense notions of a family is that its members belong to the same culture, language, and country. Given how deeply rooted this idea of the family is, it is hardly surprising that parents force their children to assimilate to their culture and forsake the country and language of the birth mother or parents. Yet forced assimilation takes away a child's freedom to design her personhood out of her unique personal circumstances, circumstances that the white adopting parent does not share.

Does the recognition of the child's freedom by, for example, maintaining her mother tongue interfere with the closeness of an adopted child to her adopting parents? Not at all. But it does demand that we think about parental relationships differently. In particular the mother–daughter relationship—known as the mother–child dyad—has been hindered by a story of too great closeness. The mother–child dyad purportedly arises because of the child's actual dependence on the maternal body for the intake of sustenance, that is, breast milk. In fantasy, both the mother and child blend together into one body, the breast no longer being part of the mother's person but a shared materiality that obliterates any division between the two.

Although this fantasy is held to be true for both male and female children, the traditional psychoanalytic story at least gives boys a way of identifying with the father's phallus so as to violently disrupt this fantasized unity with the mother. The mother and daughter, on the other hand, are never given a symbolic intermediary for their relationship that allows them to understand each other as separate persons and allows the mother to remain both intact and in the relationship to her daughter. But in reality, the fantasy mother–child dyad of traditional psychoanalysis is just that, a fantasy. The mother is simply a person with a breast—she cannot be reduced to The Breast. There is a relationship between two people from the beginning.[11]

In erotic poems that seem daring 2,700 years later, Sappho celebrates her daughter's "magnificence" and her joys in her daughter's stride, which expresses a freedom she has never known and which she mourns for as lost to herself.[12] Sappho's erotic appreciation of her daughter is inseparable from the celebration of her daughter's physical freedom, her strength. Sappho sings of the distance between the two that makes a mother's poetic joy in her daughter's singularity possible. The daughter "whose skin of burnished gold pales the magnificence of the sun"[13] is uncapturable by the mother who cannot keep up with her daughter as she runs down the beach. This mother joys in the stride that takes her daughter into her own future, as she stays behind marvelling at the play of lights illuminating her daughter's beauty.

When we travel to Latin countries, and my daughter translates for her father and me because she is bilingual and we are not, I feel something akin to Sappho's joy in her daughter's strength. My daughter's beautiful Spanish leaves her mother, who stumbles around in the language, in awe. She has access to a culture that will never be mine. She can take me into worlds that I can never know from the inside out as she can. I joy and marvel at the richness of her universe. Like Sappho, that my daughter is worlds ahead of me, in this case when it comes to language, is not cause for sorrow. Rather, it is the source of joy in this being who is becoming her own unique person and can open my world by having her own.

V. The Imaginary Domain and the Right of Birth Mothers and Adopted Children

My argument so far has been that, even in 1999, the way in which women have been symbolically sexed is partly constituted by legal duties that have been imposed upon them. For us, our "selves" have been buried under these duties for far too long. As Luce Irigaray has written:

> Valorized by society as a mother, nurturer, and housewife (the community needs children to make up the future work force, as defenders of the na-

tion and as reproducers of society, aside from the fact that the family unit is the most profitable one for the State in that much of the work that is done within it goes unpaid, for example), woman is deprived of the possibility of interiorizing her female identity.[14]

Legal enforcement of monogamous heterosexuality has made the state and not the person the source of moral meaning of their sexuate being and how it should be lived with "all our kin."[15] Now, I want to argue, it is time we recognize that governmentally enforced sexual choices, let alone the outright denial of the right to parent to some persons because of their sexual lives, are inconsistent with the equal protection of what I call "the imaginary domain."

The imaginary domain is the moral and psychic space we need if we are to have meaningful sexual freedom. What do I mean by sexual freedom? Each one of us is formed sexually through a complex interaction with the sexual personas our culture imposes in the name of gender norms and roles that are still with us and that promote heterosexuality. By engaging with these personas in fantasy and in our actual lives, we are shaped into men and women. A human being cannot escape being formed through a web of identifications and relationships. These fundamental relationships and identifications are integral to who we are, and indeed become part of how we imagine ourselves. But what has been shaped can always be reshaped.

The imaginary domain is the moral and psychic space that allows us to become the ultimate source of how we evaluate and make sense of these identifications. Of course, we cannot simply step out of identifications the way we shed clothes. But we can engage personas so that they are remade even as they are assumed. In order to revise our sense of self and reimagine who we are as sexual creatures, we must be allowed to freely "act out" how we imagine ourselves and our relationships with others. If we have an imaginary domain provided as a matter of right we at least have the chance to individuate ourselves to become our own person.

Individuation does not imply anthropological individualism. Clearly I do not believe it does since I have argued elsewhere that who we are as sexed beings is symbolic and formed by institutions. I use the word individuation to imply that the "who" of the person cannot be conflated with any sanctioned identity, including that of gender. The imaginary domain, then, is the psychic space a person has by right and which allows her or him to take on and evaluate his or her identifications, by representing who she is sexually and forming intimate relations as she sees fit.

Would the equal protection of the imaginary domain give rights to birth mothers and adopted children? First let us take the example of "birth mothers." It is only too evident that the struggle of every woman to become who she is demands a confrontation with the connection between femininity and motherhood. For some women oppression imposed by race, class, national, and sexual identity has forced absolute separation from their children upon them. Carol Austin, who had to hide her own relationship to her lesbian lover in order for them to successfully complete an international adoption, describes the situation of the "birth mother" of their first adopted child as follows:

> A real joy for us was being able to spend a lot of time with Catherine's birth mother, Violetta, a twenty-two year old Quechua Indian who was also Julie's maid. When Violetta had become pregnant out of wedlock, she had been taken in by some distant members who struggled to care for their own five children. Living in a crowded, dirt floored home in a poverty-ridden neighborhood in Lima the family was not willing to care for another child. And if Violetta decided to keep her child, she could not work. Violetta's and her child's survival depended upon her giving up this first born baby to adoption.[16]

Violetta did not have the economic option to take custodial responsibility for her child. Austin was only too well aware that Violetta's decision to give up her child was not a choice and Austin knew that no amount of emotional support from her could make up for Violetta's loss and sorrow that she could not keep her baby. Still, to whatever degree it might help Violetta, both Austin and her partner wanted her to get to know them—to know that her baby would be safe. They showed her pictures of where the baby was to live; they left their address with her so that she could check on her baby's well-being.

Certainly these measures, as reassuring as they may have been, could not make up for Violetta's terrible either/or, a forced sexual choice in the worst sense. Some adopting mothers have spoken of their feeling that their babies were destined for them. Austin was well aware that if this baby was destined for her and her lover, then Violetta was destined to be deprived of her child by economic circumstances. Measures could be taken to ameliorate Violetta's pain, but the poverty of her life circumstances remained. Austin's sensitivity to Violetta's horrible either/or, and the economic poverty and oppression that imposed it, came in part from her own struggles as an adopting lesbian parent.

Austin describes her pain at having to be disappeared in order to adopt a child for herself and her lover. Again, economics played a major role in the lovers' choice of who was to appear as a mother. Of course, Austin's circumstances were in no way comparable to Violetta's, but she did not have the same kind of professional job as her lover, who was put forward as most suitable for the role of (supposedly) single mother because of her professional and financial standing. But, in spite of her realization that this was the best way for the two of them to adopt a baby, Austin rebelled:

> I soon found myself emotionally stranded between anger and guilt. I felt angry and totally left out by my externally forced, yet self-imposed, invisibility. And right on the heels of my anger came guilt! It was after all, Jane who was putting in hours of meeting time, and it was her financial and personal history that was being dissected. I didn't envy her, yet I began to have an all or nothing reaction. . . . Finally immersion at any level, without recognition of my existence became impossible. How naive, I had been to assume, only a few months before, that my invisibility would not be a problem. The entire adoption situation had forced open some of my raw childhood wounds.[17]

Austin's emotional pain at being forcibly rendered invisible sensitized her both to a birth mother's need to be seen and understood, and to the adopted child's need to be in touch with her national heritage.

Could a birth mother who chose or was forced to give up primary custody still know herself at the deepest recesses of her person to be a mother? Testimony from birth mothers have answered yes to that question. To rob her of her chance to struggle through what meaning being a mother still has for her is to make the state, and not the woman, the master over the construction of her sense of who she is. Birth mothers have rights, not as birth mothers, but as persons who, like all others, must be allowed the space to come to terms with their own life defining decisions about sexuality and family.

Lorraine Dusky is only one of many birth mothers who have described their anguish at the enforced separation from their child. In her case she also knew that there was crucial information that the adopted parents needed to have about her daughter. Dusky had taken birth control pills during the early stage of her pregnancy before she realized that she was pregnant. The pills were found to cause serious gynecological problems in the next generation. She tried to get the agency which had handled the adoption to pass the crucial information on to the adopting parents; she was desperate to know that her daughter received the proper medical attention. The agency told her that her daughter was fine. Tragically, the information was never passed along to her daughter's adopting parents. The adopting parents were, as it turned out, trying to locate Dusky because, although she did not suffer from gynecological problems, Dusky's daughter had suffered severe seizures, almost drowning twice: The adopting parents were desperate to communicate with Dusky about her medical history. Dusky finally found her daughter through the illegal adoption underground. The adopting mother recognized her as Jane's other mother, and Dusky has for many years now had a relationship with her daughter.

Dusky's story had a happy ending. But why did Dusky, white, middle-class, and on her way to becoming a successful journalist give her baby up in the first place? The story of her decision is inseparable from the sexual shame imposed upon women in the 1950s who did not get pregnant in the proper way; that is, within legal marriage. Abortion was illegal, and, like many women who hoped against hope that they were not pregnant, she put off an abortion. By the time she got access to an illegal abortion in Puerto Rico it was too late. Adoption was her only option. It had become her only option because abortion was illegal, and because of the blending of personal and political morality which made it close to impossible at that time for an unmarried white, middle-class woman to be a single mother. Dusky's decision exemplifies the enforced sexual choice that arises from denying women their equivalent chance to claim their person, and to represent their own sexuate being.

What should a "birth mother" relinquish when she relinquishes primary custody of her child? Only that, primary custody. The equal protection of the "birth mother"'s imaginary domain out of which she can construct her personhood at least demands that she be allowed access to any information she desires to have about her child, and to have the chance to meet and explore with the child what kind of relationship they can develop.

Let me now turn to the rights of adopted children ensured by the imaginary domain. The child should have the same right to access information about his or her biological mother and father as the biological parents have to their child. Again, once we accept that even a primordial sense of self is not just given to us, but is a complicated lifelong process of imagining and projecting ourselves over time, we can see how important it is to have access to one's family history, if one feels the need for it. If the meaning of that history is inseparable from the struggle of postcolonial nations to achieve meaningful economic and political independence, then that history is political from the outset. Heritage is more than genetic. The break with the nation, culture, and language of one's birth, which is inevitably imposed by an international adoption, has to be available for symbolization. Under our current law an internationally adopted child is already subjected to second-class citizenship. Certain rights of citizenship, including the right to run for president of the United States, are denied. But even if we were to remove the taint of second-class citizenship, the child still needs to make sense of the break, to have the chance to recover herself and the meaning of keeping in touch with the linguistic and cultural traditions of her country of origin through her own imaginary domain.

Children should not have to show cause, let alone that they are emotionally disturbed because of their adoptive status. The demand to show cause is just one more way in which people who do not fit neatly into the purportedly natural heterosexual family are pathologized. Again, the imagined heterosexual adopting family is privileged as the one deserving of protection of the state, even against the child who is a member of it. My only serious disagreement with some of the literature written by birth mothers is the idealization of biological ties. There is an old Italian saying that blood seeks blood. But blood also robs, rapes, and murders blood. As Dorothy Roberts has also eloquently argued, the idealization of genetic ties is also intertwined with the most profoundly racist fantasies, including the desire for racial purity.[18]

To conclude, adopted children and birth mothers should be allowed access to each other as part of the equal protection of their imaginary domain. We should have public records in which all adopted children and birth parents can register. A birth mother who was forced to give up her child obviously did not have her right to represent her own sexuate being protected. She had a decision thrust upon her either because of economic circumstances or, as in Dusky's case, because of the sexual hypocrisy that dominated this country in the 1950s. *Her right ought to be based on her personhood, not on the fact of her biological motherhood.* If, in spite of circumstances, she still represents herself as a mother who has given up primary custody but only that, she should be allowed to follow through in her efforts to reach her child. The fear of the hysterical birth mother is just that, a fear; the adoption resolves the issue of primary custody except in the few states where lesbian lovers are allowed joint custody. Dusky did not try to steal her daughter, Jane, from her adopting parents. She knew she could not undo what she had done. Jane has two mothers, and she has had to come to terms with that. She calls Lorraine by her first name and not "mother," perhaps to recognize the differential relationship between the two mothers. Yet everyone agrees that it is better "this way."

What of the woman who when she gives up primary custody also wishes to escape entirely from any imposition on her self of the role of mother? Such a woman should be allowed her refusal to register. If the past teaches us anything, many birth fathers will continue to wish to elude acknowledgment of their fatherhood by refusing to claim paternity or meet its responsibilities. But the law cannot make it illegal for the child to track down the "birth mother." In the end it is between them. This is an example of why I argue that we should not expect law to do more than provide us with the space to work through and personalize our complicated life histories.

Some "birth mothers" who have given up their babies for adoption have undergone a trauma. A legal system that makes the cut from her child absolute blocks any hope for recovery from this trauma, for the mother certainly, and maybe for the child. What the best law can do for adopted children and "birth mothers" who feel compelled to seek out one another is to provide them with the space to work through the traumatic event that has to some extent formed them. It cannot erase the past. It certainly cannot provide a magical "cure" to the emotional difficulties we all face in our intimate associations. Some adopted children will want to search for their birth parents and some will not. Some birth parents will want to be found; others will not.

Law cannot take the passion and complexity out of emotionally fraught situations. Still, the imaginary domain will give to the persons involved in an adoption the space to come to terms with their history and the meaning it has for them and the possibilities it yields for new ways of imagining themselves. It cannot heal trauma. It cannot protect a birth mother who is tracked by her child from the pain of confrontation with her child. Such a confrontation with her child could undoubtedly challenge her sense of who she has struggled to become. The protection of the imaginary domain demands that space be open to explore and establish relationships; it cannot provide the moral content of those relationships without delimiting the space that its justification demands be kept open.

VI. Family Law—Some Concluding Notes

If family law is to protect the imaginary domain, family law reform must be rooted in the transformation of women's civil identity and must be rid of all traces of patriarchy as well. What would be fair guidelines for a family law that protected the full civil identity of all who fell under its governance?

First and foremost the state could not impose any form of family as *the* good family, and so could not reenforce the heterosexual and monogamous nuclear family, even if such families continued to be one way in which people organized their sexual life and their relationships to children. Gays, lesbians, straights, and transvestites would all be able to organize their sexuality as it accorded with their own self-representation at the time.

But what about intergenerational relationships? Obviously children need care. And this means long-term commitment. How are we, as a society, to provide for the reproduction of the next generation given the need young children have for stable, lasting relationships? A considerable amount of time and devotion is needed to bring a child up. In our society the nuclear heterosexual family has been the institution assigned primary, if not the entire responsibility for the raising of children.

One popular justification for the heterosexual family is that it is in the best interests of the child to have two parents, a man and a woman, who live together. Statistically, we know that the divorce rate means that many children of heterosexual parents do not live in such families.[19] Is there any reason to think that living as a heterosexual makes one a better parent? There is absolutely no evidence other than that grounded in homophobia that this is the case.[20] Open gay and lesbian parenting is so new that there are few studies available. Those that exist show that gay and lesbian parents tend to have less conflict in the family, and that in itself may benefit children. They may also be, overall, economically more stable than their heterosexual counterparts. Moreover, their children are wanted. Both economic stability and the intense desire to parent have been noted as factors that have helped create healthy and happy children in these families.[21] These preliminary studies should certainly assuage any legitimate fears that gays and lesbians will not be committed parents.

What would a nonheterosexist family law contribute to securing care for children? The interests of the state in securing care for children would have to be consistent with the equivalent evaluation of each one of us as a free and equal person, and children would be recognized as persons whose scope of rights would mature with time. I will suggest a reform structure consistent with the limit that must be placed on family law by the recognition of our full equality as persons, not specific legislative proposals. But I would argue that, to be legitimate, specific proposals would have to be guided by this structure.

First, regulation of the family should protect all lovers who choose to register in civil marriage, or some other form of domestic partnership. Many gays and lesbians have argued against the mimicry of heterosexuality inherent in the very idea of marriage.[22] I am sympathetic to this line of reasoning. Still, it is consistent to demand as a right what you choose under your own construction of your own person never to exercise. The denial of this legal recognition is an illegitimate incorporation of moral or religious values into the basic institutions of a constitutional government. Moreover, because the government has no legitimate interest in monogamy it cannot enforce coupling. Simply put, if in the name of equality polygamy is to be allowed, so is polyandry, including multiple, civilly recognized sexual relationships amongst women.

Secondly, the government must provide a structure for custodial responsibility for children. If the government has no legitimate interest in a particular form of family life it should also have no legitimate interest in linking custodial responsibility only to those people who are in a sexual relationship. Two women friends who were not sexually involved could assume parental responsibility for a child; three gay men could also assume parental responsibility for a child; and finally, a traditional heterosexual couple could also assume parental responsibility for a child. The difference would be that custody would not be a given fact of their sexual unit. In other words, a man skittish about becoming a parent could choose to stay married to his partner and yet also choose not to share full custodial responsibility for his child, leaving his partner to take on custodial responsibility with another friend, or for that matter, a woman lover rather than himself.

To achieve the needed stability for children, the assumption of custodial responsibility would carry with it all that it does now—financial support, limits on movement, and so forth. Parents would be legally established at the time they assumed custodial responsibility; each child would have a legally recognized family. If there were others who, because of sexual affiliation with one of the custodial parents, wanted to assume legal status as a parent, it would be up to the initial group to decide whether or not they should be allowed to do so. The procedure would be similar to that of current stepparent adoptions. Custodial responsibility would remain for life; legal responsibility to custodial children would continue regardless of the sexual lives of the members of the custodial partnership or team. From my standpoint as a mother, I would prefer a "team," but I understand that only to be my preference.

Those persons who have recently argued against divorce have done so because the stability of children is often profoundly undermined in divorce, let alone in an ugly custody battle. Divorce, or an end to a sexual liaison of one of the partners in the team, would not in any way affect custodial responsibility. The only reason for a partner or a team to legally sue to terminate someone else's custodial responsibility in the partnership, or team, would be what we now call the doctrine of extraordinary circumstances, for example, sexual or physical abuse. Children could also sue to separate themselves from one custodial partnership or team, but under the same doctrine. Under the age of majority the only requirement would be that they choose another custodian. Would adults owe financial support to other adults in this arrangement, if for example one member of the partnership or the team chose to stay home during the early years of the child's life? My answer would be only by contract.

Once signed on, you have signed on for life, which is why I believe that this conception of custodial responsibility meets the state's as well as the children's interest in stability. But could you add on? I have already advocated that you should be able to do so. For example, could you, as an adopting mother, embrace the birth mother in a relationship of shared custody? Could it be the other way around? It already is the other way around in lesbian couples, where the birth mother and her lover seek joint custody together.

The current often tortuous process of adoption has been eloquently observed by lesbian parents. The birth mother is a mother by birth. Her lover is denied parental status in most states. In states where she can achieve it, the birth mother frequently must give up her rights in order for her lover to adopt. This case forces us to confront how difficult it is for our society to conceive of two mothers raising a child together. We keep imposing a choice when it's the last thing the mothers want. It is only in a culture that imposes monogamous heterosexuality because it is only in that culture that the existence of two mothers is such a problem.[23] Patriarchy, as Irigaray eloquently describes, lets the man, not the woman, determine his line. Two mothers causes a problem only when a society is organized around patrilineal lineage. If both women are to be accorded civil status, then it follows that they are free as persons to assume custody together. This would end the pain associated with lesbian adoption.

Lesbian mothers are obviously in a relationship with one another. But so are adopting mothers who never meet the birth mother. The fear of the "return of the birth mother" haunts adoptions. But why? If she has signed away primary custody, she cannot take the child back. Why wouldn't this return be envisioned as a good thing, as it turned out in the case of Lorraine Dusky? As Dusky describes, "all of us long ago made peace with our places in Jane's life. She calls me Lorraine. "Mom" is her other mother."[24]

There is a deep and profound sense that we do not own our children. All children can escape the confines of what we would make of them. That children are not property is recognized by their inclusion in the moral community of persons from birth. Obviously this idea of custodial responsibility and children's rights demands that we stretch our imaginations. It demands that we struggle to free ourselves from the picture of the family as "Mommy and Daddy and baby makes three." But if we are to truly take seriously what it means to treat each one of us as an equal person and thus not insist on a proper family or "normal" relations between the sexes, then we have to have the courage to do so. It is what is demanded of us by our civil duty.

I have little doubt that it is in the best interests of the children. Certainly it would meet the goal of ending the horrendous tragedy of a woman losing her children because she does not live up to some fantasy conception of what her duty as a mother is. If a woman was living up to her custodial responsibility it wouldn't matter whether she had one lover or many. It certainly wouldn't matter that she currently, or in the past, had another woman as lover. But rather than entitling women through the reciprocal right of mothers and children, I would do so through the reciprocal right of custodial partners and children. I would advocate this conception of parental entitlement because any state regulation based on normalized conceptions of femininity, including those of the mother as caretaker, is inconsistent with the equal protection of the imaginary domain.

The third legitimate state interest is the equitable distribution of the burdens of reproduction and the equal protection of the health of young children. Obviously we would have to have provisions for health care for children. I would also argue that we would have to have income maintenance for families. Mothering should no longer be a class privilege. In order to support oneself beyond the level of a guaranteed income, people have to work. Therefore, we would need to provide some kind of publicly funded child care as part of parental entitlement.

The structure of these reforms would provide stability to children and sexual freedom to adults. Since there would be no state-enforced normalized family, children who fall outside the norm would not be stigmatized. There wouldn't be any normal family, as if such a thing has ever existed. Part of the difficulty for adopted children is that they have fallen outside of the norm. By lifting the norm we lift the stigma.

VII. Brave New Families

Are these brave new families? In *Brave New World* Aldous Huxley fantasized about the totalitarian horror of the state outlawing families as dangerous sites of intimacy. In Huxley's tale, embryos were processed as so many duplicate prints to stamp out beings individuated enough to be persons. Love was outlawed, and indeed, the hero's great crime against the state is that, as a sign of individuality, he falls in love.

Like all totalitarian states, the brave new world fought valiantly to defeat the imaginary domain, the place of retreat, that kept the person, uncapturable, individuated from the regime. The regime's method of torture, similar to what Orwell imagined in *1984*, articulates the centrality of defeating the imaginary domain in a totalitarian state. The state reaches into that sanctuary, breaking the divide between fantasy and reality by actualizing the victims' worst nightmares. The message is clear—there is no sanctuary from the state.

A family law that insists that this sanctuary is crucial to the protection of our inviolability clearly and firmly rejects the state control of persons of the brave new world. That state fears eros. In contrast, an equivalent law of persons that would allow us to initiate and set forth our own lives as lovers and parents celebrates eroticism.

Families are special because they offer a space for eroticism in which love and life can flourish.[25] Whether they are created through biology, technology, or adoption,[26] or some combination of each, the specialness of erotic connection will obviously make families different from other associations in civil society in and out of which people move freely. By erotic connection I do not just mean actual sexual attraction and relationships between adults. As I suggested in my reading of Sappho, mothers and daughters are erotically connected although this eroticism is rarely recognized. To recognize this connection is to get in touch with the possibility that one becomes a woman by loving another woman rather than by disavowing our love for her and more particularly our primordial longing for the mother's body. This disavowal is supposedly made necessary by the Oedipal complex which in turn assumes the child's normal progression to heterosexuality. What would the possibilities of love and attachment be once the enforcement of heterosexuality was no longer the law? Many of us are now at work in both dreaming up and trying to realize more varied forms of attachment and love within our own families.

I have argued strongly that adopted children and "birth mothers" should have access to each other if they seek it. The idea of the "birth mother" and an adopting mother living together as lovers is still obviously a brave new family to some. All that protecting the imaginary domain can do is to give us the space to try to dream up and live out love in our relationships to other adults and with our children. But this recognition would be a big step toward the dissolution of Hades, where those who have been denied their right to represent their own sexuate being have been banished.

1. Catharine A. MacKinnon, *Toward a Feminist Theory of State* (Cambridge, Mass.: Harvard University Press, 1989).

2. Diana Jean Schemo, "The Baby Trail: A Special Report; Adoptions in Paraguay: Mothers Cry Theft," *New York Times* (19 March 1996), sec. A.

3. Lorraine Dusky, *Birthmark* (New York: M. Evans, 1979).

4. See Susan and Elton Klibanoff, *Let's Talk About Adoption* (Boston: Little, Brown, 1973), chapter 16.

5. Ibid.

6. Ibid.

7. Ibid.

8. Dorothy Roberts, "The Genetic Tie," *University of Chicago Law Review* 62, no. 1 (Winter 1995).

9. E. Valentine Daniel, *Charred Lullabies: Chapters in an Anthropology of Violence* (Princeton, N.J.: Princeton University Press, 1996).

10. This demands the maintenance of dual citizenship, at least through childhood. Currently, the U.S. allows such dual citizenship for adopted children until the age of twenty-one.

11. One major contribution of feminist psychoanalytic theory has been to critically undermine the truth of the fantasy of psychoanalytic theory. See Jessica Benjamin, *Like Objects, Love Objects: Essays on Recognition and Sexual Difference* (New Haven, Conn.: Yale University Press, 1995).

12. Excerpts from the poems of Sappho, translated by Emma Bianchi, unpublished manuscript on file with author.

13. Ibid.

14. Luce Irigaray, *I Love to You: Sketch of a Possible Felicity in History*, trans. Alison Martin (New York: Routledge, 1996), 47.

15. I borrow the phrase from Carol Stack's well-known book. Stack's ethnographic study of African American families showed that "kin" was a much broader concept than that which has dominated the white middle-class community. Stack's ethnographic work showed that biological ties did not define the parameters of the family. See Carol Stack, *All Our Kin: Strategies for Survival in a Black Community* (New York: Harper and Row, 1974).

16. Carol Austin, "Latent Tendencies and Covert Acts," in *The Adoption Reader: Birth Mothers, Adoptive Mothers, and Adopted Daughters Tell Their Stories*, ed. Susan Wadia-Ellis (Seattle: Seal Press, 1995).

17. Austin, "Latent Tendencies," 106.

18. Roberts, "The Genetic Tie."

19. Judith Stacey, *In the Name of the Family: Rethinking Family Values in the Postmodern Age* (Boston: Beacon Press, 1996).

20. See testimony in *Baehr* v. *Miike*, WL 694235 (Hawaii Cir.Ct. 1996).

21. Stacey, *In the Name of the Family*, chapter 5. See also Linnea Due, *Joining the Tribe: Growing Up Gay and Lesbian in the 90s* (New York: Doubleday, 1996). Lesbian partners show the most egalitarian patterns in sharing household responsibilities. This example of integration of work and home life has seemed to be particularly beneficial to the self-esteem and general life outlook of girls raised by lesbians.

22. Morris Kaplan, *Sexual Justice* (New York: Routledge, 1997), chapter 7.

23. Same-sex parenting seems incomprehensible only to a culture that imposes heterosexuality as the norm. Consider sociologist David Eggebeen's testimony in *Baehr* v. *Miike*, at 7, "[S]ame-sex marriages where children [are] involved is by definition a step-parent relationship because there is one parent who is not the biological parent of the child."

24. Lorraine Dusky, "The Daughter I Gave Away," *Newsweek* (30 March 1992).

25. It is crucial to note that families have historically been sites of abuse and pain. See Richard J. Gelles, *Family Violence* (Newbury Park, Calif.: Sage, 1987); and Raoul Felder and Barbara Victor, *Getting Away with Murder* (New York: Simon and Schuster, 1996).

26. For some, the realization of their desire to parent demands reliance on technology; lesbian couples frequently rely on sperm banks; many gay and straight men have turned to surrogates. Straight couples have also sought out reproductive technology. This kind of technology is extremely costly and obviously class limits who has access to it. Dusky worries that human beings born of this new technology are missing a piece, "like androids out of science fiction, they lack a full human parentage, that connection with our past that forms such a large part of our present. They fill the hole in their identity with rage."

But what is "full human parentage"? Isn't it better that we leave it to each of us to work through what it means to be lovers and parents, rather than have the state impose limits that will exclude some from representing their own sexuate being? Children born into love are the lucky ones. But I would at least hope that no one in 1999 would argue that natural sexual intercourse is necessarily loving. Can the act of artificial insemination be a loving act, as joyous to the lovers as any sex that transpires between heterosexual couples? The answer is, of course. It is not the body parts that make the love. I find nothing "out of kilter" about planning babies.

Paula M. Cooey

"Ordinary Mother" as Oxymoron:
The Collusion of Theology, Theory, and Politics in the Undermining of Mothers

If "ordinary" has anything to do with meeting one's own emotional needs or finding fulfillment through work in the public arena, "ordinary mother" is a contradiction in terms in contemporary Western culture. If "ordinary" connotes class status, usually middle class and, sometimes, working class above the poverty line, then the motherhood of the wealthy, the working poor, and the unemployed ceases to count. If "ordinary" defaults to heterosexual orientation and practice, then lesbian mothers are likewise excluded.

If being ordinary involves characterological flaws, making serious, sometimes tragic mistakes while bearing or rearing children, or leaving one's children while working outside the home, then mothers must be extraordinary. Due to cultural romanticizing of both motherhood and childhood, U.S. society expects nothing less than extraordinary mothers as normative. Furthermore, "extraordinary" requires that a mother working in the public arena must accomplish as a parent what she would have accomplished had she worked full time solely in the home. Anything less renders a woman liable to negative social responses ranging from blame for the breakdown of "the" family to outright demonization.

This demonization of women who fail to meet the standards of extraordinariness, often grounded in ultra-conservative Christian theology or secular social theory, seriously complicates how religious, social service, and legal institutions respond to real moral problems that emerge during pregnancy and childrearing. In addition, negative valuation, as exemplified by political polemic and controversy surrounding family values, further complicates how legislative bodies and government agencies formulate social policy intended to address indigence, maternal child abuse, teen pregnancy, childbearing and childrearing out of wedlock, and abortion. As a consequence, individual mothers and social institutions alike fail to address the many serious problems ordinary mothers face, from economic hardship and lack of good parenting skills to alcoholism and other forms of drug addiction. Ordinary mothers, in any meaningful sense of the word "ordinary," thus do the work of mothering caught in the crosshairs of both the church and the state.

Feminist theologians and theorists in growing numbers are challenging cultural construals that romanticize motherhood and childhood, while demonizing actual mothers. In addition, we are beginning to confront critically the harsh realities involved in parenting as ordinary women, that is, as busy, flawed, needy women, for many of whom one's survival and the survival of her children are major accomplishments. To evade critical confrontation is to contribute by our silence to cultural romanticizing, thus further obscuring the richness of women's agency, as well as the obligations of parents to their children. In order to take on these sobering realities of mothering directly, however, we must first debunk the "authorities" that obscure them.

Extraordinary Mothers

The penalty for a mother's failure to meet cultural idealizations of motherhood is, as I said, demonization. This demonization likewise appears particularly as cultural representation of the "bad mother," dialectically played off against the idealizations. The effects of this dialectic upon those who fail to meet social expectations vary from the production of individual social and emotional disorder to political punishment of women, differing according to class and ethnicity.

Christian theology and psychoanalytic theory fuel this dialectic of romanticizing and demonizing. Both play central roles in the formation of the individual identities of women as mothers and in the social construal of motherhood. Just as Christian theology represents divinely authorized interpretation of scripture and church teaching for many religious women; so psychoanalytic theory pervades both religious and secular therapeutic relationships provided women by psychiatrists, psychologists, clergy, and psychiatric social workers of both genders throughout the country. Psychoanalytic theory further permeates social policy, as well as numerous self-help books on mothering. Its appeal to science as authoritative knowledge, however debatable, makes it every bit as problematic for women as appeals to divine authority on the part of the theologians. Both theological and secular authorities are extremely pernicious in their effects upon actual mothers and their children. *Theological* critique is of particular importance, given the number of women affiliated with traditional religious communities.[1]

Christian Theology

The religious right which defines itself as a pro-family movement represents a loose coalition of politically conservative groups comprising predominantly Protestant Christians. The family that the religious right seeks to promote is a modern version of the patriarchal family, that is, a male-dominated, heterosexual nuclear family. According to the theologians of the right, the male dominates by divine authority as manifested in Christian scripture. As head of household the male as husband and father has ultimate authority over the family, though the female as wife and mother may have full responsibility for all domestic matters, as well as shared economic responsibility for keeping the family going. Though women may work outside the home due to economic necessity, their primary responsibility is within the home as helpers to their husbands and mothers to their children. As helpers and mothers women ideally rear their children to be obedient to divine, civil, and familial authority, almost exclusively represented as male; they further rear their children according to stereotypically defined gender differences.[2] Within this context, motherhood replicates the fifties media creations of family life.

The theology of Stu Weber, a conservative evangelical minister active in the "pro-family" movement, serves as a case in point.[3] A former Green Beret and Vietnam veteran, Weber, along with his wife, Linda, cofounded the Good Shepherd Community Church in Oregon. Together they travel throughout the countryside speaking at Family Life marriage and parenting conferences. Weber has also spoken at "Promise Keeper" rallies. Weber formulates his theological position in *Tender Warrior: God's Intention for a Man*, further described as "Every man's purpose, every woman's dream, every child's hope." On the cover Dr. Robert Lewis, pastor of the Fellowship

Bible Church in Little Rock, Arkansas, describes *Tender Warrior* as a "soul-stirring masculine manifesto." As a masculine manifesto, it calls Christian men to their duties and responsibilities to their families. Weber's explication of these duties and responsibilities has far-reaching effects, direct and indirect, for both religious and secular women, particularly for mothers working in the public arena.

Weber acknowledges the validity of what he understands to be feminist critique of male failure to live up to the responsibilities of fatherhood, as well as the validity of the men's movement in its search for better forms of masculinity and better relations among men, as characterized by Robert Bly's *Iron John*.[4] From Weber's perspective, however, what lies at the heart of cultural and social crisis is the failure of men to assume their God-ordained role as providers and heads of the household. Instead men have abandoned, abused, misunderstood, or neglected their wives and children. Weber argues alternatively for a specifically Christian masculinity. He appeals to the story of Adam and Eve and to the New Testament passages counseling wives to submit to their husbands as authoritative for establishing male "headship" of the family, and to the story of the friendship of Jonathan and David as paradigmatic of male friendship. He theologically integrates his interpretations of these narratives under the rubric of what he perceives to be the masculinity of Christ as the divinely authorized pattern for all males.

The chief characteristics of Christian masculinity, as implied in the title, are toughness and tenderness necessary to lead effectively a two-parented, nuclear family. Christian men are tender warriors who lead not because they are superior to women in value. Rather, from Weber's perspective, God proclaims throughout scripture, from the Genesis account to the New Testament, leadership both in the home and in the public arena to be men's job. Indeed this job defines them as men. This leadership entails not only providing for the family and assuming final responsibility for all family decisions; leadership also includes involvement with childrearing, but only insofar as possible, given public commitments. Leadership further requires practiced sensitivity to gender difference which Weber understands to be grounded in nature, as well as ordained by God. Sensitivity to gender difference according to Weber involves learning to speak "woman." Learning to speak "woman" entails making women feel special, cutting them slack when they are at the mercy of their hormones, acknowledging their special gifts as the ones who are oriented toward relationship rather than toward accomplishing goals, and under no circumstances responding to them abusively. In respect to the children, fathering involves bringing them up according to their gender as God the Father brought up his child with a love that is willing to sacrifice everything including one's own child if duty requires it. For Weber this personally meant having to suspend his immediate childrearing responsibilities when called to serve in Vietnam.

Heading a nuclear family forms the base of a pyramid that represents a theologically justified political and social hierarchy. Real men not only play a strong role within their families as heads of the household, they are also conscientious workers, obedient citizens who patriotically serve their country, and active leaders in their congregations. All of these activities exemplify true faithfulness and service to God. This strong commitment to the public arena as well as to the domestic one requires cultivating a deep loyalty to other men; hence, Weber spends considerable time addressing male friendship by appealing to the biblical story of David and Jonathan, though there is no mention of establishing friendship between males and females. Weber emphasizes that this loyalty is highly personal as well as principled and is necessary to fighting wars abroad as well as confronting problems at home. What begins with an identification of human fatherhood with the Fatherhood of God culminates in loyalty to Christ as the truest most complete image of God's vision of authentic masculinity. In other words, the significant feature defining God, and through God Christ, is masculinity. For Weber all men, whether actual fathers or not, are identified through their divinely intended masculinity with divine masculinity itself. Their role is to serve as fathers in public life, if not always domestic life.

The appeal of Weber's position lies in his focus upon one of the major problems women and children confront, namely, neglect and abandonment by fathers and husbands. This focus manifests itself in the sincerity of his concern for the well-being of families, the energy he puts into reeducating men to be more responsible in all facets of their existence, and his adamant rejection of violence in the home in any form. Nevertheless, his position suffers serious problems—as much from what he does not take into consideration as from what he does consider.

In terms of what Weber does consider, his theology is first and foremost a monument to idolatry. The status he grants masculinity, although his view of it is hardly stereotypically macho, places it at the definitive center of who God is. In other words, Weber legitimates male leadership and the subordination of women to that leadership, both inside and outside the home, by identifying men with his own interpretation of the masculinity exemplified in the maleness of Christ and the fatherhood of God. In addition, by identifying leadership both in the home and in the public arena so definitively and exclusively with masculinity, he identifies the will of the father in the home and the will of male political leadership with the divine will, thus idolizing the male-headed nuclear family and governmental authority as well.

Idolizing maleness as constitutive of the divine flies in the face of the prohibition against making graven images "in the form of any figure, the likeness of male or female" (Deuteronomy 4:16), not to mention Jesus' injunction to call no man father (Matthew 23:9). Idolizing patriotism and the family follows in the same vein. Both his view of patriotism and his conception of the family disregard the ambiguity of the status of both civil and family connections found throughout the New Testament. For example, the earliest followers of Jesus refused to serve in the Roman military, for which they were persecuted. Furthermore, for some of the earliest followers, notably the disciples, following Jesus meant giving up any primacy of family ties. These various forms of idolatry that permeate Weber's position exemplify a self-serving use of scripture, however unintended, to justify power arrangements from which he as male directly benefits.

Weber's goal of converting men to taking responsibility for their involvement in reproductive life as well as productive life is laudable. There are clearly a number of women who find Weber's view of domestic and public life satisfactory.[5] Certainly the position he takes encourages men to assume more responsibility for economic provision for the family and encourages a relative respect for, sensitivity to, and appreciation of women as feminine beings. Women who wish to enter into such arrangements, however, should be cognizant of the risks involved. For example, what happens when a husband is unable for reasons beyond his control to make economic provision? Suppose he gets laid off by his place of employment, or is injured and has little or no disability compensation. In addition, the respect, sensitivity, and appreciation toward women that Weber espouses depends heavily upon relegating them as feminine beings to the realm of caretaker without consideration for other kinds of traits and aspirations according to which women might wish to define themselves. There are other problems as well—among them Weber's naïveté regarding domestic abuse (essentially, "just say no").

Women who do not want to enter into the arrangements Weber espouses also suffer, for neither they nor Weber live solely in their own families or in closed religious or secular communities. Weber's view that men should dominate the public arena affects this arena, including the women, particularly working mothers, active within it. That masculinity for Weber includes no reference to friendships between men and women implies that women are not only excluded from public leadership, but also valued largely, if not exclusively, for their sexuality and potential reproductive capacities. Needless to say, Weber's view of the workplace as grounded in male bonding precludes friendship among women altogether—friendship upon which the professional survival of women increasingly depends. Men who hold such views create yet one more handicap for the women who have to work with them in the public arena.

Weber, not surprisingly, avoids any recognition whatsoever of homosexual men and women, extended families, single-parented families, divorced and remarried families, and single people, regardless of their sexual preference, who have never married. Nowhere in *Tender Warrior* does Weber address any of these people. His "vision" focuses solely on how to recreate the nuclear family. Heterosexuality resulting in marriage and preferably children, in the form of a nuclear family, is simply assumed to be the divinely ordained norm for human existence.

It may be that most families in this country remain two-parented, heterosexual families even though in many cases the two parents have been married previously as well. More often than not, however, both parents work outside the home, by economic necessity, by choice, or by a combination of both. These families face enormous difficulty as parents seek to juggle work outside the home with childrearing and household responsibilities, civic responsibility, and faithfulness within their religious communities. This juggling act is especially complicated by how culture, including the Christian traditions that Weber represents, defines gender difference.

Weber and those who share his views have constitutional rights to hold such views; they likewise have the right to seek to persuade others to join their cause. They have no right, however, to impose legislation that impinges on the freedom directly or indirectly of those who disagree. So, for example, seeking to dismantle the Legal Services Corporation because it assists poverty-stricken women who seek divorce, or proposing to legally require the notification of the father of a fetus prior to an abortion, goes beyond persuasion to an infringement of the rights of others.[6] Insofar as this kind of legislation reflects specific religious convictions regarding divorce and abortion, it privileges one form of religious conviction and practice over other, conflicting religious and secular convictions and practices. This privileging not only violates the free exercise of those whose convictions and practices differ, it has the effect, if not the intention, of establishing a state religion.

Psychological Theory[7]

Women in the middle and working classes still have primary responsibility for the care of their children and the home. When such women enter the public arena, they must find decent day care. Unless they hold jobs that support an upper middle class lifestyle that includes hiring outside help (an exception, rather than a rule), entering the workforce often means that a woman holds down two full-time jobs or, where domestic work is shared with the husband, still assumes disproportionate domestic responsibility. The reasons for this disproportionate burden range from guilt on the part of many mothers for what they perceive to be neglect of their traditional duties, to mothers' senses of obligation because they are often paid less than men and therefore contribute less to overall household expenses, to men's refusal to share in what is traditionally viewed as women's work and for which men are not held accountable. Guilt and an overweening sense of obligation find strong reinforcement in a society whose alternative to religious authority is psychological therapy, clothed ostensibly in the authority of scientific theory.

Theologically and politically conservative evangelical women are likely to turn to their ministers or to psychotherapeutic practices informed by conservative Christian theology for psychological counsel.[8] By contrast, women who understand themselves as religious or spiritual, but not within this particular theological framework, are more likely to seek secular counseling in one of its various forms. While secular therapists are not necessarily themselves theorists, they nevertheless have most likely been trained within a particular theoretical school of thought. What society holds to be a psychologically healthy person, woman, and mother is to some extent determined by sociopsychological theory as transmitted through therapeutic practice. Both theory and practice, however secular and "scientific" in contrast to theology, work to reinforce the identity of woman with mother, whether actual or potential. Like theology, they insist that mothering manifest itself in ways that are detrimental to women and ultimately to children. In fact, sociopsychological theory and practice work alongside theology to perpetuate oppressive political environments in both conservative and liberal manifestations.

Because mothering has received the most attention of all the roles defining women, representations of the bad mother, as contrasted with idealizations of the good mother, abound in the secular theoretical literature that most psychotherapeutic training presupposes. Marie Ashe and Naomi Cahn include an extensive critical review of these representations in their work in legal theory. Their analysis, taken in conjunction with Linda Gordon's social history of family violence and Patricia J. Williams' reflections on the interplay of race and class in the social production of motherhood makes glaringly clear the ahistorical nature of most psychoanalytic theory, feminist as well as nonfeminist. These writers collectively raise several issues of relevance to theological discussions of what it means for mothers to be caught between the demand to be extraordinary and the actual difficulties encountered in rearing children.[9] These issues include class and ethnicity, the contradiction between what is considered normative adult subjectivity and the expectations placed on the good mother, and the theoretical construction of motherhood as exemplifying exclusively the perspective of the child. Ashe, Cahn, Gordon, and Williams, however, do not address a fourth related issue, namely, theoretical construals of the peculiarities of mother–daughter relations in regard to female psychological development. While all of the concerns they do address bear on any discussion of the demonization of mothers, the issue of mother–daughter relations is especially important to understand the production of violence in women toward their own children and parents.

Consider class. Whereas many professionals tacitly assume that affluent women are less likely to abuse their children, theoretical constructs of good mothering reflect or idealize conventional expectations placed on middle-class mothers and assume middle-class economic structures. Yet women who make it into the therapeutic, social service, and judicial systems come disproportionately from the working classes, the working poor, and the unemployed. This gap appears to reflect obvious differences in economic resources that might go to child care or to therapeutic treatments of any perceived problems rather than criminal procedures. However, I suggest the gap also reflects a tendency on the part of those who report neglect and abuse, as well as those in the legal and social systems who deal with the mothers directly, to perceive neglect and abuse as more characteristic of mothering by working-class and poor women, irrespective of ethnicity; in other words, to expect abuse in the context of poverty.[10] Professional expectations and theoretical representations are mutually reinforcing. This kind of class bias perpetuates lateral violence by middle-class women upon women from the underclasses (keep in mind that the social service professions are heavily staffed by white, middle-class women). It further fails to address middle-class women's vulnerability to frustration, rage, and subsequent guilt in respect to their own childrearing. Whereas we expect bad mothers to be a product of poverty and ignorance, an expectation that may well be "read in" when poverty-stricken mothers encounter social service and legal professionals, we expect mothers from affluent environments to fulfill successfully the needs of their children without ever losing control, and to enjoy doing so.[11] Thus we commit injustices against mothers regardless of class, though in different ways according to class. Though Gordon does not pursue race and ethnicity at great length in her studies, Williams' analysis confirms that related issues concerning the significance of racial and ethnic difference are at least as problematic.[12]

Even assuming that there could be a single normative psychological type for mothering, a theoretical contradiction emerges between normative subjectivity and normative mothering. Ostensibly good mothers are not vulnerable either to emotional complexity or to moral ambiguity, traits normally associated with mature adult subjectivity in the abstract. Thus, Ashe and Cahn point out that, according to widely accepted interpretations of Freudian theory, good mothering requires women to suppress aggression, sexual sensuality, and nonmaternal creativity. They go on to point out that even the "good enough" mothering of object-relations theory demands self-sacrifice, as well as total, exclusive involvement with the child for an extended, albeit finite, period of time.[13] This contradiction presents a no-win situation for actual mothers. Being a good mother by definition precludes acting like an ordinary, mature adult subject to moral and emotional complexity.

This contradiction pervades the lives of all women insofar as we are vulnerable to being perceived as potential mothers. All women are vulnerable to the denial by others of their status as subjects, whenever they are expected by men and women alike to fulfill exclusively or primarily nurturing roles that they may be reluctant at the time to fulfill. To the extent that women reject such roles as centrally determining their identities, they are further subject to being stereotyped as bad or inadequate, as if they were bad or inadequate surrogate mothers.

Thirdly, theory plays a central role in the social construction of the identification of "woman" with "mother." Susan Suleiman suggests that psychoanalytic theory in general is a theory of childhood, a concept picked up by Ashe and Cahn and applied as a category of analysis to feminist critiques of theories of mothering as well, notably the work of Dorothy Dinnerstein and Nancy Chodorow.[14] Indeed, Ashe and Cahn argue at length that almost all theoretical representations of mothering, feminist or otherwise, are intentionally or unintentionally views from the perspective of the child.[15] This perspective not only renders most psychoanalytic theory ahistorical, it also excludes theoretical representation of mothering or of childhood from the perspective of actual mothers (or for that matter any other adults as adults).

This theoretical elision reflects and in turn influences social attitudes, values, and power arrangements. In ordinary human interaction, a child's perspective is not necessarily restricted to children; adult humans of both genders frequently view reality through the lenses of their experiences of unmet needs as children and carry childhood memories, conscious or unconscious, of unmet needs into their personal and professional relations.[16] As we shall shortly see, adults acting politically out of their experiences of unmet needs as children can have devastating effects on the lives of mothers and their children in terms of how these unmet needs get translated into models for governments. In regard to theory, Ashe and Cahn pose an alternative theoretical discourse on mothering: an incorporation of multiple perspectives or voices, including the voices of mothers who have, in the eyes of various social institutions, failed to meet legal, moral, and other social expectations of mothers, as well as those who advocate in their behalf.

Lastly, the absence of multiple voices holds serious implications for daughters, the one condition all women share, as well as for mothers, the role women are unlikely to escape, regardless of whether they bear children. One of the most striking features of theoretical literature on child development is its almost universal and emphatic insistence upon the necessity for the child's rejection of the mother in the formation of identity.[17] So, as recently as 1987, Julia Kristeva wrote without irony, "For man and for woman the loss of the mother is a biological and psychic necessity, the first step on the way to becoming autonomous. Matricide is our vital necessity, the sine-qua-non condition of our individuation, provided that it takes place under optimal circumstances and can be eroticized."[18] She went on to add that this project is much more difficult for daughters than for sons, given the identification of the female child with the mother through the female body.

This claim can be read in at least two conflicting ways. One could read Kristeva's call for matricide as a metaphorical statement regarding the necessity for all children ultimately to give up expecting all their needs to be met by the person most likely to have met most needs from infancy on; this would be tantamount to saying that human beings need to "kill" the image of their mothers and, later, other human beings, especially women, projected by the perspective of a needy, egocentric child. Such a reading at least carries echoes of a mother's voice as well as that of the child. Such a reading nevertheless requires a subtlety in determining meaning, as well as a generosity in granting good intentions simply not explicit in the text. The easier and more likely reading is that maturity begins with a much more hostile and conflict-laden attack directed not so much at the subject's no longer appropriate expectations, but at the object of those expectations, the mother, and that furthermore this hostility and conflict are to be expected as normative, even desirable.

To theorize that daughters (or for that matter sons) differentiate in such a manner is not simply to describe, but to prescribe as well. Children who do not differentiate accordingly are pathological. Both this construal and the threat of diagnosis place daughters in a peculiar double jeopardy, given that they have the confusing task of differentiating as subjects *from* their mothers, while identifying *with* their mothers, not only through the female body, but also as potential mothers.

A critique of the theoretical literature, feminist or otherwise, suggests two important features concerning the significance of ordinary mothering. First, the perception of adult women, by men and women alike, through the lens of the unmet needs of the child, appears to lie at the heart of demonizing and romanticizing women through mythological projection (though no doubt sexual ambivalence reflected in the sexual objectification of women also plays a key role). Indeed, even adult mothers likely speak with "double" voices, for they also often rear their children as women who view the world from the perspective of the unmet needs of their childhood, as well from the internalized voices of culture that expect extraordinary mothering.[19] Second, the contradictions and resulting conflicts that surround mother–daughter relations and the development of daughters into mature adult women constitute breeding grounds for internalizing misogyny and may generate some of the rage driving actual women's violence both in the home and in the public realm.

Theorists and practitioners alike view the mother–child relation as necessary and normative to early human development and make every effort to socialize women to cultivate it. Thus the good mother allegedly puts herself entirely at the disposal of the infant. This expectation of actual mothers becomes problematic when "healthy" development later requires that the subject "kill" the mother. Of course, killing the mother does not necessarily kill the childhood need, which is no longer met, perhaps never was met, or perhaps could never possibly have been met by an ordinary human being. Cultural projection of the "bad mother" then provides at least one alternative as a sublimation of these unmet needs; unfortunately, as we all know, cultural artifacts reciprocate by re-making their makers.[20] Mythological bad mothers in particular and mythological bad women in general serve as available interpretations of any ordinary woman who rejects traditional or conventional views of womanhood.

Psychological matricide, considered in theory as a necessary beginning to the development of mature subjectivity, has further implications for daughters. Not only are psychological matricide and its correlative autonomy complete abstractions without reference to any historical context, linking matricide to autonomy builds misogyny into what it means to be human. In regard to daughters, this linkage at best presupposes that, in order to be subjects, women must first exercise self-hatred. Later down the line, should a daughter wish to become a mother, she necessarily submits to becoming an object of her child's hatred for the sake of the child's "maturity."

Theoretical discourse, regarded as authoritative for what is normative, perpetuates a serious conflict in the formation of actual women's identities. I suggest that understanding these conflicts as rooted in the exclusion of women's voices, particularly the voices of "bad" and ordinary mothers' accounting for their own highly complex behavior, helps to understand better the cultural expectation of extraordinary mothering as normative for motherhood. Just as important, I suggest that the contradictions, created by postulating that differentiation from the mother requires matricide and that this matricide is normative for women's development, may themselves contribute to actual women's violence as mothers, daughters, sisters, sexual partners, and criminalized social rebels.

Politics

In addition to the role of theology in shaping religious institutions and the role played by theory in the therapeutic environment, political discursive practices serve as central means by which theology and theory shape and reflect cultural assumptions about mothering and about women's identities as mothers. In *Moral Politics: What Conservatives Know That Liberals Don't*, George Lakoff argues cogently that people project how government should run from their idealizations of family.[21] What conservatives know that liberals don't is that people vote their values, even if they do not necessarily practice them. These values are rooted in conceptions of an ideal family, the same conceptions that I am arguing interact reciprocally with theory and theology to mystify and undermine mothering. This process of conception based on idealization remains largely unconscious and unintentional. In addition, this process generates for the religious their conceptions of God and moral life. Lakoff goes on to develop two types of family that set the conceptual limits for American political discourse and practice—the patriarchal family and the (ostensibly) egalitarian nurturant family.

Like a good typologist Lakoff stresses that these types of family structure represent the limits of a range of possibilities rather than isolable actualities themselves; hence, no individual family is likely to fulfill exclusively the characteristics of a single type. For example, Stu Weber's patriarchal version of the family instantiates Lakoff's patriarchal type modified to include, but subsume, nurture as a masculine quality. By contrast, the psychoanalytic theoreticians of motherhood and child development represent well the nurturant type as modified by the patriarchal tendencies to absolutize and to enforce relative norms—in this case an unachievable extraordinariness, found even in such models as the "good enough" mother.

Lakoff reveals more than even he intends, however. Both types of family presuppose some form of welfare state, though who gets subsidized, and how, differs drastically according to type. So, for example, middle-class families, more likely to fit the patriarchal type, are subsidized through income tax deductions and credits, while single-parented families in poverty may find assistance through Aid for Families with Dependent Children. As welfare states, both reflect the exclusion of theory, theology, and politics from the perspective of an adult woman or an adult egalitarian parent of either gender. That is, the patriarchal type reflects the interests of men committed to the preservation of male domination and the women convinced that this arrangement benefits them. The nuturant type projects a vision of care exclusively through the lens of the unmet needs of the child (of either gender) that undermines a serious commitment to mothers as persons and to fathers who commit to nurture their children as central to their identities as persons.

In the first case, the state becomes the subsidizer and enforcer of family relations narrowly defined as a heterosexual, nuclear, and male-headed household; in the second case, government, however ostensibly egalitarian and benevolent, becomes "big mother," establishing control by intruding into the lives of those who seek assistance in the name of protecting their children. In addition, the patriarchal type of the state or government directly punishes single and poor mothers and their children, because they fall outside the patriarchal norm, by relegating access to job training, medical care, day care, and other basic necessities to the domain of private charitable institutions with their own varying agendas and inadequate funds. Whereas the patriarchal state devalues and damages single-parented families in need and ignores the issue of children's rights, the nurturant state all too often abuses the rights of single parents in need, usually mothers, to involve themselves in emotionally and sexually satisfying relations and to discipline their children as they determine fit. For these women, living daily with the bureaucratic red tape involved in seeking assistance and the concomitant invasion of privacy, not to mention the shame of being publicly identified as on assistance, for example, through food stamps, renders life difficult, demeaning, and demoralizing.

In regard to both types, the kind of state generated by idealization of the family leaves little room for ordinary women to mother ordinarily, that is, to mother in addition to other things that women might have to do or want to do. On the contrary, mothering and its social regulation, in striking contrast to fathering, become the central, defining obsessions of religious, legal, social, and political institutions in the social production of gender difference. How to be better parents in any circumstances is a serious issue. Nevertheless, much of the discussion concerning parenting and family focuses too exclusively on issues of gender, as if the most pressing issues families face had to do with how to distinguish masculinity and femininity from one another, rather than with parenthood. (Weber's book is typical in this respect.)

My own experience as a parent teaches me that both gender difference and parents are made rather than born and that we as a society do a poor job of preparing and supporting adults as parents. It is difficult under the best of circumstances to know how to find that balance that both fosters a child's creativity and sets needed limits commensurate with the child's own temperament and development. It is likewise difficult to find that balance within mother–child relations that validates what are the sometimes conflicting needs of both. This is especially difficult for parents in response to a first child or an only child. As a working mother who shared childrearing responsibilities with the father of our child insofar as a male-dominated culture of work would permit, I found that even under optimal circumstances childrearing while working outside the home was extremely difficult. One of the greatest difficulties I faced was the contradiction of working in a culture that insisted upon defining me first and foremost in terms of my status as mother, while ignoring the material needs of childrearing, like the needs for more time to do my work, for child care when our son was sick, and for companionship with other working parents, particularly professional women married to working-class men with strong commitments to parenting.

All the same, my own experience of family life as what I consider to be a fairly ordinary mother and wife does not even begin to address the full magnitude of the tragedy of what it can mean to be ordinary mothers. Does ordinariness have to do with the circumstances that define a mother's existence or with the qualities and characteristics of her mothering, regardless of the circumstances? If "ordinary" means doing the best one can under the circumstances, and if "ordinary mothering" means mothering with the hope that one's children will flourish, what then does it mean when interpersonal relationships fail, when work is either not there or not rewarding, when the body breaks down, when the psyche is wounded far beyond simple mending, when one has lost control over one's own agency and yet is somehow responsible? The increasingly ordinary circumstances of rearing children by oneself, assuming primary responsibility for elderly family members while rearing children, having to teach children how to respond to racial and ethnic slurs or humiliation based on gender, parenting in poverty, fleeing for one's safety or the safety of one's children, and being responsible for a family while homeless set the agenda for many mothers in this country. The problems I and others like me confront should not be trivialized in any respect; nevertheless, they are, after all is said and done, the problems and struggles of one who has a full-time partner who shares her values, one who has productive labor in the public sphere, one who has chosen to bear and rear a child, one who, though she has consciously chosen work in a service profession over the fast track to material success, can be considered by most standards to be materially affluent. Such a configuration of circumstances is hardly ordinary.

Conclusion

What kinds of mothers, then, qualify as ordinary? What positive role, if any, might theology and theory have to play in fostering a political environment in which ordinary families might prosper?

In light of the foregoing critique, the first question becomes ironically easy. Ordinary mothers are the mothers we find among us in all their variability and with all their functional and dysfunctional strategies for survival. Like the ancient mothers of Hebrew and Greco-Roman literature, they struggle with domestic violence, sexual abuse, sibling rivalry, inheritance rights, marriage arrangements and their dissolution, adultery, homelessness, economic disaster, abandonment, exile, and a host of other tragedies. Like ancient mothers they struggle with ethnic prejudice and class injustice. Unlike ancient mothers they perhaps struggle more often with work in the public sphere and more explicitly with issues of gender equity and sexual preference, both in the home and in the workplace.

To restrict "ordinary" to the context of two-parented, heterosexual working families, albeit more egalitarian than patriarchal, simply replicates, in the opposite direction, the move made by the religious right in insisting on the two-parented, heterosexual, patriarchal family as normative (ordinary?). While the problems families confront will differ according to different family structures, all mothers are at economic, psychological, and spiritual risk in a society defined by the romanticization of motherhood and the demonizing of actual mothers. This risk is the bottom line, in response to which all critique of culture addressing family issues should begin.

As for the positive role that theology and theory might play, economic, psychological, and spiritual risk should provide a, if not the, starting point for future constructive theologizing and theorizing about mothering. Furthermore, theologians and theoreticians should engage in ongoing dialogue to serve as resources for one another. Whereas theologians have both intentionally and unintentionally drawn on social theory in all its forms in their theological critique and construction,[22] secular theoreticians have, for the most part, failed to take sufficient account of the roles played by religious faith, religious practice, and theology in the formation of human identity and values, particularly women's identities and values. Quick to note early on the problems and failures produced by religious life and belief, with much justification, I might add, secular theoreticians from Marx and Freud to the present have tended to regard religious commitment as simply pathological or otherwise negligible.[23] Nevertheless, many intelligent women in this country continue to find some form of religious faith and practice integral to who they are in ways that nurture them and allow them to function creatively in an often oppressive society, even to the point of challenging its oppression.

For those adult women who mother, who are looking for an alternative symbolic order that addresses their needs as persons, including their deepest spiritual needs, as well as their needs as workers inside and outside the home, not only will the religious right ultimately fail them, it will likely damage them. As social theoreticians and theologians of the left we have contributed to the damage, insofar as we have failed to provide any other constructive alternatives. In my view, a focus on the meaning of work, both in the home and in the public sphere, and its relation to religious faith or spirituality, must lie at the heart of these alternatives. Such discussion must attend to the prevalent sociocultural disregard for the economic implications of work in the home in preference for work in the public sphere, which combines with an economic privileging of workers without family commitments and obligations, to produce the feminization of poverty.[24]

For women for whom Hebrew and Christian scriptures are authoritative texts, scripture itself is an ambiguous, nevertheless potentially constructive resource. The narrators of both Hebrew and Christian scriptures view work ambivalently—sometimes as a consequence of disobedience of the divine will, as in the case of the Genesis account of the exile from Eden (Genesis 3:16–19, NRV)—sometimes as a competitor with human trust in divine providence, as in the sayings attributed to Jesus in reference to the lilies of the field and to the sparrows (Matthew 6:25–33 and Luke 12:22–31, NRV). By contrast, the "wisdom" literature of Proverbs provides an image of mother and wife as an extremely powerful and successful small-business owner, landowner, and compassionate benefactor of the oppressed, a woman who laughs at the future, who speaks with wisdom and kindness, who "fears the Lord" (Proverbs 31:10–31, NRV). The narrator further counsels that such a woman be given "a share in the fruit of her hand," as well as praise in the city gates (v. 31). While such texts clearly arise from and reflect an ancient patriarchal society, they nonetheless vividly portray a politically empowered woman as the sociocultural ideal. In this particular example, the ideal includes husband and children and obviously exemplifies a privileged economic class. However, interpreting such a text in conjunction with prophetic injunctions against the oppression of workers and the neglect of the widowed and homeless (for example, Isaiah 58:3–9, Amos 2:6–8, NRV) militates against privileging class and marital status.

All the same, most especially in regard to work, all the dialogue in the world will not suffice if we do not develop structures that simultaneously incorporate into the academy the voices of ordinary mothers as I have here defined them, while moving us as academics into those places we do not normally frequent, namely, out of our offices into jail cells, housing projects, worship services, and boardrooms, wherever ordinary mothers can be found. I suspect, however, that it will be harder to get ourselves to the jail cells, the housing projects, and perhaps the worship services, than to the boardrooms.

I am indebted to my colleague, a scholar of Hebrew Bible, Professor Francisco O. Garcia-Treto of Trinity University's Department of Religion for helping me locate representative scriptural references.

1. According to the National Opinion Research Center's General Social Survey (1994 data), 92.1 percent of the 1,625 women surveyed consider themselves "somewhat religious" to "strongly religious." 87.2 percent identify themselves as Christian. 35.1 percent of those surveyed specifically consider themselves to be fundamentalists. These percentages should reflect closely the general female population in this country.

2. The clearest and most extensive manifesto of the agenda of the religious right in the U.S. can be found in Ralph Reed's *Mainstream Values Are No Longer Politically Incorrect: The Emerging Faith Factor in American Politics* (Dallas: Word, 1994).

3. Much of this material appears in altered form in a different context in Paula Cooey, *Family, Freedom & Faith: Building Community Today* (Louisville, Ky.: Westminster Press/John Knox Press, 1996), 47–52. *Family, Freedom & Faith* critically analyzes the political rhetoric of family values characteristic of both the religious right and, more recently, the "centrists" of the Democratic Party; it also provides a constructive theological alternative response to contemporary family issues.

4. Robert Bly, *Iron John: A Book About Men* (Reading, Mass.: Addison-Wesley, 1990).

5. According to the Religious News Service women make up 55 percent of the Christian Coalition rank and file. See "The Christian Coalition: Who Are They?" *San Antonio Express-News* (11 November 1995), sec. 10A.

6. Reed, *Mainstream Values*, 99–100, 228.

7. A much abbreviated form of this analysis of psychoanalytic theory appears in a different context in Paula Cooey, "Bad Women: The Limitations of Theory and Theology," in *Differing Horizons: Essays on Feminist Theory and Theology*, ed. Rebecca Chopp and Sheila Davaney (Philadelphia: Fortress Press, 1997).

8. Recently women's groups affiliated with the Promise Keepers have emerged in part to "help" women adjust to men assuming their "proper" role as head of the household. Suitable Helpers, for example, provides counseling; likewise, Heritage Keepers "teaches women how to 'let go of the reins' of family control upon the return of a fired up Promise Keepers man." "The Promise Keepettes," *New York Times Sunday Magazine* (27 April 1997), 15.

9. See Marie Ashe and Naomi R. Cahn, "Child Abuse: A Problem for Feminist Theory," *Texas Journal of Women and the Law* 2, no. 1 (1993): 75–112; Marie Ashe, "The 'Bad Mother' in Law and Literature: A Problem of Representation," *Hastings Women's Law Journal* (1992); Linda Gordon, *Heroes of Their Own Lives: The Politics and History of Family Violence, Boston 1880–1960* (New York: Viking, 1988); and Patricia J. Williams, *The*

Rooster's Egg: On the Persistence of Prejudice (Cambridge, Mass.: Harvard University Press, 1995). See also Mary Becker, "Maternal Feelings: Myth, Taboo, and Child Custody," *Review of Law and Women's Studies* 1 (1992): 133–222; and Zillah R. Eisenstein, *The Female Body and the Law* (Berkeley and Los Angeles: University of California Press, 1988).

"Theory" for Ashe and Cahn includes not only mainstream psychoanalytic and psychological theory, but all feminist accounts subjectivity. This is, of course, a bit of an overstatement. See, for examples, historicist, historical, and cultural construals like Elisabeth Badintur's *Mother-Love Myth and Reality: Motherhood in Modern History* (New York: Macmillan, 1981); Ellen Ross's *Labor and Love in Outcast London* (Oxford: Oxford University Press, 1993); and Patricia Bell-Scott et al., eds., *Double Stitch: Black Women Write About Mothers and Daughters* (Boston: Beacon Press, 1991).

10. Gordon argues this thesis very persuasively throughout *Heroes*. Williams' work in *Rooster's Egg* on the interaction of race and class further reinforces this claim. Our national mythology assumes that most poor people are from ethnic and racial minorities, but this assumption reflects racial and ethnic bias rather than actuality. The element of class bias reflected in this gap plays a crucial role in both feminist and nonfeminist theoretical silence on the issue. This silence masks the extent to which theoretical expectations surrounding mothering, including both the good and the bad mother, differ greatly according to class.

11. This is no less true in the case of object-relations theory than in the case of previous analytic thought, the so-called good-enough mother notwithstanding. See Janice Doane and Devon Hodges, *From Klein to Kristeva: Psychoanalytic Feminism and the Search for the "Good Enough" Mother* (Ann Arbor: University of Michigan Press, 1992).

12. Many of the early cases that Gordon analyzes in *Heroes* represent immigrants, and in the period she examines, race later becomes more of an issue.

13. Ashe and Cahn, "Child Abuse," 91–92. See Sigmund Freud, "Female Sexuality," in *The Standard Edition of the Complete Psychological Works*, ed. James Strachey (New York: W. W. Norton, 1976), 223–243; and D. W. Winnicott, *The Maturational Process and the Facilitating Environment* 49 (New York: International Universities Press, 1965).

14. Melanie Klein was the first to suggest that children fantasize "good" and "bad" mothers, initially as good and bad body parts, particularly breasts, and to distinguish such representations from actual mothers; see especially "The Oedipus Complex in the Light of Early Anxieties," in *Love, Guilt and Reparation and Other Works, 1921–1945*, vol. 1 of *The Writings of Melanie Klein*, ed. R. E. Money-Kyrle, B. Joseph, E. O'Shaughnessey, and H. Segal (London: Hogarth Press and the Institute of Psychoanalysis, 1975), 370–419. For Suleiman's take on the situation see "Writing and Motherhood," in *The (M)other Tongue: Essays in Feminist Psychoanalytic Interpretation*, ed. Shirley N. Garner, Claire Kohane, and Madelon Springnether (Ithaca, N.Y.: Cornell University Press, 1985), 352, 358; see Ashe and Cahn, "Child Abuse," 92. For Dinnerstein and Chodorow, see, respectively, *The Mermaid and the Minotaur* (New York: Harper and Row, 1977), and *The Reproduction of Mothering: Psychoanalysis and the Sociology of Gender* (Berkeley and Los Angeles: University of California Press, 1978).

15. Such theoretical representations explicitly propose or at the least imply an essentialism definitive of what constitutes the human, namely, an inner child, more or less continuous throughout one's existence as part of one's identity; in fact, rather than describing or explaining what it means to be a human subject, such theoretical discourse is producing certain kinds of human beings—namely, ones who fancy themselves entitled to have all their infantile needs met. The most extreme example Ashe and Cahn give is that of the writings of Alice Miller. See, among other of her works, *Thou Shalt Not Be Aware: Society's Betrayal of the Child*, trans. Hildegaard Hannum and Hunter Hannum (New York: NAL-Dutton, 1986). There are nevertheless a growing number of exceptions. See, for example, Diane E. Eyer, *Mother–Infant Bonding: A Scientific Fiction* (New Haven, Conn.: Yale University Press, 1992); Sara Ruddick, *Maternal Thinking: Toward a Politics of Peace* (Boston: Beacon Press, 1989); and Jane Swigart, *The Myth of the Bad Mother: The Emotional Realities of Mothering* (New York: Doubleday, 1991). These works and others of their genre nevertheless do not include the voices or the concerns of actual bad mothers.

16. A child, by virtue of being a child, will focus exclusively upon her or his needs and the extent to which they are met. The needs of a child, while very real, cannot realistically be met entirely, not by one person alone and perhaps not met by an entire flotilla of people, were they available. Furthermore, maturation into adulthood means in part learning what it means not to have all needs met. In moments of extreme crisis, adults may forget this very hard lesson.

17. Simone de Beauvoir formulated the contradictions inherent in women's development in *The Second Sex* (New York: Alfred A. Knopf, 1961).

18. Leon S. Roudiez, trans., *Black Sun: Depression and Melancholia* (New York: Columbia University Press, 1989), 27–28. The context for this claim is her construal of the cultural identification of the maternal with death and of femininity with immortality. Her overall project includes elaborating what she calls the "dead mother complex."

19. I am indebted to my colleague Mary Ellen Ross for pointing out during a conversation on January 14, 1997, that how one mothers may well reflect her own perception of her unmet needs as a child. Thus a mother's voice is never univocally adult any more than any other adult's voice.

20. On the reciprocation of artifacts see Elaine Scarry, *The Body in Pain: Making and Unmaking the World* (New York: Oxford University Press, 1986), 310–311, 318.

21. George Lakoff, *Moral Politics: What Conservatives Know That Liberals Don't* (Chicago: University of Chicago Press, 1996).

22. For a recent example of the intentional use of psychoanalytic theory for theological purposes, see Bonnie Miller-McLemore, *Also a Mother: Work and Family as Theological Dilemma* (Nashville, Tenn.: Abingdon Press, 1994).

23. Actually Marx and Engels saw the religion of oppressed classes as a witness to oppression as well as an opiate. In addition, they saw it as, on occasion, a revolutionary force, albeit in mystified form. See, for example, Friedrich Engels, "On the History of Early Christianity," in *Marx & Engels: Basic Writings on Politics & Philosophy*, ed. Lewis S. Feuer (Garden City, N.Y.: Doubleday, 1959).

24. For sustained attention to the implications of privileging of workers who do not commit to sustained involvement in the rearing of children, see Joan C. Williams, "Deconstructing Gender," in *Feminist Jurisprudence*, ed. Patricia Smith (New York: Oxford University Press, 1993), 521–558.

Peggy Cooper Davis

A Reflection on Three Verbs:
To Father, To Mother, To Parent

Introduction

Law is a telling aspect of a culture. It can teach us where we collectively stand with respect to any number of issues—what standards of conduct we expect, how we sort out competing interests, whom we protect, and whom we blame. Seeing this, legal scholars, who at one time thought of law only in narrowly instrumental terms (What can I learn from this rule that will further a client's interests or alert a client to risk of liability?), are also reading law as a sign of the culture—asking what a statute or judicial opinion teaches about the context in which clients, and all the rest of us, move. It is in this new spirit of legal scholarship that I approach the subject of parenting.

In Part I of what follows, I examine the relationship between our ideas about gender and constitutional decisions about the violability or sanctity of the parental bond. As I will show, drawing the contours of the right to parent has been badly complicated by the fact that we have, but have not faced up to, conflicting and problematic understandings of what it means or should mean to mother and what it means or should mean to father: Mothering is understood to involve omnipresent nurture, while fathering is understood to involve no more than impregnation. This difference in the law's understanding of what it is to mother and what it is to father is, as I show in Part II, replayed and complicated in the law's regulation of the civic obligations of parents.

In Part II I examine the special laws affecting families whose children are thought or found to have been neglected or abused and the psychological parent theories that have so deeply influenced public policy with respect to those families. As I will show on the basis of this examination, legal standards applied to families enmeshed in the child welfare system reflect a prevailing cultural fantasy associated—destructively and unreasonably, as I will argue—with mothering; they reflect, that is, the standard that thinkers like Nancy Chodorow, Adrienne Rich, and Jessica Benjamin would associate with the idealized Good Mother. Two consequences typically follow: First, the child welfare system is wary of returning children to parents who fail to meet its idealized standard. But the system flounders in the quest for an omnicompetent nurturing substitute, so significant numbers of children are cut off from their families and inadequately nurtured by the state. After building arguments in support of these unhappy conclusions, I will suggest a way out of the catch-22. Guided by the work of Jessica Benjamin, I will urge a child-care standard that escapes the cycle of imagining an impossibly good mother, and then rejecting actual and possible parents, and then imagining again. As Benjamin's work shows, this cycle is replicated in the psychological lives of children who grow to expect a world peopled with omnicompetent, omnipresent, selfless, and benevolent (m)others, and it is as destructive of their psychological health as it is dysfunctional in the child welfare context. The alternative, in both contexts, is to imagine that adults can be simultaneously agents with minds and wills of their own and loving caregivers for the children they help to rear. Imagining in this way, we can develop a standard of fair engagement between loving-but-autonomous caregivers—singular or plural, male and female—and children growing to appreciate the wonderful mysteries of engagement with other autonomous souls. Imagining this way, we might also learn to narrow the gap between what we expect of those who mother and what we expect of those who father.

I. Defining the Constitutional Right to Mother

The right to parent is fundamental in our constitutional scheme. The Supreme Court has held that the parental role can not be compromised by excessive government regulation of children's education and upbringing,[1] and that a parent may not be deprived of custody, or of legal recognition as a parent, without being afforded special procedural protection,[2] or without good reason.[3] Still, what counts as excessive regulation within what ought, we think, to be the parental domain, or sufficiently special process when a parent is at risk of being displaced, or good enough reason for a displacement, is contested and entirely uncertain.

The largest category of Supreme Court cases exploring the contours of the right to parent is the category known until very recently as the unwed father cases. In them, the Court has struggled to determine when, and by what process, displacement of an unmarried parent is justified. Taken together, these cases yield confusing and contradictory accounts of the nature and limits of the parental right. They also provide an illuminating case study in the relationship between culturally ingrained ideas about gender and the development of legal doctrine.

The first of the Supreme Court's unwed father cases, *Stanley* v. *Illinois*, resulted in a strong affirmation of parental right. Peter and Joan Stanley lived together intermittently over a period of eighteen years before Joan Stanley's death. They had three children. They were not legally married. Under Illinois law, the fathers of children born out of wedlock were presumed to be unfit parents. As a result, these children became wards of the state upon the death of their mothers. When Joan Stanley died, and the three children were committed to state care, Peter Stanley sought their return, claiming that he had a constitutional right to care for his biological children unless he was found unfit to do so.

The case was closely decided. Some of the justices thought the Illinois presumption entirely reasonable. They argued that the distinction between unmarried fathers and all other parents was reasonable and consistent with the teaching of "[c]enturies of human experience" that "unwed fathers rarely burden either the mother or the child with their attentions or loyalties." But a bare majority disagreed. Characterizing the parental right as "essential," "basic," and "far more precious than property rights," the Court held that the Illinois statutory scheme violated due process requirements in its summary denial of the parental rights of men in Peter Stanley's situation.

Peter Stanley's parental status was preserved in 1972 by a vote of five with two justices not participating. In 1977 a unanimous court rejected the claim of Leon Webster Quilloin, another unwed father seeking the right to maintain responsibility for his offspring. Leon Quilloin had not lived with his child, but had supported him intermittently and maintained a visiting relationship. Both father and child wished to continue their relationship. Quilloin's parental rights were placed at risk when the child's mother consented to adoption by a man whom she had married some time after the child's birth. Like Stanley, Quilloin faced termination of parental rights without any allegation of fault or wrongdoing, a fate against which mothers, but not fathers, were protected by state law. Although not required under applicable law to do so, the trial judge gave Quilloin the hearing that Stanley had been denied. Quilloin was not found to be an unfit parent, but adoption was found to be in the best interests of the child, and Quilloin's parental rights were extinguished. Stressing the fact that the termination had protected the status and wishes of an intact family, the Supreme Court held that the state procedure constituted no violation of due process.[4] The Court acknowledged that the due process clause would be offended were the state to force the breakup of a natural family "for the sole reason that to do so was thought to be in the children's best interests." The biological relationship between Quilloin and his son was, however, outside the Court's conception of a "natural family."[5]

Two years later, in *Caban* v. *Mohammed*, a bare majority of the Court invalidated a New York adoption law in response to the challenge of another unwed father. Like Quilloin, Abdiel Caban was a fit parent who sought to preserve his parental rights in the face of a stepparent's petition to adopt. Had he been a female, or a divorced parent, he would have had the right under New York law to veto the adoption. The majority applied heightened scrutiny because the statute involved a gender-based classification, giving unwed mothers, but not unwed fathers, the power to bar adoption of their children. No mention was made of the possibility that rigorous scrutiny might be applied by virtue of the status of the parental right, and the Court "expressed no view" concerning the question whether, without gender discrimination, the state might order adoption over the objection of a fit parent.

Justice Stevens, joined by Chief Justice Burger and Justice Rehnquist, filed a more impassioned dissent, vigorously defending the authority of states to terminate rights of biological fathers in the process of settling their children in suitable homes. Stevens' argument was built from the perspective of child welfare officials. It assumed that these officials served the interests of children when they acted to secure their adoption and to extinguish their ties with biological fathers. In Stevens' view, biologically determined differences fully justified the difference in treatment of men and women with respect to parental rights outside of marriage. The central factor driving his opposition to the claims of unmarried fathers was a fear that requirements of paternal consent would disrupt the adoption process, with consequences for children that he thought tragic in light of what he perceived as their need for "legitimation." Justice Stewart also dissented, arguing that the state's interest in addressing the "formidable handicaps" of illegitimacy is important and that the decision to permit adoption with the consent of one parent was easily justified. For the unwed father, Stewart argued, parental rights "do not spring full-blown from the biological connection" but must be earned, usually by marriage to the mother.[6]

The dissenters in *Caban* have, it seems, been more influential than the justices who supported the opinion of the Court. Each of the Court's subsequent cases involving the parental rights of unwed fathers has resulted in a rejection of the father's claim.

In response to the *Caban* decision, the State of New York enacted a new statute, improving the notice requirements for unwed fathers in proceedings to terminate their rights and effect the adoption of their children. In 1983 the Court heard the claim of an unwed father who had fallen between the cracks of this new system. Justice Stevens wrote for the majority, vindicating the claims he had pressed so vigorously in his *Caban* dissent and assuring that adoption procedures were no further complicated than *Caban* had strictly required. Indeed, the opinion in this case, *Lehr* v. *Robertson*, constricts the rights established in *Caban*. Abdiel Caban sought and won the right to maintain parental ties until and unless he consented to their dissolution or was found unfit. Caban had received what Jonathan Lehr claimed: the right simply to be heard concerning his child's best interests before adoption could be ordered. Lehr had filed a paternity proceeding, seeking orders of filiation, visitation, and support, but had not filed the instrument that gave rise to notice requirements under the adoption statutes: a notice of *intent to file a paternity proceeding*. His failure to fall within other categories of persons entitled to veto or to have notice of proceedings concerning the adoption of their children was the result of matters outside his control. Lehr alleged, but was never given the opportunity to prove, that he had lived with the mother for two years before the child's birth. The mother had repeatedly acknowledged his paternity and told him that she had reported it to the Department of Social Services. Lehr had visited the mother and child daily when they were hospitalized for the birth, but upon discharge from the hospital the mother had hidden her whereabouts and those of the child. During the first year of the child's life, Lehr was occasionally able to find, and permitted to visit with, the child. The mother and child then disappeared for a year. When Lehr found them, with the help of a detective, the mother had married another man. She rejected his offers of financial assistance and threatened him with arrest if he attempted to see the child. Having received notice from Lehr's attorney that legal action was contemplated, the mother and stepfather commenced adoption proceedings. The majority failed to mention these allegations. It mentioned with approval the fact that state laws commonly prefer the "formal family." It also mentioned the primary role that the state has traditionally had in governing the family. It then established for unwed fathers a sliding scale of constitutional protection:

> When an unwed father demonstrates a full commitment to the responsibilities of parenthood by "com[ing] forward to participate in the rearing of his child," his interest . . . acquires substantial protection under the Due Process Clause. At that point it may be said that he "act[s] as a father toward his children." But the mere existence of a biological link does not merit equivalent constitutional protection.

Lehr's Equal Protection claim was dismissed for similar reasons: The Court thought discrimination against those with no more than a biological link to the child reasonable and lawful. Only three members of the Court—Justices White, Marshall, and Blackmun—thought Joseph Lehr entitled even to be heard.[7]

The sliding scale of paternal rights was applied and reaffirmed in 1989 when Justice Scalia wrote for the Court to dismiss the constitutional challenge of a biological father and daughter who sought to maintain their legal relationship and the opportunity it would provide for visitation. This father, known in the litigation as Michael H., faced a different legal difficulty than Caban, Quilloin, and Lehr had faced: Whereas Caban, Quilloin, and Lehr needed to block or qualify orders of adoption by men who married the mothers of their children after the children's births, Michael H. needed to block or qualify California's "presumption of legitimacy," by which it was presumed as a matter of law that his biological child was the child of the mother's preexisting marriage. Quoting *Lehr*, Justice Scalia said that "[t]he [constitutional] significance of the biological connection is that it offers the natural father an opportunity that no other male possesses to develop a relationship with his offspring." According to Justice Scalia, that opportunity was legitimately trumped by a state decision to prefer to afford parental rights to a cohabiting husband of the mother.[8]

Then, in 1996, the Court faced a case in which a divorced mother sought to preserve her parental rights in the face of a petition for adoption by the subsequent wife of her former husband. The precise issue before the Court was whether the mother, known in the litigation as M.L.B., could constitutionally be barred by her inability to afford the costs of appealing an adverse ruling at trial. But the circumstances of the case, and the arguments for giving special constitutional deference to M.L.B.'s situation, were analogous to the unwed father cases. M.L.B. participated fully in the proceedings for adoption of her children. The presiding judge found, in the language of the statute authorizing termination of parental rights, that there had been a "substantial erosion of the relationship between the natural mother . . . and the minor children," and that the erosion was caused, at least in part, by her "serious neglect, abuse, prolonged and unreasonable absence or unreasonable failure to visit or communicate with her . . . children"; accordingly, the judge terminated M.L.B.'s parental rights and authorized adoption by the children's stepmother.

In upholding M.L.B.'s right to appeal this judgment, the Supreme Court did not mention its holdings with respect to unwed fathers' rights to be notified or heard in comparable proceedings. In discussing the nature of the interests at stake in M.L.B.'s potential appeal, the Court, in an opinion by Justice Ginsburg, spoke differently of the parental right than it had spoken in the unwed father cases. Drawing on cases concerning the right to appeal convictions for crimes, the Court spoke of the shame and stigma associated with a termination. Was M.L.B. entitled to appellate review, the Court asked, "before she is forever branded unfit for affiliation with her children?" The answer was in the affirmative. Termination of M.L.B.'s parental rights was an "accusatory state action . . . barely distinguishable from criminal condemnation in view of the magnitude and permanence of the loss she faces." "She is endeavoring," the Court said, "to defend against the State's destruction of her family bonds, and to resist the brand associated with a parental unfitness adjudication. Like a defendant resisting criminal conviction, she seeks to be spared from the State's devastatingly adverse action."[9] True, this rhetoric is natural to the criminal cases by which any expansion of an indigent's right of appeal would necessarily be measured. And, of course, the holding of *M.L.B.* will be equally applicable to men and to women. Still, one cannot help but wonder whether the rhetoric of *M.L.B.* would have rung as true to the justices had the aggrieved parent been a man. Indeed, reading the unwed father cases together with *M.L.B.*, it is not unreasonable to imagine that in the Court's view the parental rights of fathers are a set of opportunities that may be seized or lost, whereas the parental rights of mothers are claims of honor, such that their loss constitutes a profound *and stigmatizing* loss. We should not, I think, wish to diminish our cultural sense that the parental claim is a claim of honor and obligation. But we should, I think, give close attention to the ways in which the components of honor and obligation are gendered. To further explore this question, we turn now to cases in which the law seeks to enforce the duty to nurture.

II. Defining the Civil Obligation to Mother

Although the parenting rights of mothers seem, as a constitutional matter, to be firmly entrenched, those rights are severely limited, and sometimes extinguished, when a parent is accused, or is found guilty of neglecting or abusing her child. The 1997 enactment of federal laws reducing support for parents of children in foster care was but a step in a continuing process by which the center of child welfare efforts has shifted more and more dramatically to a goal of child rescue rather than a goal of family stabilization. Relying in large part on an influential set of ideas known as psychological parent theory, child welfare professionals dealing with children in foster care have downplayed hopes for family reunification in favor of the goal of identifying, as quickly as possible, a psychological parent—be it the original caregiver or a new one—who will become the child's "good mother."

Psychological parent theorists argue that children are inevitably and deeply harmed by separation from their psychological parents and by any interference with psychological parents' authority to exclude other adults from their children's lives.[10] Working from this premise, Joseph Goldstein, Anna Freud, and Albert Solnit urged that child welfare policies and laws be reformed to protect children against disruption of psychological parent relationships and against any contact (in the form, for example, of court-ordered visitation) unwanted by the psychological parent. They counseled noninterventionist policies to deter unnecessary disruptions of families of origin, but once disruption had occurred, they counseled action to protect the dyadic relationship between each child and the "psychological parent" then providing day-to-day care.[11]

The recommendations of Goldstein, Freud, and Solnit were enthusiastically embraced with respect to children in foster care. In the years following publication of their recommendations, permanency planning became the preoccupation of child welfare, and terminations of parental rights skyrocketed as agencies attempted to free children for adoption.[12] Indeed, termination rates continue to escalate. Martin Guggenheim's recent empirical analysis of termination of parental rights in Michigan and New York reveals that the number of children whose parental rights had been legally severed rose in Michigan from approximately 1,700 in 1986 to 3,030 in 1992, a 78 percent increase. In New York 1,119 children were freed for adoption in 1987 and 2,082 were in that status in 1991, an 86 percent increase. As the Guggenheim study establishes, termination remains an uncertain route to permanence: "The number of children freed for adoption goes up every year; the number of children adopted fails to keep pace with the number of adoption-eligible children; and the total number of orphaned children not adopted continues to increase fastest of all."[13]

What are the theoretical bases of the argument that children need, above all else, the uninterrupted nurturance of one psychological parent? I will first sketch out the theory and review its bases. I will then turn to recent research and theoretical advances to explore whether they improve or weaken the case for child welfare policies built upon the premise that the need for an autonomous caregiver surpasses all other needs of children in substitute care. I hope to persuade you that the approach of psychological parent theorists should be moderated to take account of two developments in the human sciences: (1) rejection of the "monotropic" view of child development in favor of a family system view, and (2) a growing conviction that cognitive and emotional growth require encouragement of child–caregiver relationships in which the child learns to recognize and accept the autonomy of others. I will argue that the reality of children's multiple bonds and the importance of children's developmental need to learn to recognize (and be recognized by) other independent minds require that we acknowledge, and allow them to acknowledge and resolve, their attachments, whether they are old or new, and whether or not they can promise to be uninterrupted.

Psychological parent theory parallels the work of attachment theorist John Bowlby. Bowlby's enduring and increasingly appreciated theoretical contribution to the understanding of child development was his recognition that healthy growth depends upon social interaction as well as upon physical care—that attachment behaviors are not, as Sigmund Freud had argued, secondary to the gratification of physical needs, but evidence of a primary need for social interaction. For reasons that may have more to do with Bowlby's personal and cultural perspectives than with the logic of his analysis, this theoretical insight was stimulated by, and developed in relation to, studies of childhood separation trauma. Significant among these studies were the observations of Dorothy Burlingham and Anna Freud during their experiences caring for children sheltered in residential nurseries to escape war and Nazi persecution, and studies in the 1950s and 1960s of English children undergoing residential care as a result of maternal hospitalization or homelessness.[14] Bowlby's work was not, however, grounded exclusively in data concerning separations that were extended or traumatic. Detailed elaborations of the effects of everyday separations were developed in a large body of influential work pioneered by M. D. S. Ainsworth.[15] Bowlby, and other students of human attachment and child development, drew heavily upon the Ainsworth research. They thought the reactions of young children to the inevitable, brief separations of everyday life were of a kind with longer-term and crisis-related separations. Bowlby described them as prototypes of human sorrow and keys to the understanding of a variety of human sufferings. As a result of the linking of everyday and crisis-related separations, attachment theorists seemed to portray virtually all child–caregiver separations not initiated by the child as comparable and poignant harms.[16]

Although attachment theorists addressed in their early work separations that varied in duration and circumstance, they were constant in their choice of the object in terms of which the child would count itself separated or whole: It was the mother. Early attachment research focused almost exclusively on mother–child separations, giving little or no attention to the effects of separation from fathers, siblings, and other caregivers. This focus was justified by what Bowlby described as the child's natural monotropism— the tendency to select, and to be possessive of, a principal attachment figure who, in the cultures Bowlby focused upon, was usually, but not always, the mother.[17]

Although Bowlby saw mother–child separation as the prototype of human sorrow and the key to understanding a wide range of human emotional disturbance, he was somewhat cautious concerning the implications of studies of separation trauma and the prognosis for children who experienced separations.[18] Psychological parent theorists were more confident. They argued that children have "a marked intolerance for postponement of gratification or frustration, and an intense sensitivity to the length of separations." They regarded "[c]hanges of parent figure" as "hurtful interruptions" in the child's development that would lead the child to "regress along the whole line of . . . affections, skills, achievements, and social adaptation." They argued that children lack the capacity to "maintain positive emotional ties with a number of different individuals [who are] unrelated or even hostile to each other," and, taking a position consistent with Bowlby's theory of monotropy, concluded that children need above all else to be under the exclusive authority and constant care of a primary psychological parent.[19]

Psychological parent theorists made the child the active participant in the developmental (as opposed to the physical, nurturing) work occurring within the child–caregiver dyad. They acknowledged, but did not emphasize, the fact that interaction with a caregiver stimulates development.[20] In this respect they held Sigmund Freud's focus on attachment as a by-product of the quest for physical gratification rather than Bowlby's focus on social stimuli and interaction as independent needs. The caregiver, or mother, was characterized as a solid source of support and affection—as symbol and assurance of gratification—rather than as a developmental catalyst. Their policy prescriptions were built on the belief that the child's developmental initiatives are painful and therefore "need to be offset by stability and uninterrupted support from external sources."[21]

Psychological parent theorists traced the developmental harms of separation from infancy through adulthood, arguing that at each phase of growth, separations impaired the child's successful accomplishment of age-appropriate developmental tasks by removing the context of security and uninterrupted support out of which the child might comfortably take developmental initiatives. In describing the hypothesized harms of separation in infancy, psychological parent theorists seemed to take the concept of "uninterrupted support" quite literally. Consistent with attachment theorists' tendency to equate everyday and traumatic separations, psychological parent theorists argued that in infancy, "any change in routine" was harmful "even if the infant's care is divided merely between mother and baby-sitter." Infants and toddlers "abandoned by the parent" became incapable of emotional attachment. For young children, "separation from the familiar mother" or "the psychological parent" was said to cause regressions in such achievements as toilet training and the development of speech.[22]

Although the empirical research supporting attachment theory was based primarily upon research concerning infants and toddlers, and, to a lesser extent, on research concerning preschool children, psychological parent theorists extended their analysis to argue that later separations are not only the distressing echoes of the prototypical mother-loss experienced by infants unable to anticipate return, but also a source of independent developmental harm. School-age children who "feel abandoned" by "their psychological parents" were said to fail to identify with those parents, causing a break in superego development with resultant dissocial or criminal behavior.[23] The harm caused to adolescents by separation was not explicitly explained in terms of developmental tasks, but it was said that the adolescent's attainment of an individual identity (the developmental task most prominently associated with adolescence) depended upon ever available caregivers from whom the adolescent separated only upon his or her own initiative: "For a successful outcome it is important that the breaks and disruptions of attachment should come exclusively from . . . [the child's] side and not be imposed on him by any form of abandonment or rejection on the psychological parents' part."[24]

Implicit in this description of the harms of separation is a model of ideal parenting—a model in which maternal images loom large. If infants are harmed by "any change in routine," including the division of care between mother and baby-sitter, and young children are harmed by any separation from "the familiar mother," then the ideal parenting arrangement for infants and young children must be an omnipresent mother. In describing the harms flowing from separation experiences of children over six, the psychological parent theorists began to speak of parents in the plural, shifting from an implicit focus upon the dyad of child and single, maternal caregiver to an implicit focus upon the oedipal triad. School-age children are harmed, psychological parent theorists contended, if they feel abandoned by their parents, and adolescents are harmed if they feel unable to control the process of separation. The implicit ideal is a mother and father who, like the mother of the child's younger years, are as available as the child feels they should be.

Despite the positing of a triad as the parenting ideal for older children, psychological parent theorists argued, as we have seen, that in the event of family disruption, it is in the best interests of children not to restore or replace each leg of the triad (or to restore the original dyad), but to give legal recognition and permanence to a dyad consisting of the child and the adult who was in the immediately preceding period most responsible for the child's day-to-day care and supervision. The restorative ideal, like the maternal ideal, is a figure who will provide perfect "[c]ontinuity of relationships, surroundings, and environmental influence."

There is no definitive study that tells us whether separation per se causes lasting psychological harm to children. Two developments in recent literature do, however, offer guidance. They do not begin to answer the question whether children are more in need of one set of parents or the other; they help us to see why that is the wrong question. And they help us to see why we have asked for so long a question that could not have been answered and may not have mattered to the best interests of our children. The first development is the emergence of a consensus within the human sciences that a child's security comes not from a single, constant individual, but from a familiar milieu and a network of attachments. The second development is the emergence of informed and realistic answers to the question Michael Rutter urged in the 1970s that psychologists probe more deeply: what a "good mother" is and what she does. Let me discuss these two developments in turn and then attempt to show how they are related and what implications they hold for child welfare policy.

Challenges to Monotropism

Some child development experts have long insisted that children are dependent on a network of attachments rather than on a single psychological parent. The Group for the Advancement of Psychiatry (GAP) was the most prominent early advocate of this view. Based on the clinical experiences and theoretical assumptions of its members, GAP argued in 1980 that there was "no evidence for the existence of a single 'psychological parent' with whom the tie is critically more important than with the rest of the [child's affiliational] network" and that children suffered adverse emotional consequences when part of their network was cut off and labeled as bad.[25]

The broader consensus that milieu is more fundamental than the mother bond has come as a result of a number of convergent research findings. It has grown out of empirical work concerning basic attachment theory, a growing body of research concerning the nurturing tasks of fathering, extensive research concerning the attachments and adjustments of children of divorced parents, and cross-cultural comparisons of child–caregiver interactions.

In order to describe the effect of basic attachment research upon views concerning children's bonding patterns, it is necessary to provide some background concerning the investigation of attachment behaviors during child–caregiver interactions and during and after short-term separations. I have said that attachment theory was greatly influenced by the systematic investigations of everyday separations that were conducted by M. D. S. Ainsworth. Ainsworth recorded the behavior of very young children as they interacted with their mothers and then were introduced to strangers, left briefly in the strangers' care, and returned to the care of their mothers. In the course of this research, Ainsworth observed distinct types of reactions to mother–child separation and reunification.[26] Some of these reaction patterns are deemed indicative of insecure attachments to the mother; others were deemed indicative of secure attachments. At the risk of gross oversimplification, it can be said that attachments are deemed insecure if the child reacts too much or too little to an everyday separation and secure if the child's reaction is moderate, involving neither avoidance of the familiar caregiver or clinging upon the caregiver's return. Subsequently it was discov-

ered that insecure reaction patterns correlated with behavioral and adjustment problems, while secure reaction patterns correlated with an absence of
those behavioral and adjustment problems. The body of research documenting child behavior before and after everyday separations and correlating reaction patterns with behavioral and adjustment patterns does not address
the longer-term effects of separation. It does not tell us whether everyday
separations are developmental impediments or developmental triggers; it
simply describes separations, draws conclusions concerning the quality of
attachment, and examines correlations between attachment quality and aspects of psychosocial functioning.

The Ainsworth measures of attachment quality have been used widely
and in a range of cultural settings. Increasingly they have been used to assess
the quality of children's attachment to caregivers other than the mother. As
a result it has been determined that children can be securely attached (as
Ainsworth defines the concept) not only to their mothers, but also to fathers
and to other caregivers.[27] "Infants form attachments with many people, including fathers, siblings, and babysitters. [Moreover,] . . . many of these relationships can be characterized as secure."[28]

The Ainsworth measures of attachment quality are, of course, limited
in that they are applicable only to older infants and toddlers and test only a
narrow aspect of the child's relationships.[29] Investigations into the roles and
relationships of fathers have considered a wide range of evidence to assess the
quality of children's bonds to men who are, and men who are not, primary
caregivers. These studies provide evidence both of the capacity for and of
the fact of close, nurturing relationships between fathers and children of all
ages. They therefore support the conclusions that children of all ages may
be bonded to both of their parents and that both bonds are important to
their emotional well-being. Fathers have been found "capable of emotionally responsive, nurturant caregiving" and of "biorhythmic synchronicity"
during their children's first three months. Fathers have been found to evoke
little or no stranger reaction and to interact similarly to the mother with
their three- to six-month-old infants. Mother and father interactions with
five- to ten-month-old children have been found to be comparable, and fathers who are nonprimary caregivers have been thought to play a special role
in the development of children between fifteen and twenty-four months.[30]
Although mothers in the United States have been found to spend more time
with children, to take more responsibility for their care, and to interact with
them more, mothers and fathers have been found equally competent at the
time of their child's birth to care for the child, and children with highly in-

volved fathers have been found to be "characterized by increased cognitive competence, increased empathy, . . . and a more internal locus of control."[31] A large and apparently well designed study of father custody found "no differences . . . between custodial fathers and mothers on . . . measures of nurturance and involvement."[32]

Research concerning the adjustment of children after the divorce of their parents is complex and often ambiguous, for it is impossible to account for all the variables that might affect well-being. Nonetheless, the results of this research are consistent with the conclusion that bonds to both parents are strong and developmentally significant. Whether in father-custody or mother-custody, children experience distress at the time of family dissolution, and children of divorced parents seem almost invariably to hold reunification fantasies.[33] There is substantial, although not uncontradicted, evidence that children of divorced parents fare better if they are able to maintain positive contact with both parents.[34] Moreover, children in joint custody arrangements report greater satisfaction and seem to fare at least as well as children in sole custody arrangements. A four-year longitudinal study of 1,124 divorcing families with children between the ages of six and fourteen found that child satisfaction was greatest in dual residence custodial arrangements. Children in mother-, father-, and dual-custody "were quite similar in their self-reported levels of adjustment, and judging from the absolute level of their ratings, most appeared to be functioning well within the normal range."[35]

Studies of different cultures and subcultures have also undermined belief in the primacy of the single psychological bond, for they have shown that children's reactions to everyday separations vary according to whether they have been acculturated to expect multiple caregivers. A study of Kipsigi children in western Kenya found that although infants "as in other communities, are often upset when their mothers leave them for short periods, this response does not last long. They become accustomed to care by several people, and so maternal absence by itself does not occasion distress." Studies across five cultures have shown that "after the universal emergence of distress at separation . . . at about 1 year of age [coinciding with the emergence of "a cognitive ability to detect and evaluate (and therefore sometimes fear) unusual and unpredictable events"], there is considerable diversity among cultures in its decline in the second and third years of life." American and Botswanan children who were cared for almost exclusively by their mothers continued beyond the thirtieth month to show distress upon everyday separations; for children, like the Kipsigi children, from communities "where siblings or other persons play an important role in the day-to-day care of infants and toddlers, there is a more rapid decline in the amount of distress."[36] Similar differences have been observed between children who have and children who do not have nonworking parents. Jessica Benjamin has reported from her research that "when one-year-old babies were left alone with the stranger in the Ainsworth experiment . . . the babies of working mothers who had regular sitters related to and 'used' the stranger to remain calm. Of the babies in exclusive-mother care, most showed stranger anxiety and became upset when left by mother with the stranger. All babies were upset when left completely alone, as expected."[37]

Shirley Brice Heath's descriptions of two communities in the American South convey a "feel" for cultural differences that might aggravate or mitigate the child's reactions as s/he becomes able to appreciate that the familiar caregiver is absent. In the first of these communities, a white, working-class neighborhood in the southern United States, access to the child is rather carefully controlled:

> Neighbors, church people, and relatives come to visit the new mother and baby. . . . Female relatives of the new mother are in charge of visitors, and they usher visitors in to see the sleeping baby and allow some close relatives to hold the baby for a feeding or while the bottle is being prepared.

Heath reports that in this community "[y]oung mothers home alone, with their first child in particular, often have many hours with no one around to talk to. They talk to their babies." In the second community, a nearby Black working-class neighborhood, children are "almost never alone and very rarely in the company of only one other person." A crying baby is "fed, tended, held, and fondled by anyone nearby." Each child seems to be the concern of each adult. "There is great joking about those who hold a new baby awkwardly, and men and women demonstrate willingly how to hold a baby as though 'he's a part of you'"; crawling babies and curious toddlers "are constantly under the watchful eye of someone in the community."[38]

Rejection of the monotropic view of infant and child bonding has been widespread, affecting the views of research scientists, clinicians, and child welfare practitioners alike. As Jessica Benjamin has noted, "the literature on attachment has long since disconfirmed . . . [Bowlby's] original theory that attachment devolves on only one person in favor of the idea of multiple attachment figures."[39]

Some researchers have concluded not only that multiple bonds are characteristic of most children, but also that they are beneficial. Scholars engaged in a comprehensive, international research program on attachment and bonding have, as a result of their own findings and their extensive reviews of the findings of others, shifted from what it calls the monotropy of earlier bonding theories to an "extension hypothesis." They have come to believe that

> the optimal caregiving arrangement would consist of a network of stable and secure attachment relationships between the child and both its parents and other persons such as professional caregivers, members of the family, or friends. In research, attachment should be considered in light of a network of relationships the child builds up in the first years of life.[40]

As these researchers point out in an analysis of the deficiencies of Bowlby's monotropy thesis:

> [P]ermanent actual presence of the (primary) caregiver is virtually impossible in a family in which there is (often) more than one child to be cared for, and in which the caregiver has to fulfill other responsibilities than bringing up children. In most families, help provided by baby-sitters, neighbors, relatives, friends, acquaintances and especially the partner is indispensable. Given the inevitability of temporary separations, the optimal rearing context will, from the child's perspective, be made up by more or less stable relationships with several different caregivers who all act as attachment figures. For if only one specific caregiver has developed into an attachment figure, each separation will appear to be a very severe event, since the child has no one else to turn to. On the other hand, in an extended rearing context, a separation from an attachment figure does not automatically imply a separation as perceived by the child: there are a number of caregivers who may provide the same source of security in potentially threatening situations.[41]

The implications of rejection of the monotropic view have been brought to bear upon clinical and legal practice. James Bray writes:

> In contrast to popular ideas and viewpoints within the legal system, research indicates that children develop multiple attachments to caregivers who can help them cope with separation anxiety and stress. The idea of "one psychological parent" or "the primary parent" is a concept often emphasized by custody evaluators and within legal circles. This notion is controversial and has very little empirical support. There is usually a hierarchy of attachment figures, each of whom may have qualitatively different . . . relationships with the child, although children may prefer one attachment figure over another. Thus, the relationships between parents, other caregivers and children . . . are of importance in determining children's . . . reactions to custodial arrangements and visitations.[42]

A careful review of research concerning post-divorce visitation and custody arrangements concluded, "the contention . . . that the child's relationship with the custodial or 'psychological parent' may be damaged by the continued coequal involvement of the non-custodial parent does not appear to be necessarily true."[43]

We must be very careful in drawing out the implications for psychological parent theory of rejection of the monotropic view. Psychological parent theorists accept the possibility of multiple bonds. They are monotropists in two rather limited senses. First, the work of psychological parent theorists does not acknowledge cultural and subcultural differences (and arguably underestimates age differences[44]) in the reaction of children to separations. As a result psychological parent theorists fail to acknowledge the variability of reactions to everyday separations and to longer-term separations not associated with permanent loss or other trauma. Thus, in contrast to Bowlby's acknowledgment that separation distress is significantly mitigated by the presence of a familiar companion other than the absent caregiver or by nurturing care from an unfamiliar caregiver,[45] and in contrast to the findings of cross-cultural studies that separation effects vary according to the experiences and expectations of the child, psychological parent theorists see intense distress or lasting harm even in everyday separations. Second, although psychological parent theorists acknowledge, if only in the case of older children, that children may be importantly bonded at least to both of two parents, they minimize the importance to the child of all but the most intense current bond. Believing that children can only maintain bonds to adults who are positively related to one another, they counsel that older bonds be severed in service of the autonomy of the primary caregiver. As a result of these two stances, psychological parent theorists propose policies that leave children in the consistent (if not constant) care of adults with exclusive authority to limit their interactions with others.

Child welfare practitioners and policymakers influenced by the milieu or family systems perspective on attachment and bonding take a different approach. Like Goldstein, Freud, and Solnit, they recognize that family disruptions are traumatic, combining separation from familiar caregivers with the trauma of official intervention and an uprooting from familiar surroundings.[46] But they aspire not to provide a single, substitute bond, but to provide an expanded milieu and opportunities to conquer feelings of betrayal and loss. Despite somewhat mixed research findings, sociologists prominent among researchers addressing divorce custody issues have expressed a conviction, grounded in theories of child development, that "when parents are able to cooperate in childrearing after a divorce and when fathers are able to maintain an active and supportive role, children will be better off in the long run."[47] In contrast to the "out of sight, out of mind" theory that seems to underlie the recommendations of psychological parent theorists, clinicians responsive to multiple bonds have worked to develop ways for children to "mourn" or otherwise come to terms in explicit ways with feelings about their families of origin.[48] Practitioners working in the foster care system have developed devices like the "Fami-O-Graph" or "Lifebook" to help young children in placement to record and come to terms with all of their biological and fictive kinship ties.[49] Open adoptions have been recommended for children who cannot return to their families of origin.[50] For older children, a policy of "family integrity" has been recommended. This policy stems from the recognition that residential placement can interfere with developmentally significant processes of family interaction, thus "disempower[ing] the family as a unit" and disrupting healthy development. Under the family integrity system, the child's substitute caregivers encourage interaction with the family of origin:

> Family or significant care-givers would not be given an opportunity to . . . withdraw on any permanent basis. The task of residential placement would be to ensure that the family, no matter what, is unrelentingly confronted with their responsibility and their value to the young person's well-being. Families would be given continuous recognition of what they can now contribute to their young person.[51]

Constructive interaction among original caregivers, substitute caregivers, and children would presumably meet with the approval of psychological parent theorists so long as it was voluntarily engaged in by the primary custodial caregiver.[52] Their claim is not that interaction with former caregivers is inherently bad for children, but rather that children cannot profit, but will suffer, from interactions with adults about whom the psychological parent is negative or hostile and with whom the psychological parent does not want the child to interact. This claim is not unreasonable. It finds apparent support in the consistent findings of research concerning the adjustment of children of divorce that animosity between parents correlates with behavioral problems and poor adjustment.[53] The difficulty, of course, is that these findings do not tell us whether children are harmed by the fact that important figures in their lives are in conflict or by an inability to interact with those figures when they are in conflict. If one takes the older view that the primary bond is of overwhelming importance, then one is drawn to minimize the child's desire or need to maintain other ties and shelter the psychological parent–child dyad. If one takes the family system perspective, believing that children profit from multiple bonds and suffer the repression or denial of separation distress, then one is drawn to minimize the value of an autonomous dyad and keep the child's world open to preexisting attachment figures.

Challenging the Omnicompetent Ideal

Theoretical work concerning the nature of the "mother bond" is like the more recent work concerning patterns of multiple attachments in that it suggests, although it does not compel, modifications of psychological parent theory. Attachment theory was originally grounded in study of trauma surrounding mother–infant separations. It is carried in our minds, I believe, with an image of a baby crying for its mother. It grew naturally from the observation, made by Bowlby in a 1951 report concerning neglected children in postwar Europe, that "maternal love" is as important to mental development as nutrients are to physical development.[54] Despite important differences between the views of Anna Freud and John Bowlby,[55] psychological parent theory shares this lineage.[56] The first image of the psychological parent is the mother whose familiar patterns of feeding, handling, and comforting the child cannot, without cost, be interrupted, even by the use of a babysitter. The parental function, as described by psychological parent theorists, changes little over time. Although the developmental needs of the child change, the parent continues to act as an omnipresent base of security and comfort.[57] More recent theoretical work concerning child development and the "mothering" function provides new models of parenting. These models are built on two insights. The first is recognition that the requirement of omnipresence is infeasible, a product of denial generated by the fantasy of the "perfect" mother. The second is recognition that infants and children need (and want), not only a measure of comfort and security, but also the challenge of interacting with other minds—minds that prove their "otherness" in that they do *not* act invariably in fulfillment of the child's wishes.

Just as attachment theorists have recognized the impossibility—and questioned the desirability—of "permanent actual presence of the primary caregiver," women striving to include the perspective of the parent in child development research have questioned the mothering ideal implicit in many theories of attachment. Nancy Chodorow and Susan Contratto have identified a culturally dominant image of the mother as all powerful—always idealized, and, as a result, always blamed when things are not well. They quote Adrienne Rich's description of the need mother is imagined to fulfill as "a need vaster than any single human being could satisfy, except by loving continuously, unconditionally, from dawn to dark, and often in the middle of the night."[58] They help us to see that the job of parenting implicit in the psychological parent theorist's ideal is a job only imaginable for woman, and, upon reflection, not imaginable at all. Sara Ruddick, focusing on the intellectually demanding work of mothering, describes the stories of real mothers:

> The "dream of plentitude"—a mutually embracing, mutually desiring mother-child couple—often disappears in mothers' tales of babies who can't be made happy, jealous older siblings, altered sexual and love relationships, financial worries, and the general emotional confusion and sleeplessness that tend to mark the early weeks of mothering. To be sure, many mothers also remember moments of passionate infatuation with an astonishingly marvelous infant. But these mothers, if they are at all effective in their work, are unlikely to remember themselves as absorbed lovers in a baby couple. As Madeleine Sprengnether has remarked, "the concept of mother-infant symbiosis is an obvious absurdity, for a mother can only act as a mother if she perceives herself as such, as separate and different from her infant. A mother who felt in every way like an infant would be worse than useless as a caretaker."[59]

The fantasy of the perfect and all powerful mother is held so dearly that women who make these statements (and we who report them) must seem churlish spoilers. Yet a great deal can be learned from those who speak with an experienced and loving mother's realism about the possibility, and wisdom, of living up to the fantasy. Jessica Benjamin, mother, psychoanalyst, and scholar, looks beyond the "omnicompetent angel of the house"[60] who is our mother fantasy to imagine a parent who excites a child's capacity for interaction with an independent mind.

Developmental theorists are helping us to see that the developmental work of infancy occurs as a baby learns, beginning as early as four months, to recognize, and then to relate to, other minds.[61] Language, interpersonal competence, and personality all follow the baby's profound recognition that s/he interacts with someone who has independent thoughts, moods, and intentions. Benjamin works from Bowlby's recognition of the social character of early attachment behaviors, and, relying upon the subsequent insights of Margaret Mahler, Daniel Stern, and D. W. Winnicott, proposes a theory of intersubjectivity.[62] In Benjamin's view, the infant has an ability to recognize, to enjoy, and to grow in reaction to the experience of the mother's subjectivity. The expectation that mother will be omnipotent and subject to the child's will leaves the child in a dominating isolation, with an illusion of "mastery" but no sense of otherness. Moreover, it leaves the child unable to address in a constructive way the anger and fear aroused when s/he is disappointed—to contend with forces imagined to be all powerful but unpredictable, rather than to learn to negotiate with an independent mind.

From Benjamin's theory of intersubjectivity there flows an understanding of a role for caregivers beyond the provision of physical care and comfort. A caregiver "stimulates an incipient recognition of otherness, difference, discrepancy, and this pleases the infant, who likes the excitement that a brush with otherness brings."[63] The excitement of recognition of another mind is not only pleasurable, but necessary to the child's development:

> If the mother is unable both to set a clear boundary for the child and to recognize the child's intentions and will, to insist on her own separateness and respect that of the child, the child does not really "get" that mother is also a person, a subject in her own right. Instead, the child continues to see her as all-powerful, either omnipotently controlling or engulfingly weak . . . [and] the process of mutual recognition has not been furthered.[64]

It is in the play of intersubjectivity that a child learns to manage separations, and to manage them without resorting to displacement of negative feelings into fantasied scenarios of the omnipotent but evil caregiver or the omnipotent self who annihilates the other's will:

> The child who can imaginatively entertain his own and his [caregiver's] part—leaving and being left—has attained a space that symbolically contains negative feelings so that they need not be projected onto the object (she is dreadful) or turned back upon the self (I am destructive). The mother has . . . helped the child to contain and share these feelings, has provided a space in which they can be understood as fantasy.[65]

The work of parenting—of caring for children and helping them to grow— includes the work of meeting their physical needs and providing basic comfort. But it is not the work of protecting the illusion of the omnipotent mother who satisfies all wants. It is the work of helping them—gently, lovingly, playfully—to grow in health and to learn to relate in health to other independent minds.

I have described a process of rethinking the nurturing role to take account of the impossibility of uninterrupted symbiosis, and of the child's need for intersubjective exchange. This rethinking has two implications for psychological parent theory: It removes some of the stigma of separation, and it suggests that separation is an issue that children should be encouraged to confront rather than deny. Each of these implications needs to be drawn with a very careful line of argument.

If the denial of an earnest wish to be omnipotent makes a mother seem churlish, any suggestion that the harms of childhood separation have been overstated by psychological parent theorists seems cruelly perverse. Let me first cabin the statements. When I speak of mitigation of the stigma of separation, I do not mean to suggest that it is all right to impose upon children the obvious harms of long-term and other traumatic separations from familiar caregivers. It does seem, however, that everyday separations can be understood as constructive learning experiences rather than as inflictions of inevitable damage. As attachment theorists have pointed out, and as cross-cultural analyses demonstrate, everyday separations can be mitigated by a supportive milieu in which caregiving is shared among several adults with whom the child is familiar. As Benjamin's work suggests, they can provide opportunities for healthy—and even pleasurable—brushes with the concept of an independent other.

It is in pursuit of Benjamin's suggestion that I say children should be encouraged to confront rather than deny separation. If we accept the possibility of a constructive approach to everyday separations, we are led to rethink the stance we take with respect to all separations. The inevitable separations of daily life are aggravated by our tendency to pretend that they are evitable. We imagine that "mother" need never go away, and so we fail to provide the support of alternate caregivers or to apply our minds to encouragement of the child's capacity to adapt. In thinking through the needs of foster children, perhaps we have been captured again by the image of the perfect mother. All of us have imagined everyday separations as small crimes and want to pretend that mother could avoid them by always being there for her child. Perhaps we have also wanted to pretend that we could erase the conflicted feelings associated with the greater "crime" of family disruption by calling forth a new mother, by giving the child "permanence" and a new symbiosis. Of course, this is a fantasy. Enduring symbiosis is a womb state; wherever a child goes, s/he will meet the challenge of separations. Moreover, many, many foster children retain deep feelings for the families they have lost. The fantasy of a new symbiosis is no cure for the conflict associated with those feelings.

Conclusion

The variables in a child's life are many, and measures of well-being are imprecise. Numbers will not tell us which interventions will help and which will hurt. Case studies are also inconclusive. They invite us to generalize from fact patterns that may be rare or idiosyncratic. Nonetheless, case studies are a useful way of filling in explanatory stories suggested by empirical and theoretical work. To this end, Rita Eagle has published a moving account of the course of therapy with a boy who spent most of his childhood in foster care.[66] Eagle chronicles this child's abiding attachment, manifested in alternating expressions of acceptance and rejection, to his family of origin; his similar, but increasingly fragile, attachments to foster parents and to institutional caregivers; his moments of relative comfort when he is made to feel secure and permitted to speak openly about his lost families; and his anguish as institutional caregivers disappear and foster families change. This child was preoccupied with a toy spaceship given to him by his mother, and he repeatedly drew pictures of spaceships. When Eagle suggested on one occasion that he draw an airplane, the child said, "Airplanes are no good—they run out of fuel and crash. Only spaceships are good, because they don't fail. They just stay in orbit." Eagle believes that the child was telling her that "like airplanes, real mothers and real foster mothers run out of 'fuel' (love and caring) and 'crash' (fail to provide for, protect, and stay with him). Like spaceships, however, the 'good mother' of his reunion fantasies would stay aloft and remain forever with him."[67]

As the child moved from one foster setting to another, he was never able to talk about and work through his feelings about the homes he had left. Never able to come to terms with those who had failed him, he remained captured by the image of a good mother who would never fail. Struggling to find ways to address this child's needs, Eagle suggests that the agencies and policies that shaped his life harmed him by clinging themselves—and by implicitly encouraging the child to cling—to the fantasy of a "good mother" who would never "fail." Consistently with what she describes as "strong evidence," Eagle argues that "past ties are tenacious, that they may have persisting effects in children's lives, and that respect for these ties by new caretakers may help, rather than hinder, the development of new relationships."[68] She therefore gives cautious support to recognition of multiple caregivers and a policy of access between children and families of origin.

If, as recent research and theory would have us believe, children profit more from the care of several caregivers than from the exclusive care of one; are bonded to old caregivers; and need to put aside fantasies of omnicompetent mothers in favor of loving engagement with imperfect others, how should the law respond? How should we as a people and a culture respond? When we think about the rights and obligations of parenting, perhaps we should train ourselves to think less of mothering and fathering and more of parenting and caregiving. When we attempt to address the needs of foster children, perhaps we should transcend differences of class, race, history, and parenting capacity to provide as cooperative a network of care as the children's decidedly disadvantageous circumstances will allow.

1. *Wisconsin* v. *Yoder*, 405 U.S. 645 (1972); *West Virginia* v. *Barnette*, 319 U.S. 624 (1943); *Pierce* v. *Society of Sisters*, 268 U.S. 510 (1925); *Meyer* v. *Nebraska*, 262 U.S. 390 (1923).

2. *Santowsky* v. *Kramer*, 455 U.S. 745 (1982); *Lassiter* v. *Department of Social Services*, 452 U.S. 18 (1981).

3. *Stanley* v. *Illinois*, 405 U.S. 645 (1972).

4. Ibid.

5. *Quilloin* v. *Walcott*, 434 U.S. 246 (1978). The Court declined, on procedural grounds, to consider Quilloin's sex discrimination claim. It found no unlawful discrimination by virtue of the more privileged position given married and divorced fathers.

6. *Caban* v. *Mohammed*, 441 U.S. 380 (1979).

7. *Lehr* v. *Robertson*, 463 U.S. 248 (1983).

8. *Michael H.* v. *Gerald D.*, 491 U.S. 110 (1989).

9. *M.L.B.* v. *S.L.J.*, 117 Sup.Ct. 555 (1996).

10. Joseph Goldstein, Anna Freud, and Albert J. Solnit, *Beyond the Best Interests of the Child* (New York: Free Press, 1973), 31–34. Psychological parents were defined as persons who provided uninterrupted day-to-day care to a child for minimum periods that varied depending on the age of the child (Ibid., 17–19).

11. Joseph Goldstein, Anna Freud, and Albert J. Solnit, *Before the Best Interests of the Child* (New York: Free Press, 1979), 15–18, 399–351.

12. Peggy C. Davis, "Use and Abuse of the Power to Sever Family Bonds," *N.Y.U. Review of Law and Social Change* 12 (1984): 562, reporting an increase in New York State terminations of parental rights from 92 in 1968 to 1,719 in 1980.

13. Martin Guggenheim, "The Effects of Recent Trends to Accelerate the Termination of Parental Rights of Children in Foster Care—An Empirical Analysis in Two States," *Family Law Quarterly* 29, no. 121 (1995):

11, 13–14; see also Margaret Beyer and Wallace Mlyniec, "Lifelines to Biological Parents: Their Effect on Termination of Parental Rights and Permanence," *American Law Quarterly* 20 (1986): 233.

14. Jessica Benjamin, *The Bonds of Love* (New York: Pantheon Books, 1988), 17, arguing that Bowlby, together with object-relations theorists, "offered psychoanalysis a new foundation: the assumption that we are fundamentally social beings" (John Bowlby, *Attachment and Loss*, vol. 1, *Attachment* [New York: Basic Books, 1973], 216–220). For an excellent description of attachment theory, its influences, and its shortcomings see Marinus H. Van Ijzendoorn and Louis W. C. Tavecchio, "The Development of Attachment Theory as a Lakatosian Research Program: Philosophical and Methodological Aspects," in *Attachment in Social Networks: Contributions to the Bowlby-Ainsworth Attachment Theory*, ed. Louis W. C. Tavecchio and Marinus H. Van Ijzendoorn (Amsterdam: North-Holland, 1987), 3, 6–12, 8–10, concluding that "[s]ocial factors . . . intellectual climate . . . and personal experiences . . . form in brief the foundation of Bowlby's preoccupation with attachment relationships, separation and loss."

15. For descriptions of this work, see ibid., 39–47.

16. See Bowlby, *Attachment and Loss*, vol. 2, *Separation*, 30–56, especially 30–31, describing the importance of separation research and the relevance of "the comparable [to responses to long term separations in times of trauma] but far less intense responses that are to be seen in young children during the course of everyday living."

17. See Bowlby, *Attachment*, 308–309, arguing that although children have multiple bonds, "there is a strong bias for attachment behavior to become directed mainly towards one particular person and for a child to become strongly possessive of that person."

18. See Bowlby, *Separation*, 3–22; Bowlby, *Attachment*, 3. "When removed from mother by strangers young children respond usually with great intensity; and after reunion with her they show commonly either a heightened degree of separation anxiety or else an unusual detachment. Since a change in relations of one or other of these kinds, or even of both compounded, is frequent in subjects suffering from psychoneurosis and other forms of emotional disturbance, it seemed promising to select these observations as a starting-point; and . . . to 'follow it up through the material as long as the application of it seems to yield results,'" citing Sigmund Freud, *Repression* [1915], in vol. 14 of *The Standard Edition of the Complete Psychological Works of Sigmund Freud*, ed. James Strachey (New York: W. W. Norton, 1976); see also Bowlby, *Separation*, 5: "Most children who have had experiences of these kinds recover and resume normal development, or at least they appear to do so. Not infrequently, therefore, doubts are expressed whether the psychological processes described are in reality related so intimately to personality disturbances of later life. Pending much further evidence, these are legitimate doubts."

19. Goldstein et al., *Beyond the Best Interests*, 11, 12, 18.

20. This failure to attribute intellectual work to the mother was characteristic until the last decade of virtually all theoretical analyses of infant and child development. See Sara Ruddick, "Thinking Mothers / Conceiving Birth," in *Representations of Motherhood*, ed. Donna Bassin, Margaret Honey, and Meryle Mahrer Kaplan (New Haven and London: Yale University Press, 1994), 29–33, describing the failure of theorists to conceive the mother as a thoughtful, social being; see also Goldstein et al., *Beyond the Best Interests*, 18, acknowledging the child's "demands for affection, companionship and stimulating intimacy," and, 31–34, emphasizing the child's need for continuity.

21. Ibid., 32.

22. Ibid., 33, citing studies of wartime separations and enuresis.

23. See Bowlby, *Separation*, 33–56, citing the social history of a condemned murderer as recited in a judicial opinion.

24. Ibid., 34.

25. *Divorce, Child Custody and the Family*. Material formulated by the Committee on the Family Group for the Advancement of Psychiatry (New York: Mental Health Materials Center, 1980), 80–81.

26. The number and the definitions of the types have varied as the research has continued. For a description of both the older and the newer categories, see Marinus H. Van Ijzendoorn, Susan Goldberg, Pieter M. Kroonenberg, and Oded J. Frenkel, "The Relative Effects of Maternal and Child Problems on the Quality of Attachment: A Meta-Analysis of Attachment in Clinical Samples," *Child Development* 63 (1992): 840.

27. See Van Ijzendoorn et al., "The Relative Effects"; Kathleen J. Sternberg and Michael E. Lamb, "Evaluations of Attachment Relationships by Jewish Israeli Day-Care Providers," *Journal of Cross-Cultural Psychology* 23 (1992): 285; Marinus H. Van Ijzendoorn and Pieter M. Kroonenberg, "Cross-Cultural Patterns of Attach-

ment: A Meta-Analysis of the Strange Situation," *Child Development* 59 (1988): 147; Rosanne Kermoin and P. Herbert Leiderman, "Infant Attachment to Mother and Child Caretaker in an East African Community," *International Journal of Behavioural Development* 9 (1986): 455, examining attachments to mothers and to child caregivers and finding East African children securely attached to both mothers and child caregivers at rates comparable to mother attachment rates in U.S. studies; Robert Marcus, "Attachments of Children in Foster Care," *Genetic, Social, and General Psychology Monographs* 117 (1992): 367, examining attachments to foster mothers and foster fathers; Jeffrey Scott Applegate, "Beyond the Dyad: Including the Father in Separation-Individuation," *Child and Adolescent Social Work* 4 (1987): 92.

28. Kermoin and Leiderman, "Infant Attachment to Mother," 468; see also Louis W. C. Tavecchio and Marinus H. Van Ijzendoorn, "Perceived Security and Extension of the Child's Rearing Context: A Parent-Report Approach," in *Attachment in Social Networks: Contributions to the Bowlby-Ainsworth Attachment Theory*, ed. Louis W. C. Tavecchio and Marinus H. Van Ijzendoorn (Amsterdam: North-Holland, 1987), 35, 42, reporting studies establishing that "children may have similar attachment relationships with several different adults, i.e., father, mother, and professional caregivers."

29. For a discussion of the possibilities and problems of using the Ainsworth measures in the evaluation of older children, see Ann Easterbrooks, Cherilyn E. Davidson, and Rachel Chazan, "Psychosocial Risk, Attachment, and Behavior Problems Among School-Aged Children," *Development and Psychopathology* 5 (1993): 389.

30. Applegate, "Beyond the Dyad," 95–99.

31. Michael E. Lamb, "The Emergent American Father," in *The Father's Role: Cross-Cultural Perspectives*, ed. Michael E. Lamb (Hillsdale, N.J.: Lawrence Erlbaum, 1987), 3, 11, 15–16. Research in the United States has suggested that fathers interact differently with children than do mothers in that fathers are more playful and less nurturant (Ibid., 10). Research in a different cultural setting has found otherwise: see Barry S. Hewlett, "Intimate Fathers: Patterns of Paternal Holding Among Aka Pygmies" in *The Father's Role*, 295, reporting findings that among the Aka men engage regularly in nurturing behavior and that vigorous play is not characteristic of interactions between children and male caregivers.

32. Richard Warshak, "Father-Custody and Child Development: A Review and Analysis of Psychological Research," *Behavioral Science and the Law* 4 (1986): 181, 194.

33. Ibid., 191; Judith S. Wallerstein and Joan B. Kelly, *Surviving the Breakup: How Children and Parents Cope with Divorce* (New York: Basic Books, 1980), 35; P. Lindsay Chase-Lansdle and Mavis Hetherington, "The Impact of Divorce on Life-Span Development: Short and Long Term Effects," in *Life Span Development and Behavior*, vol. 10, ed. David L. Featherman and Richard M. Lerner (Hillsdale, N.J.: Lawrence Erlbaum, 1990), 105; Warshak, "Father-Custody and Child Development," 192, reporting a study in which "virtually all the children attributed reconciliation wishes to the child in their projective story."

34. For evidence that positive relationships with noncustodial parents are related to well-being, see E. Mavis Hetherington, "Family Relations Six Years After Divorce," in *Remarriage and Step-Parenting, Current Research and Theory*, ed. Kay Pasley and Marilyn Ihinger-Tallman (New York: Guilford Press, 1989), 185. For evidence that there is no correlation, see Frank F. Furstenberg, Jr., S. Philip Morgan, and Paul D. Allison, "Paternal Participation and Children's Well-Being After Marital Dissolution," *American Sociological Review* 52 (1987): 695.

35. Eleanor E. Maccoby, Christy Buchanan, Robert Mnookin, and Sanford Dornbusch, "Post-Divorce Roles of Mothers and Fathers in the Lives of Their Children," *Journal of Family Psychology* 7 (1993): 24, 34; see also Robert D. Felner and Lisa Terre, "Child Custody Dispositions and Children's Adaptation Following Divorce," in *Psychology and Child Custody Determinations*, ed. Lois A. Weithorn (Lincoln: University of Nebraska Press, 1987), 106, 128: "In general . . . [studies examining the differences in adjustment as a function of being in joint or sole custody] report no clear differences among family types as they relate to Children's adjustment."

36. Charles M. Super and Sara Harkness, "The Development of Affect in Infancy and Early Childhood," in *Cultural Perspectives on Child Development*, ed. Daniel A. Wagner and Harold W. Stevenson (San Francisco: W. H. Freeman, 1982), 1, 7, 9, 15 (table 1–4). Similarly, stranger anxiety is more pronounced in cultures in which children are exposed to few strangers. Thus, American children who see many strangers but have a single caretaker were found to be less anxious about strangers, but more anxious about separations, than were Kipsigi children who had multiple caretakers but saw few strangers.

37. Benjamin, *The Bonds of Love*, 209.

38. Shirley Brice Heath, *Ways with Words: Language, Life and Work in Communities and Classrooms* (Cambridge and New York: Cambridge University Press, 1983), 74–76, 116–17, 121.

39. Benjamin, *Bonds of Love*, 210. As Benjamin also notes, Bowlby himself came to acknowledge, to some extent, the importance of a child's bonds to multiple caretakers; see Bowlby, *Attachment*, 304: "During their second year of life a great majority of infants are directing their attachment behavior towards more than one discriminated figure, and often towards several. Some infants select more than one attachment-figure almost as soon as they begin to show discrimination; but probably most come to do so rather later."

40. Marinus H. Van Ijzendoorn and Louis Tavecchio, "The Development of Attachment Theory as a Lakatosian Research Program: Philosophical and Methodological Aspects," in Tavecchio and Ijzendoorn, *Attachment in Social Networks*, 1, 24–25.

41. Tavecchio and Ijzendoorn, *Attachment in Social Networks*, 39–40; see also Warshak, "Father Custody and Child Development," 198, reporting findings that for children of divorced parents "contact with additional caretakers was positively related to the child's behavior toward the custodial parent."

42. James H. Bray, "Psychosocial Factors Affecting Custodial and Visitation Arrangements," *Behavioral Sciences and the Law* 9 (1991): 419.

43. Felner and Terre, "Child Custody Dispositions," 106, 140.

44. Attachment theory is largely undeveloped with respect to children above the age of two. See Easterbrooks et al., "Psychosocial Risk," discussing the difficulties of assessing attachment behaviors of five- to seven-year-olds.

45. Bowlby, *Separation*, 16.

46. See Martha Morrison Dore and Eleanor Eisner, "Child-Related Dimensions of Placement Stability in Treatment Foster Care," *Child and Adolescent Social Work Journal* 10 (1993): 301, 303: "[A]ny child who enters out-of-home placement, whether traditional or treatment foster care, is experiencing significant trauma by virtue of the loss of familiar surroundings and relationships, no matter how detrimental these may seem to an outside observer. This trauma is compounded by further changes in placement, as when a child is moved from one foster home to another or from a temporary shelter to a foster home"; Grant Charles and Jane Matheson, "Children in Foster Care: Issues of Separation and Attachment," *Community Alternatives* 2 (1990): 37, 39–40: "The experiences of repeated separations and abandonments, as is often the case with a child in care, will elicit ever-increasing anger and related dysfunctional responses."

47. Frank F. Furstenberg, Jr., and Andrew J. Cherlin, *Divided Families: What Happens to Children When Parents Part* (Cambridge, Mass.: Harvard University Press, 1991), 73.

48. For a review of these clinical strategies, see Rita S. Eagle, "Airplanes Crash, Spaceships Stay in Orbit: The Separation Experience of a Child 'In Care,'" *Journal of Psychotherapy Practice and Research* 2 (1993): 318, 319–320.

49. Linda L. Katz, *An Overview of Current Clinical Issues in Separation and Placement, Child and Adolescent Social Work Journal* 4 (1987): 209, 219.

50. See Lawrence W. Cook, "Open Adoption: Can Visitation with Natural Family Members Be in the Child's Best Interest?" *Journal of Family Law* 30 (1991–92): 471; Carol Amadio and Stuart L. Deutsch, "Open Adoption: Allowing Adopted Children to 'Stay in Touch' with Blood Relatives," *Journal of Family Law* 22 (1983–84): 59.

51. Philip E. Perry, Grant P. Charles, and Jane E. Matheson, "Separation and Attachment: A Shift in Perspective," *Journal of Child Care* 2 (1986): 9, 23.

52. Goldstein et al., *Beyond the Best Interests*, 116–121.

53. See Daniel S. Shaw and Robert E. Emery, "Parental Conflict and Other Correlates of the Adjustment of School-Age Children Whose Parents Have Separated," *Journal of Abnormal Psychology* 15 (1987): 269, finding acrimony between parents independently related to problems of children; Felner and Terre, "Child Custody Dispositions," 115, reporting that continuing family conflict is important to negative outcomes for children of divorce; Shaw and Emery, "Parental Conflict," finding parental conflict correlated with behavior problems and with low perceived cognitive competence.

54. Ijzendoorn and Tavecchio, "The Development of Attachment Theory," 7, citing John Bowlby, *Maternal Care and Mental Health* (1951).

55. See Bowlby, *Separation*, 388–390, describing Anna Freud's adherence to her father's view that attachment behaviors were secondary to physical drives rather than primary, as Bowlby argued.

56. The influence upon psychological parent theorists of attachment theorists, including Bowlby, is acknowledged in Goldstein et al., *Beyond the Best Interests*, 201–202.

57. Goldstein et al., *Beyond the Best Interests*, 32–34.

58. Nancy Chodorow and Susan Contratto, "The Fantasy of the Perfect Mother," in *Rethinking the Family:*

Some Feminist Questions, rev. ed., ed. Barrie Thorne (Boston: Northeastern University Press, 1992), 191, 203–204.

59. Ruddick, "Thinking Mothers / Conceiving Birth," 29, 32–33, quoting Madeleine Sprengnether, *The Spectral Mother* (Ithaca, N.Y.: Cornell University Press, 1990), 239.

60. Benjamin, *The Bonds of Love*, 211.

61. See Jessica Benjamin, "The Omnipotent Mother," in *Representations of Motherhood*, ed. Donna Bassin, Margaret Honey, and Meryle Mahrer Kaplan (New Haven and London: Yale University Press, 1994), 133; Jerome Bruner, *Actual Minds, Possible Worlds* (Cambridge, Mass.: Harvard University Press, 1986), 59–62, 73–77.

62. See Benjamin, *The Bonds of Love*, 11–50.

63. Benjamin, "The Omnipotent Mother," 133.

64. Ibid., 135.

65. Ibid., 138.

66. Eagle, "Airplanes Crash" (*Clinical and Research Reports* 2 [1993]: 321–331).

67. Ibid., 323.

68. Ibid., 331.

PART 4

Beginning Again—
Conversations of Mothers

Bonnie J. Miller-McLemore

Ideals and Realities of Motherhood:
A Theological Perspective

Recently I heard a telling story of the lie mothers find themselves living. Faced with an important meeting and no child care, a friend of mine took her young child with her. Strategically armed with a bag of M&Ms, she placed the child on the floor at her knee. After several minutes of surreptitiously dishing out candies under the table, she raised her hands only to discover that, in her words, "They lied! M&Ms do melt in your hands." The milk chocolate mess was not the only lie she encountered in that moment. Current myths suggest a mother ought to be able to have a life alongside motherhood. Yet combining children and adult work seldom happens without some minor or major fiasco.

At the beginning of this century Sigmund Freud argued that the unconscious mind refuses to acknowledge human mortality; on one level, people truly do not believe that they will some day die. Similarly, with mothering, no one really wants to admit that there are no easy answers. Indeed, some of the most powerful lies have been told about mothering, whether the lie of the happy stay-at-home mother of the 1950s or the lie about the ease of breast-feeding while returning to paid work of the 1990s. Mothers would often rather lie, it seems, than openly admit what they endure. More accurately, mothers lie about the pain of childbirth or the complexities of parenting to protect themselves and others or out of fear that we have not lived up to the incessant stream of images of the perfect mother. We lie without meaning to because the realities of mothering seem impossible to depict within the limits of modern language and the confines of a still incumbent patriarchy.

Religion has had a lot to do with bolstering lies about motherhood. However, in the name of religion people have also doggedly pursued truth, even within a postmodern context that radically undermines such an enterprise. During different historical periods, religion has served to moderate and even unveil the lies people tell and put prophetic visions of abundant life in their place. More than other areas of cultural reflection, theology has attempted to comprehend this lying *and* truth-seeking dynamic of human behavior. Psychology is a close second in its analogous focus on the tension between ideals and realities and in its practice of therapeutic intervention.

Since religion has had a lot to do with both bolstering old lies about motherhood and creating new standards, attempts to critique and reconstruct ideals of motherhood require an understanding of religious theory, even for secular publics. Unfortunately, more often than not, religion is bracketed, ignored, or misunderstood. In the first section of this essay I explore this problem in both the secular and liberal religious discussion. Participants in current debates over motherhood, I observe, now seem all too ready to assert that there are no answers, perhaps more than we realize falling under the influence of Freud's reality principle and his advice about stoic resignation to death. But debunking lies about the traditional family and motherhood, including those inspired by religion, does not resolve dilemmas of mothering, I argue, and leaves some difficult questions. People need ideals and myths by which to live, even if these often degenerate into untruths and fabrications. In the second section, I briefly consider recent work in psychoanalytic psychology that provides a way to understand the longing for answers. This leads nicely into a discussion of the contributions of religion to ideals of motherhood as understood primarily through the work of feminists in religion. Theology and psychology, especially under the influence of feminist theory, can help us understand some of the reasons people lie and perhaps correct simplistic answers. They also suggest that people are sustained by the hope of answers. And theology, attempting to go still further, circles around what good answers look like, even if it can no longer pretend to define exhaustively their content.

The nature of the contributions of religion to matters of mothering and the need to understand these contributions are at least twofold—historical and normative. First, current dilemmas cannot be understood without comprehension of the historical impact of religious practices and beliefs. Although public education in the United States has conventionally omitted the study of religion as a result of the separation of church and state, one cannot grasp, for example, either the settlement of this country or the development of our constitution without some knowledge of religion. Similarly, as I will develop below, one cannot grasp ideals of mothering without some knowledge of the effects of religion on their formulation. Second, religious beliefs and practices will continue to have complex normative consequences for human ideals of fulfillment. While many of these ideals are particular to the faithful, public arguments for such values as justice, equal rights, responsibility, democracy, and so forth will gain clarity, viability, and endurance from the study of religion. Public dismissal of religion as a field of study is unfortunate because it leaves an entire spectrum of human behavior and history untouched and misunderstood. This is even more troubling when rather limited views of "Christian" values, such as those proposed by the Christian Coalition, are those most equated with Christianity or even religion. The media's tendency to portray religion in sound bites is partly responsible for such misperceptions. In contrast to subjects like geometry and sociology, religion is one subject about which many feel free to claim expertise and yet most are strikingly ignorant. Beyond my specific theses about myths and realities, sharpening sensitivity to the contributions of religion is an additional agenda for this essay.

I should clarify at this point that while my central subject is mothers I do not separate sharply reflection on mothers from reflection on families and disagree with some literature on mothers that tends to do so. My desire to reconnect the two results from a philosophically influenced nonseparative or connective definition of the self and reality and a theologically influenced conviction that motherhood is fundamentally social and relational, involving women in family constellations, minimally of child and mother and, in some shape and form, a male partner (even if only as a source of sperm). Adequate mothering can hardly happen without several concentric circles of supporting relationships, extending from mother and child outward to the wider social context.

Oversight of Religion

Secularization theories and Enlightenment belief in scientific rationalization have encouraged widespread ignorance about the influence of religion on mothers and families in contemporary American culture. While I am not attempting to provide extended evidence of the disregard for religion here, I do want to identify a few interesting books as examples of the questions and distortions that arise when religion is simplified and dismissed or simply overlooked. My first two examples are books specifically on the myths of motherhood and would be the most likely place to expect attention to religion. I have chosen two other examples of research on the more general subject of the family primarily because their authors are influential in discussions of mothers, gender, sexuality, and families. Their inattention to religion and the consequences of this inattention are typical of much of the literature on issues that, as I will attempt to argue, can never be entirely separated from religious ideas.

The cover of a book contesting the myths of motherhood, *Representations of Motherhood*, edited by Donna Bassin, Margaret Honey, and Meryle Mahrer Kaplan, is designed to provoke an immediate reaction from the reader. It portrays a miniature 1940s mother strapped in an infant swing, gazing up at an imposing, cherubic toddler twice her size. In an attempt to rescue the "hostage mother from her swing" and return her to her rightful proportions, the collection of essays examines sentimentalized and distorted images of motherhood in art, film, literature, the social sciences, and history. Mothers, it argues, must be viewed as subjects in their own right.

This is great as far as it goes. But it does not go far enough. Implicit ethical and quasi-religious questions drive the book: One of its aims is to challenge the "predominant image of the mother in white Western society . . . the ever-bountiful, ever-giving, self-sacrificing mother."[1] However, if the intent encompasses disputing the institutionalization of unconditional love, the study of religion and theology is sorely missing.

The authors of *Representations of Motherhood* establish that mothering is indeed a complex experience. Is this enough? The editors "want a mother who is a real person." But what is a real person? What and who defines personhood, much less motherhood? And if this question cannot be answered, from what vantage point does one hope to question cultural notions of the mother? Feminists have often seen religion as parochial and patriarchal, and often enough this is the case. The omission of religion in *Representations of Motherhood* is also partly related to the editors' identities as psychologists who are by discipline less mindful of the import of normative discourse. But if feminists hope to move beyond analysis and critique and, as Bassin, Honey, and Kaplan themselves desire, to "push forward a *vision* of the maternal place as generative for women's psychological development as well as for cultural and political change," some kind of ethical, religious, theological, and philosophical discourse becomes almost inevitable.[2] To dismiss religion heedlessly is to miss its continued influence and to fail to recognize feminist scholars in religion as important partners in the U.S. debate about mothers and families.

A single-authored volume, *The Myths of Motherhood*, is a nice exception to the rule. Also a psychologist, Shari L. Thurer does include religion alongside the arts, history, and psychology in her attempt to restore the mother to her right proportions and reveal the "useless and ephemeral" character of many of our cherished ideals of parental excellence. She intends to establish that "there are no easy answers, no magical solutions, no absolutes" and to encourage "decent people . . . to mother in their own decent way."[3] Nonetheless, despite her thorough analysis, two questions surface that also characterize my other examples. First, how might we understand the human need for answers, solutions, and absolutes? Second, having exposed cultural myths, from where will we get adequate normative ideals and stories to determine and convey the parameters of human decency?

Shere Hite's survey on female sexuality in the mid-1970s attracted a lot of attention. More recently her turn to the family, in *The Hite Report on the Family: Growing-Up Under Patriarchy*, promises to hold similar public interest. In contrast to other critics, I am more troubled by her inaccurate assumptions about religion than her controversial survey methods. On the first page she blames the problems of current families on our sad attempts to model ourselves after the " 'holy family.' " If this "archetype" is so powerful, and I partly agree that religious ideology pervades our thinking more than we acknowledge or understand, then one might expect further investigation of "the icons of Jesus, Mary and Joseph." However, beyond criticizing fundamentalist views of families and beyond using religious imagery as a straw horse, Hite pays religion little further attention. Had Hite considered religion more closely, she might have discovered that the processes of democratization that she admires and certain religious beliefs are not polar opposites. She portrays them as mutually exclusive because she sees religion only as a fundamentalist reactionary force. Ignoring the plurality of religious traditions in the United States, she claims that the religious tradition of "the Church" "has as its basic principle, at its heart, the political will of men to dominate women."[4] Yet, as I argue below, religious feminists are themselves working from within a variety of religious traditions toward new family models of equality and justice that Hite herself seeks. The very ideals of democracy she applauds are found within selected religious traditions.

Thoughtlessness about actual religious traditions does not mean that Hite refrains from moral and quasi-religious reflection of her own. In her projection of new normative ideals of love and family, she exemplifies remarkable naivete. She concludes the family is not struggling; it is simply changing. Pluralism in family relationships "should be valued and encouraged; far from being a sign of the breakdown of society, it is a sign of a new, more open and tolerant society springing up."[5] Hite's conclusion is partially appropriate and grows out of a justified fear of conservative alliances. But it is also precariously unenlightened about, first, the growing trend among previously "liberal" social scientists and politicians alike toward documenting the negative consequences of family disruption for children,[6] and second, the complexity and everyday influence of conservative Christian alliances.[7] Angry, unreflective dismissal of both phenomena as backlash leaves Hite unable to counter conservative arguments with any comparable or substantive contrasting religious and social interpretations. She ignores the potential deleterious effects of family disruptions on children and overlooks the possible positive role of liberal religion in family democratization or in reinterpreting biblical traditions.

Definitions of motherhood and family are hotly debated because they are not just functional or descriptive. In her history of the family, Stephanie Coontz declares that the family is foremost an ideological conception, "an *idea*, a 'socially necessary illusion'" that justifies particular social, economic arrangements.[8] The family is a battlefield located at the crossroads of biology and culture, involved in the formation of persons and values. Debate over motherhood, and more recently, fatherhood, is often at the center of the conflict. In two sequels to her first book on the history of families, *The Way We Never Were* and *The Way We Really Are*, Coontz herself changes hats from historian to social prophet under the pressure of the family debate. Myths about the duration of marriage or the high incidence of teen pregnancy have many harmful consequences: They erode solidarity, foster guilt and nostalgia, and diminish the confidence of those already beleaguered. When "memories" of traditional family life "never existed or existed in a totally different context," she points out, ideals become rigid and onerous.[9] As historical prophet, Coontz banishes many cherished illusions about the "Leave It to Beaver" ideal and shatters dominant myths about the self-reliance of American families, the links between feminism and family disruption, and so forth.

Coontz's efforts to debunk family myths are enlightening. But, once again, are they sufficient? She is highly critical of definitions that turn to biological or religious dimensions to give the term *family* an absolutistic quality that keeps people from questioning its social construction and renegotiating its demands. She demonstrates effectively the extent to which the prescriptive role of the term makes its definition both a political and religious venture, for good and for ill. But she focuses almost solely on the negative consequences of religion and in her latest two books barely mentions religious traditions except when they cast a destructive light on a case. In the end she fails to comprehend either the power of myths to lure and enrich life or the appropriateness of the human appetite for myth making. Her kind of prophetic history provides sobering but limited resources when it comes to constructing new ideals and solutions to parental struggles. Ultimately, she wants some kinds of myth—"we need to invent new family traditions," she notes.[10] But how, beyond discarding romanticized ideals? Can history and sociology alone provide sufficient help to today's families? In her eyes, traditions and communities which endorse religious traditions have little, if any, positive or constructive role. But do traditions only "hold families back," as one of her chapter titles asserts?

The oversight of religion, I readily acknowledge, should be partly laid at the doorstep of liberal religion and theology itself. Until recently, feminist religion scholars themselves have tended to neglect families and the mother-as-subject. Other crucial tasks, whether addressing violence or reconstructing doctrines of God, Christ, and human nature, have absorbed a great deal of attention. The ground swell of protest over powerful, reverberating ideals of the all-giving mother, it is worth noting, has occurred primarily outside the study of religion. The increased interest in a variety of disciplines in mothers as subjects in the 1980s has only slowly appeared in the study of religion in the 1990s. Many theologians are mothers and many advocate maternal god imagery and language, but few have investigated actual mothering and what is learned about theology from this vantage point. Fortunately, this is changing. And there have been some important, even if neglected, exceptions to this charge in the work of Kathryn Rabuzzi, Margaret Hebblethwaite, and a few other individual essays and collections.[11]

Oversight of religion can also be explained by the silence, hesitancy, and ambiguity about change within the less conservative, mainline congregations and those on the religious left. As vexing as the presumptuousness of the Christian right that they speak for all Christians on family matters is the vacuous discussions of families and parenting among the Christian left.[12] This leaves secular society and the media to assume that any discussion on the family, mothers, fathers, and religion necessarily entails the conservative values of Pat Robertson, James Dobson's Focus on the Family, or the Promise

Keepers. This is a sad misrepresentation of the richness of religious traditions for which those in the mainline and on the religious left are also responsible.

Attempts to set the agenda for families in Coontz and Hite, and attempts to counter myths of mothering in *Representations of Motherhood* and Thurer raise some tough questions about the ideals and realities of mothering. What do children need, and mothers need in relation to them? To what extent do parents have a moral responsibility as adults to recognize that their decisions shape the lives of their children for better and for worse and, through them, the wider community? To what extent should they alter their actions on their children's and society's behalf? And what is the father's role in all this?

Beyond questions of parental practice are riskier theoretical questions. One of the key problems that those who identify themselves as feminist must face, as well as those who wish to promote an adequate family theory in general, is how to preserve what is good in the institutions of family, marriage, and parenthood without preserving patriarchy?[13] Are all forms of heterosexual monogamy oppressive and, if not, what forms are not and how might they be sustained? Can we after all devise alternatives to the patriarchal family which find an appropriate place for the institutions of male–female sexual intimacy, commitment, and responsible parenting without merely reinforcing heterosexism, gender stereotypes, and sexist exploitation? Are proposals supporting the nontraditional approach of egalitarian parenting possible if one also wants to support diversity in family form?

These kinds of questions can be answered, of course, without recourse to religion. But, I believe, more adequate answers will evolve if feminist scholars in religion participate in the discussion. Practically, answers are more likely to have an impact on human behavior if supported by religious narratives and practices. Theoretically, if feminists intend to reconstitute motherhood as a more complex reality, their task should include an understanding of the evolution of ideals. Moreover, feminists, including feminist scholars in religion, should continue to define not only the ambiguities of good mothering but new constructive ideals and future possibilities. Of course, the construction of ideals is a questionable task in a postmodern context deeply suspicious of truths of any kind, much less religious truths.

The Need for Truth and Ideals in a Postmodern Context

In *Escape from Paradise*, religion scholar Kathleen Sands outlines a powerful critique of wishful thinking in theology. Escaping paradise, according to

Sands, means admitting the tragic dimension of all experience to an extent precluded by conventional theology, including feminist theology. In a postmodern context, we can no longer expect to "encounter truth and goodness unaccompanied by the most profound questions of violence, conflict, and loss."[14] As she remarks, "no single feature has marked the theology of this century so deeply as the encounter with the radical evils washed up by the receding tide of modernity."[15] No ontological truth can define the good since social interests construct truth rather than the other way around.

Mainstream and feminist Christian theology hide the evil, ambiguity, and inevitable tragedy of human experience behind one of two kinds of religious solutions: Christian rationalism and its shadow, Christian dualism. Either one hopes monistically that being is good and evil is the privation of good, or nonbeing. Simply put, one refuses to acknowledge evil's real existence and beings are ranked hierarchically according to their degree of goodness, with women and children below men. Or reality is construed as a battle between two relatively equal forces of good and evil in which good eventually triumphs and evil is blamed on the Other. Lest the nonreligious think they have escaped unscathed, the categories cover modern variations. The Enlightenment progress-oriented view of evil as "bias"—that is, an accident to be remedied by objectivity and universal imperatives—is simply a version of Christian rationalism. And certain forms of feminism have dualistically aligned the bad with the "White Male System" and the good with "Women's Reality."[16]

Philosophically, Sands has put to rest the dream of truly knowing the good and seeking moral perfection. The good, she writes, is an "entirely human, entirely fragile creation,"[17] and therefore theology involves the interrogative mode of a "tragic heuristic." A tragic heuristic requires asking questions more than suggesting answers and coming face to face in the stories of our lives with irredeemable loss and irresolvable conflict rather than denying them. It requires people to relinquish ideals and create what right and wrong they can in radically plural contexts. Moral judgments then become "strategic, contextual judgments about how the diverse goods of life might best be integrated and unnecessary suffering minimized in a particular place and moment."[18]

In all this, Sands strikes a responsive chord in the postmodern heart. While her analysis is disturbing, it is not unusual or atypical of much of postmodern conversation in liberal religion. And in some ways it fits well with the arguments against myths of motherhood discussed above. The secular discussion of mothering would find in Sands much confirmation of their suspicion of theological ideals and religious myths. She lends religious support to Coontz's decisive conclusion in *The Way We Really Are:* "The biggest lesson of the past is that there are no solutions there."

On one very important account, however, the approach to ideals that Sands' work exemplifies is limited. She offers little in the way of reconstructed alternative religious traditions and beliefs. While she hopes to illuminate ethical discourse and enhance the vitality of religious feminism, her contemporary version of a situation ethic is minimalist. One is overwhelmed with a sense of the inescapable nature of evil in the world and left with little account of the motivation to combat it. To return to our central subject, how are families and mothers in particular to live between recognition of the radical nature of evil and the yearning to eradicate its presence? Building moral commitments in the ruins of postmodernity involves not just intellectual finesse but psychological insight and awareness. If one is to practice compassion—the closest Sands comes to resurrecting a religious ideal—how does one know compassion when one sees it, much less how to exercise it? Neither the recognition of tragedy nor the respect for diversity relieves people of the responsibility of making ethical distinctions between delightful and destructive actions. In fact, recognition of and guidance for the many, many ways to be a good mother and the many ways in which mothering goes wrong calls for an even more than usually dogged, sophisticated, complicated pursuit of adequate truths and ideals.[19]

Psychoanalytic Reflections

The postmodern rejection of ideals in secular feminism and Sands' theology is not entirely psychologically tenable. Freud, of course, relegates ideals and religious hopes about love and work, including motherhood, to the terrain of the superego, the pathological, and the delusional.[20] By contrast, psychoanalytic self-psychologist Heinz Kohut suggests that people need answers by which to live, even answers that wax over into lies.[21] Whereas Freud saw ideals as defenses against drives and sought to penetrate the unconscious by overcoming defenses and resistance, Kohut seeks to establish "self structure" by comprehending defense and resistance and reclaiming the significance of ideals. The self yearns for structure for its very survival, and ideals are an important element in this process of creating structure. In this view, some lies may actually be a necessary defense against self-demise rather than a regressive behavior in need of exposure.

According to Kohut, human pathology results not from repressed instincts and oppressive superego constructs, but from an insufficiently structured self or from a defect in the establishment of a coherent self at the pre-oedipal level. Healthy narcissism is crucial to the development of the coherence of the self. Narcissism, defined in classical psychoanalytic theory as the libidinal cathexis or investment in the self, or in nontechnical terms as self-love, is not something that must be outgrown or replaced by object-love or love for others. Rather, Kohut argues, narcissism has its own independent line of development, distinct from ego development.

Kohut distinguishes three primary narcissistic needs: mirroring, or the need for admiration; twinship, or the need for those like us; and, most important for my purposes, idealization. These needs are neither defensive maneuvers to escape aggressive and sexual drive-wishes in psychoanalytic terms nor, in religious terms, destructive signs of selfishness or fallacious tyrannical assertions of absolutes. On the contrary, a child begins to develop a cohesive self only as significant others respond empathically to her developing narcissistic needs.

Alongside the need for mirroring and twinship, "a person needs something general to respect."[22] When an infant meets the inevitable shortcomings of parental care, one way she compensates is through the idealization of a perfect, admired omnipotent "self-object," a person who is experienced as part of her self, often a parent. The central experience of the child is "You are perfect, but I am a part of you."[23] Over time, with empathy that includes in-tune understanding and discipline as much as sympathy and positive regard, and with necessary but not traumatic failures in empathy, the infant incorporates the function of the idealized object into the structure of the self in transmuted form. This is not a simple one-time phenomenon. Under adequate conditions, dependence on progressively more mature and expansive idealizable self-objects continues throughout life. From this idealization comes the capacity for sustained commitment and value-oriented behavior.

Almost anything can serve as an idealized self-object and psychology itself creates such ideals. The idea of the "good enough" mother illustrates an attempt in psychoanalysis to name that range of behavior that is less than ideal but adequate. Like other ideals, even this benevolent ideal is capable of its own degeneration: D. W. Winnicott himself sometimes uses the term to describe a mother who is uncannily perfect in her responses.[24] Yet both Winnicott and Kohut emphasize an intriguing twist: Failure is a requisite dimension to ideals and to ideal parenting. Failures in parenting, like empathic "breaks" in therapy, are actually primary sites for the creation and internalization of healthy self-structure, but only when they are nontraumatic and part of a larger context of understanding and explanation. The dynamic interplay of illusion and disillusionment, seen most clearly in the use of transitional objects, is essential for mature development.[25]

In short, people tend to create ideals, even in a postmodern context of ambiguity and pluralism, as one means to soothe, comfort, and sustain the self and its relationships. People may create ideals that fade into lies to protect themselves and survive, to retain a semblance of control over life and self, or, in more troubling cases of family violence, addictions, racism, and class arrogance, to maintain power over others as well as control over themselves. While religion and morality still can operate in illusional or delusional ways, they also serve as sources of self and social cohesion. A villain in many cases, religious discourse is also, as Martha Nussbaum remarks, "in multiple and powerful ways, a major source of hope for women's futures."[26] Many people will worship and deny gods; the important question is what kind.

Religious and Theological Reflections on Ideals of Motherhood

Representations of self-sacrificing motherhood in Western society are not just a result of nineteenth-century Victorian values. They are intertwined with older historical and religious notions—Christian edicts of suffering servanthood, Jewish ideals of maternal self-sacrifice, Aristotelian and Christian codes defining the relationship between subordinate and superior family members, and other powerful motifs. Furthermore, ideals of motherhood are not only intertwined with religious teachings. They are embedded in the formative religious practices of men as elders and priests, in prayers, doxologies, and creeds imaging a male deity, in the exclusion of women and mothers from leadership in sacred rituals, and in continued resistance to change in all of these areas.

The impact of religion in the United States has not declined nearly as much as popular opinion has led people to believe. These practices continue to have a hidden yet persuasive influence because they are embodied physically in word and in deed and repeated weekly in ritualized ceremonies of conviction and proclamation in settings that are unique in their cross-generational participation of children, youth, adults, and the elderly. For many people, worship is *the* primary encounter with particular family and gender ideals and, at the very same time, the last place for critical reflection on these ideals. Genuine worship requires an immersion in participation that often forbids a more distanced evaluation. So young and old alike absorb a great deal in ritual practices that remains unnoticed, hidden, unanalyzed.

The impact of religion extends beyond religious beliefs and practices internal to faith communities. The influence of Christianity on the national scene is hardly more apparent and yet more overlooked by the general public than in marriage and family law. As law and ethics professor John Witte observes, "Much of what we call the traditional family and the classic law of the family was forged by Roman Catholic theologians and canon lawyers in the first half of this millennium, then reforged by Protestant theologians and jurists in the middle of this millennium and transmitted with periodic reforms into the 20th century."[27] The Roman church played a key role in shifting control over marriage from the clan to the couple and in privileging monogamy over polygamy, divorce, and adultery. Sacramental interpretations elevated the status of the bond between woman and man above ties to parent, other family members, government, or parish. As a sacrament, marriage could only be received voluntarily by the consent of the individual. Others argue that this Western Christian principle of consent "created an assumption that individuals have a right to accept or reject the conditions of their lives, an assumption that was very different from that which prevailed among cultures committed to clan-controlled marriages."[28]

The need for a proclamation of consent to validate marriage is only one example of a church action that sparked more extensive social reform, including the gradual weakening of the control of fathers over wives and children. As fundamental to the current status of marriage was the Protestant Reformers' move to put a social model of marriage in place of the sacramental model, making marriage a public and civic estate and the family a social unit as important as church and state. Each of these historical examples suggests a more general observation. Current contractual law can adjudicate the specific rights of parties involved in families, marriages, and partnerships, but a broader moral vision is necessary to inspire and shape the large range of obligations that surround mothers, fathers, children, marriage, family, and community. Moreover, if people used religion to construct visions of family life, it will take an understanding of religion to undo and redo them.

Assuming that religion continues to have an impact on lives through religious practices and edicts and through its historic influence over social and legal arrangements, what does reflection on religion offer specifically to our discussion of the myths of motherhood and the longing for ideals by which to live? I will limit my comments to four topics. First, theologians themselves have long debated the complex relationship between ideals and reality. The present and the not-yet quality of grace is a core constituent of Christian faith as is the Reformed premise that all human answers are partial. I will merely allude to some of this discussion. Second, radical mutuality in parenting, even as helpfully reconceived by feminist theologians, is easier said than achieved. The nature of mutuality in nonequal relationships of parents and children and other dependencies and transitional hierarchies must be more clearly understood by religious and secular feminists alike. Third, with discussion of mutuality in mind, I believe we should reconsider, as one illustration of the importance of reinterpreting Christian ideals, a major roadblock to genuine mutuality in Christian marriage—the disturbing and much maligned "household codes," or New Testament passages that spell out the rules for relationships within the family. Finally, feminist theory has emphasized new understandings of the experience as distinct from the patriarchal institutionalization of motherhood. Yet the opposition between experience and institution has not proven adequate to the complex reality of motherhood. In religious circles the family and motherhood are still considered crucial social institutions. These institutions must somehow come to contain the rich diversities and ambiguities of families within structures that enhance the common good without repudiating the experiences of mothers.

First then, the relation between ideals and reality. In our work together on *From Culture Wars to Common Ground*, Pamela Couture shed light on the use and misuse of religious ideals in the U.S. history of marriage and families. The purpose of an ideal, she states, "is to point us beyond the immediacy of our concrete existence toward a vision for which we can hope."[29] However, few people approximate ideals and the way we do depends heavily upon the actual circumstances of our lives. Even the separate gender spheres of the Victorian ideal were in actuality less distinct than the ideal and appeared in many variations across the United States. Based on a historical study of U.S. families and religion—Puritan ideals of the northeast, Anglican and Calvinist patterns of the Southeast, Wesleyan and revivalistic values of Western movements as well as the imposition and moderation of these ideals among Native Americans and African Americans—Couture contends:

> It is important to distinguish between cultural ideals and their concrete variants which arise when people shape ideals in tension with their contexts. The danger in formulating ideals is that their concrete versions will be invested with ultimate status. Sometimes, concrete variations of family

life identified with Christianity have been imposed on new situations as if they had the status of an ideal, even when, in the new context, the model actually violates the ideal of Christian love and justice. . . .

The most oppressive form of the use of ideals occurs when norms derived from concrete realities are applied by people in power, as if they were ideals, to judge situations in which people cannot possibly attain the ideal because their situation is so different. Frequently, this abuse of an ideal occurs across race and class line.[30]

Ideals can be destructive when invested with ultimacy and absolutism. This does not in itself invalidate the premise of ideals such as justice or love. Ideals can also be used constructively and subversively by less powerful groups to challenge the status quo. Analogous to their healthy role in psychological development, ideals provide a vision by which new cohesive patterns and structures emerge and evolve.

Paula Cooey makes a similar point. "We cannot live without some pattern to social life in order to establish responsibility for child rearing and the care of the elderly," she observes, "but most family patterns, *when taken as absolute*, often wreak havoc on the lives of the people they are supposed to protect and nourish."[31] Codes have only a provisional nature and must be responsive to the particularities of context. Nonetheless, patterns and guides are necessary. This is an important step once removed from Sands' tragic ethic or Coontz's resignation to a history that ultimately yields no answers. The psychoanalytic code of the "good-enough family," as adapted by those in religion, defines an ideal family which "is less than its own ideal and yet competent enough to raise reasonably adequate children." Minimally, the norms of such a family include nurturing children into healthy adulthood and strengthening the personhood of the parents. From a Christian perspective, they include the ideals of hospitality, compassion, justice, and reconciliation.[32]

These claims rest in part on a long-standing tension in the history of Christian theology between vision and realism. Denominational differences as well as the differences between theologians surface around this tension. Lutherans, for example, tend to believe that "the finite is capable of receiving the infinite," or that ideals can become realities; and the Reformed tend to hold that "the finite is not capable of receiving the infinite!" or that humans are too limited and fallen to realize ideals.[33] A few theologians, like Reinhold Niebuhr with his understanding of the ironies of history, for example, or his definition of sin as inevitable but not necessary, bring together the two traditions in a jointly enriching way.[34]

Let me turn to my second point, the ideal of radical mutuality in parenting. In seeing mutuality as a relatively easy human achievement next to the impossibility of agapic or sacrificial love, Niebuhr himself grossly oversimplifies the significance of mutuality in Christian love. Radical mutuality is a transformative Christian ideal with potentially more dramatic consequences for families than sacrificial love. While feminist theologians have propounded this ideal in various forms for the last three decades,[35] only a few have attempted to modify it to fit the distinctiveness of family relationships. Christine Gudorf continues an early feminist theological challenge to doctrines of sin as prideful self-assertion by asserting the importance of self-fulfillment in the very act of giving to one's children. She recognizes the transitional sacrifices necessary for adequate mothering but holds mutuality as the goal rather than sacrifice. Here she argues for the relevance of Catholic ideas of charity that do not exclude the self over traditions shaped by Protestant views of self-interest as invalidating Christian love (in Luther, Kierkegaard, Niebuhr, Anders Nygren, for example).[36] The meaning of Jesus' death itself assumes a different interpretation under this view. Less a sacrifice and more an unavoidable consequence of the love of others, the cross calls people to renewed relations (that may require moments of sacrifice) but not to self-sacrifice in and of itself. This may sound like a slight distinction but it makes all the difference in the world in people's lives and in mothering. And this change in understanding is one of the hardest to implement in ritual practice and the interpretation of the cross that accompanies the act of the Eucharist or communion that stands at the center of most Christian worship.

Feminist theological discussion of mutuality has sometimes been sloppy. First, more often than not, the proclamation of mutuality assumes a relationship between two relatively equal adults. However, in the practice of parenting as well as many other practices, such as teaching, counseling, and so forth, equal relationships are rare. More difficult questions arise when one strives to maintain the ideal of mutuality within nonequal relationships. Second, with the free and easy use of the term "mutuality" these days, concrete pragmatic details of maintaining life are often dropped from the equation. The movement from rhetoric to reality in the practical equality between women and men and between mothers and fathers has to reckon with factors as diverse as the limits of time, the competing values of a capitalistic market economy, the economic disparity between the races, classes, and gender, and the demands for geographic mobility.[37] Both oversights lead to a neglect of the tricky question of how and where certain sacrifices become requisite, either in unequal relationships or in the midst of the practical demands of equal relationships, as a means to maintain mutuality and equality.

Nonetheless, Christian feminist theology has effectively established radical mutuality as more than a humanitarian interest. Mutuality has ontological or divine warrant in a Trinitarian, relational godhead where God is understood as three-persons-in-one and in need of human relationship.[38] In other words, at their core, images of the divine exemplify relationality rather than project an omnipotent, all-powerful but basically independent supreme being. Mutuality also has biblical warrant in the early Christian communities.[39] Despite the patriarchal character of the ancient societies in which Christianity arose and despite the ways in which the Christian tradition has perpetuated ideals of male dominance in the centuries since, Elisabeth Schüssler Fiorenza, for example, claims that in Mark's gospel women emerge as the "true Christian ministers and witnesses" and the most courageous of all his disciples.[40] Others join her in confirming the prominent role of women in early Christianity.[41] Still others explain the contradiction between Paul's insistence on the silence of women in the church in I Cor. 14:34–35 and the radical inclusivity of his message elsewhere as a concession to the prevailing values of his time or even as the imposition and addition of someone else's words. In other words, over against social convention certain kinds of egalitarian premises characterized the early Christian movement. I am not arguing, of course, that all mothers must believe and abide by these particular tenets of Christian faith to realize good mothering and mutuality. Rather, I am simply observing that to the extent that religious ideals shape mothering, then ample grounds exist for alternative ideals within Christianity to shape culture and families in new directions.

In the light of Christian ideas of mutuality, the hardest texts to contend with and the texts that have most influenced the ideals and institution of the family in the Western world are the household codes of the New Testament. Household codes is a term applied to scriptural passages that sought to order family relationships among early Christian converts in two Deutero-Pauline letters (letters attributed to but not authored by Paul) of the Christian New Testament, Colossians and Ephesians. Typically, in these letters, family members are exhorted to certain behaviors in relation to one another, most specifically, subordinates (e.g., wives, slaves, children) to their superiors (e.g., husbands, masters, fathers). The term sometimes alludes to similar or related codes in I Timothy, Titus, and I Peter, although these passages are less tightly structured and related to broader guidelines for congregations and communities.

These texts are particularly problematic for feminist interpretations of mutuality in sex, gender, and parenthood. From at least the Reformation, if not earlier, to the last century, they have given supernatural sanction to patriarchal family roles in which men lead and women follow. More recently, the household codes echo in the background of the handbook for the Promise Keepers' movement. Similarly, points no. 2, 3, and 6 of the "Danvers Statement" issued by the Council on Biblical Manhood and Womanhood formed in 1989 among the Christian right declare gender roles ordained by God, including Adam's headship in marriage, and redemption as consisting in loving leadership by husbands and willing submission by wives.

There are sufficient grounds for arguing, however, that the codes were not intended to bolster but to reverse ancient heroic models of male authority in families.[42] Historians have documented a genderized pattern of honor-shame throughout the Mediterranean world during the period of Roman Hellenism as a prominent backdrop for these texts. Male honor and reputation was gained through winning and through protecting the privacy and "shame" of women in their household. Male dishonor or shame occurred through losing and intrusion into the private realm.[43]

Taking the household codes in Ephesians as an example, we see that the author borrows and yet transforms the metaphors of the surrounding male culture of strength, dominance, and conflict to suggest new virtues of peace, humility, patience, and gentleness. The husband is called to the self-giving love of Christ and a sort of mutual subjection not found in similar Aristotelian codes. The logic of the Aristotelian household codes is changed, if not subverted. The code in Ephesians balances compliance with the patriarchal social mores of the times with new innovations about male submission and reciprocity introduced by the Christian proclamation. The very need for household codes in the Deutero-Pauline letters may itself testify to the disruptive reality of a new family ethic evolving in the early Christian house church movement.[44]

Over history, it is this accent on male subordination that has been most overlooked. Instead, women, more than men, have heard and absorbed the message of sacrifice and submission. Feminists in religion have tended to deride the codes as a reversal of the more inclusive message of equality within the early Christian community under the social and political pressures of the patriarchal society of that time. The passage in Ephesians itself only finally obtains a modified or benevolent patriarchy, failing to articulate new roles for women in leadership and charity. Nonetheless, the hierarchical patterns of the Greco-Roman world, if not completely challenged, were at least mitigated in the household codes as well as in some important aspects of the Jesus movement and in some of the practices of the early church.

Finally, let me turn to my fourth observation on the contributions of religion to the discussion of myths and ideals of motherhood, an insistence upon the institutional dimensions of motherhood and families. In 1976, in *Of Woman Born*, Adrienne Rich made a crucial distinction between motherhood as experience and motherhood as institution. In Rich's words, the institution is superimposed on the experience and aims at ensuring that the "*potential relationship* of any woman to her powers of reproduction and to children . . . remain under male control."[45] She had historical and political reason to see the institution as evil and the experience as good. The institution of motherhood under patriarchy thwarts women's freedom, alienates them from their bodies, and corrupts fatherhood. It does so through three generic precepts: "All women are seen primarily as mothers; all mothers are expected to experience motherhood unambivalently and in accordance with patriarchal values; and the 'nonmothering' woman is seen as deviant." Yet, as Rich establishes so well, all mothers feel ambivalent, some women choose not to mother, and "a lesbian can be a mother and a mother a lesbian."[46] Through the courage and intensity of her prose, readers encounter the mother as a person with needs, desires, and thoughts of her own. To her credit and those who have followed, some of the patriarchal dimensions of the institution have less hold than they once did.

The ensuing years have shown, however, that the relationship between the institution and the experience of motherhood is more complex than Rich assumes in viewing the institution as the problem and women's experience as the grounds for fighting it. One never has, it seems, raw experience unshaped by institutions. Debunking the patriarchal myths of motherhood is, in the end, only one half of a job well done. As in the story of the melting chocolates, new myths and institutions rather quickly replace the old. The task is not simply breaking silences, although under a resilient but weakened patriarchy this remains crucial. The task also involves distinguishing poor institutions and ideals from more adequate ones and creating institutions of family, marriage, partnership, and motherhood that secure the good of mothers and the good of others.

The ways in which reproduction has been controlled by men and suffered by women is not adequately addressed, as theological ethicist Lisa Cahill points out, "by speaking as though sex and birth have no intrinsic social dimension at all."[47] From the perspective of Catholic ethics, the liberal emphasis on personal autonomous choice tends to disassociate sex from parental fulfillment and social responsibility. While sexual pleasure and intimacy between individuals and couples has an importance of its own, valuing them should not mean the neglect of the social meanings of the body realized through kinship and parenthood. A strength of the Catholic tradition is its strong social vision that connects sexual pleasure, intimacy, and parenthood. The personal sexual relationship is situated at the center of a series of concentric circles that emanate out from the joy of sexual exchange to the parental relationship to the family and finally to the family's critical contribution to the common good. In Cahill's words, parenthood is a "specifically sexual mode of social participation"; procreation is "the social side of sexual love."[48] Family choices are social and moral through and through.

In contrast to Rich, then, the choice is not between patriarchal institutions and nature or maternal experience but "between oppressive institutions and institutions that are life enhancing." In this regard, as Jewish theologian Judith Plaskow argues, feminist theology offers a viable path beyond the dichotomies that arise in feminist liberal and radical theory between rejection of women's body experience and exaltation of it.[49] Feminist theologians generally have not found either of these an attractive or sufficient option. In part this is because they have grappled with complex historical images of women, the valuable and ambiguous contributions of social institutions, and religious traditions in which intricate human relationship is mediated through the flesh.

This holistic or antidualistic understanding of flesh and spirit as inseparable is a particular reading of experience or nature and institution or culture shared by feminist readings of Jewish and Christian traditions. Maternal experience is neither a mechanical reflex of biology upon which family ideals rest nor solely a male or social construction with no biological referents. Childbirth and even childrearing are to some extent "bio-social" events. Roles and duties in parenting and sexuality are social and physical arrangements women and men must constantly renegotiate in face of both natural circumstance and historical, social contingency. Maternal stereotypes and perfectionist absolutes signal an onerous breakdown in this process with negative consequences for all involved.

There is much to be learned about the role of biblical and theological practices and beliefs in current dilemmas that surround mothers and families. Until we wrestle with the religious dreams and ideals deeply rooted in specific traditions and institutions that continue to shape North American culture and psyches, authentic change in the visions of mothering, sacrifice, compassion, and responsibility will remain fortuitous and superficial. Even less appealing ideals may fill the vacuum left by the demise of conventional religious and social institutions. While a reconstructed religion alone and Christianity in particular will not give answers to the complex contemporary quandaries about mothering, one can hardly confront representations of motherhood in Western culture without confronting those that emerge from particular religious world views. Recent reflection among feminists in religion suggests that positive insights and visions for mothers and families will emerge from reinterpreted religious understandings.

1. Donna Bassin, Margaret Honey, and Meryle Mahrer Kaplan, eds., "Introduction," in *Representations of Motherhood* (New Haven and London: Yale University Press, 1994).

2. Ibid., 10 (emphasis added).

3. Shari L. Thurer, *The Myths of Motherhood: How Culture Reinvents the Good Mother* (New York: Houghton Mifflin, 1994), xii.

4. Shere Hite, *The Hite Report on the Family: Growing-Up Under Patriarchy* (New York: Grove Press, 1995), 359.

5. Ibid., 2.

6. See, for example, Sara McLanahan and Gary Sandefur, *Growing Up with a Single Parent: What Hurts, What Helps* (Cambridge, Mass.: Harvard University Press, 1994); Judith S. Wallerstein and Sandra Blankeslee, *Second Chances: Men, Women, and Children a Decade After Divorce* (Boston: Houghton Mifflin, 1990); Barbara Dafoe Whitehead, "Dan Quayle Was Right," *Atlantic Monthly* (April 1993): 47–84; William A. Galston, "Beyond the Murphy Brown Debate: Ideas for Family Policy" (New York: Institute for American Values, 1995); *Marriage in America: A Report to the Nation* (New York: Council on Families in America of the Institute for American Values, 1995).

7. See, for example, Bill Bright et al., *Seven Promises of a Promise Keeper* (Colorado Springs, Colo.: Focus on the Family, 1994); Brian Paul Kaufman, "Promise Keepers Rallies Men to Commitment," *Christianity Today* (September 1992): 57; Douglas DeCelle, "Among the Promise Keepers: A Pastor's Reflections," *Christian Century* 113, no. 21 (July 3–10, 1996): 695–697.

8. Stephanie Coontz, *The Social Origins of Private Life: A History of American Families, 1600–1900* (New York: Verso, 1988), 12–14.

9. Stephanie Coontz, *The Way We Never Were: American Families and the Nostalgia Trap* (New York: Basic Books, 1992), 5.

10. Ibid., 278.

11. Kathryn Allen Rabuzzi, *Motherself. A Mythic Analysis of Motherhood* (Bloomington: Indiana University Press, 1988); Kathryn Allen Rabuzzi, *Mother with Child: Transformations Through Childbirth* (Bloomington: Indiana University Press, 1994); Margaret Hebblethwaite, *Motherhood and God* (London: Geoffrey Chapman, 1984); Anne Carr and Elisabeth Schüssler Fiorenza, eds., *Concilium: Motherhood: Experience, Institution, The-*

ology (Edinburgh, Scotland: T & T Clark, 1989); Christine Gudorf, "Parenting, Mutual Love and Sacrifice," in *Women's Consciousness, Women's Conscience: A Reader in Feminist Ethics*, ed. Barbara Hilkert Andolsen, Christine E. Gudorf, and Mary D. Pelauer (San Francisco: Harper and Row, 1985), 175–191; see also Margaret L. Hammer, *Giving-Birth: Reclaiming Biblical Metaphor for Pastoral Practice* (Louisville, Ky.: Westminster Press/ John Knox Press, 1995) and my own book, *Also a Mother: Work and Family as Theological Dilemma* (Nashville, Tenn.: Abingdon Press, 1994).

12. For further reflection on this see Paula Cooey, *Family, Freedom, and Faith: Building Community Today* (Louisville, Ky.: Westminster Press/John Knox Press, 1996), 5–6.

13. Karen Green, *The Woman of Reason: Feminism, Humanism and Political Thought* (New York: Continuum, 1995), 5–6.

14. Kathleen Sands, *Escape from Paradise: Evil and Tragedy in Feminist Theology* (Minneapolis: Fortress Press, 1994), 6.

15. Ibid., 25.

16. Anne Wilson Schaef, *Women's Reality: An Emerging Female System in a White Male Society* (New York: Harper and Row, 1981).

17. Sands, *Escape from Paradise*, 64.

18. Ibid., 15.

19. For a development of this argument, see Wendy Farley, *Eros for the Other: Retaining Truth in a Pluralistic World* (University Park: Pennsylvania State University Press, 1996).

20. Sigmund Freud, *The Future of an Illusion* (Garden City, N.Y.: Doubleday Anchor, [1927] 1964), and *Civilization and Its Discontents* (New York: W. W. Norton, [1930] 1962); see also Stephen Mitchell, *Relational Concepts in Psychoanalysis* (Cambridge, Mass.: Harvard University Press, 1988), chapters 2, 3; James W. Jones, *Religion and Psychology: Psychoanalysis, Feminism, and Theology* (New Haven, Conn.: Yale University Press, 1996), chapter 1.

21. Heinz Kohut, *How Does Analysis Cure?* (Chicago: University of Chicago Press, 1984), 64–66.

22. Lawrence Friedman, "Kohut: A Book Review Essay." *Psychoanalytic Quarterly* 49 (1980): 400.

23. Heinz Kohut, *The Analysis of the Self* (New York: International Universities Press, 1971), 27. For a fruitful overview of Kohut's work from the perspective of religion, prior to the publication of *How Does Analysis Cure?*, see "Religion and the Self-Psychology of Heinz Kohut: A Memorial Symposium," *Journal of Supervision and Training in Ministry* 5 (1982): 89–205.

24. D. W. Winnicott, *The Maturational Processes and the Facilitating Environment* (New York: International Universities Press, 1965); see also Janice Doane and Devon Hodges, *From Klein to Kristeva: Psychoanalytic Feminism and the Search for the "Good Enough" Mother* (Ann Arbor: University of Michigan Press, 1992).

25. Kohut, *How Does Analysis Cure?*, 70; D. W. Winnicott, *Playing and Reality* (New York: Tavistock, 1971), 10–13.

26. Martha Nussbaum, "Religion and Women's Human Rights," *Criterion* 36, no. 1 (Winter 1997): 11.

27. John Witte, Jr., "Consulting a Living Tradition: Christian Heritage of Marriage and Family," *Christian Century* (November 1996): 1108; see also his "The Transformation of Marriage Law in the Lutheran Reformation," in *The Weightier Matters of the Law: Essays on Law and Religion*, ed. J. Witte and Frank S. Alexander (Atlanta: Scholars Press, 1988), 57–97, and *From Sacrament to Contract: Marriage, Religion, and Law in the Western Tradition* (Louisville, Ky.: Westminster Press/John Knox Press, 1997).

28. James Q. Wilson, *The Moral Sense* (New York: Free Press, 1993). See also Robert W. Shaffern, "Christianity and the Rise of the Nuclear Family," *America* (May 1994): 13–15; David Herlihy, *Medieval Households* (Cambridge, Mass.: University of Massachusetts, 1985).

29. Pamela Couture, "The Use and Misuse of Ideals of Marriage and Families," delivered at the Religion and the American Family Debate Conference, September 1996, Chicago, and partly incorporated into chapter 3 of *From Culture Wars to Common Ground: Religion and the American Family Debate* (Louisville, Ky.: Westminster Press/John Knox Press, 1997).

30. Ibid.

31. Cooey, *Family, Freedom, and Faith*, 21 (emphasis added).

32. Herbert Anderson and Susan B. W. Johnson, *Regarding Children: A New Respect for Childhood and Families* (Louisville, Ky.: Westminster Press/John Knox Press, 1994), 70–72.

33. Gabriel Fackre, "What the Lutherans and the Reformed Can Learn from One Another," *Christian Century* 114, no. 18 (June 4–11, 1997): 558–561.

34. Reinhold Niebuhr, *The Nature and Destiny of Man*, vol. 1 (New York: Charles Scribner's Sons, 1941), 251, 263, and *The Irony of American History* (New York: Charles Scribner's Sons, 1952).

35. See Valerie Saiving Goldstein, "The Human Situation: A Feminine View," *Journal of Religion* (April 1960): 100–112; reprinted in *Woman Spirit Rising*, ed. Carol Christ and Judith Plaskow (New York: Harper and Row, 1980), 25–42; Barabara Hilkert Andolsen, "Agape in Feminist Ethics," *Journal of Religious Ethics* 9 (Spring 1981): 69–83; and Beverly Harrison, "The Power of Anger in the Work of Love: Christian Ethics for Woman and Strangers," *Union Seminary Quarterly Review* 36 (1981): 41–57.

36. Gudorf, "Parenting, Mutual Love, and Sacrifice," 182. For a renowned statement of Christian love as complete self-giving, see Anders Nygren, *Agape and Eros*, trans. Phillip S. Watson (Chicago: University of Chicago Press, 1982).

37. Herbert Anderson, "Between Rhetoric and Reality: Women and Men as Equal Partners in Home, Church and the Marketplace," in *Word and World* 17, no. 4 (Fall 1997): 376–386.

38. See, for example, Elizabeth A. Johnson, *She Who Is: The Mystery of God in Feminist Theological Discourse* (New York: Crossroad, 1992); and Catherine La Cugna, *God for Us: The Trinity and Christian Life* (New York: Harper, 1991).

39. See, for example, Elisabeth Schüssler Fiorenza, *In Memory of Her: A Feminist Theological Reconstruction of Christian Origins* (New York: Crossroad, 1984); see also Warren Carter, *Households and Discipleship: A Study of Matthew* 19–20 (Sheffield, England: Sheffield Academic Press, 1994).

40. Elisabeth Schüssler Fiorenza, "In Search of Women's Heritage," in *Weaving the Visions: New Patterns in Feminist Spirituality*, ed. Judith Plaskow and Carol P. Christ (New York: Harper & Row, 1989), 31.

41. See, for example, Elisabeth M. Tetlow, *Women and Ministry in the New Testament* (New York: Paulist Press, 1980); Ben Witherington, *Women in the Ministry of Jesus* (New York: Cambridge University Press, 1984); and Virginia Ramey Mollenkott, *Women, Men, and the Bible* (Nashville, Tenn.: Abingdon Press, 1977).

42. This argument draws on chapter 5, "Honor, Shame, and Equality in Early Christian Families," in *From Culture Wars to Common Ground*.

43. J. H. Neyrey, *The Social World of Luke–Acts* (Peabody, Mass.: Hendrickson, 1991); Bruce Malina, *The New Testament World: Insights from Cultural Anthropology* (Louisville, Ky.: Westminster Press/John Knox Press, 1993); David Cohen, *Law, Sexuality, and Society* (Cambridge: Cambridge University Press, 1991).

44. David Balsh, *Let Wives Be Submissive: The Domestic Code in 1 Peter* (Atlanta: Scholars Press, 1981); see also Rosemary Radford Ruether, *Sexism and God-Talk: Toward a Feminist Theology* (Boston: Beacon Press, 1983), 141–142, and "Church and Family 1: Church and Family in the Scriptures and Early Christianity," *New Blackfriars* (January 1984): 4–14.

45. Adrienne Rich, *Of Woman Born: Motherhood as Experience and Institution* (New York: W. W. Norton, 1976), 13 (italics in text).

46. Adrienne Rich, "Motherhood in Bondage (1976)," in *On Lies, Secrets, and Silence: Selected Prose, 1966–1978* (New York: W. W. Norton, 1979), 197.

47. Lisa Sowle Cahill, *Sex, Gender and Christian Ethics* (New York: Cambridge University Press, 1996), 61.

48. Ibid., 206–207.

49. Judith Plaskow, "Woman as Body: Motherhood and Dualism," *Anima* 8 (1981): 57, 65.

Jennifer Nedelsky

Dilemmas of Passion, Privilege, and Isolation:
Reflections on Mothering in a White, Middle-Class Nuclear Family

Next to falling in love with my husband, having my two children is the best thing that ever happened to me. As a woman who came of age in the sixties and became active as a feminist in 1970, it seems embarrassing, even shocking, to write such a sentence in a public, feminist essay. In my early days as a feminist, much scorn and opprobrium was heaped on marriage and the nuclear family—and with good reason. The fact that my own nuclear family is now the center of my life is central to many of the dilemmas of motherhood that I experience in my daily life.

I was delighted to be asked to write an essay for this volume, since I have wanted to write about my experiences of mothering since the infancy of my first child. But until this invitation I had not made the time or figured out the appropriate forum for exploring my ideas. And when I first started to work on this essay, I was uncertain whether most of the many things I wanted to write about were actually dilemmas. Indeed, there are important things that I have learned from mothering that don't fall into that category.[1] But as I thought back over the key issues that have emerged for me over the eleven years of raising my children, they do center around dilemmas. That is, they center around struggles to find solutions that are morally, psychologically, and politically adequate to problems that are intensely personal, yet structured in ways that are beyond our immediate control. My dilemmas have been those of isolation, of public and private responsibility, of caretaking, and of balance in my life. Of course, these are many of the same issues that generated the early critique of the nuclear family. These issues continue to pose dilemmas because fully adequate solutions are not possible at the individual level; the necessary systemic changes have still not taken place. For me, however, the dilemmas are framed by the passion that I feel for my children—something I never heard about in the feminism of my young adulthood. I am glad finally to bring my scholarly attention to the issues so central to my life. I offer my reflections on these dilemmas as they have come to me: by thinking back over my experiences from conception to my efforts to balance my needs and commitments while mothering my eight- and eleven-year-old boys.

Conception and Birth

My decision to try to conceive a child was embedded in my complex relation to my work, and my ability to make that decision was the first step in what proved to be a miraculous improvement in that relationship once my first child was born. Because my life still seems consumed by the struggle to find a proper balance among the competing pulls of work and family, I sometimes forget that this struggle is played out on a solid base made possible by the shift that came with Michael's birth.

When my husband, Joe, first suggested that we try to conceive, we had been married about six months (a second marriage for both of us, with no children by the previous marriages). I had been denied tenure at Princeton the previous year, and I was still not making much progress on the book that I had been avoiding writing for six years. At the time we were both visiting at the University of Toronto and looking for two permanent jobs in the same place. I was thirty-six, Joe was forty, and Joe persuaded me that we were too old to wait until all the material circumstances of our lives were sorted out. And in any case, he said, none of those circumstances really mattered in the decision about having a child. Something would work out. We could have a child whether I finished my book (and had an academic career) or not. That realization was the first step in the shift in my relationship to my work. Finishing the book did not define me or my life or control my most basic decisions.

In my ambivalence and ignorance, I managed not to know I was pregnant for six weeks. By then it was just two weeks before I was to begin teaching full time at the University of Toronto. I had to find a doctor, negotiate the terms of my maternity leave, and because I was thirty-seven, I thought I needed to find out about prenatal testing. A friend of mine had told me that with CVS (Chronic Villi Sampling) instead of amniocentesis, one could get the results in the third month. Since the thought of facing a decision about whether to have an abortion in my fifth month seemed too horrible to contemplate, I spent many hours searching out information and ultimately arranging to fly to Chicago to have the test done.

But even in the midst of harried phone calls, I realized that I was busily arranging for something about which I had deep ambivalence. Almost immediately upon finding out that I was pregnant I began to feel fiercely protective of the baby growing inside me. I knew that miscarriage in the first three months was very common, and I desperately wanted *this* baby to be all right, to grow safely within me.[2] It felt deeply wrong to take this precious and precarious gift and ask some doctor to ascertain if it was good enough. When I faced the same decision about whether to undergo testing three years later with my second child, it infused the early months of my pregnancy with a deep sadness. There was not the same hecticness of trying to make the arrangements in time, and I was left simply with a kind of low-level despair that I could not find a way around doing something that violated my sense of wonder, gratitude, and attachment to a precious new life.

I called my friend who had waxed eloquent about the advantages of CVS and asked her, didn't it feel terrible, didn't it feel like taking God's gift and saying that first you wanted to check out if it was good enough. To my relief, she said that of course it had felt like that. She went on to say that perhaps it would be different in a different world where there were more forms of collective support for families facing exceptional demands of care. We talked for some time about the terrible strain on families of severely disabled children and about people who are able to rise to the challenge. The conversation gave me a context for making sense of a decision that felt painful and not entirely "right."

I didn't dwell on the difficult choices I might face. I focused on my sense that there were some few conditions, such as those where the baby would certainly die very shortly after birth, where it would be clear to me that I would have an abortion. And the statistics on the chances of some abnormality were frightening, especially for my second pregnancy, when I was forty. But I'm not sure all of that would have been enough for me to go through with the testing if it hadn't been that Joe was absolutely certain that he couldn't face the anxiety of a pregnancy without the testing. I felt as though in some way I had no real choice but to have it done, and I went ahead without any sense of having resolved my feelings about it.

Part of what I am struck by when I think back on this early dilemma of mothering is that when my friend Lynn first told me about CVS she didn't tell me about the pain and sadness of having any kind of test. Similarly, in the counseling sessions that preceded the test, I never encountered any discussion of how a decision to test could be both right and painful. And I find, thinking back over the years, that when I have talked about it, I haven't talked about my unresolved grief and distress. I continue to behave as though it is self-evident that after a certain age a pregnant woman will want some form of genetic testing—and that therefore the only issues are technical ones of choice of method. This seems to me to be one of many forms of the unwillingness to be forthright about confronting the dilemmas of motherhood that inspired this book. I have tried to figure out both why I don't talk about the sadness and what I think the optimal solutions would be.

I am sure that part of the reason for my silence is the discomfort of discussing intense and unresolved personal pain. But I think I also fear making another woman feel guilty. She might feel that my revealing my sadness and unease implies that there is something wrong about her planning testing. Or she might not feel such sadness and then think that my experience implies that there is something wrong with her for not feeling that the decision to test is a painful and difficult one.

I think part of what we need culturally are better means for acknowledging and dealing with the grief that some of our decisions bring. We need to know that the grief we feel over the decision to have prenatal testing or to have an abortion does not mean that we are making the wrong decision. As long as the pain is interpreted as a signal for guilt, it will be hard to find constructive ways to work through the pain. I do think that the distress is a signal that something very serious is at stake. Although I know that not all feminists agree, I think there is something wrong with treating lightly the decision to have an abortion or to undergo testing for the purpose of a possible abortion. Perhaps something is wrong structurally that makes us construct our options as we do. Optimal collective means for reflecting on the pain of our decisions would allow for working through the personal grief and for reflecting on the social structures involved. I would include in such means informal norms of conversation, as well as information about feelings of sadness or grief available where genetic testing is done. Such means might run the risk of making some women feel that if they did not feel distress that something was wrong with them. In this, as in so many other issues, part of what is important is for women to know more about how they feel and how other women feel by having the opportunity to talk openly among themselves. Then we could explore the differences and the similarities and come to a better understanding of both the personal and the structural dimensions of the problems.

In focusing on the pain of the genetic testing, I do not want to deny the ways in which it lessened my anxiety during the pregnancy. I spent little time worrying about whether my baby would be all right. I have sometimes wondered whether that sense of security left me even less prepared for a traumatic birth. I had worried about how I would handle the pain of labor, but it never occurred to me that my baby might die.

After a terrible labor, beginning with five hours of diarrhea and vomiting, the baby's heartbeat dropped, and I was rushed off to an emergency delivery. Against all expectations, a cesarean was not necessary; a high forceps delivery brought Michael out. But he was clearly in bad shape and the anaesthesiologist, after suctioning him out, whisked him off to an intensive care unit without even letting me see him—despite protests from the obstetrician. As it turned out, Michael had aspirated a great deal of meconium (fetal stool) in the womb. It had coated his lungs, making it very difficult for him to breathe.

Several hours later a "transition team" brought him to me en route to an intensive care unit in the neighboring children's hospital. He looked wonderful under his little oxygen tent, and for the first time I felt excited and happy. When they took him away again, they left me with a Polaroid picture of him. The next day I visited him in the morning and got to put my hands on him through the special openings in his enclosed bed. Although he was attached to lots of monitoring wires he looked great to me. But that afternoon he got worse, and he went downhill for forty-eight hours until they could find a respirator that worked for him. Babies in his condition often die, having worn themselves out trying to breathe. Had we been anywhere but in a hospital with the latest high-tech equipment, he would not have made it.

In the midst of my grief and anxiety, I formed a passionate attachment to Michael. I felt again the urgent sense that I wanted *this* baby to be all right. I could feel the particularity even in the womb, and now it was even more intense. It would not be better for him to die if he were brain damaged. I didn't want to know anything about the possibility of such consequences. I only wanted him to be okay, to live. When I visited him, I focused all my energies on extending healing, love, and security through my hands. And I was rewarded by seeing his overworked heart slow to a better rhythm under my touch. After a week, he had improved enough that I could hold him and nurse him for the first time. After three agonized, exhausting weeks I was able to bring him home. He became a strong and healthy baby with no physical effects from his ordeal.

I think this traumatic entry into motherhood shaped my experience in a variety of ways. First, I think this near brush with losing Michael ensured that I never took having my children for granted. For a long time after he was home I felt a daily sense of relief, gratitude, and wonder at his birth and survival. Even now, when he and his brother are eleven and eight, Joe and I marvel almost daily at these wonderful boys who seem a good fortune beyond our wildest dreams. Perhaps some of that sense also comes from having had children late, so that even getting pregnant was not something I took for granted. I cherish this capacity to enjoy my children and to sustain a sense of wonder at the gift of sharing their lives. And I feel a daily sense of gratitude for the privilege of my circumstances that makes the sense of pleasure easily available, not swamped by fatigue, need, or despair.

Michael's birth was also a dramatic instance of the isolation that has characterized my experience of motherhood. We had only been in Toronto for about eighteen months when Michael was born. We had not made close friends and our families were in the United States. When we called to make announcements of his birth to our university faculties, there was a strong pressure to say that he was okay, or that he would be okay. Neither of us were able to communicate what was really going on. As a result very few, if any, of our colleagues knew what we were going through. So we went through it alone. Our midwife was really the only person who visited us regularly. I still cry when I tell the story of Michael's birth with any degree of openness, and I think that is in large part because there is still so much grief that I could not find ways of working through in the isolation and pressure of those early days.

The Astonishing Joy and Stress of Infancy

Once Michael was home I was overwhelmed by joy and by chaos. Over and over again I wondered why no one had told me how wonderful it was to have a baby. I fell in love with Michael with a passion and intensity that took me completely by surprise. Part of the astonishing joy was being consumed by a love that had no quid pro quos, no contractual dimension, no fairness or reciprocity issues. I realized that I had been plagued by anxieties about my capacity for such feelings, at the same time that I was unsure whether they were possible for anyone. I saw myself as obsessed with self-protection, vigilantly guarding the precarious balance of equal power relations with Joe, wary and subtly hostile toward those with power over me. But now I reveled in an all-consuming attentiveness to Michael's needs, an endless fascination with the bond between us. I felt fulfilled to overflowing with my love for him: There was no issue of what I was "getting back." I had never had that experience before and it felt like a miracle that sustained itself day after day. I think there is something miraculous about the love one can feel for a baby, how it can bring out the best in you beyond what you thought was possible. And I think there was also something in my particular psyche that made the experience so powerful, so unexpected. But I also think that part of the wonder of having a baby is that when one falls in love like that, one experiences a kind of relationship whose possibility is subtly but relentlessly denied by the pervasive market mentality of negotiated self-interest as the foundation of human affairs.[3]

I never experienced my absorption in Michael as selflessness (a truly bizarre term for a virtue), although it did provide me with my first taste of what could happen when ordinary care for myself seemed completely unable to have a claim compared to the needs of the baby: I realized in the first week home with him that days had gone by without my finding time to brush my teeth. I remember this sometimes when I hear stories of women who go for years and years without attending to their own needs. But for me self-sacrifice was not what the intense focus on Michael was about. I realized this early on when another mother of an infant Michael's age referred to nursing as "a nice thing to do for your baby." This struck me as the most extraordinary way of referring to what I experienced as one of the most pleasurable and satisfying experiences of my life.

Nursing, like so many other choices, was not something I did "for" Michael. I made these choices because they were what I wanted. At least in the early years, I was able to attend deeply to his needs by following my own heartfelt desires. My wants were not, of course, identical to his, but they were intertwined. My need to be with him was related to his need for me. But I did not experience myself as giving up my needs for his, but as following a thread of passionate desire in my relationship to him.

Being tuned in to Michael in ways that kept our needs and desires intertwined may have come in part from my intense efforts to connect to him in his first precarious days of life in the incubator when I comforted and healed him with my hands. But some of the capacity for tuning in was also the result of a kind of discipline. I especially remember the pull to watch TV or read when I was nursing. But I learned that if I kept my attention on him and our interaction, it was rewarding and fulfilling. And if I were distracted by thoughts of all the other things I ought to be doing rather than relaxing and enjoying holding him after he had eaten, I would lose a precious connection as well as pleasure. Learning that the connection was not just automatic, that it took a kind of effort and discipline, was a crucial lesson that has remained important (though more complicated to implement). Although I never exactly felt like I simply "had" the time to focus on my baby—there was always the pull of work I was behind on, both academic and household—I was grateful that I had enough support (first from Joe and then from Merilyn, our nanny) to be able to learn the lesson of the link between connection and focus.[4] I think it was in part my success in being tuned in to my children when they were infants that made infancy the time of passionate engagement that it was.

The astonishing joy of infancy ultimately brought its own dilemma. The surprise of the intensity of the pleasure and passion brought with it a kind of anger and resentment: The question of why no one had told me about this was not just rhetorical. I felt a sort of sense of collective betrayal by my feminist sisters. Why hadn't I read dozens of stories and articles about this special joy, why hadn't all my friends, colleagues, and acquaintances with children raved to me about their experiences? Sometimes people are puzzled when I tell them about this sense of not having been told; after all, the culture is full of various forms of glorifying motherhood. But, in fact, I think there is relatively little detailed depiction of the special bond of infancy. And I must have dismissed the depictions of motherhood (however ostensibly positive) in popular culture as a kind of propaganda for the patriarchal nuclear family. The sources I would have believed, feminist literature and associates, seemed to me to have been silent on the subject. Why had they kept it from me?

Of course, I have finally come to realize that not everyone experiences infancy the way I did. My closest friend who had had children before I did loves being a mother, but simply did not have my experience of the early years as an explosion of unlooked-for joy. But I think my sense of a silence was not simply the result of these variations in experience. In the beginning I told everyone within earshot how wonderful it was having a baby. I taught feminist theory the fall after Michael was born and talked about my experiences in class whenever the opportunity arose. But gradually I became anxious about the message I was sending. Was I subtly (or not so subtly) implying that no woman should miss this experience? And did that, in turn, imply that a woman without children was not a real or full woman? Was this the "pro-natalism" some feminists were concerned about? As the years passed I said less and less in class, where these anxieties were particularly acute. But then I realized that I also muted or reduced what I said to colleagues and acquaintances, even to some friends. If the woman didn't have children, I didn't know if it was because she had been unable to, or because her partner didn't want to, or she didn't have a partner. The related issues seemed highly charged and once I focused on them, I could not find a way to be forthright about my own experiences without running the risk of causing inadvertent pain. The occasions on which I felt invited to talk about my feelings about motherhood became rarer and rarer. And even talking to another mother, or a woman planning to have children, I often constrained my expression because I knew that not every woman experiences motherhood as I have. I did not want to make a woman feel bad if her feelings were more ambivalent than my own. In the end, I find myself complicit in the silence that had so angered me in the beginning.

And that is where it has stood for some years now. I have not been able to figure out a way to share my experiences in the way I wished other women had shared theirs with me. Recently I talked about this with a woman reveling in the joys of mothering an infant; she told me she had shared my sense of not knowing because no one talked about it. She said, "I almost missed this." She had seriously considered not having children and now felt that she might have made that decision with no real sense of what she was giving up. I now think that this noncommunication is part of a broader pattern of isolation and privatization, which I discuss in the last section. In terms of my own path through this dilemma, the process of writing about it has persuaded me to try again to communicate my experiences to those who express an interest. I am still most unsure about the classroom where I feel both the urgent need for honest storytelling about motherhood and anxieties about pressures from one in authority. I think the remaining unease is in part a recognition that I really do not have a very balanced view of the subject. Barring wartime or other social or political crisis, it is hard for me to understand any woman deciding not to have a child if she could (financially, physically, emotionally). There is nothing in my own life that could possibly have been more important or a greater source of joy and fulfillment. I recognize this as a limitation that many years of conversations have done little to shift.

————

I don't want to leave the impression that the early years with my children were simply a path of smooth delight. I was overwhelmed by the chaos generated by a new infant. I was as ignorant of the demands as I was of the joys of infancy, and completely unprepared for them. We had bought a new house without any appliances and planned to move in right after Michael's birth. I had thought that it was just as well that we would need to shop for appliances since I wouldn't really have much to do in the first few weeks. I simply had no idea of the exhaustion of sleep disruption and the amount of time and energy an infant requires.[5] I felt as though I got a sense of how men who have never undertaken child care can completely fail to understand its demands. "What does she do all day?" echoed in my own voice as, "What *have* I done all day?" Why is there dirty laundry piled up, dirty dishes, a chaotic household and I'm still exhausted? I thought I was someone who set no store by housekeeping and would not be embarrassed by unwashed dishes. Yet I found I needed to keep rereading books that assured me that this state was common and that my rest and enjoyment of the baby were more important than a tidy house. The despair over the chaos reached truly epic proportions when we moved to a new house when Michael was six weeks old, three weeks after he had come home from the hospital.

Later I realized that although I had always mouthed the line that "homemakers" have a set of skills that are valuable in the paid workforce, I had not really had any idea what that meant until I was confronted with my own lack of the organizational skills necessary to make a household with young children run reasonably smoothly.

When Daniel was born, it turned out that I had managed to forget the chaos of infancy. I had planned not to try to get any research or writing done in the summer months following his birth. And so I imagined, once again, that I would have time on my hands—since this time I had tenure, we were not moving house, and we had a full-time nanny instead of no help. I envisioned sitting in the backyard with a friend whose baby was due about the same time, sipping wine and idling away a relaxing summer. I had forgotten the chaos and the sleep deprivation, and I had underestimated the demands of an infant and a toddler. I think this failure of anticipation must also have been, in part, the result of not having had many conversations with other mothers.

I was also surprised and extremely anxious to find that I did not fall in love with Daniel in the same way I had with Michael. I loved him, was delighted to have an infant again, felt the joy of the special uncomplicated love; but I did not experience the same kind of passion. I worried about it a lot.

Finally, when Daniel was a few months old, a colleague who was over for dinner told me that the same thing had happened with her second child and that it was quite common. She reassured me that it didn't mean anything, that I would love him just as much. (And she turned out to be completely right.) It mattered enormously to me to get that reassurance, from someone who I saw as a very engaged and devoted mother. And I was struck again at how little information I really had about mothering, and that practically my only resources were books.

Care and Responsibility
Child Care

I did know that I needed to figure out what to do about child care. Throughout my pregnancy we did not know whether Joe would have a job for the coming academic year. Because my income was the only certain one, I did not consider taking more than the seventeen-week paid leave that the Unemployment Act provided for (and the University topped to provide 95 percent of my salary). We talked about Joe doing the child care if he didn't get the job he had applied for, but I think both of us fervently hoped it wouldn't come to that.

While I was pregnant Joe and I went to visit a day-care center near us. The toddlers seemed engaged and happy, but the children under two seemed rather lost. It was a parent co-op day care, and none of the staff there that day seemed to be trying to engage the little ones who were on their feet, but not part of group play. It made me sad to think of my baby there. Perhaps I was already anticipating the powerful sense I would come to have of not wanting to be apart from him. Of course I did not actually believe that my one visit constituted a thorough investigation of the day-care option. I remembered a colleague talking enthusiastically about the infant care at a center far from where we lived, but didn't have the heart to pursue it. Even before I really knew why, I didn't want Michael in day care. We never visited another center.

My next plan was to share a nanny with neighbors who were expecting a baby at the same time. We spent quite a bit of time discussing the arrangement and, at their suggestion, drawing up a contract for a prospective nanny. The plan was for both babies to be at the neighbors' house. But once Michael was born and home from the hospital, I knew I couldn't bear to be away from him eight hours a day—even if he was just around the corner. I wanted to be around him as much as possible, to know what he was doing, when he was crying, when playing happily even if I wasn't looking after him. I just wanted to be as close to him as possible, as much of the time as possible. Ultimately I realized that I wanted to be able to take short breaks seeing him, whenever I felt like it, with no planning or preparation. I knew that it would feel completely different to me to have to get my coat on, leave the house, walk over to some other place to see him. It would be much harder to justify such an interruption in my work, and it would feel like more of an interruption than going downstairs to see him for a few minutes whenever I wanted to.

Michael was born on April 10. My classes were over (having compressed some earlier in the term). The long academic summer allowed us several months of paralysis around what we were going to do about child care. Finally in July we got sufficiently panicked about what we were going to do when classes started in September that I called a couple of colleagues who seemed to be happy with their nannies (as the Canadians still call full-time child minders). I got the names of four or five women their nannies knew who were looking for work and interviewed them. We found the process extremely painful. It was clear that some of the women desperately needed the job, but I cried at the thought of any of them caring for Michael. After relaying my sad tale to the receptionist at my chiropractor's (my neck having gone into spasm from the strain), she ended up sending her best friend to see us.

Merilyn was a white Canadian of working-class background, a few years older than I, who had gotten married and had children when she was eighteen. Now divorced, her children were grown and she had just finished an intensive "transition year program" which simultaneously gave her a high school diploma and admission to the University of Toronto. She did not want to go back to her accounting job in a bank and was tired of living in student poverty. In our first conversation we discovered that she and I were reading the same books, both novels and Jungian psychology. I was delighted to find someone whom I felt I could really talk to. And she seemed delighted to be with Michael.

By the time I met Merilyn I had figured out that I wanted someone who would feel comfortable handing Michael over to me whenever I felt like being with him. And while I was with him, I wanted her to do whatever household tasks needed doing (excluding cleaning the house, for which we hired someone else). Fortunately, I was able to talk to Merilyn about how it was going to feel to each of us to be in this relationship, which was such a complex mix of employee/employer and quasi-familial. After I offered her the job, we had a long conversation (I can still remember the sidewalk café, since it was rare for me to be out anywhere without Michael) and I raised the awkwardness I felt about asking someone else to do the "shitwork." At the same time, I explained, it was clear to me that every minute I didn't have to spend doing housework was time I could have for my baby. Merilyn said, "somebody has to do it," and, in fact, we were able to develop a fluid and comfortable relationship of shifting care for Michael among Joe, me, and Merilyn. It felt like Michael had three primary caregivers who loved him and were intensely engaged with him, and in most circumstances he seemed equally happy to be cared for by any of us. I found that very reassuring and it gave me the flexibility and support I wanted to do my work and have lots of time with Michael. I think perhaps it was because I had so much time with Michael that I found the intensity of the bond between him and Merilyn comforting rather than threatening. And it helped, too, that we were able to talk to each other about how we were feeling.

By the time Michael was two and a half, it was clear that he needed more contact with other kids. We enrolled him in a parent co-op play school for five mornings a week. Between us, Joe and I worked at the play school three to four mornings a month. That was enough to allow us to continue to feel very connected to his daily routine. At four and a half, he entered the public school kindergarten for two more years of morning school before starting a full day in first grade. Although I missed the sense of knowing his routines, his classmates, his favorite activities, I was also relieved not to have the demands of working at the co-op. At first I thought I would volunteer at his school to maintain the sense of contact, but I never did.

The relationship with Merilyn was quite close and intense for all of us. I think that very closeness made it hard for us to come to terms with the fact that from the time Daniel was born (Michael was three and in play school), neither she nor Joe and I were really happy with how things were working out. While she found her absorption in Michael as a baby rewarding, she found caring for two children a strain. She became very attached to Daniel, but the days left her exhausted. Later she suggested that Daniel's birth brought up some of the strains she had felt with her own second child. In any case, although there were clear signs that things were no longer working out so well, it took us another two years (one of them with her working half-time) before she left. Although we had not been able to end the working relationship when we should have, I have always been grateful to have had Merilyn's loving presence in the tense early years when I was trying to finish my book. And I think she felt that, at least for the first three years, working for us had satisfied important needs for her.

When we knew Merilyn was leaving, we decided to hire another nanny through an agency. We thought that would give us a wide range of choices, with a fair amount of background information before an interview, but would not overwhelm us. (A colleague had put an ad in the paper and received over 200 calls.) We were delighted to find Nancy. She had grown up in Toronto in a working-class Portuguese family. Although she was only twenty-three, she seemed exceptionally mature and responsible. She had a B.A. from the University of Toronto and experience working in day care. It was only the poor state of the economy and the underfunding for day care that made her available for a nanny job. Indeed, we often felt like we had hired a private preschool teacher for our kids. She was full of creative ideas for projects for them, comfortable with lots of kids in the house, and excellent at organizing their day into an orderly routine. For the first time we had someone in the house who had the organizational skills to make the household run smoothly. We realized that Merilyn's skills in this regard were no better than our own, and that we had all muddled along in a fairly constant state of low-level chaos until Nancy arrived.

Nancy started working for us in January, and Daniel was to start the play school the following September, when Michael entered first grade. Our understanding was that at that point she would take over the housecleaning as well as the child care, laundry, cooking a weekly dish we could eat as leftovers, and daily tidying of the downstairs. I was intent on being very clear, again, about the mix of child care and other responsibilities and explaining that I worked at home a lot and wanted to spend time with the kids during the day. Nancy had two other job offers and came back for a second conversation after we had offered her the job (as well as talking to Merilyn at our suggestion). We were very happy she chose us and very happy with her care of the kids and the household. We never developed the kind of intense personal relationship we had with Merilyn, but in many ways it seemed easier to be less closely involved with her life outside our home. (Neither Merilyn nor Nancy lived with us.) We told Nancy at the start that we hoped she would work for us until Daniel entered first grade. The timing turned out to work just right for all of us. Nancy and her husband had a baby the June that Daniel finished kindergarten, and we planned to spend most of the summer away.

At one level, I have always been happy that I was able to figure out what I wanted in terms of paid help with the multiple daily demands of household and child care. I knew I wanted to see a lot of my kids on a daily basis and

I knew that I couldn't spend as much time with them as I wanted unless I got help with all the other household work. But even though I was able to get that help in relationships that were characterized by mutual warmth and respect and a kind of social equality, the understanding we worked out together could not solve the deeper problem of inequality that sits at the base of the nanny relationship.

One day when Michael was about eight, our minister was talking to the children in church about fairness. She said it's not fair if one person ends up having to do all the crummy work. Michael responded, that's the way it is in our house. I gasped silently, wondering what he had in mind. Certainly there was no such division between Joe and me. Then he said, "Nancy our nanny has to do all the crummy work." I felt embarrassed and also proud of him for being able to see that and recognize it as an example of unfairness. When I talked to him later I told him that we wanted Nancy to do that work so that we could spend more time with him and Daniel. He said, "You never have enough time for us." Rather taken aback, and feeling generally unsettled and uncertain, I just said that it would be even worse if Nancy didn't help us with the work that needed to be done to take care of the household. I left it at that since I really didn't have a very good answer for these questions. I also told Nancy about the conversation so she would know how Michael saw things and how I had tried to respond.

Recounting this unease reminds me of an unsettling conversation I had at a women's center in Halifax, Nova Scotia, in 1974. I was arguing for the importance of dividing responsibility for child care equally between men and women. A woman in her thirties responded that whenever she heard someone say that the father and mother should share child care equally, it really meant that they were going to hire someone else to do it. To this day that remark brings the shock of being caught in an unconscious contradiction. Although I almost never feel that I have found the right balance in the time I spend with my children, Joe, my work, my colleagues, my friends, I do feel that I found the kind of child-care arrangements that suited my needs. The problem is that it is not a solution that could be made available to everyone, or even everyone who would want it. And it is a solution that relies on being paid a lot less for child care than for being a university professor. What I wanted, and basically got, was made possible by privilege that I would not want to justify.

What I take very seriously about my experience is that institutionalized day care, even excellent day care, would not have been what I wanted. It would have helped a lot to have had excellent day care in the same building as my university office, so that I could still take my breaks during the day with my kids. If that had been an option, I might well have tried it, especially if lots of my colleagues had had young children so that the day care would have been a shared point of connection. I certainly wish there were children around the law school on a daily basis. I think it would transform the environment to have faculty, staff, and students interacting with their kids in the same building where classes are taught. The realities of caretaking might become part of the milieu of legal education.

But in the absence of such a potentially transformative option, having day care even a ten-minute drive from my house would not have met my needs. From the start it was clear to me that I was not making a judgment about whether good day care could meet Michael's needs. It was my needs, my desire to have him close by me as much as possible that drove my choice of child care. The daily flexibility of access and the trade-off of doing more child care and less home care myself only seemed possible with a nanny. I missed Michael after even short absences, and an uncharacteristic five-hour separation would fill me with longing. Having him away from me for many hours a day on a routine basis would have deprived me of the contact and proximity I passionately desired.

It has become clear to me over the years that different women want different things in the way they structure paid work, child care, and household work. Among my colleagues who have the same advantages of flexibility and affluence that I have there is a range of choices of child-care arrangements. When I got pregnant, there was only one other woman on the law faculty who had children. She was in her office eight hours a day. Now there are lots of young faculty with young children. Few of them are in the office quite as much as she was, and none is away as much as I am. Most have nannies, some use day care, some use both. I know that my needs are not those of everyone, but I think they are among the range of needs that it should be possible to meet. Day care, as it is usually organized, could not have met my needs. Trying to imagine solutions that would have, that were not based on exploitation or inequity, that could be available to everyone only serves to reveal the depth of the changes that would be necessary in our society to create the range and variety of child care that were truly optimal for everyone. In the absence of those changes, I live with a low-level awareness (heightened from time to time) that many women cannot enjoy their children in the ways I have because as a society we have not offered them the necessary support. And I live with the distress of having chosen solutions that seemed vitally important to me, but which rested on structures of unjustifiable inequality.

Caretaking and the Bonds of Connection

One of the most important insights I got from having my children was the importance of routine physical caretaking for forming the basic bonds of connection. Even feminists who talk about the importance of caretaking sometimes assume that the mundane activities such as changing diapers and taking out the garbage can be done by anyone; they are of no consequence in the formation of self or relationships. I came to understand their consequence in a visceral sort of way by not doing a lot of the mundane caretaking when Michael was an infant.

When Michael was born I did not have tenure and the terms of my job were explicit: I had to finish my book or lose my job. In July, when Michael was three months old, Joe gave him his first bottle so that I could go to my office to work in the mornings. I would come home and nurse him at noon and try to work in all the interstices of time for the rest of the day. After a while we established a pattern: I would go upstairs to work after dinner every night, leaving Joe with all the evening clean-up. He would also get Michael ready for bed and, usually, put him to sleep after I had come down to say goodnight to him. I nursed him and played with him, but for the following year I did less and less of the "mundane" caretaking. I worked every day, including weekends, and every evening for eighteen months until I finished my book. (I still remember that I celebrated that day by walking over to Woolworths to buy Michael clothes for the first time.) In many ways I was satisfied with my capacity to write, teach full time, and have quite a lot of time for Michael (I remember calculating it once as about six hours a day). But I felt the loss of the connection through caretaking. The diaper changing, the feeding, the dressing turned out to have been an essential part of the intimate bond I had formed with him. As I did less of it, I felt less connected. I felt that I had to give it up to get my book done. But it turned out that my ability to turn mundane chores over to others was not a simple benefit, freeing me to work or to play with Michael, but a real loss. (I felt it with my dog, too. During those tense months I asked Merilyn to walk her, and after a while I realized that the time gained was a connection lost.)

Joe, in turn, formed a very powerful bond with Michael by doing so much of the caretaking when he was an infant.[6] He enjoyed changing diapers, and remembers those times as satisfying ways of caring for Michael. I think it was an important kind of intimate, physical connection of satisfying basic needs, when nursing monopolized so much of that primal contact. When Daniel was an infant Joe was trying to catch up for all the time spent away from his work while I was writing my book. He spent much less time at the basic caretaking (though he still did a lot of rocking and carrying in the early hours of the morning when Daniel was colicky). And I think Joe had a less intense and intimate connection with Daniel when he was an infant. (It was also true that Daniel seemed to want only me from very early on. It's very hard to tell what was cause and what was effect.)

I recently had a male student express complete disbelief that diaper changing could be an important source of connection. There seems to be a widespread general sense that diaper changing is simply one of the unpleasant and unfortunately necessary parts of having a baby—which everyone hopes someone else will do. But I expect that many mothers will share my sense that diaper changing is part of a complex physical-emotional bond with a baby. Nevertheless, that sense does not always carry over to an understanding of the broader link between mundane physical caretaking and the bonds of connection. Over the years my initial insight about caretaking and connection with children broadened into a belief that physical caretaking is part of what roots us in the world and permits us to feel a connection with the material foundations of life, from the care the earth requires to respect for the labor that permits us to live as we do. The dominant culture of North America treats virtually all forms of physical caretaking with contempt. The more successful we are, the less caretaking we do—of our children, our houses, our cars, our material possessions.[7] The definition of being successful is that our time is too important for mundane work.

Until there is a shift in this basic stance, those who do the caretaking will be treated with contempt: They will be paid little and defined as unsuccessful. If caretaking were actually valued, there would be a revolution in the structure of our society. But when the people in power have less and less experience with the knowledge and connection brought by caretaking, the transformation is less and less likely.

One might think that there must be limits to this argument: What does one get out of cleaning one's own toilet? But I get glimpses of the sense of connection that can come even from cleaning toilets. My labor has made an essential part of my home clean, attractive, sanitary. I know what it takes for others to do the job. I know the satisfaction of doing it well. And I feel a satisfaction in contributing to making our home a pleasant, comfortable place to be. I get a sense of the value of being a "homemaker," of devoting one's energies to creating a home, a space of comfort, beauty, utility, peace, and play for the people I love most. The most mundane physical labor translates into complicated values. Of course that translation is disrupted when the labor is treated with disdain and the outcomes ignored or taken for granted. I don't wish to do this kind of labor full time, even with the best of translations. And the dilemma arises here because actually I do it hardly at all (except during the summer at our cottage[8]). But I do have some sense of what I am missing and the costs to the culture as a whole of the pattern I participate in.

I find the contradictions here to be perhaps the most acute of any I have discussed here. I think this issue of the relationship to caretaking is of great importance, and I notice when feminist discussions of care miss the significance of doing mundane, physical caretaking. But on a daily basis, the pain and conflict are submerged below consciousness. I regularly treat some things as merely mundane, such as laundry, cleaning the house, and much of the cooking. Sometimes I wish that I had time to do this work myself, but mostly I feel grateful that I can afford to hire someone else to do it. I continue to buy time by treating physical caretaking as something to be farmed out to others. The only way I know how to do my job and have some fraction of the time I want for my family is to participate in what I see as one of the most destructive features of our culture. Not only do I deprive myself of the connections and knowledge that mundane caretaking brings, but I send the message to my boys that these "chores" have no value. I tacitly affirm to them that successful, important people do not do the life-sustaining work that the culture despises.

Transformation

While having my children generated these tensions of contradiction around the work of caretaking, my troubled relationship to my academic work underwent a miraculous transformation after Michael was born. It is both a blessing and a curse of scholarship, and other "chosen work,"[9] that no one else will determine for you when, how, or whether you do it. The same privilege of flexibility that allowed me to spend so much time with my kids, had for years permitted an intermittent state of paralysis. I had been struggling to turn my dissertation into a book for eight years. Most of that time I was anxiously, actively not-writing. I had had a short, important burst of productive work when I was on leave three years earlier. And I had managed to send off a rough manuscript and get an advance book contract the following year. But then the work ground to a halt again. Something very powerful in me was preventing me from being able to write. I made some important headway in understanding those forces through therapy the year before I got pregnant, but the insights didn't translate into written work. I was anxious all through my pregnancy, because I had the strong sense (and several people had told me) that I had better get the book done before the baby was born. I was nauseous twenty-four hours a day during the first trimester, so I pinned my hopes on an energetic middle trimester. But it came and went with only my teaching getting done. I was very tired in the last trimester, so when Michael was born I had still done nothing with the original manuscript I had submitted. The anxiety was particularly acute since Joe had given up his job to stay in Toronto and we didn't know whether he would get a job at the University of Toronto until a few weeks before Michael was born. So my incapacity to write looked like it might mean that soon neither of us would have a job.

When Michael was three months old I started to work on the book and worked steadily and extremely effectively for the eighteen months it took to write it. It had become clear to me that the only book I could write was the book I wanted to write—half of which was new, not in the dissertation. I wrote exactly the book I wanted to and was incredibly happy with how it turned out. After eight years of incapacity, the steady satisfying flow of work was amazing. It was also a grueling eighteen months and hardly a model of how I wanted to work. But the break in the logjam of my writing was permanent. Of course, I still have my struggles with deadlines, with inability to make time for my own work in the constant press of demands (which seems to escalate every year). There is still a residual barrier to the free flow of my creativity. But the eight-year block was lifted with Michael's birth. Far from being unable to get anything done once he was born (as warned), I was able to work well for the first time since I started teaching at Princeton.

Of course there were other factors. The move to Toronto gave me a collegial environment that was both stimulating and supportive. Being at Princeton had been terribly damaging to me, and the one other time I had gotten some work done on the book was when I was away in New York for eight months. And, as I noted, I think I laid the groundwork for the change in my therapy. But neither therapy nor Toronto had brought forth the flow of writing. Michael did.

I think that part of the block had been a fear that if I wrote my book I would become a tenured professor—and lose my soul.[10] I would become caught up in the demands and allures of professional academic life, and lose touch with what really mattered. I would live entirely in the realm of what the academy recognizes as reason, and lose the capacities I had been slowly developing of a different way of seeing the world, its multiple dimensions and connections. My spirit would wither, perhaps die, in the busyness of a successful academic career.

Once Michael was born I knew that danger had passed. I knew that nothing could ever be as important to me as my child. My bond to him would keep me grounded in what mattered. My ability to tune in to him would remind me of the essential and invaluable gift of knowing through a form of cognition completely different from what I practiced at work. With that confidence, I wrote my book.

As the years have passed, I find that there are some periods in which I am more in tune with these alternate forms of seeing and knowing, and some when I feel a pull toward a more conventional mode of analytic thought, and some when I just get lost in the busyness. But I have been able to incorporate some of the other kind of vision and capacity into both my writing and my teaching. I almost never feel a full integration of my different capacities, but rather a switching back and forth between them. And I wonder, somewhat anxiously, whether my analytic preoccupations of the past few years are connected to my boys' getting older. Perhaps the tuning in to young children helped keep my other capacities vibrant and alert. They seem a bit dormant at the moment. But I retain the confidence that came with Michael's birth: It is possible for me to have a successful academic career without losing my soul.

Isolation, Engagement, and the Need for Community

On a day-to-day basis, I have no sense of having given up anything to have my children. Indeed, when I would hear this issue raised, I used to joke that the only thing I ever gave up was broccoli (while I was nursing). And that about captured my sense of the trade-offs. But in fact I have practically given up my social life. I rarely spend time with friends or colleagues. And I do feel a pain, disappointment, and frustration in my isolation. It is a particular irony that isolation is so central to the balance I strike given the emphasis on relationship in my scholarship.

When Michael was eight months old I took a dramatic step in furthering that isolation. I packed up my office and moved home to do my work. I can still remember the moment of decision. I had gone down the hall to get my mail and ended up in a half hour conversation about nothing in particular with a colleague. By the time I got back to my office I was in a rage. I had just wasted half an hour in which I was not with my baby and not writing my book. I decided I didn't have that kind of time to waste, and it is only a slight exaggeration to say that I haven't had a hallway conversation with a colleague since. Of course one cuts oneself off from a lot of information about what's happening in the institution by eliminating hallway exchanges. And there is a loss of genuine intellectual stimulation as well. There is a loss to the institution as well as to me, so I cannot entirely fault my colleagues for being annoyed. (The Faculty of Law, like many law schools, has much stronger norms about working in one's office than most arts and science departments.) I get occasional snide remarks about how long it's been since they have last seen me. And once as I strode along in my characteristic haste, a senior colleague shook his head as I passed and said, "She doesn't even have time to say hello."

I miss the informal exchange of students dropping by my office as well. Generally they know there will be a line-up for office hours so they come for specific purposes, not to chat. One student, surveying a particularly long line-up, said she had never known a professor who was so accessible, and yet so inaccessible.

I regret these losses and often think that I should spend more time at school now that the kids are older. But the ever increasing press of academic "chores" makes the uninterrupted time for writing at home seem indispensable. In the end, at least tacitly if not entirely self-reflectively, I continue to think that the loss of casual exchange with colleagues and students is a price worth paying. In particular, it is more important for me to write and to be with my kids than to be "in the loop" of hallway information. What I regret most is my relative unavailability to junior colleagues and the ways in which I limit the opportunities for casual conversation to develop into friendship.

I experience the loss of time with close friends as the greatest failure of the balance I strike. I am trying to learn not to let the busyness of both home and work overwhelm the importance of sustaining those connections.

My pattern of isolation as a "solution" to the ongoing dilemmas of the competing demands of work and family is in part made possible by the flexibility of an academic job. I have never been faced with the choice of having to be away from my children for long hours in order to do the work I love. (Virtually all jobs require eight hours and law firms and other professions now have norms of ten-hour days and weekend work.) It has been quite easy for me to arrange my classes and office hours so that I can work at home until around 1 p.m. three days a week. Most weeks I can plan meetings so that I only have to go in for part of one additional day. I do almost all my work, even bureaucratic paperwork, at home. I only go in to teach or to meet with students or colleagues. Even among academics this pattern is on the far end of the continuum. It replicates that of my academic father, who was home and available to us most of the time (although not involved in "mundane" caretaking).[11] His life was also characterized by a lot of involvement with his children and ultimately a kind of isolation I find it painful to think about.

Despite the ways in which my degree of isolation is peculiar to the freedom of academics and my idiosyncratic choices, I see it as part of a broader culture of privatization that shapes motherhood, at least for middle-class professionals. Middle-class affluence removes a whole network of public, community engagement that was once part of the routine of childhood. We rent videos instead of going to the movies, we buy books instead of going to the library, in Canada many families go to cottages instead of public parks in the summer.[12] The school-yard conversations with other parents are eliminated if baby-sitters pick up the kids or they go directly into day care. In general, the opportunities for unplanned, but routine, encounters with other parents become very limited.

One of the consequences I think is that I and many middle-class mothers do their mothering without a "community of judgment" in which to ground the daily decision making of motherhood. The term *community of judgment* is derived from Hannah Arendt's argument that when we judge, we do so by imagining how others in our judging community would judge. We compare our initial approach with those of multiple others, and in forming our judgment we imagine persuading them. It is this relation to the judgment of others that gives judging its distinctive nature as fully subjective and yet "valid" for the judging community. As I interpret this insight, we can only engage in the process of judgment if we are routinely engaged in conversation with members of our community. The part of the process that draws on imagination can only work if it is based on the experience of actual exchange.[13]

The 1970s critiques of the nuclear family often focused on the isolation of mothers within the private realm of the family. While this was surely an important problem, I think it too narrowly construed the forms of "public" life. Mothers who met regularly in the playground or for coffee must have formed judgment communities of mothering. Even if the histories of consciousness-raising groups show that the playground forums were not sufficient for women to form considered judgments about their marriages and the division of labor in the home, or the conventional public–private divide of home and "work," I think they must have enabled women to compare their experiences of childrearing. The judgments they had to make, that all mothers make all the time, about how to handle the challenges of raising their children, could be made in the context of ongoing exchange of information.[14] The casual forums in which this exchange took place formed an important kind of public space, the basis for a judgment community of mothering.

Ironically, the important public dimension that my academic career brings me has worked to exclude me from the public spaces of motherhood. (Or to be fair, my adaptation to the competing demands excludes me.) Whenever I do manage to hang out for a while in the school yard, I not only enjoy the company of other mothers, I often learn important things about how others are making choices about schools, teachers, after-school activities, discipline, sibling conflict, etc. But even knowing that, I usually feel the press of other demands and either don't go or hurry home.

There is another dimension of the privatization of modern professional life that undermines the creation of judgment communities that feminist mothers (and probably all women) need. A simple way to capture it is to say that psychotherapy has replaced consciousness-raising groups.[15] I have found that my own behavior is characteristic of that of many of my female colleagues: When the constant struggle to balance family and work collapses into crises such as divorce, acute anxiety, or disabling work patterns we go to see a therapist. We share our experience, if at all, with a close friend, but not with friendly colleagues. While I think a trained therapist is important for many kinds of problems,[16] the reciprocal obligations of friendship create bonds of community as well as the knowledge we need of each other's experiences. When therapy replaces mutual exchange, we buy a kind of time at the cost of connection: We deal with our problems without having to listen to those of others.[17] As a result, we each experience our struggles as if they were exclusively a private problem, requiring a private solution. We cannot see their systemic character because we never share our experiences.[18] It is as though the basic lessons of consciousness raising have been lost; we cannot see how the personal is embedded in the political.

I do not think organized consciousness-raising groups are necessarily the solution. I have in mind a shift in norms about what we talk about with our female colleagues. All of the issues I have discussed here, from genetic testing to taking time for school-yard exchange, could be transformed if there were ongoing conversations about these issues. We need to be able to situate the dilemmas of motherhood in their social context through engagement that is regular and sustained enough to create communities of judgment for ourselves. The consciousness-raising groups of the 1970s created alternative communities of judgment that, by developing a different frame of reference, literally changed how women saw and experienced their lives. They also pointed to structural change that was necessary. If we could create new norms of exchange, perhaps we could see some of the intractable dilemmas in a different way. We could think more creatively about individual solutions, as well as seeing the systemic forces that need to be changed. Perhaps the hope of fostering new norms will finally induce me to participate in hallway conversations again.

This story of isolation does have a counterpart. My children have also been an important path into community for me. I moved to Toronto twelve years ago, when I was thirty-six. Prior to that I had not lived in the same city longer than six years since I had left home to go to college when I was seventeen. I never really felt part of a neighborhood or a community. In a way I have felt that I have had to create my identity as teacher-scholar-mother-wife without a model, and without a clear sense of how this identity-in-process fits into any of the institutions I am a part of. Although I found in the University of Toronto an institution I am very happy with, I never feel a simple, clear sense of belonging. I feel respected and sometimes appreciated, but also somewhat marginal. Of course my strategy of isolation and my appointment to three different departments[19] contribute to this, but I think there is some deeper sense that the life I am trying to create does not fit neatly into the established professional norms.

But I am finally beginning to feel at home, to feel part of communities that I have found because of my children. Before they were born, I followed my spiritual path largely by myself. I then came to feel strongly that I wanted to find a way of including them. Against all my expectations (having not been raised going to church), I found a small church that has become a core community I belong to. I was motivated to find it for my kids and I chose it initially because it was so welcoming to children, but now it is one of the most important parts of my life. Co-organizing the children's programs was the first form of community work I took up after the boys were born.

I have also come to feel part of the community at their public school, despite the limited time I spend in the playground or volunteering. I know the other mothers who are active in the school (few of whom work full time), and the school is another place where I feel at home. (I enjoy my identity as "mother" there.) The school and the boys' friends there have, in turn, been a path into a neighborhood. At the cost of seemingly endless disruption and disorder, we moved to a house on a family-oriented block close to the boys' school and friends. Now not only do they enjoy a rare urban freedom to go out by themselves, but Joe and I know lots of our neighbors and enjoy increasing casual social contact. (I seem to be trying to replicate a childhood pattern again. I grew up in Hyde Park on the south side of Chicago on a block where children ran free, secure in the sense of attentive, caring neighbors. My parents' friends in the neighborhood were a far more important source of community than my relatives, whom I rarely saw.)

My relationship to the larger world is yet one more dimension to the complexities of connection, engagement, and isolation. Once I had my children, I felt a kind of empathy with other mothers in the world that seemed new to me. Often when I had to get up in the night with a sick child, I would sit rocking him, comforting him, settling him back to sleep, and tears would come to my eyes for all the mothers around the world who did not have what they needed—food, medicine, safe shelter—to comfort their children. I have felt a kind of urgency about the importance of providing women with what they need to care for and enjoy their children. I experienced the stories of war abroad and the casual cruelty of North American "welfare" systems in a different, more immediate, more impassioned way.

The irony is that while my affective relation to the world increased in intensity when my children were little, I also felt a strong inward turning, away from active involvement in things outside my home. Those years were the least politically active for me since adolescence. I felt the need for changes in the world more keenly and did less to promote them than ever before. And as my bonds with my children shift, as they become less all consuming and more complicated, I find I experience that sharp pain of the unmet needs of women and children less frequently. It is as though the special capacity I had to connect to my babies provided a kind of connection to people I have never met. Both of those forms of connection have changed. But now I find myself willing and able to go to demonstrations over funding cuts to education and social services, to write a maternity leave policy for my law faculty, and generally to take small steps of action in the world. The issues that rouse me to action remain those that especially affect women and children. I think there is a lot to be explored about this shifting dynamic. For example, I think that what I experienced as a new kind of empathy is an important indication of the ways in which "generalization" can take place in very different ways. I had a long-standing concern with the inequalities that forced many to live in poverty. But my experience of concern for the particular plight of mothers who could not give their children what they needed had a very different quality to it. It was a sort of generalization from my experience, but it did not feel abstract even though there was no actual, particular mother I had in mind. The question remains what difference this form of concern and connection makes for political action.[20]

And that, of course, is the dilemma I want to point to. The kind of life I wanted with my children and my work precluded active political involvement for years. The sense of the tension between my passionate attachment to my children and my incapacity to help other mothers and children enjoy what I had seemed a real problem. It was one factor in my acquiescence in the decision not to have a third child. Not only would a third child (which I longed for) exacerbate my ongoing struggle to find enough time for the things that seemed essential to my personal life. A third child would mean I would have that much less time to fulfill my responsibilities to the wider world.

But despite this unease, I think my choices may reflect a pattern that should be respected. As we think about what optimal forms of democratic participation would look like, and try to ensure an equal role for women, I think it is important to recognize that participation may vary with different stages of life. The inward turning that I felt when my children were under six seems valuable to me. Optimal institutions of work and of collective decision making would make space for such periods (which might arise at other times in life as well). There is, of course, the additional challenge of trying to ensure that this experience of intense bonding with young children, and the gifts of pleasure and insight it brings, is not restricted to women. I feel certain that this is a dimension of life that men should experience in order, among other things, to have the kind of information and insight they need to make good public policy.[21]

At the beginning of this essay I noted that expressions of the passionate joy of mothering were missing from my experience of feminism in the 1970s. I think a large part of the reason must have been that for many women who had children and were active feminists, the joys of their children were bound up with anger and pain over having to do all the work of childrearing without help or recognition. My own joys are centrally shaped by sharing the work, the joy, the anxiety with Joe. The joys of mothering are powerful, elemental, and yet fragile. They can so easily be overwhelmed by unmet needs, fear, anxiety, and simple exhaustion. Even in the affluence of the United

States and Canada, the structures of support for mothers are so poor that the passion they feel for their children is often a source of pain rather than joy. When I proclaim the joys of mothering, I want to make sure that my views cannot be construed as grounds for arguing that women should do the work of childrearing cheerfully and stop complaining if men miss out. The same holds true for the special satisfactions and significance of physical caretaking. I doubt that it is possible for caretaking, of children or of the material world, to be fully valued when it is organized around a gendered division of labor. And until it is properly valued, it will not be adequately supported (or compensated). And, in any case, a gendered division of labor would deprive men of knowledge and experience crucial to human flourishing as well as to informed policymaking. My joys, and the range of options I get to struggle with, are possible because in my own household we have largely transcended the traditional division of labor.

I want my story to be read as one of joy and of pain, each framing the other. The pain of compromise, contradiction, and isolation forms the context of my life, but I suppress it much of the time. On a daily basis I experience immense joy, satisfaction, and gratitude for my extraordinary good fortune. I love my life in my nuclear family. Amidst the usual family squabbles, and more than the usual disorder, we all take an enormous amount of pleasure in each other's company. I love being with Joe and watching my boys grow and thrive. They are wonderful brothers to each other and a joy to play with, to read to, to be with. I also experience a constant sense of struggle amid competing pulls, but almost all of the things that claim my time are things I care about and enjoy doing. I never forget the good fortune, and the privilege, that makes that possible, even when I am not in touch with the pain of the dilemmas.

What would it take to sustain the joy and satisfaction, to make them available to all, and to dissolve the dilemmas they are embedded in? Of course a full answer would require a sketch of a utopia and the means to get there. What I offer instead, by way of conclusion, is the links between the threads that run through this reflection: silence and isolation reinforcing one another, both fostered by the increasing pace of professional life. These threads at least point in the direction of solutions.

Silence was a central part of my story about my feelings of sadness around genetic testing, and of the gradual muting of the way I talk about the joy of my children. I have never had a fully open conversation with other mothers about my feelings about the inequities and denigration of caretaking that are part of my child-care arrangements.[22] In all these cases I think the silence arises out of anxiety over imperfect solutions to intractable problems and out of fear and anxiety about difference.

It is hard to talk about practices that do not seem fully defensible. But the dilemmas of motherhood are genuine dilemmas because there are no fully adequate solutions to them available. We cannot see the possibilities for change, if we do not talk openly about how we experience our dilemmas and how we feel about the imperfect solutions we have arrived at.

Similarly, it is hard to talk about feelings we have not fully acknowledged to ourselves or sorted through. I think here about genetic testing and the pain many women feel about being apart from their children. I think also about the role of status and money in the choices I make about how much time I spend on professional work and how much on family. But, of course, unless we talk about these issues with others, we cannot understand them. And if we only talk about them with therapists, we cannot create the collective knowledge we need.

These difficulties and anxieties are compounded by the fear that our feelings will not be shared by others. We may fear both censure and causing pain when others feel differently, make different choices. For example, in singing out the joys of the time I spend with my children, I fear the pain of those who are faced with choices I am not: Work long hours or lose your job or hope of promotion. And I fear the pain and anger of women who are not in the professions and do not have any of the options I have discussed. Because the structure of work and societal inequities have generated such imperfect solutions to child care, the subject is fraught for most women. It is hard to have an open conversation when there is such a high possibility of causing pain, anger, or disapproval. Finally, I think women avoid talking about their pain and struggles with colleagues for fear of appearing weak, inadequate, incompetent. If their experiences are not shared, their vulnerability may be dangerous as well as painful.

But the silence isolates us. It makes it impossible for us to know what we need to know either to make our own immediate (imperfect) choices or to figure out how to change things. Communities of judgment cannot emerge from silence. And the isolation and privatization of contemporary professional life make it harder to break the silence. (Ironically, if more workplaces provided the flexibility of academic life, it might increase the isolation even as it made possible better connection with family.)

All solutions to the mutually reinforcing silence and isolation take time. And this means finding time in lives already strained by the impossibility of achieving a healthy balance given the escalating demands. I am certain that the strain is exacerbated by the isolation, the lack of the energy that comes from connection around shared concerns. But on a day-to-day basis, I find it extremely hard to choose to take the time for the quasi-public connection that I think is required.[23] The increasing pace of professional life exacerbates the existing problems and makes it harder to grasp even the short-term available solutions of better connection among women.

But it is this solution, the connection of open dialogue, the constitution of new forms of community, that seems the best hope for understanding and coping with existing dilemmas and for their ultimate transformation.

1. I can't resist naming two. 1. It is the nature of living things to change. The search for stability is illusory if it is understood as stasis. No solutions last because the problems transform. 2. Life is characterized by difference. When I observed how surprised I was that my pregnancies were not the same, and the ongoing amazement I felt over the differences between my two boys, I realized that I had somehow absorbed a sort of social science expectation that the particulars within general categories would be the same.

2. Ursula Le Guin has a beautiful story that circles around the theme of the particularity of "this" baby, "this" child: "Half Past Four," *The New Yorker* (28 September 1987), 34–56.

3. See Virginia Held on the "contractual paradigm" in *Feminist Ethics: Transforming Culture, Society and Politics* (Chicago: University of Chicago Press, 1993), chapter 10.

4. On the basis of a small sample of anecdotal evidence, I think that men often fail to learn this lesson. Because they don't know how to tune in to their preverbal children, they spend their time with them "babysitting" with the TV or radio on or a newspaper close to hand. This rather boring and distracting form of interaction then reinforces the sense that there is nothing very interesting or compelling about caring for very young children.

5. I just heard a young colleague say that she also had envisioned having time on her hands when she had her first baby. This confirms my sense that at least women academics do not talk to each other enough about the terrible stress of the chaos and disorientation of having a baby.

6. The title story in Jane Smiley's *Age of Grief* offers a moving picture of the intense, physical bond a father forms with his children through his daily engagment with their care (New York: Ivy Books by Ballantine Books, 1987; see especially 164, 168–169).

7. I believe that exceptions, like gardening, are popular because they provide the relatively affluent with a rare experience of the satisfaction of physical caretaking. And the status of gardening as a respectable hobby doesn't threaten the rule that the successful hire others to do their caretaking for them. Their time can still be claimed as too important for mundane work.

8. My life at the cottage is a cherished exception to almost all of the patterns I describe here. For two

months we hire no help with child care or physical caretaking (except construction). I enjoy cooking in a way I never do during the year, I see neighbors on a regular, casual basis. Last summer I had a balance in my life amidst natural beauty that left me grief-stricken at returning to my Toronto work routine. I did not, however, get the writing done that I wanted to. I am hoping that greater discipline will solve that problem this year.

9. Sara Ruddick and Pamela Daniels, eds., *Working It Out: 23 Women Writers, Artists, Scientists, and Scholars Talk About Their Lives and Work* (New York: Pantheon Books, 1977).

10. I wrote about this fear and the transformation Michael brought in the preface to my book, *Private Property and the Limitations of American Constitutionalism* (Chicago: University of Chicago Press, 1990). I wanted readers to know about my struggle and Michael's role in making the book possible.

11. My academic brother follows this pattern as well.

12. I owe this insight to Francis Coombs, Minister, Bathurst Street United Church, Toronto, Ontario.

13. "Embodied Diversity: Challenges to Law," *McGill Law Review* 42 (1997): 91.

14. Of course, like all cases of judging communities, problems of conformity with dominant norms arise.

15. Leslie Thielen Wilson, "Agency and the Feminist Therapization of the Oppressed," delivered at Women in Philosophy Annual Meeting, Dalhousie University, September 1997.

16. Working with therapists has certainly been important to me.

17. I want to thank Julia Hanigsberg for this point.

18. Even though a good therapist can point out the systemic connections, I do not believe that builds the same kind of collective knowledge as exchanging experiences with other women.

19. The Faculty of Law, Political Science Department and Women's Studies program.

20. Jean Elshtain at the University of Chicago is working on research that will illuminate this issue.

21. I am less certain about the difference that pregnancy and nursing make to the formation of these bonds.

22. I haven't even mentioned in this essay the strain that pregnancy and infancy put on marriages, another subject where the pervasive silence is destructive.

23. My argument here finally impelled me to take an afternoon off the final editing to attend a symposium for women faculty and librarians on balancing work and family. I learned a lot (about the virtues of day care among other things) and made plans with some other senior faculty about how we could make our voices heard more effectively.

Bibliography

Abramovitz, Mimi. *Regulating the Lives of Women*. Boston: South End Press, 1988.

Adams, Christine. "Mothers Who Fail to Protect Their Children from Sexual Abuse: Addressing the Problem of Denial." *Yale Law and Policy Review* 12 (1994): 519.

Alvarez, Lizette. "Mother of Girl Missing a Year Won't Face Murder Charges." *New York Times* (24 February 1997): B3.

Amadio, Carol, and Stuart L. Deutsch. "Open Adoption: Allowing Adopted Children to 'Stay in Touch' with Blood Relatives." *Journal of Family Law* 22 (1983–84): 59.

American Academy of Pediatrics, Committee on Substance Abuse. "Drug Exposed Infants." *Pediatrics* 86 (1990): 639.

Amott, Theresa. "Black Women and AFDC: Making Entitlement Out of Necessity." In *Women, the State, and Welfare*. Edited by L. Gordon. Madison: University of Wisconsin Press, 1990.

Anderson, Herbert. "Between Rhetoric and Reality: Women and Men as Equal Partners in Home, Church and the Marketplace." *Word and World* 17, no. 4 (Fall 1997): 376–386.

Anderson, Herbert, and Susan B. W. Johnson. *Regarding Children: A New Respect for Childhood and Families*. Louisville, Ky.: Westminster Press/John Knox Press, 1994.

Andolsen, Barbara Hilkert. "Agape in Feminist Ethics." *Journal of Religious Ethics* 9 (Spring 1981): 69–83.

"APALC Responds to Welfare Changes," *Asian Pacific American Legal Center News* 14, no. 4 (Winter 1997): 1, 5.

Applegate, Jeffrey Scott. "Beyond the Dyad: Including the Father in Separation-Individuation." *Child and Adolescent Social Work* 4 (1987): 92.

Ashe, Marie. "The 'Bad Mother' in Law and Literature: A Problem of Representation." *Hastings Women's Law Journal* (1992).

Ashe, Marie, and Naomi R. Cahn. "Child Abuse: A Problem for Feminist Theory." In *The Public Nature of Private Violence*. Edited by Martha A. Fineman and Roxanne Mykitiuk. New York: Routledge, 1994. First published in *Texas Journal of Women and the Law* 2, no. 1 (1993): 75–112.

Austin, Carol. "Latent Tendencies and Covert Acts." In *The Adoption Reader: Birth Mothers, Adoptive Mothers, and Adopted Daughters Tell Their Stories*. Edited by Susan Wadia-Ellis. Seattle: Seal Press, 1995.

Ayalon, Ofra. "The Daughter as a Sexual Victim in the Family." In *Child Abuse*. Edited by Amnon Carmi and Hanita Zamrin. Berlin, N.Y.: Springer-Verlag, 1984.

Badinter, Elisabeth. *Mother-Love Myth and Reality: Motherhood in Modern History*. New York: Macmillan, 1981.

Balsh, David. *Let Wives Be Submissive: The Domestic Code in 1 Peter.* Atlanta: Scholars Press, 1981.

Banks, Rae, and Assata Zerai. "Maternal Drug Abuse and Infant Health: A Proposal for a Multilevel Model." In *African-American and the Public Agenda: The Paradoxes of Public Policy.* Edited by Sedrick Herring. Newbury Park, Calif.: Sage, 1997.

Bartlett, Katharine. "Rethinking Parenthood as an Exclusive Status: The Need for Legal Alternatives When the Premise of the Nuclear Family Has Failed." *Virginia Law Review* 17 (1984): 879.

———. "Re-Expressing Parenthood." *Yale Law Journal* 98 (1988): 293.

Bassin, Donna, Margaret Honey, and Meryle Mahrer Kaplan, eds. "Introduction." In *Representations of Motherhood.* New Haven and London: Yale University Press, 1994.

Beauvoir, Simone de. *The Second Sex.* New York: Alfred A. Knopf, 1961.

———. "Sex, Society, and the Female Dilemma." *Saturday Review* (14 June 1975): 18.

Becker, Mary. "Maternal Feelings: Myth, Taboo, and Child Custody." *Review of Law and Women's Studies* 1 (1992): 133–222.

Belfiore, Constance. "The Case for Becoming a Full-time Parent." *Washington Lawyer* (May/ June 1988): 46.

Bell-Scott, Patricia, et al., eds. *Double Stitch: Black Women Write About Mothers and Daughters.* Boston: Beacon Press, 1991.

Benjamin, Jessica. *The Bonds of Love.* (New York: Pantheon Books, 1988).

———. "The Omnipotent Mother." In *Representations of Motherhood.* Edited by Donna Bassin, Margaret Honey, and Meryle Mahrer Kaplan. New Haven and London: Yale University Press, 1994.

———. *Like Objects, Love Objects: Essays on Recognition and Sexual Difference.* New Haven, Conn.: Yale University Press, 1995.

Benson, Paul. "Feminist Second Thoughts About Free Agency." *Hypatia* 5, no. 3 (Fall 1990): 47–64.

Bernstein, Fred A. "This Child Does Have Two Mothers . . . and a Sperm Donor with Visitation." *New York University Review of Law and Social Change* 22 (1996): 1–58.

Bérubé, Michael. *Life as We Know It: A Father, a Family, and an Exceptional Child.* New York: Random House, 1996.

Beyer, Margaret, and Wallace Mlyniec. "Lifelines to Biological Parents: Their Effect on Termination of Parental Rights and Permanence." *American Law Quarterly* 20 (1986): 233.

Biel, Steven. *Down with the Old Canoe: A Cultural History of the Titanic Disaster.* New York: W. W. Norton, 1996.

Blume, Sheila B. "Sexuality and Stigma: The Alcoholic Woman." *Alcohol, Health and Research World* 15, no. 2 (1991): 139–146.

Bly, Robert. *Iron John: A Book About Men.* Reading, Mass.: Addison-Wesley, 1990.

Bonacich, Edna. "Asians in the Los Angeles Garment Industry." In *The New Asian Immigration in Los Angeles and Global Restructuring.* Edited by Paul Ong, Edna Bonacich, and Lucie Cheng. Philadelphia: Temple University Press, 1994.

Bonavoglia, Angela. "The Ordeal of Pamela Rae Stewart." *Ms.* (August 1987).

Boswell, John. *The Kindness of Strangers: The Abandonment of Children in Western Europe from Late Antiquity to the Renaissance.* New York: Pantheon Books, 1988.

Bowker, Lee H., et al. "On the Relationship Between Wife Beating and Child Abuse." In *Feminist Perspectives on Wife Abuse.* Edited by Kersti Yllo and Michele Bograd. Newbury Park, Calif.: Sage, 1988.

Bowlby, John. *Maternal Care and Mental Health.* New York: Schocken Books, 1966.

———. *Attachment and Loss,* vol. 1, *Attachment.* New York: Basic Books, 1973.

———. *Attachment and Loss,* vol. 2, *Separation.* New York: Basic Books, 1973.

Bray, James H. "Psychosocial Factors Affecting Custodial and Visitation Arrangements." *Behavioral Sciences and the Law* 9 (1991): 419.

Bright, Bill, et al. *Seven Promises of a Promise Keeper.* Colorado Springs, Colo.: Focus on the Family, 1994.

Bruner, Jerome. *Actual Minds, Possible Worlds.* Cambridge, Mass.: Harvard University Press, 1986.

Buber, Martin. *Tales of the Hasidim: Later Masters.* New York: Schocken Books, 1948.

Cahill, Lisa Sowle. *Sex, Gender and Christian Ethics.* New York: Cambridge University Press, 1996.

Cahn, Naomi R. "Civil Images of Battered Women: The Impact of Domestic Violence on Child Custody Decisions." *Vanderbilt Law Review* 44 (1991): 1041–1057.

Calhoun, Cheshire. "Family's Outlaws: Rethinking the Connections Between Feminism, Lesbianism, and the Family." In *Feminism and Families.* Edited by Hilde Lindemann Nelson. New York: Routledge, 1997.

Callahan, Sidney. "Gays, Lesbians, and the Use of Alternative Reproductive Technologies." In *Feminism and Families.* Edited by Hilde Lindemann Nelson. New York: Routledge, 1997.

Caplane, Ronnie. "Choosing Domesticity over Depositions." *Legal Times* (3 April 1995): 54.

Card, Claudia. "Caring and Evil." *Hypatia* 5, no. 1 (1990): 101–108.

Carr, Anne, and Elisabeth Schüssler Fiorenza, eds. *Concilium: Motherhood: Experience, Institution, Theology.* Edinburgh: T. & T. Clark, 1989.

Carse, Alisa L., and Hilde Lindemann Nelson. "Rehabilitating Care." *Kennedy Institute of Ethics Journal* 6, no. 1 (1996): 19–35.

Carter, Warren. *Households and Discipleship: A Study of Matthew.* Sheffield, England: Sheffield Academic Press, 1994.

"Case of Culture Clash; Actions of Mexican Couple Under Fire in U.S." *Austin American-Statesman* (19 February 1996): B2.

Caspi, Mishael Maswari, and Sascha Benjamin Cohen. *The Binding of (AQEDAH) and Its Transformations in Judaism and Islam: The Lamps of God.* Lewiston, N.Y.: Mellen Biblical Press, 1995.

Center on Addiction and Substance Abuse at Columbia University *Annual Report*, 1994.

Center on Addiction and Substance Abuse at Columbia University *Substance Abuse and the American Woman*, 1997.

"Charges Dismissed Against Dad of 14-Year-Old's Son." *Austin American-Statesman* (18 June 1996): B3.

Charles, Grant, and Jane Matheson. "Children in Foster Care: Issues of Separation and Attachment." *Community Alternatives* 2 (1990): 37.

Chase-Lansdle, P. Lindsay, and Mavis Hetherington. "The Impact of Divorce on Life-Span Development: Short and Long Term Effects." In *Life Span Development and Behavior*, vol. 10. Edited by David L. Featherman and Richard M. Lerner. Hillsdale, N.J.: Lawrence Erlbaum, 1990.

Chavkin, Wendy. "Drug Addiction and Pregnancy: Policy Crossroads." *American Journal of Public Health* 80, no. 4 (April 1990): 483–487.

Chira, Susan. *A Mother's Place: Taking the Debate About Working Mothers Beyond Guilt and Blame.* New York: HarperCollins, 1998.

Chodorow, Nancy. *The Reproduction of Mothering: Psychoanalysis and the Sociology of Gender.* Berkeley and Los Angeles: University of California Press, 1978.

Chodorow, Nancy, and Susan Contratto. "The Fantasy of the Perfect Mother." In *Rethinking the Family: Some Feminist Questions*, rev. ed. Edited by Barrie Thorne. Boston: Northeastern University Press, 1992.

"The Christian Coalition: Who Are They?" *San Antonio Express-News* (11 November 1995): sec. 10A.

Clinton, Hillary Rodham. *It Takes a Village: And Other Lessons Children Teach Us.* New York: Simon and Schuster, 1996.

Coakley, Tom. "Christian Science Couple's Conviction in Death Overruled." *Boston Globe* (12 August 1993): 1.

Cohen, Cynthia P., and Howard A. Davidson, eds. *Children's Rights in America: U.N. Convention on the Rights of the Child Compared with United States Law.* Chicago: American Bar Association Center on Children and the Law, 1990.

Cohen, David. *Law, Sexuality, and Society.* Cambridge: Cambridge University Press, 1991.

Collins, Patricia Hill. *The Meaning of Motherhood in Black Culture and Black Mother / Daughter Relationships.* Newbury Park, Calif.: Sage, 1987.

———. *Black Feminist Thought.* New York: Routledge, 1990.

———. "Shifting the Center: Race, Class, and Feminist Theorizing About Motherhood." In *Mothering: Ideology, Experience, and Agency.* New York: Routledge, 1994.

Committee on the Family Group for the Advancement of Psychiatry. *Divorce, Child Custody and the Family.* New York: Mental Health Materials Center, 1980.

136 Congressional Record S14416–11417. (Daily ed. October 3, 1990).

Cooey, Paula. *Family, Freedom & Faith: Building Community Today.* Louisville, Ky.: Westminster Press/John Knox Press, 1996.

———. "Bad Women: The Limitations of Theory and Theology." In *Differing Horizons: Essays on Feminist Theory and Theology.* Edited by Rebecca Chopp and Sheila Davaney. Philadelphia: Fortress Press, 1997.

Cook, Lawrence W. "Open Adoption: Can Visitation with Natural Family Members Be in the Child's Best Interest?" *Journal of Family Law* 30 (1991–92): 471.

Coontz, Stephanie. *The Social Origins of Private Life: A History of American Families, 1600–1900.* New York: Verso, 1988.

———. *The Way We Never Were: American Families and the Nostalgia Trap.* New York: Basic Books, 1992.

Couture, Pam. "The Use and Misuse of Ideals of Marriage and Families." Delivered at the Religion and the American Family Debate Conference, September 1996, Chicago. Partly incorporated into chapter 3 of *From Culture Wars to Common Ground: Religion and the American Family Debate* (Louisville, Ky.: Westminster Press/John Knox Press, 1997).

Cranston, Maurice. *Jean-Jacques: The Early Life and Work of Jean-Jacques Rousseau, 1712–1754.* Chicago: University of Chicago Press, 1982.

———. *The Solitary Self: Jean-Jacques Rousseau in Exile and Adversity, 1763–1778.* Chicago: University of Chicago Press, 1997.

Crenshaw, Kimberlé W. "Mapping the Margins: Intersectionality, Identity Politics, and Violence Against Women of Color." In *The Public Nature of Private Violence.* Edited by Martha A. Fineman and Roxanne Mykitiuk. New York: Routledge, 1994.

Cugna, Catherine La. *God for Us: The Trinity and Christian Life.* New York: Harper, 1991.

Dale, Suzanne. "Born on Crack and Coping with Kindergarten." *New York Times* (7 February 1991): A1.

Dallas Morning News (11 August 1996): 1J.

Daniel, E. Valentine. *Charred Lullabies: Chapters in an Anthropology of Violence.* Princeton, N.J.: Princeton University Press, 1996.

Darling, Rosalyn Benjamin. *Families Against Society: A Study of Reactions to Children with Birth Defects.* Beverly Hills, Calif.: Sage, 1979.

———. "Parent-Professional Interaction: The Roots of Misunderstanding." In *The Family with a Handicapped Child: Understanding and Treatment.* Edited by M. Seligman. New York: Grune and Stratton, 1983.

———. "Parental Entrepreneurship: A Consumerist Response to Professional Dominance." *Journal of Social Issues* 44, no. 1 (1988): 141–158.

Davidson, Howard A. "Child Abuse and Domestic Violence: Legal Connections and Controversies." *Family Law Quarterly* 29 (1995): 357, 362.

Davis, Kingsley. "Wives and Work: A Theory of the Sex-Role Revolution and Its Consequences." In *Feminism, Children, and the New Families*. Edited by Sanford M. Dornbusch and Myra H. Strober. New York: Guilford Press, 1988.

Davis, Peggy C. "Use and Abuse of the Power to Sever Family Bonds." *N.Y.U. Review of Law and Social Change* 12 (1984): 562.

DeCelle, Douglas. "Among the Promise Keepers: A Pastor's Reflections." *Christian Century* 113, no. 21 (3–10 July 1996): 695–697.

DiFranza, Joseph R., and Robert A. Lew. "Effect of Maternal Cigarette Smoking on Pregnancy Complications and Sudden Death Syndrome." *Journal of Family Practice* 40 (1995): 385.

Dinnerstein, Dorothy. *The Mermaid and the Minotaur*. New York: Harper and Row, 1977.

Doane, Janice, and Devon Hodges. *From Klein to Kristeva: Psychoanalytic Feminism and the Search for the "Good Enough" Mother*. Ann Arbor: University of Michigan Press, 1992.

Dohrn, Bernardine. "Bad Mothers, Good Mothers, and the State: Children at the Margins." *University of Chicago Law School Roundtable* 2 (1995): 1–8.

Donovan, Patricia. "Can Statutory Rape Laws Be Effective in Preventing Adolescent Pregnancy?" *Family Planning Perspectives* 29, no. 1 (January / February 1997).

Dore, Martha Morrison, and Eleanor Eisner. "Child-Related Dimensions of Placement Stability in Treatment Foster Care." *Child and Adolescent Social Work Journal* 10 (1993): 301.

Doyle, Roddy. *The Woman Who Walked into Doors*. New York: Viking, 1996.

Dubler, Ariela R. "Monitoring Motherhood." *Yale Law Journal* 106 (1996): 935.

Due, Linnea. *Joining the Tribe: Growing Up Gay and Lesbian in the 90s*. New York: Doubleday, 1996.

Dugger, Celia W. "Litany of Signals Overlooked in Child's Death." *New York Times* (29 December 1992): A1.

Dusky, Lorraine. *Birthmark*. New York: M. Evans, 1979.

———. "The Daughter I Gave Away." *Newsweek* (30 March 1992).

Eagle, Rita S. "Airplanes Crash, Spaceships Stay in Orbit: The Separation Experience of a Child 'In Care.'" *Journal of Psychotherapy Practice and Research* 2 (1993): 318. Also in *Clinical and Research Reports* 2 (1993).

Easterbrooks, Ann, Cherilyn E. Davidson, and Rachel Chazan. "Psychosocial Risk, Attachment, and Behavior Problems Among School-Aged Children." *Development and Psychopathology* 5 (1993): 389.

Eaton, John P., and Charles A. Haas. *Titanic: Destination Disaster, The Legends and the Reality*. New York: W. W. Norton, 1996.

Edin, Kathryn, and Laura Lein. "Work, Welfare and Single Mothers' Economic Strategies." *American Sociological Review* 62 (1997): 253–263.

Eggebeen, David, and Alan J. Hawkins. "Economic Need and Wives' Employment." *Journal of Family Issues* 11 (1990): 48–49.

Eisenstein, Zillah R. *The Female Body and the Law.* Berkeley and Los Angeles: University of California Press, 1988.

Ellwood, David. *Poor Support.* New York: Basic Books, 1988.

Elshtain, Jean Bethke, et al. "A Communitarian Position on the Family." *National Civic Review* 82, no. 1 (Winter 1993): 25–35.

"Embodied Diversity: Challenges to Law." *McGill Law Review* 42 (1997): 91.

Engels, Friedrich. "On the History of Early Christianity." In *Marx and Engels: Basic Writings on Politics and Philosophy.* Edited by Lewis S. Feuer. Garden City, N.Y.: Doubleday, 1959.

English, Bella. "No Excuses for Child Abuse." *Boston Globe* (30 November 1992): 13.

Erdrich, Louise. *Love Medicine.* New York: Harper-Perennial, 1984, 1993.

Erickson, Nancy S. "Battered Mothers of Battered Children: Using Our Knowledge of Battered Women to Defend Them Against Charges of Failure to Act." In *Current Perspectives in Psychological, Legal and Ethical Issues: Children and Families: Abuse and Endangerment.* Edited by Sandra A. Garcia and Robert Batey. London: Kingsley, 1991.

Etzioni, Amitai. *The Spirit of Community: Rights, Responsibilities, and the Communitarian Agenda.* New York: Crown, 1993.

Everson, Mark, et al. "Maternal Support Following Disclosure of Incest." *American Journal of Orthopsychiatry* (April 1989): 197.

Eyer, Diane E. *Mother–Infant Bonding: A Scientific Fiction.* New Haven, Conn.: Yale University Press, 1992.

———. *Motherguilt: How Our Culture Blames Mothers for What's Wrong in Society.* New York: Times Books/Random House, 1996.

Fackre, Gabriel. "What the Lutherans and the Reformed Can Learn from One Another." *Christian Century* 114, no. 18 (4–11 June 1997): 558–561.

Farley, Wendy. *Eros for the Other: Retaining Truth in a Pluralistic World.* University Park: Pennsylvania State University Press, 1996.

"A Father Is Accused of Gluing Eyes Shut." *New York Times* (20 August 1995): 19.

Featherstone, Helen. *A Difference in the Family.* New York: Basic Books, 1980.

Felder, Raoul, and Barbara Victor. *Getting Away with Murder.* New York: Simon and Schuster, 1996.

Felner, Robert D., and Lisa Terre. "Child Custody Dispositions and Children's Adaptation Following Divorce." In *Psychology and Child Custody Determinations.* Edited by Lois A. Weithorn. Lincoln: University of Nebraska Press, 1987.

Ferguson, Philip M., and Adrienne Asch. "Lessons from Life: Personal and Parental Perspectives on School, Childhood, and Disability." In *Schooling and Disability—Eighty-Eighth Yearbook of the National Society for the Study of Education, Part II.* Edited by Kenneth J. Behage. Chicago: University of Chicago Press, 1989.

Fernandez, John P. *Child Care and Corporate Productivity: Resolving Family / Work Conflicts.* Lexington, Mass.: Lexington Books, 1986.

Fineman, Martha A. "Dominant Discourse, Professional Language, and Legal Change in Child Custody Decisionmaking." *Harvard Law Review* 101 (1988): 727, 767 n. 161.

———. *The Illusion of Equality: The Rhetoric and Reality of Divorce Reform.* Chicago: University of Chicago Press, 1991.

———. "Images of Mothers in Poverty Discourse." In *Mothers in Law: Feminist Theory and the Legal Regulation of Motherhood.* Edited by Martha A. Fineman and Isabel Karpin. New York: Columbia University Press, 1995.

———. *The Neutered Mother, The Sexual Family and Other Twentieth-Century Tragedies.* New York: Routledge, 1995.

Frank, Deborah A., and Barry S. Zuckerman. "Children Exposed to Cocaine Prenatally: Pieces of the Puzzle." *Neurotoxicology and Teratology* 15 (1993): 298–300.

Frank, Deborah A., Karen Breshahn, and Barry S. Zuckerman. "Maternal Cocaine Use: Impact on Child Health and Development." *Advances in Pediatrics* 40 (1993): 65–99.

Frankel, Ellen. *The Classic Tales: 4,000 Years of Jewish Lore.* Northvale, N.J.: Jason Aronson, 1993.

Fraser, Nancy. "Talking About Needs: Interpretive Contests as Political Conflicts in Welfare-State Societies." *Ethics* 99, no. 1 (January 1989): 291–313.

Freud, Sigmund. *Repression* (1915). In vol. 14 of *The Standard Edition of the Complete Psychological Works of Sigmund Freud.* Edited by James Strachey. New York: W. W. Norton, 1976.

———. *Civilization and Its Discontents.* New York: W. W. Norton [1930] 1962.

———. *The Future of an Illusion.* Garden City, N.Y.: Doubleday Anchor [1927] 1964.

———. "Female Sexuality." In *The Standard Edition of the Complete Psychological Works of Sigmund Freud.* Edited by James Strachey. New York: W. W. Norton, 1976.

Friedman, Lawrence. "Kohut: A Book Review Essay." *Psychoanalytic Quarterly* 49 (1980): 393–422.

Frye, Marilyn. *The Politics of Reality.* Trumansburg, N.Y.: Crossing Press, 1983.

Fuchs, Rachel G. *Abandoned Children: Foundlings and Child Welfare in Nineteenth-Century France.* Albany: State University of New York Press, 1984.

———. *Poor and Pregnant in Paris: Strategies for Survival in the Nineteenth Century.* New Brunswick, N.J.: Rutgers University Press, 1992.

Furstenberg, Frank F., Jr., S. Philip Morgan, and Paul D. Allison. "Paternal Participation and Children's Well-Being After Marital Dissolution." *American Sociological Review* 52 (1987): 695.

Furstenberg, Frank F., Jr., and Andrew J. Cherlin. *Divided Families: What Happens to Children When Parents Part.* Cambridge, Mass.: Harvard University Press, 1991.

Galston, William A. *Liberal Purposes: Goods, Virtues, and Diversity in the Liberal State.* New York: Cambridge University Press, 1991.

———. *Beyond the Murphy Brown Debate: Ideas for Family Policy.* New York: Institute for American Values, 1995.

———. "Needed: A Not-So-Fast Divorce Law." *New York Times* (27 December 1995).

Gambone, Philip. "The Kid I Already Have: On Considering Fathering a Child with a Lesbian." In *Sister and Brother: Lesbians and Gay Men Write About Their Lives Together.* Edited by Joan Nestle and John Preston. New York: HarperSanFrancisco, 1994.

Gelles, Richard J. *Family Violence.* Newbury Park, Calif.: Sage, 1987.

Gellmann, Jerome I. *The Fear, The Trembling, and the Fire: Kierkegaard and Hasidic Masters on the Binding of Isaac.* Lanham, Md.: University Press of America, 1994.

Geshan, Shelley. "A Step Toward Recovery, Improving Access to Substance Abuse Treatment for Pregnant and Parenting Women." *Southern Regional Project on Infant Mortality* (1993): 1.

Gillespie, Cynthia. *Justifiable Homicide.* Columbus: Ohio State University Press, 1988.

Ginzberg, Louis. *Legends of the Jews.* Translated by Henrietta Szold. Philadelphia: Jewish Publication Society of America, 1938.

Glendon, Mary Ann. *Rights Talk: The Impoverishment of Politics.* Cambridge, Mass.: Harvard University Press, 1991.

Glenn, Evelyn Nakano. *Issei, Nisei, War Bride: Three Generations of Japanese American Women in Domestic Service.* Philadelphia: Temple University Press, 1986.

Golden, Marita. "Why I Sent Him Away." *Washingtonian* (December 1993): 31–33.

Goldstein, Joseph, Anna Freud, and Albert J. Solnit. *Beyond the Best Interests of the Child.* New York: Free Press, 1973.

———. *Before the Best Interests of the Child.* New York: Free Press, 1979.

Goldstein, Valerie Saiving. "The Human Situation: A Feminine View." *Journal of Religion* (April 1960): 100–112. Reprinted in *Woman Spirit Rising*, edited by Carol Christ and Judith Plaskow, New York: Harper and Row, 1980.

Gomby, Deanna S., and Patricia H. Shiono. "Estimating the Number of Substance-Exposed Infants." *Future of Children* 1, no. 1 (Spring 1991): 17–25. Los Altos, California, Center for the Future of Children, The David and Lucile Packard Foundation.

Gomez, Laura E. *Misconceiving Mothers.* Philadelphia: Temple University Press, 1992.

Goodwin, Joanne L. *Gender and the Politics of Welfare Reform: Mothers' Pensions in Chicago, 1911–1929.* Chicago and London: University of Chicago Press, 1997.

Gordon, Linda. *Heroes of Their Own Lives: The Politics and History of Family Violence, Boston 1880–1960.* New York: Viking, 1988.

———. *Pitied But Not Entitled.* New York: Free Press, 1994.

Gordon, Linda, and Nancy Fraser. "Decoding 'Dependency': Inscriptions of Power in a Keyword of the U.S. Welfare State." In *Restructuring Political Theory: Feminist Perspectives*. Edited by Mary Lyndon Shanley and Uma Narayan. University Park: Pennsylvania State University, 1997.

Gordon, Mary. "The Good Mother." *New York Times Book Review* (28 April 1996): 7. Reviewing Roddy Doyle, *The Woman Who Walked into Doors*, New York: Viking, 1996.

Gould, Stephen J. "Carrie Buck's Daughter." *Natural History* (July 1984).

Gowans, Christopher W. *Innocence Lost: An Examination of Inescapable Moral Wrongdoing.* New York: Oxford University Press, 1994.

Green, Karen. *The Woman of Reason: Feminism, Humanism and Political Thought.* New York: Continuum, 1995.

Grey, Mike. *Drug Crazy.* New York: Random House, 1998.

Gross, Jane. "Confrontation in the Gulf: New Home Front Developing as Women Hear Call to Arms." *New York Times* (18 September 1990): A1.

Gudorf, Christine. "Parenting, Mutual Love and Sacrifice." In *Women's Consciousness, Women's Conscience: A Reader in Feminist Ethics*. Edited by Barbara Hilkert Andolsen, Christine E. Gudorf, and Mary D. Pelauer. San Francisco: Harper and Row, 1985.

Guggenheim, Martin. The Effects of Recent Trends to Accelerate the Termination of Parental Rights of Children in Foster Care—An Empirical Analysis in Two States. *Family Law Quarterly* 29, no. 121 (1995): 11, 13–14.

Hammer, Margaret L. *Giving-Birth: Reclaiming Biblical Metaphor for Pastoral Practice.* Louisville, Ky.: Westminster Press/John Knox Press, 1995.

Hanigsberg, Julia E. "Power and Procreation: State Interference in Pregnancy." *Ottawa Law Review* 23 (1991): 35.

———. "Homologizing Motherhood and Pregnancy: A Consideration of Abortion." *Michigan Law Review* 94 (1995): 371.

Harrison, Beverly. "The Power of Anger in the Work of Love: Christian Ethics for Woman and Strangers." *Union Seminary Quarterly Review* 36 (1981): 41–57.

Harrison, Kate. "Fresh or Frozen: Lesbian Mothers, Sperm Donors, and Limited Fathers." In *Mothers in Law: Feminist Theory and the Legal Regulation of Motherhood*. Edited by Martha A. Fineman and Isabel Karpin. New York: Columbia University Press, 1995.

Hartog, Hendrick. "The Constitution of Aspiration and the Rights That Belong to Us All." *Journal of American History* 74, no. 3 (December 1987): 1013.

Heath, Shirley Brice. *Ways with Words: Language, Life and Work in Communities and Classrooms.* Cambridge and New York: Cambridge University Press, 1983.

Hebblethwaite, Margaret. *Motherhood and God.* London: Geoffrey Chapman, 1984.

Held, Virginia. *Feminist Ethics: Transforming Culture, Society and Politics.* Chicago: University of Chicago Press, 1993.

Herlihy, David. *Medieval Households.* Cambridge, Mass.: University of Massachusetts, 1985.

Hetherington, E. Mavis. "Family Relations Six Years After Divorce." In *Remarriage and Step-Parenting, Current Research and Theory.* Edited by Kay Pasley and Marilyn Ihinger-Tallman. New York: Guilford Press, 1989.

Hewlett, Barry S. "Intimate Fathers: Patterns of Paternal Holding Among Aka Pygmies." In *The Father's Role: Cross-Cultural Perspectives.* Edited by Michael E. Lamb. Hillsdale, N.J.: Lawrence Erlbaum, 1987.

Hill, Amy. "Applying Harm Reduction to Services for Substance Using Women in Violent Relationships." *Harm Reduction Coalition* 6 (Spring 1998): 7–8.

Hill, Kate. "Mothers by Insemination: Interviews." In *Politics of the Heart: A Lesbian Parenting Anthology.* Edited by Sandra Pollack and Jeanne Vaughn. Ithaca, N.Y.: Firebrand Books, 1987.

Hite, Shere. *The Hite Report on the Family: Growing-Up Under Patriarchy.* New York: Grove Press, 1995.

Hoagland, Sarah. "Some Concerns About Nel Noddings' *Caring.*" *Hypatia* 5, no. 1 (1990): 109–114.

Hoffman, Jan. "Pregnant, Addicted and Guilty?" *New York Times Magazine* (19 August 1990): 53.

Hossfeld, Karen J. "Hiring Immigrant Women: Silicon Valley's 'Simple Formula.'" In *Women of Color in U.S. Society.* Edited by Maxine Baca Zinn and Bonnie Thornton Dill. Philadelphia: Temple University Press, 1994.

Hudson, Mike. "With Neglect Charge Behind Her, Mother Intent on Staying Clean." *Roanoke Times* (17 September 1991).

Ifill, Gwen. "Tenacity and Change in a Son of the South: William Jefferson Clinton." *New York Times* (16 July 1992): A1, A14.

Ikemoto, Lisa. "The Code of Perfect Pregnancy: At the Intersection of the Ideology of Motherhood, the Practice of Defaulting to Science, and the Interventionist Mindset of Law." *Ohio State Law Journal* 53 (1992): 1206–1306.

"Iraqi Accused of Forcing Teen Daughters to Marry." *San Antonio Express-News* (11 November 1996): 5A.

Irigaray, Luce. *I Love to You: Sketch of a Possible Felicity in History.* Translated by Alison Martin. New York: Routledge, 1996.

Jablow, Martha Moraghan. *Cara: Growing with a Mentally Retarded Child.* Philadelphia: Temple University Press, 1982.

Jamieson, Kathleen H. *Beyond the Double Bind: Women and Leadership.* New York: Oxford University Press, 1995.

Jetter, Alexis. "Mom Given 5–15 Years in Tot Death." *Newsday* (27 February 1990): 4.

Johnson, Elizabeth A. *She Who Is: The Mystery of God in Feminist Theological Discourse.* New York: Crossroad, 1992.

Jones, Charisse. "A Casualty of Deficit: Center for Addicts." *New York Times* (14 January 1996).

Jones, James W. *Religion and Psychology: Psychoanalysis, Feminism, and Theology.* New Haven, Conn.: Yale University Press, 1996.

Jos, Philip H., Marshall Jos, and Martin Perlmutter. "The Charleston Policy on Cocaine Use During Pregnancy: A Cautionary Tale." *Journal of Law Medicine and Ethics* 23 (1995): 120–128.

Kagan, Shelly. *The Limits of Morality.* Oxford: Clarendon Press, 1989.

Kamerman, Sheila, and Alfred J. Kahn. *Starting Right: How America Neglects Its Youngest Children and What We Can Do About It.* New York: Oxford University Press, 1995.

Kandall, Stephan R. *Substance and Shadow, Women and Addiction in the United States.* Cambridge, Mass.: Harvard University Press, 1996.

Kaplan, Morris. *Sexual Justice.* New York: Routledge, 1997.

Karst, Kenneth. "The Freedom of Intimate Association." *Yale Law Journal* 89, no. 4 (1980): 624–693.

Katz, Linda L. *An Overview of Current Clinical Issues in Separation and Placement. Child and Adolescent Social Work Journal* 4 (1987): 209, 219.

Kaufman, Brian Paul. "Promise Keepers Rallies Men to Commitment." *Christianity Today* (September 1992): 57.

Kelly, Virginia. *Leading with My Heart.* New York: Simon and Schuster, 1994.

Kermoin, Rosanne, and P. Herbert Leiderman. "Infant Attachment to Mother and Child Caretaker in an East African Community." *International Journal of Behavioural Development* 9 (1986): 455.

Kertzer, David I. *Sacrificed for Honor: Italian Infant Abandonment and the Politics of Reproductive Control.* Boston: Beacon Press, 1993.

Kierkegaard, Søren. *Fear and Trembling.* Translated by Alastair Hannay. London: Penguin Books, 1985.

Kittay, Eva Feder. "Dependency Work, Political Discourse and a New Basis for a Coalition Amongst Women." Lecture. *Women, Children and Poverty: Feminism and Legal Theory Workshop.* Columbia Law School and Barnard College Institute for Research on Women, 6 June 1995.

———. "Human Dependency and Rawlsian Equality." In *Feminists Rethink the Self.* Edited by D. T. Meyers. Boulder, Colo.: Westview Press, 1996.

———. *Love's Labor: Essays on Women, Equality and Dependency.* New York: Routledge, 1999.

Klein, Melanie. "The Oedipus Complex in the Light of Early Anxieties." In *Love, Guilt and Reparation and Other Works, 1921–1945*, vol. 1 of *The Writings of Melanie Klein.* Edited by

R. E. Money-Kyrle, B. Joseph, E. O'Shaughnessey, and H. Segal. London: Hogarth Press, Institute of Psychoanalysis, 1975.

Klibanoff, Susan, and Elton Klibanoff. *Let's Talk About Adoption.* Boston: Little, Brown, 1973.

Kohut, Heinz. *The Analysis of the Self.* New York: International Universities Press, 1971.

———. "A Memorial Symposium." *Journal of Supervision and Training in Ministry* 5 (1982): 89–205.

———. *How Does Analysis Cure?* Chicago: University of Chicago Press, 1984.

Koren, Gideon, Karen Graham, Heather Shear, and Tom Einarson. "Bias Against the Null Hypothesis: The Reproductive Hazards of Cocaine." *Lancet* (1989): 1440–1442.

Lait, Matt. "Teen-Adult Weddings Draw More Criticism." *Los Angeles Times*, Orange County Edition (11 September 1996): A1.

———. "Agency Helps Some Girls Wed Men Who Impregnated Them." *Los Angeles Times*, Orange County Edition (1 September 1996): A1.

Lakoff, George. *Moral Politics: What Conservatives Know That Liberals Don't.* Chicago: University of Chicago Press, 1996.

Lamaze, Ferdinand. *Painless Childbirth: Psychoprophylactic Method.* Chicago: H. Regnery, 1956.

Lamb, Michael E. "The Emergent American Father." In *The Father's Role: Cross-Cultural Perspectives.* Edited by Michael E. Lamb. Hillsdale, N.J.: Lawrence Erlbaum, 1987.

Lassor, Laura M. "When Success Is Not Enough: The Family Rehabilitation Program and the Policies of Family Preservation in New York City." *Review of Law and Social Change* (forthcoming).

Le Guin, Ursula. "Half Past Four." *The New Yorker* (28 September 1987): 34–56.

Leibowitz, Nehama. *New Studies in Bereshit (Genesis)* 189. Translated by Aryeh Newman. Jerusalem: Eliner Library, Hemed Press.

Lessing, Doris. *The Fifth Child.* New York: Alfred A. Knopf, 1988.

Levenson, Jon D. *The Death and Resurrection of the Beloved Son: The Transformation of Child Sacrifice in Judaism and Christianity.* New Haven, Conn.: Yale University Press, 1993.

Levine, Jane, David Chambers, and Martha Minow. *Brief for Amici Curiae.* Eleven Concerned Academics, Court of Appeals, State of New York, Index no. 000692–88 (1990).

Liebrum, Jennifer. "Crime Story Winds Up as Matrimony; Judge Rules Girl, 13, Married to Man, 22." *Houston Chronicle* (17 June 1996): A1.

Liebrum, Jennifer, and Jerry Urban. "'He Is Bewildered'; Man Does Not Understand Illegality of Relationship with Girl." *Houston Chronicle* (27 January 1996): 30.

Liebrum, Jennifer, and Jo Ann Zuniga. "Deportation Possible for Girl and Husband." *Houston Chronicle* (18 June 1996): A11.

"Life Sentence in Girl's Death." *New York Times* (8 June 1995): A27.

Lindesmith Center. *Cocaine and Pregnancy.* 1997.

Lipsky, Dorothy Kerner. "A Parental Perspective on Stress and Coping." *American Journal of Orthopsychiatry* 55 (October 1985): 614–617.

Lord, Walter. *A Night to Remember.* New York: Bantam Books, 1995.

Lutiger, B., K. Grhan, T. R. Einarson, and G. Koren. "Relationship Between Gestational Cocaine Use and Pregnancy Outcome: A Meta-Analysis." *Teratology* (1991): 44, 405–414.

Maccoby, Eleanor E., and Robert H. Mnookin. *Dividing the Child: Social and Legal Dilemmas of Custody.* Cambridge, Mass.: Harvard University Press, 1992.

Maccoby, Eleanor E., Christy Buchanan, Robert Mnookin, and Sanford Dornbusch. "Post-Divorce Roles of Mothers and Fathers in the Lives of Their Children." *Journal of Family Psychology* 7 (1993): 24, 34.

MacKinnon, Catharine A. *Toward a Feminist Theory of State.* Cambridge, Mass.: Harvard University Press, 1989.

Mahoney, Martha R. "Legal Images of Battered Women: Redefining the Issue of Separation." *Michigan Law Review* 90 (1991): 1, 5.

Mairs, Patricia A. "Bringing Up Baby: Attorney / Mothers Are Increasingly Leaving Their Jobs, Saying Motherhood and Law Don't Mix." *National Law Journal* (March 1988): 1.

Malina, Bruce. *The New Testament World: Insights from Cultural Anthropology.* Louisville, Ky.: Westminster Press/John Knox Press, 1993.

March of Dimes Report: Hearings Before Senate Committee on Judiciary, 101st Cong., 1st. Sess., pt. 2 (1990): 142.

Marcus, Robert. "Attachments of Children in Foster Care." *Genetic, Social, and General Psychology Monographs* 117 (1992): 367.

Marital Status and Living Arrangements: U.S. Dept. of Commerce, Series P-20, no. 461 (March 1991).

Marriage in America: A Report to the Nation. New York: Council on Families in America of the Institute for American Values, 1995.

Marshall, Allison. 1992, 1993, 1994 Legislative Update. In *National Association for Families and Addiction Research and Education Update.* Chicago, 1993, 1994, 1995.

Martin, Judith. "Maternal and Paternal Abuse of Children: Theoretical and Research Perspectives." In *The Dark Side of Families: Current Family Violence Research.* Edited by David Finkelhor et al. Beverly Hills, Calif.: Sage, 1983.

Mason, Mary Anne. *From Father's Property to Children's Rights.* New York: Columbia University Press, 1994.

Maybaym, Ignaz. "The Sacrifice of Isaac: A Jewish Commentary." *Leo Baeck College Publication*, no. 1. London, 1959.

Mayes, Linda C., R. H. Granger, M. H. Bornstein, and B. Zuckerman. "The Problem of Cocaine Exposure, A Rush to Judgment." *Journal of the American Medical Association* 267 (1992): 406.

McDonnell, J. T. "Mothering an Autistic Child: Reclaiming the Voice of the Mother." In *Nar-*

rating Mothers: Theorizing Maternal Subjectivities. Edited by B. O. Daly and M. T. Reddy. Knoxville: University of Tennessee Press, 1991.

McLanahan, Sara, and Gary Sandefur. *Growing Up with a Single Parent: What Hurts, What Helps*. Cambridge, Mass.: Harvard University Press, 1994.

Meiselman, Karin C. *Resolving the Trauma of Incest*. San Francisco: Jossey-Bass, 1990.

Miccio, Kristian. "In the Name of Mothers and Children: Deconstructing the Myth of the Passive Battered Mother and the 'Protected Child.' " Child Neglect Proceedings, *Albany Law Review* 58 (1995).

Miller, Alice. *Thou Shalt Not Be Aware: Society's Betrayal of the Child*. Translated by Hildegaard Hannum and Hunter Hannum. New York: NAL-Dutton, 1986.

Miller-McLemore, Bonnie. *Also a Mother: Work and Family as Theological Dilemma*. Nashville, Tenn.: Abingdon Press, 1994.

Minow, Martha. "We, The Family: Constitutional Rights and American Families." *Journal of American History* 74, no. 3 (December 1987): 959–983.

Minow, Martha, and Mary Lyndon Shanley. "Revisioning the Family: Relational Rights and Responsibilities." In *Reconstructing Political Theory: Feminist Perspectives*. Edited by Mary Lyndon Shanley and Uma Narayan. University Park: Pennsylvania State University, 1997.

Mintz, Steven, and Susan Kellogg. *Domestic Revolutions: A Social History of American Family Life*. New York: Free Press, 1988.

Minuchin, Salvador. *Families and Family Therapy*. Cambridge, Mass.: Harvard University Press, 1974.

Mitchell, Stephen. *Relational Concepts in Psychoanalysis*. Cambridge, Mass.: Harvard University Press, 1988.

Mollenkott, Virginia Ramey. *Women, Men, and the Bible*. Nashville, Tenn.: Abingdon Press, 1977.

Morrison, Toni. *Beloved*. New York: Alfred A. Knopf, 1987.

Murphy, Sheigla, and Marsha Rosenbaum. *Pregnant Women on Drugs: Combating Stereotypes and Stigma*. New Brunswick, N.J.: Rutgers University Press (forthcoming).

Murray, Charles. "The Coming White Underclass." *Wall Street Journal* (29 October 1993): A14.

NAPARE. Policy statement no. 1, "Criminalization of Prenatal Drug Use: Punitive Measures Will Be Counter-Productive." *National Association on Prenatal Addiction Research*. Chicago, 1990.

Naples, Nancy A. The " 'New Consensus' on the Gendered 'Social Contract.' " The 1987–1988 U.S. Congressional Hearings on Welfare Reform. *Signs* 22 (1997): 907–945.

National Association of Alcoholism and Drug Abuse Counselors et al. Amicus brief. Submitted in *Whitner v. State*, United States Supreme Court, no. 97–1562 (1998) at *www.lindesmith.org*.

National Institute of Child Health and Human Development (NICHD) Study of Early Child Care. The study is available at *http://nih.gov./nichd/html/news/early-child/Early Child Care.htm*; for a summary, see Barbara Vobejda, "Better Behavior in Day Care; Federal Study Finds Groups Beneficial," *Washington Post* (3 April 1998): A1.

National Research Council. *Who Cares for America's Children: Child Care Policy for the 1990s.* Edited by Cheryl D. Nayes et al. 1990.

Nedelsky, Jennifer. *Private Property and the Limitations of American Constitutionalism.* Chicago: University of Chicago Press, 1990.

Nelson, Hilde Lindemann. "Resistance and Insubordination." *Hypatia* 10, no. 2 (Spring 1995): 23–40.

———. *Feminism and Families.* New York: Routledge, 1997.

Nelson, James Lindemann. "Is It Ever Right to Do Wrong?" Review of Gowans, *Innocence Lost.* In *Hastings Center Report* 25, no. 3 (1995): 48–49.

Neyrey, J. H. *The Social World of Luke–Acts.* Peabody, Mass.: Hendrickson, 1991.

Nicholson, Linda J. *Gender and History: The Limits of Social Theory in the Age of the Family.* New York: Columbia University Press, 1988.

Niebuhr, Reinhold. *The Nature and Destiny of Man.* Vol. 1. New York: Charles Scribner's Sons, 1941.

———. *The Irony of American History.* New York: Charles Scribner's Sons, 1952.

Nussbaum, Martha. "Religion and Women's Human Rights." *Criterion* 36, no. 1 (Winter 1997): 2–13.

Nygren, Anders. *Agape and Eros.* Translated by Phillip S. Watson. Chicago: University of Chicago Press, 1982.

Okin, Susan Moller. *Justice, Gender, and the Family.* New York: Basic Books, 1989.

Olsen, Tillie. "One Writer in Twelve: Women Who Are Writers in Our Century." In *Working It Out: 23 Women Writers, Artists, Scientists, and Scholars Talk About Their Lives and Work.* Edited by Sara Ruddick and Pamela Daniels. New York: Pantheon Books, 1977.

———. *Silences.* New York: Seymour Lawrence/Delacorte Press, 1978.

Ong, Paul, Edna Bonacich, and Lucie Cheng. "The Political Economy of Capitalist Restructuring and the New Asian Immigration." In *The New Asian Immigration in Los Angeles and Global Restructuring.* Edited by Paul Ong, Edna Bonacich, and Lucie Cheng. Philadelphia: Temple University Press, 1994.

Paltrow, Lynn M. "When Becoming Pregnant Is a Crime." *Criminal Justice Ethics* 9, no. 1 (Winter–Spring 1990): 41–47.

———. "Punishing Women for Their Behavior During Pregnancy." In *Drug Addiction Research and the Health of Women.* Edited by Cora Lee Wetherington and Adele B. Roman. Rockville, Md.: National Institute on Drug Abuse, 1997.

Panko, Linda. "Legal Backlash: The Expanding Liability of Women Who Fail to Protect Their Children from Their Male Partner's Abuse." *Hastings Women's Law Journal* 6 (1995): 67.

Pear, Robert. "Clinton to Offer a Child Care Plan, White House Says." *New York Times* (14 December 1997): A1.

Pearson, Carol. *The Hero Within.* San Francisco: Harper and Row, 1989.

Perry, Philip E., Grant P. Charles, and Jane E. Matheson. "Separation and Attachment: A Shift in Perspective." *Journal of Child Care* 2 (1986): 9.

Phillips, Jill A. "Re-Victimized Battered Women: Termination of Parental Rights for Failure to Protect Children from Child Abuse." *Wayne Law Review* 38 (1992): 1549.

"Physical Violence During the 12 Months Preceding Childbirth." *Morbidity and Mortality Weekly Report* 43 (4 March 1994): 132.

Pitts, Leonard. "Plight of Teenage Girls Cries Out for New Lessons in Self-Worth." *Miami Herald* (27 July 1997).

Plaskow, Judith. "Woman as Body: Motherhood and Dualism." *Anima* 8 (1981): 56–67.

Polakow, Valerie. *Lives on the Edge: Single Mothers and Their Children in the Other America* Chicago and London: University of Chicago Press, 1993.

Polikoff, Nancy. "This Child Does Have Two Mothers: Redefining Parenthood to Meet the Needs of Children in Lesbian-Mother and Other Nontraditional Families." *Georgetown Law Journal* 78 (1990): 459.

Pollack, Sandra. "Two Moms, Two Kids: An Interview." In *Politics of the Heart: A Lesbian Parenting Anthology.* Edited by Sandra Pollack and Jeanne Vaughn. Ithaca, N.Y.: Firebrand Books, 1987.

Pollack, Sandra, and Jeanne Vaughn, eds. *Politics of the Heart: A Lesbian Parenting Anthology.* Ithaca, N.Y.: Firebrand Books, 1987.

Pollitt, Katha. "A New Assault on Feminism." *The Nation* (26 March 1990).

Postow, Betsy. "Coercion and the Moral Bindingness of Contracts." *Social Theory and Practice* 4, no. 1 (1976): 75–92.

"Pregnant Runaway May Be 14 Rather Than 10; Girl Is in U.S. Illegally." *Memphis Commercial Appeal* (26 January 1996): 4A.

"The Promise Keepettes." *New York Times Sunday Magazine* (27 April 1997): 15.

Rabuzzi, Kathryn Allen. *Motherself: A Mythic Analysis of Motherhood.* Bloomington: Indiana University Press, 1988.

———. *Mother with Child: Transformations Through Childbirth.* Bloomington: Indiana University Press, 1994.

Ransel, David L. *Mothers of Misery: Child Abandonment in Russia.* Princeton, N.J.: Princeton University Press, 1988.

Rawls, John. *A Theory of Justice.* Cambridge, Mass.: Harvard University Press, 1971.

Reece, Laura E. "Mothers Who Kill: Postpartum Disorder and Criminal Infanticide." *UCLA Law Review* 38 (1991): 699.

Reed, Ralph. *Mainstream Values Are No Longer Politically Incorrect: The Emerging Faith Factor in American Politics.* Dallas: Word, 1994.

Regan, Dianne O., Saundra M. Ehrlich, and Loretta P. Finnegan. "Infants of Drug Addicts: At Risk for Child Abuse, Neglect, and Placement in Foster Care." *Neurotoxicology and Teratology* 9 (1987): 315–319.

Regan, Milton C. *Family Law and the Pursuit of Intimacy.* New York: New York University Press, 1993.

"Religion and the Self-Psychology of Heinz Kohut: A Memorial Symposium." *Journal of Supervision and Training in Ministry* 5 (1982): 89–205.

Repetti, Rena L., et al. "Employment and Women's Health: Effects of Paid Employment on Women's Mental and Physical Health." *American Psychology* 44 (1989): 1394.

Rich, Adrienne. *Of Woman Born: Motherhood as Experience and Institution.* New York: W. W. Norton, 1976.

———. "Motherhood in Bondage" (1976). In *On Lies, Secrets, and Silence: Selected Prose, 1966–1978.* New York: W. W. Norton, 1979.

Rimer, Sara. "Children of Working Poor Are Day Care's Forgotten." *New York Times* (25 November 1997): A1.

Roberts, Dorothy. "Punishing Drug Addicts Who Have Babies: Women of Color, Equality, and the Right of Privacy." *Harvard Law Review* 104, no. 7 (1991): 1419, 1422.

———. "Racism and Patriarchy in the Meaning of Motherhood." *American University Journal of Gender and the Law* 1 (1993): 1–38.

———. "The Genetic Tie." *University of Chicago Law Review* 62, no. 1 (Winter 1995).

———. *Killing the Black Body: Race, Reproduction, and the Meaning of Liberty.* New York: Pantheon Books, 1997.

Robertson, John A. *Children of Choice: Freedom and the New Reproductive Technologies.* Princeton, N.J.: Princeton University Press, 1994.

Robinson, Elise L. E., Hilde Lindemann Nelson, and James Lindemann Nelson. "Fluid Families: The Role of Children in Custody Arrangements." In *Feminism and Families.* Edited by Hilde Lindemann Nelson. New York: Routledge, 1996.

Rodriguez, Brenda. "Bills Target Men, Girls Having Sex; Teen Pregnancies Alarm Lawmakers." *Dallas Morning News* (11 August 1996): 1J.

Romero, Mary. "Day Work in the Suburbs: The Work Experience of Chicana Private House Keepers." In *The Worth of Women's Work.* Edited by Anne Statham et al. Albany: State University of New York Press, 1988.

———. *Maid in the U.S.A.* New York: Routledge, 1992.

Ross, Ellen. *Labor and Love in Outcast London.* Oxford: Oxford University Press, 1993.

Rothman, Barbara Katz. *Recreating Motherhood: Ideology and Technology in a Patriarchal Society.* New York: W. W. Norton, 1989.

Roudiez, Leon S., trans. *Black Sun: Depression and Melancholia.* New York: Columbia University Press, 1989.

Rousso, Harilyn. "Fostering Healthy Self-Esteem." *Exceptional Parent* 14 (December 1984): 9–14.

Ruddick, Sara. *Maternal Thinking: Toward a Politics of Peace.* Boston: Beacon Press, 1989, 1995.

———. "Procreative Choice for Adolescent Women." In *The Politics of Pregnancy.* Edited by Annette Lawson and Deborah Rhode. New Haven, Conn.: Yale University Press, 1993.

———. "Thinking Mothers / Conceiving Birth." In *Representations of Motherhood.* Edited by Donna Bassin, Margaret Honey, and Meryle Mahrer Kaplan. New Haven and London: Yale University Press, 1994.

———. "Injustice in Families: Assault and Domination." In *Justice and Care: The Essential Readings.* Boulder, Colo.: Westview Press, 1995.

———. "Procreative Ethics." Prepared for seminar in feminism and philosophy, Beijing, China, June 1995 (unpublished).

———. "The Idea of Fatherhood." In *Feminism and Families.* Edited by Hilde Lindemann Nelson. New York: Routledge, 1997.

———. "'Care' as Labor and Relationship." In *Norms and Values: Essays in Honor of Virginia Held.* Edited by Joram Haber and Mark Halfon. Totowa, N.J.: Rowman and Littlefield, 1998.

Ruddick, Sara, and Pamela Daniels, eds. *Working It Out: 23 Women Writers, Artists, Scientists, and Scholars Talk About Their Lives and Work.* New York: Pantheon Books, 1977.

Ruddick, William. "Parenthood: Three Concepts and a Principle." In *Family Values: Issues in Ethics, Society and the Family.* Edited by Laurence D. Houlgate. Belmont, Calif.: Wadsworth, 1998.

Ruether, Rosemary Radford. *Sexism and God-Talk: Toward a Feminist Theology.* Boston: Beacon Press, 1983.

———. "Church and Family 1: Church and Family in the Scriptures and Early Christianity." *New Blackfriars* (January 1984): 4–14.

Sanchez, Sandra. "In Texas, Worlds Collide: Expectant Couple Caught in Clash of Two Cultures." *USA Today* (29 January 1996): 1D.

Sandel, Michael. *Democracy's Discontent.* Cambridge, Mass.: Harvard University Press, 1996.

Sands, Kathleen. *Escape from Paradise: Evil and Tragedy in Feminist Theology.* Minneapolis: Fortress Press, 1994.

Sanger, Carol. "M Is for the Many Things." *Southern California Review of Law and Women's Studies* 1 (1992): 15–67.

———. "Separating from Children." *Columbia Law Review* (1996): 399–409.

———. "Separation and Abandonment." In *Mothers in Law: Feminist Theory and the Legal Regulation of Motherhood.* Edited by Martha A. Fineman and Isabel Karpin. New York: Columbia University Press, 1995.

Scarry, Elaine. *The Body in Pain: Making and Unmaking the World*. New York: Oxford University Press, 1986.

Schaef, Anne Wilson. *Women's Reality: An Emerging Female System in a White Male Society*. New York: Harper and Row, 1981.

Schemo, Diana Jean. "The Baby Trail: A Special Report; Adoptions in Paraguay: Mothers Cry Theft." *New York Times* (19 March 1996): sec. A.

Scheper-Hughes, Nancy. *Death Without Weeping: The Violence of Everyday Life in Brazil*. Berkeley and Los Angeles: University of California Press, 1992.

Schüssler Fiorenza, Elisabeth. *In Memory of Her: A Feminist Theological Reconstruction of Christian Origins*. New York: Crossroad, 1984.

———. "In Search of Women's Heritage." In *Weaving the Visions: New Patterns in Feminist Spirituality*. Edited by Judith Plaskow and Carol P. Christ. New York: Harper and Row, 1989.

Sears, Brad. "Winning Arguments / Losing Themselves: The (Dys)functional Approach in *Thomas S. v. Robin Y.*" *Harvard Civil Rights–Civil Liberties Law Review* 29 (1994): 559–580.

Segura, Denise A. "Working at Motherhood: Chicana and Mexican Immigrant Mothers and Employment." In *Mothering: Ideology, Experience, and Agency*. Edited by Evelyn Nakano Glenn et al. New York and London: Routledge, 1994.

Sexton, Joe. "Poor Parents' Summertime Blues; Choices for Children: Enforced Boredom or Street Roulette." *New York Times* (25 June 1995).

Shaffern, Robert W. "Christianity and the Rise of the Nuclear Family." *America* (May 1994): 13–15.

Shanley, Mary Lyndon. " 'Surrogate Mothering' and Women's Freedom: A Critique of Contracts for Human Reproduction." *Signs: Journal of Women in Culture and Society* 18 (1993): 618–639.

———. "Fathers' Rights, Mothers' Wrongs? Reflections on Unwed Fathers' Rights and Sex Equality." *Hypatia* 10, no. 1 (1995): 74–103.

Shaw, Daniel S., and Robert E. Emery. "Parental Conflict and Other Correlates of the Adjustment of School-Age Children Whose Parents Have Separated." *Journal of Abnormal Psychology* 15 (1987): 269.

Sherwood, Joan. *Poverty in Eighteenth-Century Spain: The Women and Children of the Inclusa*. Toronto: University of Toronto Press, 1988.

Shultz, Marjorie Maguire. "Reproductive Technology and Intent-based Parenthood: An Opportunity for Gender Neutrality." *Wisconsin Law Review* 1990 (1990): 300, 302–303.

Siegel, Reva. "Reasoning from the Body: A Historical Perspective on Abortion Regulation and Questions of Equal Protection." *Stanford Law Review* 44 (1992): 261.

Smiley, Jane. *Age of Grief*. New York: Ivy Books by Ballantine Books, 1987.

Smith, Lillian. *The Journey*. Cleveland, Ohio: World, 1954.

Spencer, Dee. "Public Schoolteaching: A Suitable Job for Women?" In *The Worth of Women's*

Work (1880). Edited by Anne Statham et al. Albany: State University of New York Press, 1988.

Spiegel, Shalom. *The Last Trial: On the Legends and Lore of the Command to Abraham to Offer Isaac as a Sacrifice: The Akedah*, 46–47. Translated by Judah Goldin. Woodstock, Vt.: Jewish Lights, 1969.

Sprengnether, Madelon. *The Spectral Mother*. Ithaca, N.Y.: Cornell University Press, 1990.

Stacey, Judith. *Brave New Families: Stories of Domestic Upheaval in Late Twentieth Century America*. New York: Basic Books, 1990.

———. *In the Name of the Family: Rethinking Family Values in the Postmodern Age*. Boston: Beacon Press, 1996.

Stack, Carol. *All Our Kin: Strategies for Survival in a Black Community*. New York: Harper and Row, 1974.

Stark, Evan, and Anne H. Flitchcraft. "Woman-Battering, Child Abuse and Social Heredity: What Is the Relationship?" In *Marital Violence*. Edited by Norman Johnson. Boston: Routledge, 1985.

———. "Women and Children at Risk: A Feminist Perspective on Child Abuse." *International Journal of Health Services* 18 (1988): 97.

Steinberg, Jacques. "Records Show Mother's Neglect Preceded a 3-Year-Old's Death." *New York Times* (5 March 1992): B3.

Sternberg, Kathleen J., and Michael E. Lamb. "Evaluations of Attachment Relationships by Jewish Israeli Day-Care Providers." *Journal of Cross-Cultural Psychology* 23 (1992): 285.

Stocker, Michael. "The Schizophrenia of Modern Ethical Theories." In *The Virtues: Contemporary Essays on Moral Character*. Edited by Robert B. Kruschwitz and Robert C. Roberts. Belmont, Calif.: Wadsworth, 1987.

Straus, Murray A., et al. *Behind Closed Doors: Violence in the American Family*. Garden City, N.Y.: Anchor Books/Doubleday, 1980.

Styron, William. *Sophie's Choice*. New York: Random House, 1979.

Suleiman, Susan. "Writing and Motherhood." In *The (M)other Tongue: Essays in Feminist Psychoanalytic Interpretation*. Edited by Shirley N. Garner, Claire Kohane, and Madelon Sprengnether. Ithaca, N.Y.: Cornell University Press, 1985.

Super, Charles M., and Sara Harkness. "The Development of Affect in Infancy and Early Childhood." In *Cultural Perspectives on Child Development*. Edited by Daniel A. Wagner and Harold W. Stevenson. San Francisco: W. H. Freeman, 1982.

Sussman, George D. *Selling Mothers' Milk: The Wetnursing Business in France, 1715–1914*. Urbana: University of Illinois Press, 1982.

Swigart, Jane. *The Myth of the Bad Mother: The Emotional Realities of Mothering*. New York: Doubleday, 1991.

Tan, Amy. *The Joy Luck Club*. New York: Putnam's, 1989.

Tavecchio, Louis W. C., and Marinus H. Van Ijzendoorn. "Perceived Security and Extension of the Child's Rearing Context: A Parent-Report Approach." In *Attachment in Social Networks: Contributions to the Bowlby-Ainsworth Attachment Theory.* Edited by Louis W. C. Tavecchio and Marinus H. Van Ijzendoorn. Amsterdam: North-Holland, 1987.

Tetlow, Elisabeth M. *Women and Ministry in the New Testament.* New York: Paulist Press, 1980.

"Texas Judge Drops Charges Against Mexican Migrant." *Reuters* North American Wire (17 June 1996).

Thorne, Barrie, and Marilyn Yalom, eds. *Rethinking the Family: Some Feminist Questions.* New York: Longman, 1992.

Thornton, Terry E., and Lynn Paltrow. "The Rights of Pregnant Patients: Carder Case Brings Bold Policy Initiatives." *Healthspan* 8, no. 5 (May 1991): 10–16.

Thurer, Shari L. *The Myths of Motherhood: How Culture Reinvents the Good Mother.* New York: Houghton Mifflin, 1994.

Tortorilla, Toni. "On a Creative Edge." In *Politics of the Heart: A Lesbian Parenting Anthology.* Edited by Sandra Pollack and Jeanne Vaughn. Ithaca, N.Y.: Firebrand Books, 1987.

Tronto, Joan. *Moral Boundaries: A Political Argument for an Ethic of Care.* New York: Routledge, 1993.

Tsing, Anna L. "Monster Stories: Women Charged with Perinatal Endangerment." In *Uncertain Terms: Negotiating Gender in American Culture.* Edited by Faye Ginsburg and Anna L. Tsing. Boston: Beacon Press, 1990.

Uchitelle, Louis. "Lacking Child Care, Parents Take Their Children to Work." *New York Times* (23 December 1994): A1.

United States General Accounting Office Report to the Chairman, Committee on Finance, U.S. Senate. *Drug-Exposed Infants, A Generation at Risk.* GAO/HRD-90–138 (June 1990).

Van Ijzendoorn, Marinus H., and Louis W. C. Tavecchio. "The Development of Attachment Theory as a Lakatosian Research Program: Philosophical and Methodological Aspects." In *Attachment in Social Networks: Contributions to the Bowlby-Ainsworth Attachment Theory.* Edited by Louis W. C. Tavecchio and Marinus H. Van Ijzendoorn. (Amsterdam: North-Holland, 1987).

Van Ijzendoorn, Marinus H., and Pieter M. Kroonenberg. "Cross-Cultural Patterns of Attachment: A Meta-Analysis of the Strange Situation." *Child Development* 59 (1988): 147.

Van Ijzendoorn, Marinus H., Susan Goldberg, Pieter M. Kroonenberg, and Oded J. Frenkel. "The Relative Effects of Maternal and Child Problems on the Quality of Attachment: A Meta-Analysis of Attachment in Clinical Samples." *Child Development* 63 (1992): 840.

Volpp, Leti. "(Mis)Identifying Culture: Asian Women and the 'Cultural Defense.'" *Harvard Women's Law Journal* 17 (1994): 57.

Walker, Lenore E. *The Battered Woman.* New York: Harper and Row, 1979.

———. *Terrifying Love: Why Battered Women Kill and How Society Responds.* New York: Harper and Row, 1989.

Walker, Margaret Urban. *Moral Understandings*. New York: Routledge, 1997.

Wallerstein, Judith S., and Sandra Blankeslee. *Second Chances: Men, Women, and Children a Decade After Divorce*. Boston: Houghton Mifflin, 1990.

Wallerstein, Judith S., and Joan B. Kelly. *Surviving the Breakup: How Children and Parents Cope with Divorce*. New York: Basic Books, 1980.

Walsh, Elsa. *Divided Lives: The Public and Private Struggles of Three Accomplished Women*. New York: Simon and Schuster, 1995.

Warshak, Richard. "Father-Custody and Child Development: A Review and Analysis of Psychological Research." *Behavioral Science and the Law* 4 (1986): 181.

Washburne, Carolyn Kott. "Happy Birthday from Your Other Mom." In *Politics of the Heart: A Lesbian Parenting Anthology*. Edited by Sandra Pollack and Jeanne Vaughn. Ithaca, N.Y.: Firebrand Books, 1987.

Weiner, Lynn Y. *From Working Girl to Working Mother: The Female Labor Force in the United States, 1820–1980*. Chapel Hill: University of North Carolina Press, 1985.

Weston, Kath. *Families We Choose: Lesbians, Gays, Kinship*. New York: Columbia University Press, 1991.

Whitehead, Barbara Dafoe. "Dan Quayle Was Right." *Atlantic Monthly* (April 1993): 47–84.

———. *The Divorce Culture*. New York: Alfred A. Knopf, 1997.

Wikler, L. "Family Stress Theory and Research on Families of Children with Mental Retardation." In *Families of Handicapped Persons: Research, Programs, and Policy Issues*. Baltimore, Md.: Paul H. Brookes, 1986.

Wilgoren, Jodi. "Challenge to Green Card Reprieve Fails." *Los Angeles Times* (30 October 1997): A3.

Williams, Bernard. "Persons, Character, and Morality." In *Moral Luck*. Cambridge: Cambridge University Press, 1981.

Williams, Joan C. "Deconstructing Gender." In *Feminist Jurisprudence*. Edited by Patricia Smith. New York: Oxford University Press, 1993.

———. "Restructuring Work and Family Entitlements Around Family Values." *Harvard Journal of Law and Public Policy* 19 (1996): 753.

Williams, Patricia J. *The Rooster's Egg: On the Persistence of Prejudice*. Cambridge, Mass.: Harvard University Press, 1995.

Wilson, James Q. *The Moral Sense*. New York: Free Press, 1993.

Wilson, Leslie Thielen. "Agency and the Feminist Therapization of the Oppressed." Speech delivered at *Women in Philosophy* Annual Meeting, Dalhousie University, September 1997.

Winnicott, D. W. *Maturational Processes and the Facilitating Environment* 49. New York: International Universities Press, 1965.

———. *Playing and Reality*. New York: Tavistock, 1971.

Witherington, Ben. *Women in the Ministry of Jesus*. New York: Cambridge University Press, 1984.

Witte, John, Jr. "The Transformation of Marriage Law in the Lutheran Reformation." In *The Weightier Matters of the Law: Essays on Law and Religion.* Edited by J. Witte and Frank S. Alexander. Atlanta: Scholars Press, 1988.

———. "Consulting a Living Tradition: Christian Heritage of Marriage and Family." *Christian Century* (November 1996): 1108–1111.

———. *From Sacrament to Contract: Marriage, Religion, and Law in the Western Tradition.* Louisville, Ky.: Westminster Press/John Knox Press, 1997.

Woodhouse, Barbara Bennett. "Hatching the Egg: A Child-Centered Perspective on Parents' Rights." *Cardozo Law Review* 14 (May 1993): 1747–1865.

———. "Out of Children's Needs, Children's Rights: The Child's Voice in Defining the Family." *BYU Journal of Public Law* 8 (1994): 321–341.

Woolf, Virginia. *The Letters of Virginia Woolf,* vol. 2, 1912–1922. New York: Harcourt Brace Jovanovich, 1975.

Yazigi, Ricardo A., Randall Odem, and Kenneth L. Polakoski. "Demonstration of Specific Binding of Cocaine to Human Spermatozoa." *Journal of the American Medical Association* 266, no. 14 (9 October 1991).

Yngvesson, Barbara. "Negotiating Motherhood: Identity and Difference in 'Open' Adoptions." *Law and Society Review* 31, no. 1 (1997): 31–80.

Young, Iris Marion. Critiquing Galston's *Liberal Purposes* in "Mothers, Citizenship and Independence: A Critique of Pure Family Values." *Ethics* (1995).

Zelizer, Viviana. *Pricing the Priceless Child: The Changing Social Value of Children.* New York: Basic Books, 1985.

Zornberg, Avivah Gottlieb. *Genesis: The Beginning of Desire.* Philadelphia: Jewish Publication Society, 1995.

Zuckerman, Barry, et al. "Effect of Maternal Marijuana and Cocaine Use on Fetal Growth." *New England Journal of Medicine* 320, no. 12 (23 March 1990): 762–768.

Contributors

Paula M. Cooey teaches at Trinity University in San Antonio, Texas, where she is Professor of Religion. She received her Ph.D. in Religion from Harvard University, her M.T.S. in Theology from Harvard Divinity School, and her B.A. in Philosophy from the University of Georgia. Author of numerous books and articles, her most recent books include *Family, Freedom & Faith: Building Community Today* (Westminster–John Knox, 1996) and *Religious Imagination and the Body: A Feminist Perspective* (Oxford University Press, 1994). She is currently engaged in research on aging, death, and dying.

Drucilla Cornell is Professor of Law, Women's Studies, and Political Science at Rutgers University. Prior to beginning her academic life, Professor Cornell was a union organizer for a number of years, working for the U.A.W., the U.E., and the I.U.E. in California, New Jersey, and New York. She played a key role in organizing the conferences on Deconstruction and Justice with Jacques Derrida, held at Cardozo in 1989, 1990, and 1993. In addition, she has worked to coordinate the Law and Humanism Speakers Series with the Jacob Burns Institute for Advanced Legal Studies and the Committee on Liberal Studies at the New School for Social Research. Professor Cornell was a professor at the Benjamin N. Cardozo School of Law from 1989 to 1994 and spent the 1991–92 academic year at the Institute for Advanced Study at Princeton. She has authored numerous articles on critical theory, feminism, and "postmodern" theories of ethics. She is the coeditor, with Seyla Benhabib, of *Feminism as Critique: On the Politics of Gender* (University of Michigan Press, 1987); and, with Michel Rosenfeld and David Gray Carlson, of *Deconstruction and the Possibility of Justice* (Routledge, 1993); and has published four books, *The Imaginary Domain: Abortion, Pornography and Sexual Harassment* (Routledge, 1995), *Beyond Accommodation: Ethical Feminism, Deconstruction and the Law* (Routledge, 1991), *The Philosophy of the Limit* (Routledge, 1993), and *Transformations: Recollective Imagination and Sexual Difference* (Princeton University Press, 1998). She is the author of the forthcoming book *At the Heart of Freedom: Feminism, Sex, and Equality.* She is also a produced playwright—productions of her plays *The Dream Cure* and *Background Interference* have been performed in New York and Los Angeles.

Peggy Cooper Davis is the John S. R. Shad Professor of Law at New York University School of Law. She is a mother, a former Family Court Judge, and the author of *Neglected Stories: The Constitution and Family Values* (New York: Hill and Wang, 1997).

Martha Albertson Fineman is the Maurice T. Moore Professor of Law at Columbia University in the City of New York and the Dorothea S. Clarke Professor of Feminist Jurisprudence at Cornell University Law School. She is a 1975 graduate of the University of Chicago Law School. In addition to numerous articles and book chapters on feminism, family law, and the regulation of intimacy and sexuality, Professor Fineman is the author of *The Neutered Mother, The Sexual*

Family and Other Twentieth Century Tragedies (Routledge, 1995) and *The Illusion of Equality: The Rhetoric and Reality of Divorce Reform* (Chicago, 1991). She is a contributor and coeditor of a number of collections of papers from the Feminism and Legal Theory Project including *Feminism, Media and the Law* (Oxford University Press, 1997), *Mothers in Law* (Columbia University Press, 1995), *The Public Nature of Private Violence* (Routledge, 1994), and *At the Boundaries of Law: Feminism and Legal Theory* (Routledge, 1991).

Julia E. Hanigsberg earned her law degrees (LL.B and B.C.L.) from McGill University. She holds a Master of Law (LL.M) from Columbia University School of Law, where she is also a candidate for a doctorate in law (J.S.D.). Ms. Hanigsberg was a clerk to the Honorable Peter Cory of the Supreme Court of Canada and an Associate in Law at Columbia University School of Law. She has published a number of articles on feminist legal theory and regulation of motherhood in American and Canadian law reviews, including the *Michigan Law Review*, the *Ottawa Law Review*, and the *Michigan Journal of Gender and the Law*. Ms. Hanigsberg works in development of justice policy as a lawyer for the government of Ontario.

Lisa C. Ikemoto is Professor of Law, Loyola Law School. She earned her B.A. in 1984 at U.C.L.A. (English and History), her J.D. in 1987 at the University of California, Davis School of Law, and her LL.M. in 1989 at Columbia University School of Law. Lisa Ikemoto uses critical theory and cultural studies to explore race, gender, and class issues. Her scholarship interests arise primarily from her community commitments which include Asians and Pacific Islanders for Reproductive Health, the National Asian Pacific American Women's Forum, the California Women's Law Center, and the Korean Immigrant Workers Association.

Eva Feder Kittay is Professor of Philosophy at SUNY, Stony Brook. She is the mother of two children, one of whom is her disabled daughter Sesha, the subject of the essay included in this volume. She has written numerous articles on issues pertaining to women, ethics, and social and political philosophy and is an expert on metaphor and the philosophy of language. She has most recently begun to publish essays on disability, including "On the Expressivity and Ethics of Selective Abortion for Disability," written together with her son, in *Norms and Values: Essays in Honor of Virginia Held* (Rowman and Littlefield, 1998). Her most recent book is *Love's Labor: Essays on Women, Equality, and Dependency* (Thinking Gender Series; Routledge, 1999). Her other books include *Women and Moral Theory*, coedited with Diana Meyers (Rowman and Littlefield, 1987), *Metaphor: Its Cognitive Force and Linguistic Structure* (Clarendon Press, 1987, 1989), and *Fields, Frames and Contrasts*, coedited with Adrienne Lehrer (Lawrence Erlbaum, 1992). While the federal welfare reform was pending, she helped organize feminist opposition to punitive welfare legislation by founding *Women's Committee of One Hundred* which lobbied Congress, initiated an ad campaign, and promoted education concerning women and welfare. She is currently the Chair of the APA Committee on the Status of Women.

Bonnie J. Miller-McLemore is Associate Professor of Pastoral Theology and Counseling at Vanderbilt University Divinity School and the mother of three boys. Her publications address major cultural issues and include *Death, Sin and the Moral Life: Contemporary Cultural Interpretations* *of Death* (Scholarly Press, 1988), *Also a Mother: Work and Family as Theological Dilemma* (Abingdon Press, 1994), and most recently, a coauthored volume, *From Culture Wars to Common Ground: Religion and the American Family Debate* (Westminster–John Knox Press, 1977).

Martha Minow is Professor of Law at Harvard Law School and teaches Family Law, Civil Procedure, and School Reform. She is author of the books *Making All the Difference: Inclusion, Exclusion, and American Law* (Cornell University Press, 1990), *Not Only for Myself: Identity, Politics and Law* (The New Press, 1997), and *Between Vengeance and Forgiving: Facing History After Genocide and Mass Violence* (Beacon Press, 1998). She has edited the book *Family Matters: Readings on Family Lives and the Law* (The New Press, 1993) and coedited, with Gary Bellow, *Law Stories* (University of Michigan Press, 1996). Her scholarship includes articles about the treatment of women, children, persons with disabilities, and members of ethnic, racial, or religious minorities. She serves on the boards of the Bazelon Center for Mental Health Law, the Covenant Foundation, and the W. T. Grant Foundation. She has served on the board of several child welfare agencies. Her daughter, Mira, was born in 1992.

Jennifer Nedelsky received her Ph.D. from the Committee on Social Thought, at the University of Chicago. She had the great good fortune of working with Hannah Arendt and is now returning to Arendt's work in her current project on judgment. She is also completing a book pulling together her previous work on relational feminism, *Law, Autonomy and the Relational Self: A Feminist Revisioning of the Foundations of Law.* She teaches at the University of Toronto in Law, Political Science, and Women's Studies. She balances the demands of all of the above with the joys of her family: her husband, Joe Carens, and her sons, Michael, eleven, and Daniel, eight, Carens-Nedelsky.

Hilde Lindemann Nelson, M.A., is the Director of the Center for Applied and Professional Ethics at the University of Tennessee. A former editor at the *Hastings Center Report*, she is the coauthor, with James Lindemann Nelson, of *The Patient in the Family* (Routledge, 1995) and *Alzheimer's: Answers to Hard Questions for Families* (Doubleday, 1996). She has edited two collections, *Feminism and Families* and *Stories and Their Limits: Narrative Approaches to Bioethics* (both Routledge, 1997). She coedits the Reflective Bioethics Series for Routledge and the Feminist Constructions Series for Rowman and Littlefield, and is currently at work on a book about narrative constructions of the self.

Lynn M. Paltrow is the director of a New York–based national advocacy campaign on behalf of pregnant and parenting women and their children, a program of the Women's Law Project. Recognized in 1991 by the *National Law Journal* as one of the "100 Most Influential Lawyers in America," Ms. Paltrow is a leading national litigator and strategist in cases involving reproductive freedom and health issues. Her writings include "Punishing Women for Their Behavior During Pregnancy: An Approach That Undermines the Health of Women and Children," in *Drug Addiction Research and the Health of Women*, edited by Cora Lee Wetherington and Adele B. Roman, published by the National Institute on Drug Abuse, Rockville, Md. (1998); "Women, Abortion and Civil Disobedience," *Nova Law Review*, vol. 13 (1989); and the Supreme Court

Amicus brief in *Thornburgh* v. *ACOG*, printed in *Women's Law Reporter*, vol. 9 (1986). Ms. Paltrow also teaches as an adjunct professor at area colleges and is a founding member of Be Present Inc., an Atlanta-based national organization devoted to empowering women and girls.

Nina Perales is a civil rights attorney in San Antonio, Texas. She is a Staff Attorney of the Mexican American Legal Defense and Educational Fund, Inc. (MALDEF), and performs class action litigation on behalf of Latinos in the area of political access. Prior to joining MALDEF in 1996, Ms. Perales worked as an Associate Counsel with the Puerto Rican Legal Defense and Education Fund, Inc., in New York City and served as the first Coordinator of PRLDEF's Latina Rights Initiative. Ms. Perales earned her J.D. from Columbia University School of Law in 1990 and her B.A. from Brown University in 1986. The views expressed in Ms. Perales's essay are her own and do not necessarily reflect the views of MALDEF.

Dorothy Roberts is a professor at Northwestern University School of Law, with joint appointments in the Department of Sociology (courtesy) and as a Faculty Fellow of the Institute for Policy Research. She received her B.A. from Yale University and her J.D. from Harvard Law School. Professor Roberts has written and lectured extensively on the interplay of gender, race, and class in legal issues concerning reproduction and motherhood. She is the author of *Killing the Black Body: Race, Reproduction, and the Meaning of Liberty* (Pantheon Books, 1997), as well as the coauthor of casebooks on constitutional law and women and the law. She has published more than forty articles and essays in books, scholarly journals, newspapers, and magazines, including *Harvard Law Review, Yale Law Journal, University of Chicago Law Review, Social Text*, and *The New York Times*. Her influential article "Punishing Drug Addicts Who Have Babies: Women of Color, Equality, and the Right of Privacy" (*Harvard Law Review*, 1991) has been widely cited and is included in a number of anthologies.

Sara Ruddick is the author of *Maternal Thinking: Toward a Politics of Peace* (Beacon Press, 1989, 1994). She coedited, with Pamela Daniels, *Working It Out: 23 Women Writers, Artists, Scientists, and Scholars Talk About Their Lives and Work* (Pantheon Books, 1977) and, with Carol Ascher and Louise DeSalvo, *Between Women: Biographers, Novelists, Critics, Teachers and Writers Talk About Their Work on Women* (Beacon Press, 1984; Routledge, 1993). She has written essays on birth and mothering, war and nonviolence, the ethics of care, Virginia Woolf, and most recently on virtues and age. She has taught for many years at the New School for Social Research in New York City.

Carol Sanger is a Professor of Law at Columbia Law School where she specializes in courses on children, child abuse, family law, gender and law, and contracts. Professor Sanger received her J.D. from the University of Michigan in 1976 and her B.A. from Wellesley College in 1970. She has taught at Santa Clara and University of Oregon Law Schools and was a visiting professor at Stanford Law School and a research scholar at the Institute for Research on Women and Gender, also at Stanford University. Her recent work has focused on the ways that law influences family formation, particularly between parents and children. She has investigated this topic in a number of areas: immigration (*Immigration Reform and Control of the Undocumented Family*), emancipation (*Minor Changes: Emancipating Children in Modern Times*), and, most recently, law's influence on decisions by mothers to leave their children (*Separating from Children* [*Columbia Law Review* and forthcoming, University of California Press]). She is particularly interested in legal procedures for teenagers, as developed in her work on emancipation and in her current project on teenage abortion hearings. She has published in a number of major law reviews.

Mary Lyndon (Molly) Shanley is Margaret Stiles Halleck Professor of Political Science at Vassar College. She is author of *Feminism, Marriage and the Law in Victorian England* (Princeton University Press, 1989), coeditor, with Carole Pateman, of *Feminist Interpretations and Political Theory* (Polity Press; Penn State Press, 1990), and, with Uma Narayan, of *Reconstructing Political Theory: Feminist Essays* (Polity Press; Penn State Press, 1997). She is currently writing a book, *Mothers and Families: Dilemmas for Feminism and the Law* (Beacon Press, forthcoming) on ethical issues in contemporary family law.

Susan Dougherty

Acknowledgments

From the time we began thinking about this book three years ago, our husbands, William Ruddick and Lorne Sossin, have also lived with our project. They were always willing to listen, advise, and edit. We have depended on their good cheer and many kinds of practical help.

Throughout the project, Jane Lazarre and Hilde Lindemann Nelson offered editorial help, general encouragement, and practical advice.

We have had two editors at Beacon Press. Marya Van't Hul encouraged our project at the outset and provided us with the security of knowing that we had a publisher committed to bringing our book into being. Amy Caldwell provided us with valuable feedback and heartened us with her enthusiasm for our authors and our goals in putting the collection together.

In the final stages of the project our assistant, Martina Sovoboda of Toronto, worked energetically, skillfully, and diligently with good cheer and enthusiasm. Without her help we could not have completed our work.

Our greatest debt is to our contributors. We are grateful to our earliest authors who embraced the conception of this collection at its inception and stuck with us through the long process of getting where we are today. We wish to thank all of our authors for their essays and for their patience, willingness to work to our deadlines, and ability to hear and respond to our comments.